THE ROUGH GUIDE TO

True Crime

by
Cathy Scott

Contents

Credits

Editors: Matthew Milton, Rob White, Andrew Lockett
Layout: Anita Singh
Design: Diana Jarvis
Proofreading: Jason Freeman
Cover: Diana Jarvis
Production: Rebecca Short, Vicky Baldwin

Forensic psychology profiles: Louis B. Schlesinger, Professor of Psychology at John Jay College of Criminal Justice, New York
Additional contributors: David Anthony, Richard Craig, David Leffman, James Smart

Picture Credits

Publishing Information

Published September 2009 by Rough Guides Ltd, 80 Strand, London WC2R 0RL
375 Hudson St, New York 10014, USA
Email: mail@roughguides.com

Distributed by the Penguin Group:
Penguin Books Ltd, 80 Strand, London WC2R 0RL
Penguin Putnam, Inc., 375 Hudson Street, NY 10014, USA
Penguin Group (Australia), 250 Camberwell Road, Camberwell, Victoria 3124, Australia
Penguin Books Canada Ltd, 90 Eglinton Avenue East, Toronto, Ontario, Canada M4P 2YE
Penguin Group (New Zealand), Cnr Rosedale and Airborne Roads, Albany, Auckland, New Zealand

Printed and bound in Singapore by SNP Security Printing Pte Ltd

The publishers and authors have done their best to ensure the accuracy and currency of all information in *The Rough Guide to True Crime*; however, they can accept no responsibility for any loss or inconvenience sustained by any reader as a result of its information or advice.

348 pages; includes index

A catalogue record for this book is available from the British Library

ISBN: 978-1-85828-385-2

1 3 5 7 9 8 6 4 2

Deception: the art of the con

Homicide

Serial killers   187

Organized crime   223

Cybercrime   305

Feature Boxes

Preface

A journalist's assignments often lead her career. Covering military news stories has taken me to the war-torn country of Somalia, to the Middle East and to Panama. And a concern for animal welfare took me to the storm-ravaged US Gulf Coast, where I spent four months investigating the fates of pets left behind in hurricane-ravaged New Orleans, Louisiana.

But it is the footprints left behind by criminals that fascinate me the most. For me, true crime is a passion – looking behind the story and picking up on the clues that lead to the perpetrators. I'm interested in getting to the facts of a case, no matter how emotive the circumstances of that case might be.

I've been to more crime scenes – and far too many homicides – than I care to count. Even so, it is the details – the demeanour of witnesses, of family, neighbours and police, and even the weather – that hold your attention. As a writer, I am something more than a bystander, but I have the bystander's vantage point: I step back and observe as the tales unfold before me.

The illegal deeds described within this book are often gritty but always fascinating, whether they are the facts of an infamous gem heist in Milan, Italy, in which thieves tunnelled into a top-end jewellery store, or the murder of an unsuspecting Oklahoma grandmother, Bertha Pippin, who was caught off-guard early one morning when there was a knock at her door. I have always gravitated towards the underdog when covering crime, attempting to give a voice to the victims.

In the latter case, I wondered why it was all but ignored by the media after the initial reports, despite its shocking nature. In the case of the murder of Susan Berman – an unsolved crime that took place in Beverly Hills in 2000 – nobody, after a flurry of early articles, appeared to be covering the story with much depth. All the more surprising, when you consider that Berman was the daughter of a mobster.

Some true cases are just plain absurd. A Las Vegas police detective once told me that reason crooks are caught is simple: they are stupid. Some leave their own belongings behind: it has been known for burglars to even leave photo ID, such as driving licenses, at the crime scene.

It doesn't get better than that for investigators – not to mention writers.

The stories within these pages include the good, the bad, the ugly, and sometimes the comical. The devil is in the details, and I hope I have achieved my goal, of bringing both the victims and the culprits to life for you, the reader.

Cathy Scott, 2009

Acknowledgements

I am grateful to Jim Cypher, my agent at the time, for leading me to this project; Susan Lee Cohen with Riverside Literary Agency for taking me under her wing; Sean Mahoney with Penguin Books for his faith in my abilities; and Rough Guides editors Andrew Lockett and Matthew Milton, from across the pond, for their careful and thoughtful massaging of the manuscript.

I salute my colleagues in the press, whose well-researched background articles helped point me in the right direction. And, as always, many thanks to my family for believing in me, especially my twin sister Cordelia Mendoza and her husband Bob; my big brother Dr J. Michael Scott and his wife Sharon; my son Raymond Somers Jr and daughter-in-law Karen; and my grand kids Claire and Jake. I don't know what I'd do without them. Also, many thanks go to my late mother, Eileen Rose Busby, a fellow author who loved a great mystery and kept our family book shelves well stocked.

OUTLAWS: "THE MONEY, OR YOUR LIFE"

Outlaws: "the money, or your life"

The criminals and crimes of the early modern age have been romanticized, stylized and celebrated time and again in print and on screen. In the first few decades of the twentieth century - and in the Depression era of the 1930s in particular - outlaws often became heroes of sorts.

The procession of high-profile public enemies began with John Dillinger – the most famous of all US bank robbers – and it included such notorious criminals as Bonnie and Clyde, Ma Barker, Machine Gun Kelly, Pretty Boy Floyd, and Baby Face Nelson. They were the first celebrity gangsters and their crimes were always front-page news during what became known as the Midwest Crime Wave or Public Enemy era.

It is still hard to tell how much of their reported exploits was hard fact and how much popular myth. Such is certainly the case with Ma Barker and her boys, whose misdemeanours have been dramatized over the years in books and in films – particularly with regard to the degree to which Barker was herself a criminal.

Not all the outlaw tales, however, were exaggerated. Bonnie and Clyde, the most famous outlaw couple of all time, may have been glamourized even more in the years since their deaths, but they were larger-than-life legends even when they were alive. It's a phenomenon for which the **FBI** itself was partially responsible: being placed on the most wanted list pumped up the crooks' status, making the criminals' reputations even more notorious. However, from John Dillinger and his gang to Ma Barker and her boys, the reality of their lives and the circumstances they lived under as they committed their crime sprees were anything but glamorous. Many of these criminals were on the lam for years, hiding out wherever they could, and terrorizing towns with kidnappings, robberies, and murders – often mowing down anyone who tried to get in their way. Because they had to keep low profiles, they lived rough, bedded down where they could and frequently didn't know when they'd eat their next meal.

There's an irony to this of course, as many of US Depression-era gangsters, such as **Pretty Boy Floyd** and **Machine Gun Kelly** were down on their luck and turned to a life of crime because, during the economic slump, there was simply no work to be found. Many were poor country boys and girls yearning for a new way of life and willing to do anything to get it, for whom shiny new cars and powerful sub-machine-guns were equally covetable tokens of success. Most died violent deaths.

OUTLAWS AND THEIR NICKNAMES

To accompany their notorious reputations, outlaws often had outrageous names bestowed upon them. Some of the names didn't exactly fit their tough-guy personas, as with Charles "Pretty Boy" Floyd and Lester "Baby Face Nelson" Gillis. Some, however, were entirely appropriate, as evidenced by the rather unimaginative but apposite monikers for George "Machine Gun" Kelly and Alvin "Creepy" Karpis (whose eventual 26-year incarceration at "The Rock" – Alcatraz – was the longest sentence the prison had ever known).

Lesser-known Western outlaws included Slim Kid, One-shot Charlie, Wild Dick and Indian Bob. Whether they were high profile or relatively unknown, the nicknames of the desperados were no accident and certainly not given with affection: assigning catchy, memorable monikers to robbers was an FBI innovation that survived the US Gold Rush days and Prohibition. The practice continues today. Just as it was done in years past for old-style Western robbers, modern-day law enforcement still give their robbers a name that sticks.

While federal agents doubtless quietly enjoy assigning the latest epithet to a robber du jour, it's actually a serious business: the names are given to help trap these hold-up artists. For instance, one robber in

The first known medieval outlaws were the Coterel gang, who, in 1328, robbed 10 shillings from, and attacked, a vicar in Derbyshire, England. On the lam for years, they were eventually pardoned in exchange for serving in the military.

Alvin Karpis: creepy enough for you?

San Diego, California, was labelled the "**Bad Breath Bandit**" by FBI agents because bank tellers reported that his breath stank. In Arizona, an unattractive criminal was nicknamed the "**Ugly Robber**". She was given the title because she used different disguises and wore a variety of colourful wigs to a dozen hold-ups. These unflattering, catchy monikers are given so the public will remember them and tip off the FBI with leads. The Ugly Robber was eventually caught after four months on the run.

In Washington State, suspects have been given names as unusual as "The Pillowcase", "Duelling Banjo" and "Attila the Bun" – the latter on account of the fact that the female suspect had a messy bun of a haircut.

Indeed, hair crops up in a lot of the FBI's name-tags. Witness the high-profile "**Ponytail Bandit**". The suspected culprit was an attractive, slender woman in her twenties, whose shoulder-length blonde ponytail stuck out from the back of her baseball cap in images captured on security video cameras. She pulled off a string of bank robberies that began on 8 May, 2007 in Austin, Texas, and were repeated in nearly identical heists in California and Washington states. During the robberies, she would ask the tellers to smile as they handed over the money. Because her photos and nickname were broadcast internationally, in February 2008 authorities, based on an anonymous tip, arrested the 21-year-old Morgan Michelle Hoke at the Cha Cha Villa Hotel in Bangkok, Thailand. The FBI did not release the dollar amount of the total take, as usual, because they typically do not want would-be robbers to look at it as a lucrative occupation. Authorities named Hoke's husband, 26-year-old Stuart Michael Romine, as her alleged partner in crime in what law enforcement described as a modern Bonnie-and-Clyde-style crime spree. The husband's complicity was suspected due to surveillance video footage in which a man looking very like him, wearing a similar baseball cap to Morgan Hoke's, could be seen holding up four Texas banks. He remains at large.

Dress sense has also earned some criminals their names. In Southern California, one robber dressed so stiffly that agents dubbed him the "**Button-Up Bandit**." And in December 2007 the Los Angeles Police Department issued a news release informing the public about a "**Tuxedo Bandit**" who lifted two expensive Rolex watches. The crime happened in mid-afternoon when the unarmed man, dressed in a dinner jacket, walked into the Saint Cross watch store in Los Angeles. Posing as a customer, he told the store clerk that he was interested in buying an engagement gift for his girlfriend. After the would-be buyer spotted a couple of Rolex watches in the display case, he asked if he could see them. Once the timepieces were in his hands, he ran out the front door and fled. He had gotten away with two "Champagne-style" Rolexes with diamond bezels, valued at a total of $60,200. The bandit and the stolen watches have never been located.

The prize for the most cumbersome of criminal nicknames must surely go to the "**Irreconcilable Differences**" bandit. Doesn't exactly trip off the tongue, does it? He earned his nickname after telling a Beverly Hills bank teller, while he was holding her up, that he was going through a divorce. He was eventually caught and held accountable for seventeen bank heists.

As long as crooks are robbing banks, it appears that the practice of assigning them unflattering handles will no doubt continue.

For further investigation

📖 **Wayne Erbsen** Outlaw Ballads, Legends & Lore (**1996**) A collection of ballads and legends of the lawless men and women of the Wild West and South.

ⓦ labankrobbers.org This site introduces you to the high-profile bank robbers, via their profiles, nicknames and photos, who have pulled off heists from Southern Californian financial institutions.

BILLY THE KID, THE US's MOST FAMOUS OUTLAW

A teenage outlaw of the Southwest, the Kid was born William Henry McCarty on 3 November 1859, in the New York area. He also went by the aliases of William Antrim and William Harrison Bonney.

Billy had a reputation for being short-tempered and was considered a vicious and ruthless killer. According to legend, he killed twenty-one men in total: one for each year of his life. In a period of just four years, he fought in at least sixteen shootouts, killed at least four men, and assisted in the murder of five others. Some historians have countered the depiction, describing Billy the Kid instead as merely a born survivor in the savage world of the Wild West, where knowing how to use a gun meant the difference between life and death. The era he grew up in was a lawless and corrupt time.

Much discussion over the years has concerned whether Billy was left- or right-handed. A famous tintype photo of him was, in fact, a reverse image, which gave the impression that the Kid was left-handed. Astute historians concluded the outlaw was right-handed, for he was holding a rifle in his left hand while a revolver was positioned on his hip near his right hand. The original tintype is now worth roughly $300,000, making it one of the most valuable historical photographs of the Old West.

Billy's mother, **Catherine McCarty**, was a widow and single mother of two – Billy had an older brother named Joseph – and the family relocated from New York to Wichita, Kansas, during Billy's early childhood. By the early 1870s, Catherine was diagnosed with tuberculosis and ordered by her doctor to move to a dryer climate, which is when the family relocated to Santa Fe, New Mexico. After his mother married **William Antrim** in 1873, the family moved again, this time to Silver City, where Billy's mother died a year later. Billy's stepfather moved the boys to Arizona, where both Billy and Joseph had to fend for themselves. He put them in foster homes, but they fled. Billy got a job washing dishes and quickly fell in with the wrong crowd.

His first criminal offence was the insignificant theft of a large tub of butter from the buckboard of a horse-drawn carriage, at the age of fourteen. After Billy tried to sell the goods to a local merchant, he was caught by the sheriff; he received a tongue-lashing and a public spanking. Next, along with the town troublemaker **Sombrero Jack**, Billy stole a large hamper of finished clothes from a Chinese laundry. He was caught with the clothing. When he refused to turn in his accomplice, the sheriff threw Billy in jail. Sombrero Jack helped him break out, and they moved to New York. When Billy, by now sixteen, and his friends got into a fight and a man was killed, one of Billy's foster parents paid for his train fare back to New Mexico.

According to legend, it was in 1879, at the Old Adobe Hotel in Hot Springs, in New Mexico Territory, that Billy hooked up with another outlaw, Jesse Evans, the leader of a band of horse rustlers called the Boys. Billy had been playing cards at the hotel when he was introduced to Jesse and Billy then joined the Jesse James gang. Billy was involved in what was called the Lincoln War, between Jesse James's gang and lawmen over the possession of horses, during which Sheriff

William Bonney, a.k.a. Billy the Kid.

GUNSLINGERS

Gunslinger (or gunfighter) was the title given to the men of the American Old West who gained their reputations as pistol-packing lawbreakers. The best-known of the gunfighters were so feared by the public that they tended to meet their ends during inglorious ambushes rather than from the gun battles so stylized in the Westerns. And they were often feared not because of their actions, but because of their hyper-inflated reputations.

Some were even putative good guys: the Earp brothers, for instance, became law enforcement deputies and marshals. Nevertheless, they were viewed by many simply as bandits-with-badges, ruthlessly enforcing their interests in Tombstone, Arizona, instead of protecting the rights of the citizens.

The most famous gunslingers' battle was the Gunfight at the O.K. Corral. The fight, in October 1881, was in a vacant patch of ground behind a corral in Tombstone. Despite only three people being killed that day, it has acquired a mythological significance unique to the history of the Old West. A newspaper headline, dated 26 October 1881, described the battle as "A Desperate Fight Between Officers of the Law and Cowboys". The paper reported that after a marshal had arrested a cowboy named Clanton for disorderly conduct, he had sworn he'd seek vengeance against the sheriff and Deputy City Marshal Virgil Earp. By 3pm that afternoon, the Earp brothers and Doc Holliday, an American dentist, gambler, and gunfighter who was staying at Fly's boarding house immediately next to the O.K. Corral, met up with the infamous Clanton brothers and two McLaury brothers, two gangs of brothers who had tough reputations. A "lively fire commenced from the cowboys" against the citizens and "about thirty shots were fired rapidly", the paper reported.

Virgil's brother Wyatt, walked away from the gun battle unhurt (unlike Virgil, who was shot through the right calf); Morgan Earp was hit by a lone bullet through the upper back above his shoulder blades, while Holliday was grazed on his hip. Billy Clanton and Tom and Frank McLaury died from their wounds. Afterward, an inquest and arraignment hearing determined that Holliday and the Earps did not commit criminal acts during the gunfight.

Doc Holliday, although he was a doctor, had turned to lawlessness because, during those treacherous cowboy days, he had felt it was a dog-eat-dog world. Following Doc's death in 1896, Wyatt Earp was quoted in a newspaper article as saying: "Doc was a dentist whom necessity had made a gambler; a gentleman whom disease had made a frontier vagabond; a philosopher whom life had made a caustic wit; a long lean ash-blond fellow nearly dead with consumption, and at the same time the most skilful gambler and the nerviest, speediest, deadliest man with a gun that I ever knew."

Tiburcio Vasquez, a colourful Californian bandit (between 1857 and 1874) who was fluent in English and Spanish, has been called a hero by some Mexican-Americans because he defied racial discrimination and ignored what he considered to be unjust laws against his fellow countrymen.

William Brady was killed. He escaped being caught, however, and became a fugitive.

Billy broke out on his own as a cattle rustler, getting his name on the "Wanted" posters down in Arizona. He wrote New Mexico governor **Lew Wallace** an impassioned letter, asking for a pardon. In the letter, he wrote: "I'm not afraid to die like a man fighting, but I would not like to be killed like a dog unarmed." The governor agreed to pardon Billy in exchange for testimony against other outlaws. As part of the agreement, Billy turned himself in. But he soon realized that the pardon would never come: he was wanted for more than just rustling and didn't stand a chance in court. Billy made his escape quite easily – more or less just walking out of the Lincoln jail to freedom.

He was caught three years later and charged for his participation in the Lincoln War. While he was by no means the only participant in the fight, Billy was the sole person tried for the murder of Sheriff Brady. On 8 April, after the one-day trial in a small adobe building, Billy stood before the bench and a jury found him guilty of gunning Brady down three years earlier. On 13 April, Billy was sentenced by Judge Warren Bristol to be hanged "by the neck until his body be dead". Instead, he escaped, and immediately headed for Fort Sumner, New Mexico, where he had friends.

On 14 July 1881, Lincoln County sheriff **Pat Garrett** shot Billy the Kid to death in an ambush at the Fort Sumner ranch home of a friend of his. The next day, Billy was buried at the nearby Old Fort Sumner cemetery on the same grave site as two fallen companions, Tom O'Folliard and Charlie Bowdre. A stone marker lists all three men, who are buried side by side, with the word "Pals" carved into the top of the tombstone.

For further investigation

📖 **Sheriff Patrick Garrett** The Authentic Life of Billy, the Kid A new edition of the original 1927 account, written by the sheriff who killed Billy.

📖 **Michael Wallis** Billy the Kid: The Endless Ride (2008) Using newspaper accounts and other historical documents, the author pieced together the facts behind Billy the Kid's life.

🎬 **William A. Graham** Billy the Kid (1989) A remake of the 1941 movie of the same name, starring Val Kilmer.

Ⓦ memory.loc.gov/wpa/19030911 Some oral history: the deposition of a lawman who met Billy the Kid in 1877 when the outlaw was jailed in New Mexico.

JOHN DILLINGER

Chicago police gunned down the outlaw John Herbert Dillinger in 1934, when he was 31 years old. He had spent most of his young life as a criminal: armed robberies were his speciality, terrorizing the good citizens of Indiana and neighbouring states. He has often been described as the US's first celebrity criminal. US Federal Bureau of Investigations agents dubbed Dillinger **Public Enemy Number One** and "a notorious and vicious thief" because of the scale of his crimes and his unpredictably violent nature. Clearly he was a force to be reckoned with; he epitomized the 1930s American gangster era and stirred mass emotion to a degree rarely seen at that time.

By modern standards, Dillinger's crimes were perhaps tame, especially when compared with some of today's criminals. Nevertheless, once the FBI was tracking him down for murder, his status became legendary. Associates of the Dillinger Gang were responsible for the fatal shootings of thirteen law-enforcement officers in 1933 and 1934 alone.

His life started out normally enough. Born John Herbert Dillinger Jr in Indianapolis, Indiana, on 22 June, 1903, there was nothing to distinguish him from any other minor crook in his early criminal years. On 4 December 1923, after serving just five months in the US Navy, Dillinger went absent without leave. In 1924, he married a child bride, sixteen-year-old Beryl Hovious.

That same year, on 16 September, Dillinger and a new accomplice, Ed Singleton, robbed a Mooresville, Indiana, grocer named Frank Morgan. Dillinger hit Morgan with an iron bolt wrapped in cloth. It was a particularly stupid crime to have attempted, given that Mooresville was only a small town of which Dillinger was a resident: he was recognized by the grocer, who was not seriously injured, and was arrested for the assault and robbery. Ten days later, he was incarcerated at the Indiana State Reformatory in Michigan City to serve out a ten- to twenty-year sentence. Singleton was sentenced to two to fourteen years. Dillinger was later transferred to the Indiana State Prison, a facility built near Michigan City, Indiana, to house prisoners of war during the Civil War. In 1929, Dillinger's wife divorced him, not wishing to remain married to a convicted felon.

The "gun", carved out of wood and blackened with boot polish, with which John Dillinger escaped jail.

While in prison, Dillinger picked up tips from fellow inmates who were seasoned bank robbers. As it turned out, prison turned out to be an excellent training ground for Dillinger, honing his smarts and toughening him up for a career as a professional lawbreaker. In May 1933, he was released on parole because his stepmother was dying, but by the time he made it home she had already passed away. Less than a month after his release, he tried out his acquired robbery tips by holding up his first bank – a stick-up job in New Carlisle, Ohio, in which he walked away with a booty of $10,600.

Within four months, he was back in jail again, this time in Lima, Ohio. He was sprung by some fellow prison gang members; they escaped, killing their jailer, Sheriff Jessie Sarber, in the process. At the end of that year, most of the gang, including Dillinger, were captured in Tucson, Arizona. This time Dillinger was incarcerated in the Lake County jail in Crown Point, Indiana. It was in that jail that the now-famous photograph of him with his arm on the prosecutor's shoulder was taken. Before his trial was to start, Dillinger, who had picked his fellow inmates' brains on the prison's workings, busted out of the so-called escape-proof county jail, embarrassing his jailers. Newspapers reported that Dillinger had made a fake gun, fashioned out of wood and blackened with shoe polish, and fooled deputies into believing he was armed.

Once out of prison, he was once again up to his old tricks and his bank robberies continued at a steady pace. Dillinger was thought to have been associated with gangs that robbed a dozen banks and stole more than $300,000, which was a huge amount during the Depression years. As he pulled off a growing list of heists, newspaper accounts began referring to him as "**Jack Rabbit**": his movements during robberies were apparently very like a jack rabbit, as he leaped over bank counters, narrowly escaping police officers. He hooked up with other robbers and the group became known as the Dillinger Gang. After Dillinger and his boys moved into Chicago territory, the Chicago Police Department established a special elite group dubbed the Dillinger Squad, headed by **Captain John Stege**, to track down the gang. While living there, Dillinger, a big sports fan, regularly attended Chicago Cubs baseball games.

He was eventually apprehended by the authorities and held on a murder charge at the Crown Point County Jail. He escaped, but it was to be the Jack Rabbit's last leap. A girlfriend of his betrayed him, tipping police off as to his whereabouts. Unaware that federal agents were lying in wait for him the gang leader was shot three times – twice in the chest and once in the neck – as he left a cinema on 22 July 1934. Dillinger died instantly.

Fans of the criminal continue to observe their annual "John Dillinger Day" on 22 July, and Dillinger's gravestone at Crown Hill Cemetery in Indianapolis, Indiana, has been pillaged for memorabilia. Some naysayers claimed that John Dillinger did not in fact die on that 22 July day, insisting that the dead man was in fact a petty criminal from Wisconsin named Jimmy Lawrence who looked a lot like Dillinger. The allegations caused a controversy which heated up even more when an autopsy revealed that the body had brown eyes but, according to police documents, Dillinger's eyes were actually grey. Furthermore, the body showed signs of a childhood disease and a rheumatic heart condition that Dillinger never had.

The police mugshot of gangster John Dillinger, and the flier giving notice of his "wanted" status.

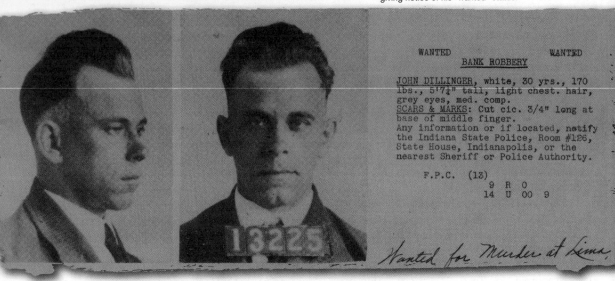

```
WANTED                          WANTED
           BANK ROBBERY
JOHN DILLINGER, white, 30 yrs., 170
lbs., 5'7¼" tall, light chest. hair,
grey eyes, med. comp.
SCARS & MARKS: Cut cic. 3/4" long at
base of middle finger.
Any information or if located, notify
the Indiana State Police, Room #126,
State House, Indianapolis, or the
nearest Sheriff or Police Authority.

     F.P.C.  (13)
                  9  R  0
                 14  U  00  9
```

Wanted for Murder at Lima,

The credibility of these claims is compromised by the fact that the body was positively identified as that of Dillinger by his sister, by a scar on his leg he received as a child. While there was substantial scarring, the postmortem fingerprints were positively identified as Dillinger's.

For further investigation

📖 **G. Russell Girardin, William J. Helmer & Rick Mattix** Dillinger: The Untold Story **(2005)** Everything you could ever want to know about the notorious John Dillinger.

📖 **William J. Helmer, Rick Mattix & Rose Keefe** The Complete Public Enemy Almanac: New Facts and Features on the People, Places, and Events of the Gangster and Outlaw Era, 1920–1940 **(2007)** A reference book covering two decades of lawlessness in American history.

Ⓦ hydeparkmedia.com/dillinger An article about Dillinger's escape from the Crown Point County Jail when he used a toy gun to break out, a move that to this day is said to embarrass the townsfolk.

PRETTY BOY FLOYD

Charles Arthur Floyd grew up on a small farm in the Cookson Hills district of Oklahoma. The family had moved there in the midst of a drought, and they struggled financially. To make ends meet, his father, Walter Floyd, got into the business of bootlegging, and Charles got into bank robberies. He bought his first gun while still a teenager. The first known crime to be committed by Floyd was at age eighteen, when he stole $3.50 in pennies from a post office, according to the 22

October 1922 issue of *Time* magazine. Unable to find work, he started robbing banks.

Three years later, at twenty-one, he was arrested in St Louis, Missouri, for a payroll robbery and served five years in prison. When paroled, he found refuge in Tom's Town, later to be renamed Kansas City. It was a rough place, a haven for hired guns, gangsters, and murderers. The city had gained a reputation as a safe port of call for criminals. To stay there, crooks had to pay off the Italian mob, which, at the time, was run by **Johnny Lazia**, the unofficial sheriff who tolerated bootlegging, prostitution and gambling, while keeping serious and violent crimes in check. It was in Tom's Town that Floyd learned how to use a machine gun.

While never a member of a gang, Floyd certainly had accomplices, and he teamed up with various outlaws he encountered in the criminal underworld of Tom's Town. He had a regular partner, George Birdwell, with whom he pulled a multitude of bank jobs close to home and, on 22 December 1931, even managed two in one day in the Oklahoma towns of Castle and Paden. As a result, the local bank insurance rates doubled, and the governor of Oklahoma placed a $56,000 reward on George Birdwell's head. He gained national recognition, becoming regularly referred to as "Oklahoma's Bandit King". At the same time, the FBI issued a poster with the following caption: "Wanted dead or alive: $4,000 for the capture of "Pretty Boy" Charles Floyd". He had become a folk anti-hero.

Pretty Boy Floyd became even more notorious when he was accused in 1933 of participating in the 17 June Kansas City **Union Station Massacre** in Tom's Town. The shootout occurred as convicted murderer **Frank "Jelly" Nash** was being escorted

HOW THE BOY BECAME PRETTY

There are two different accounts as to how he got the nickname "Pretty Boy". One story says he earned it after his first major robbery because of the description given by one witness that he was "a mere boy – a pretty boy with apple cheeks". Another account says that Beulah Baird Ash, a brothel madam in Tom's Town, give him the nickname. He was reportedly never happy with the name – much like Baby Face Nelson. But the name stuck.

through Union Square by officers, in order to return him to jail at Leavenworth, Kansas, from which he had already escaped three times. After the smoke had finally cleared over this particularly bloody event, FBI agent Raymond Caffrey, Police Chief Otto Reed, and detectives Frank Hermanson and W.J. Grooms were dead. Nash was also cut down in the bloodbath, despite the fact that his associates were supposedly trying to free him.

It was one of the most sensational stories of its time. It is believed that **Adam Richetti**, who was a friend of Nash, and two machine-gun-wielding accomplices had committed the crimes. Richetti was tried and convicted of murder in the case; he was later executed in Missouri's gas chamber.

It was believed that the other shooters were Floyd and Vernon Miller, although the truth of the matter is not known: both men denied being there, though US federal agents didn't buy their stories. With one of their own dead, the G-men wanted payback, and began tailing Floyd. On 22 October 1934, they

13

caught up with him in Ohio after spotting Floyd's car behind a bush. They surrounded his car, and when Floyd stepped out of the driver's seat with a .45 calibre pistol in hand, agents opened fire. Floyd was shot to death during the ambush. The action marked the first time that US federal agents, serving under Director J. Edgar Hoover, carried guns in the line of duty.

Pretty Boy Floyd's body was put on public display in Salisaw, Oklahoma, and there were reports of between

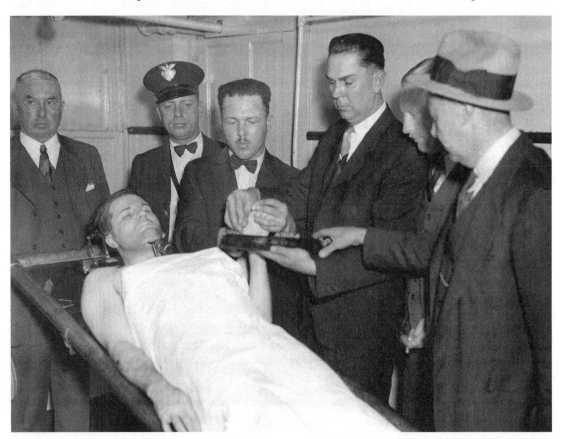

The body of Charles "Pretty Boy" Floyd is propped on a slab in the county morgue in East Liverpool, Ohio, after he was shot and killed in a gun battle with federal agents on a nearby farm on 22 October 1934.

20,000 and 40,000 people attending his funeral, the largest service in Oklahoma history. He was buried in Akin, Oklahoma.

Recent in-depth studies of Pretty Boy Floyd and the Kansas City Massacre have suggested that Floyd had been telling the truth. Author Robert Unger produced evidence that officers may have accidentally killed their own, in an incidence of what the military call "friendly fire": that it could have been Agent Lackey's handling of an unfamiliar weapon – a shotgun – that killed Frank Nash, Agent Caffrey, and Officer Hermanson.

Woody Guthrie immortalized many Oklahoma bandits in a series of songs titled the *Dustbowl Ballads* that celebrated the outlaws as populist heroes. Included was a song about the **Dalton Gang**, and another about a brazen female outlaw named **Belle Starr**. One of his most famous songs, however, was Guthrie's 1939 "The Ballad of Pretty Boy Floyd". "Come gather 'round me, children, a story I will tell", the lyrics began. "'Bout Pretty Boy Floyd, an outlaw, Oklahoma knew him well."

For further investigation

📖 **Michael Wallice** Pretty Boy: The Life & Times of Charles Arthur Floyd **(1994)** Everything you could ever want to know about Pretty Boy Floyd.

📖 **Robert Unger** The Union Station Massacre: The Original Sin of J. Edgar Hoover's FBI **(2005)** Controversial examination of the bloody fiasco at Union Station.

Ⓦ geocities.com/CapitolHill/Lobby/3935 Detailed biography of Charles Floyd.

BABY FACE NELSON

A short man at five foot six, Lester Joseph Gillis, also known as George Nelson, grew up after the turn of the twentieth century in the hard Chicago Union Stockyard district. His parents were Belgian immigrants, and he was one of seven children. They lived on North California Avenue, near Humboldt Park, and their father, Joseph, worked in the stockyards at a tannery, while their mother, Marie (or Mary, as she anglicized it), tutored schoolchildren in French. Lester was the youngest Gillis child and the smallest boy on his block, a fact that made him the target of bullies. After his parents enrolled him in a rigid parochial school, Lester began misbehaving and eventually skipping school.

In 1918, his sister, Jenny Gillis, fell victim to the deadly influenza epidemic and died. Instead of attending the funeral service, held in the front room of his home, Lester cowered on his bed, terrified of seeing his sister's lifeless body. Nevertheless, his mother pulled her nine-year-old son out of bed and forced him to look. "See now how peaceful your sister looks?" she asked him. From that day forward, Lester expressed dread whenever death was mentioned. His parents sent him off to boarding school fifty miles away, hoping it would lift him out of his depression. A month later, Lester, dirty and wet from the rain and clutching a kitten, showed up at the door of his father's tannery. His parents re-enrolled him in the local Catholic school, but Nelson again started skipping classes.

During the ensuing years, while he was in his early teens, Lester roamed the streets of Chicago with a gang of underage hoodlums, and by the age of fourteen he was an accomplished car thief, according to his FBI file. He was sent to the Cook County School for Boys, a reformatory. While there, his father committed suicide and Lester ran away again. He returned to school, but he played hooky most of the time.

Finally, Lester dropped out of high school and began hanging out with the **Halsted Street Boys**, neighbourhood gang members who took their name after the central thoroughfare in their neighbourhood, which they considered their turf.

His early criminal career, with the local wannabe thugs, included stealing tyres, bootlegging and armed robbery. He was nicknamed "**Baby Face**" because of his youthful appearance, but his demeanour was anything but soft. He was said to hate the nickname, but it stuck to him for the rest of his life.

After he was caught stealing cars and taking friends on joyrides, he was convicted of car theft in 1922. A judge sentenced him to eighteen months in the Illinois State School for Boys at St Charles. He arrived at the overcrowded and understaffed reformatory two months shy of his fourteenth birthday. While there, Lester hooked up with Roger Touhy ("the Terrible") and his gang. It was then that Lester changed his name to George Nelson.

He didn't stick around, and, through Touhy, Nelson met the notorious Chicago gangster Al Capone and became an enforcer and thug for the mob. However, after Nelson fought with Capone's top ally in New Jersey, **Anthony Accetturo** – a leader in the Lucchese crime family – Capone let Nelson go. Even in Al Capone's underworld, Baby Face Nelson was too violent and out of control for the mobster. Nelson's reputation grew: it became known that his take on sticking up a bank was to go in guns blazing, and he became the most feared robber of his time.

In 1934, Nelson gained even more prominence when he joined up with John Dillinger's gang – only Dillinger died the same year. Nelson was known to boast about having robbed a bank a day for a month, which was his way of trying to surpass Dillinger's notorious crime record. While that claim was never substantiated, Nelson was personally responsible for killing more federal agents than any other criminal during that era. A cold and brutal man, he apparently took pleasure in killing.

In 1928, when Nelson was twenty, he got to know **Helen Warwick**, a petite girl of fifteen whose immigrant parents had altered their name from Wawrzyniak. He met her at the toy store where she was a shop assistant. Within months, Helen was pregnant, and in October of that year they were married at the county courthouse. Nelson and his wife were devoted to each other and, in between George's hold-ups, lived a quiet domestic life with their two children.

In his criminal activity, Nelson was anything but gentle. Richard Lindberg, author of *Return to the Scene of the Crime*, wrote that "Gillis compensated for his physical limitations with a murderous temper and a willingness to employ a switchblade or a gun without hesitation or remorse for the intended victim." After John Dillinger died, the G-men, as FBI agents were called in those days, bestowed the vacant title of Public Enemy Number One upon Nelson.

Nelson's reign of terror ended in 1934 during a machine-gun battle with two FBI agents. On 27 November, in the town of Barrington, Illinois, Nelson engaged agents Herman Hollis and Samuel Cowley in a fierce gunfight. By all accounts Nelson's attack was motiveless, and entirely down to his hatred of lawmen.

A police mugshot of Baby Face Nelson.

Nelson, his wife Helen, and criminal associate John Paul Chase were driving down a road when Nelson noticed that there were FBI agents in a car travelling in the opposite direction: he kept a list of FBI and police licence plates, such was his loathing of the law. Nelson turned the car around and gave chase to the vehicle. Once both had stopped, he leaped from the car and fired a Thompson sub-machine-gun at both agents, who returned fire.

Reportedly, Nelson made no effort to take cover, simply walking towards the pair. He was shot and injured, but he escaped arrest that day. The following day, however, his body was found lying, swaddled in a blanket, in a ditch next to a cemetery in Niles Center, Illinois. It was assumed he had died from his injuries from the gunfight the day before; when the story broke, *The New York Times* claimed he had been shot seventeen times. George "Baby Face" Nelson was dead at age 25.

He was buried at St Joseph Cemetery in River Grove, Illinois, twelve miles from the home he grew up in, near the Union Stockyards.

For further investigation

📖 **The Federal Bureau of Investigations** Baby Face Nelson: The FBI Files (2007) This paperback contains declassified criminal investigations carried out by the FBI into Nelson. Included are documents and details concerning Nelson's infamous 1934 robbery of the Peoples Savings Bank in Grand Haven, Michigan.

📖 **Steven Nickel & William J. Helmer** Baby Face Nelson: Portrait of a Public Enemy (2002) A no-holds-barred account of Nelson's criminal career, covering all his infamous bank robberies and violent gun battles in the street.

🎬 **Scott Levy** Baby Face Nelson (1997) A nostalgic but unromanticized and violent account of Baby Face Nelson's gangster activities in Chicago, which rivalled Al Capone, the top mobster of the era.

ⓦ **s9.com/Biography/Nelson-George** A timeline of pivotal events in Baby Face Nelson's life.

BONNIE AND CLYDE

In 1932, Clyde Barrow and Bonnie Parker burst upon the American Southwest in the midst of the Great Depression. They were among a growing list of celebrity criminals of the modern era, and there have now been five movies made that tell their story, and plenty of song lyrics have been written about the notorious young killers.

Bonnie was married at the age of sixteen, and was left on her own when her husband was sent to a federal penitentiary just a year after their wedding. To get by, Bonnie landed a job as a waitress, but she was convinced there was more to life than her dead-end job, and she quit. It was around the time Bonnie left her job that she met Clyde Barrow, when she was nineteen and Clyde was twenty-one.

A number of theories have been bandied about over the years about how Bonnie and Clyde first met. The most credible version says that Clyde Barrow met Bonnie Parker in January of 1930. Bonnie was staying with a friend in West Dallas; Clyde dropped by the house while Bonnie was in the kitchen making hot chocolate. There was an immediate attraction. She stood by him when he was imprisoned shortly after they met, helping him to escape by smuggling a gun to him in jail. He was recaptured but paroled in early 1932. She remained a loyal companion to him as they carried out their crime spree for the next two years and awaited the violent deaths they saw as inevitable. Indeed, Bonnie rather prone to self-mythologizing: she wrote poetry, and some of her poems were published after her death, including two titled "The Story of Bonnie and Clyde" and "Suicide Sal". Clyde, on the other hand, wasn't nearly so interested in fame and fortune. His goal in life was to exact revenge on the Texas prison system he despised for abuses he felt he had suffered while serving time.

In 1932, Bonnie and Clyde hooked up with Raymond Hamilton, a young gunman, for a few months, before William Daniel Jones – "W.D." – replaced him as the third of their criminal trio. The following year, Clyde's brother Buck was released from the Texas State Prison where he had been serving time. He and Clyde had already committed a multitude of robberies – mostly grocery stores and petrol stations – and crimes such as safe-cracking and car theft. Buck, along with his wife Blanche, joined the gang, making them a quintet.

For two years, between 1932 and 1934, the Barrow Gang took bank employees hostage and kidnapped lawmen in the course of their headline-grabbing crime spree. They usually released any prisoners

Stick 'em up: Clyde Barrow at the wrong end of Bonnie Parker's gun.

them. The pair were also compared to Shakespeare's star-crossed lovers, being dubbed "Romeo and Juliet in a getaway car" by one writer. The pair in reality had little in common with any heroes of myth or fiction: the Barrow Gang did not hesitate to kill anyone if people got in their way. Clyde is believed to have shot and killed at least ten people. Other members of the Barrow Gang wanted for murder by the lawmen included W.D. Jones, Raymond Hamilton, Buck Barrow (Clyde's brother) and Henry Methvin.

On 13 April 1933, J.W. "Wes" Harryman, a Newton County constable, and Harry McGennis, a Joplin police detective, approached the gang's hideout – a two-storey apartment in Joplin, Missouri. There ensued a gun battle that left both men dead. But not before, however, they had wounded gang member W.D. Jones, and the trio of Jones, Bonnie and Clyde fled in Clyde's car. The gang had left most of their possessions behind inside the $20-a-month rented apartment – including a 16-gauge bloodstained shotgun, handwritten poems by Bonnie Parker, a camera, and several rolls of exposed Kodak film. The film, which contained mostly photos taken of each other, was developed by the *Joplin Globe* newspaper, and produced the now-famous photos of the members of the gang. After the photos were published, Bonnie and Clyde, who were on the lam for a month, wised up and started to cover the licence plates of their stolen vehicles with coats and hats when they posed for photos. Barrow was now wanted for murder, robbery, and kidnapping, and a massive manhunt was launched to locate him.

they took far from home, and would even on occasion give them cash so they could make it back on their own. It was a habit that contributed to the "Robin Hood" mystique that grew to surround

In January 1934, while eluding police, Clyde masterminded the prison escape of Henry Methvin,

BEING A GANGSTER: IT'S A DOG'S LIFE

Despite the glamorous images associated with the Barrow Gang, their lives were truly desperate. A recently published manuscript revealed Blanche Barrow's account of her life on the run. Clyde, the book says, drove furiously while he searched for places where they could sleep or have a meal without being noticed; even though they had thousands of dollars gained from bank heists, sleeping in beds was a rare luxury and one person was always assigned as a lookout. It wasn't exactly a stress-free environment and, far from being a roller-coaster ride, the gang's existence was characterized by arguments and bickering.

Raymond Hamilton, and several other infamous prisoners – an event that was dubbed the "Eastham Breakout". If revenge against Texas penal institutions was indeed Barrow's main criminal ambition, then he seemed to have achieved it. The Texas Department of Corrections was considerably embarrassed by the jailbreak, compounded by the fact that two prison guards were shot with automatic pistols used by the escaping prisoners. The department commissioned **Frank A. Hamer**, a six-foot-three, 230-pound former captain in the Texas Rangers, to come out of retirement to hunt down the Barrow Gang.

In April of that year, the Barrow Gang lost further sympathy in the eyes of the public when Henry Methvin and Clyde killed two young highway patrolmen near Grapevine in Texas (an area now known as Southlake); they killed a police constable in Oklahoma a few days later, where they also wounded and abducted an officer.

An FBI agent deduced that Bonnie and Clyde were probably hiding out in a remote area south of Ruston, Louisiana, which was close to the home of the Methvins. The combined efforts of the FBI and local law enforcement authorities in Louisiana and Texas turned up some trump-card information: that Bonnie and Clyde, with some of the Methvins, had thrown a party at Black Lake, Louisiana, on the night of 21 May and were going to return to the area two days later. The lawmen decided to stage an ambush.

In the early morning of 23 May, a posse composed of police officers from Louisiana and Texas, including Texas Ranger Frank Hamer, hid in bushes along Highway 154 near Sailes, Louisiana. Bonnie and Clyde were identified driving an automobile and when they attempted to escape, the officers opened fire. The pair of outlaws were killed instantly.

No warning was called out to Bonnie and Clyde, and a combined 130 rounds were shot into the car, riddling the vehicle and its occupants with bullets.

Inside the stolen car that Clyde had been driving was a cache of weapons, including automatic rifles, semi-automatic shotguns, handguns, and several thousand rounds of ammunition. There were also fifteen licence plates from a variety of US states. The bullet-riddled 1934 Ford deluxe four-door saloon was purchased in 1988 by the owner of a Nevada hotel and casino and is regularly on display in Missouri and in Nevada.

Inscribed on Bonnie's tombstone was a poem she wrote: "As the flowers are all made sweeter by the sunshine and the dew, so this old world is made

THE SHOOTING OF BONNIE & CLYDE

In a statement to the *Dallas Dispatch* newspaper on the day after the shooting of Barrow and Parker, one of the posse of policemen gave the following description of events: "Each of us six officers had a shotgun and an automatic rifle and pistols. We opened fire with the automatic rifles. They were emptied before the car got even with us. Then we used shotguns ... There was smoke coming from the car, and it looked like it was on fire. After shooting the shotguns, we emptied the pistols at the car, which had passed us and ran into a ditch about fifty yards on down the road. It almost turned over. We kept shooting at the car even after it stopped. We weren't taking any chances."

brighter by the lives of folks like you."

For further investigation

📖 **E.R. Milner** The Lives and Times of Bonnie and Clyde (2003) A readable write-up of the most romanticized pair of crims in history.

ⓦ txashideout.tripod.com/joplinapartment Photos and information about the Joplin hideout apartment on Oak Ridge Drive. The apartment is available to rent by the week.

ⓦ texashideout.tripod.com/warrencar A site that includes photos and information over the years about what has been called Bonnie and Clyde's "death car".

MA BARKER

Kate "Ma" Barker was one of the legendary American criminals of the "Public Enemy" era. While her gang's exploits were headline news at the time, Barker's notoriety has since subsided, trailing behind John Dillinger and Bonnie and Clyde. The popular view of Ma Barker as the gang's leader and its criminal mastermind has been called a myth: it was not until after Ma Barker's death that she became known as the brains behind the infamous Barker-Karpis Gang; they were only "Ma Barker and her boys" once she was in the grave.

Ma Barker was a pudgy, five-feet-two, Bible-reading fiddle player who enjoyed hillbilly songs and crossword puzzles, and a mother of four – all of whom grew up to be deadly criminals. It was the FBI that gave Ma the prestigious but undeserved title of leader of the pack, claiming that she was the mastermind behind her sons' jobs. According to the Bureau, she was the engineer of the escape routes, who then waited at home, in prayer, for her sons to return with the loot. The theory was never proven and Ma was in actual fact never even charged with a crime.

No evidence ever surfaced linking her as an active participant in her boys' endeavours. Rather, her role was to take care of gang members, who often sent her out to the movies while they committed their crimes. The FBI insisted, however, that Ma played a major criminal role, and they nicknamed her "**Bloody Mary**".

Ma's life began simply enough. She was born **Arizona Donnie Clark** in 1872, part of a poor family who lived in the Ozark hills near Springfield, Missouri. Friends called her Kate. In 1892 at the age of twenty, she

KARPIS ON MA

Alvin "Creepy" Karpis is one of the most authoritative voices to have attempted to dispel the myth that Ma Barker was the leader of the gang. And he should know. "The most ridiculous story in the annals of crime is that Ma Barker was the mastermind behind the Karpis-Barker gang", he stated. "She wasn't a leader of criminals or even a criminal herself. There is not one police photograph of her or set of fingerprints taken while she was alive ... she knew we were criminals but her participation in our careers was limited to one function: when we travelled together, we moved as a mother and her sons. What could look more innocent?"

married **George Barker**, a farm labourer.

The couple lived in a tar-papered shack in a small Missouri town not far from where Kate had been born. She gave birth to four sons, **Herman**, **Lloyd**, **Arthur**, and **Freddie**. Her husband George had a drink problem; he abandoned the family shortly after Freddie was born. The kids were badly behaved, and became juvenile delinquents. They began their criminal careers with petty crimes, but eventually graduated to bank and train robberies. The two oldest Barker boys, Herman and Lloyd, are thought to have been part of the **Central Park Gang**, which was based in Tulsa, Oklahoma, from around 1915. Herman had already been arrested several times for highway robberies, while Arthur Barker began a not altogether successful career as a bank robber in the early 1920s. In 1922, Arthur was imprisoned for the murder of James J. Sherrill, a night watchman, in

Tulsa, Oklahoma, the previous year. He was not to be released for ten years.

Throughout the 1920s, the Barker boys that were still at large were involved in a plethora of robberies and heists. All this time, their mother professed she did not believe the stories she heard about her sons. "Lies, all lies! You're all lying against my boys!", she shouted at the federal officers, as they arrested one of her sons yet again. It was a classic case of a mother's self-protective denial, flying in the face of all the evidence.

In 1927, however, Herman was stopped by police following a bank heist in Wichita, Kansas, just over the Missouri-Kansas state line. Rather than be taken into custody, Herman turned his gun on himself, committing suicide. Then, in 1932, Lloyd was sent away to the US penitentiary in Leavenworth, Kansas, to serve a 25-year term for robbing mail in Baxter Springs, Kansas. Fred Barker had also been arrested and served time between 1927 and 1931. During his time inside he had met **Alvin "Creepy" Karpis**, who had been convicted of car theft. Alvin was the son of Lithuanian immigrants, was said to have a photographic memory and had gained his nickname from his smile – supposedly a sinister sight. Upon the pair's release, they teamed up, formed a gang, and committed a series of successful bank robberies. Although Herman Barker was dead and Lloyd was in prison, Arthur rejoined his brother Fred in the gang in late 1932.

The Barker-Karpis gang turned to kidnapping in 1933. Their first victim was **William Hamm** – the rich owner of Hamm's Beer – and they got away with $100,000 in ransom money. But the kidnapping of **Edward G. Bremer**, a wealthy Minnesota businessman, was to prove the gang's downfall. Although the kidnapping was successful – the gang

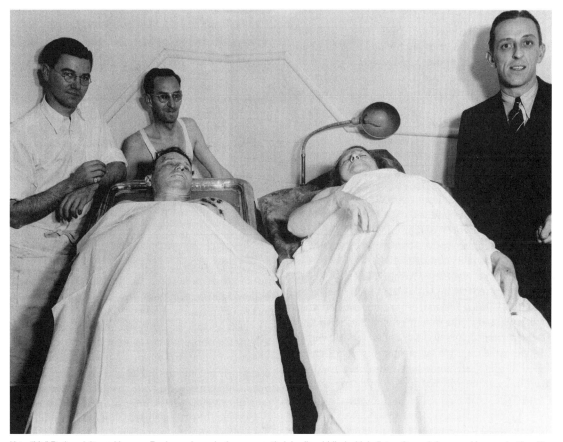

Kate "Ma" Barker, right, and her son Fred, are shown in the morgue, their bodies riddled with bullets, after a six-hour machine-gun battle with federal agents in Ocklawaha Florida, on 16 January 1935.

scored a large ransom and released Bremer unharmed – it was an affront too far. The Bureau redoubled their efforts to take the gang down. They arrested Arthur Barker on 8 January 1935, in Chicago. They then managed to track down the matriarch of the Barker

clan via letters that she had sent.

The G-men, dressed in black suits and armed with Tommy guns, surrounded a two-storey house in Ocklawaha, a small Florida community, on 16 January 1935. They called out to Ma Barker, telling her that if she and her son surrendered, no one would get hurt. Instead, Freddie fired shots from the second floor. Federal agents returned fire and a six-hour gun battle ensued with fourteen FBI agents. When it was over, the feds had pumped a hundred rounds into the dwelling. Afterward, all was quiet. An agent went in, then quickly returned. "They're dead", he shouted. With that, the G-men broke out in applause – at least that's how the tale has been handed down.

Kate and Freddie's bullet-riddled bodies remained for eight months at the Ocala funeral parlour, waiting to be claimed. While there, FBI agents were photographed with the bodies. Eventually, George Barker, Ma's estranged husband, went to the mortuary and arranged for the burial of Kate and his son Freddie in Welch, Oklahoma.

In 1936, the FBI arrested Alvin Karpis in New Orleans. Three years later, Arthur Barker was fatally shot during an attempted escape from the federal prison on Alcatraz Island, off the coast of Northern California. Lloyd, the only surviving Barker son, was released from prison in 1947, after serving out his 25-year sentence. Two years later, his wife shot and killed him in their home in Westminster, Colorado. For the crime, his wife was sent to an insane asylum.

For further investigation

Robert Winter Mean Men: The Sons of Ma Barker (2007) This book, though now out of print, is well worth the search in used online bookstores.

Bill Karn Ma Barker's Killer Brood (1960) This lurid film depicts the Barker Gang's exploits in the 1930s South and Midwest; no-holds-barred in its rather sensationalist dramatizing of their kidnappings, robberies, and murders.

digital.library.okstate.edu/encyclopedia/entries/B/BA038
A historical, thorough account of the Barker Gang.

ATTILA AMBRUS: TRANSYLVANIA'S WHISKY ROBBER

When a career criminal was taken down in Budapest in January 1999, the scene was one that was straight out of a cops-and-robbers movie. The police, decked out in combat gear that included bulletproof vests and sub-machine-guns, stood guard at the cordoned-off roads leading out of the capital. Their colleagues combed the bus and railway stations, and, with helicopters circling overhead, tirelessly searched out their target. The high speed train to Bucharest was boarded by fifty officers, who had orders to open fire if they found their man and he was armed. The elite law-enforcement unit was after **Attila Ambrus**, a bandit who had earlier busted out of Gyorskocsi utka, a maximum-security prison. Following his escape, Ambrus had become known as Eastern Europe's most famous thief.

A decade earlier, in 1988, Ambrus had crossed Romania's borders into Hungary by riding underneath a freight train. So determined was he to escape his homeland that he had positioned himself between a grate and a wide steel bar that connected two train carriages, putting himself six inches off the ground. The train chugged into Hungary; he had made it intact.

Ambrus had grown up in a one-street village in Eastern Transylvania. He applied for political asylum and citizenship in Hungary, which was granted in 1994. A year earlier, in 1993, Ambrus had committed his first Post Office robbery – one near the flat where he lived. A string of 27 robberies followed – at least that is what he has admitting to doing – which included extending his range to banks and travel agents too.

In the life he led outside his criminal activities, he landed work as a gravedigger, pelt smuggler, Zamboni driver, and professional hockey goalie. He was, however, by all accounts a terrible goalkeeper, once letting in 23 goals in a single game. But, while a hockey player on the **Hungarian National Hockey** team, he never missed a practice. Whether the job was legal or illegal, he was a hard worker. All told, he stole about 299 million in Hungarian forints, or about $1 million.

Before Attila's arrest, websites in Hungary had popped up celebrating his exploits, put there by his cult-like following, rooting for him on the sidelines. Despite his large fan base, it was just a matter of time before he was caught, as his face had become too familiar thanks to the heavy media coverage of his crimes. He became known as the "Whiskey Robber" after he was spotted a couple of times downing shots of Johnnie Walker whiskey at pubs before commit-ting his crimes. Attila, who was eighteen months old when his mother deserted him to become a Jehovah's Witness, was also known as a ladies' man, because of his penchant for handing flowers to tellers during the bank heists.

He also mailed a bottle of wine to a police chief and, to pull off one particular job, he disguised himself as the head of a police department's robbery division. Indeed, Ambrus himself was not at all impressed with the Budapest police department's lengthy tactics in

arresting him. "I didn't think they were that good", he told reporters.

However, on Wednesday 27 October 1999, the police finally closed in on Attila, ending his career in crime. A special unit had been set up specifically to nail him. It had taken police three months to catch Attila, even though he was living in a downtown Budapest apartment. He was caught following a robbery at which police were able to find clues that led to his hideout. The arrest came at the end of what has been called the largest manhunt in modern Eastern European history.

Today, he remains jailed in a maximum-security prison in northeast Hungary in a town called Satoraljaujhely, where he regularly posts to an Internet blog. He was widely liked as an anti-Establishment figure, helped enormously by the fact that he did not hurt anyone when carrying out his robberies. Even a national newspaper sang his praises. "He didn't rob banks", opined the Hungarian daily *Magyar Hirlap* upon Ambrus's arrest. "He merely performed a peculiar redistribution of the wealth that differed from the elites only in its method."

For further investigation

📖 Julian Rubinstein Ballad of the Whiskey Robber (2004) The Johnnie-Walker-glugging heist-puller gets his own myth-making bio.

Ⓦ ce-review.org/99/19/gusztav19_ambrus A lengthy article concerning Ambrus's capture.

Ⓦ myspace.com/thewhiskeyrobber Attila's blog, which he updates (when he can) from prison.

NED KELLY

Hanged in Melbourne in 1880 when he was 26, Edward "Ned" Kelly had already become a legend, a man whose gang had carried out two daring bank robberies before being cut to pieces during a siege in rural country Victoria. His story has since struck a deep chord with Australians, always ready to identify with the ordinary man standing up against persecution by officialdom.

Born of an Irish convict father in 1854, Kelly's first serious brush with the law came in 1870, when he served six months hard labour for brawling with a neighbour and then mailing a pair of calf testicles to the man's wife. Fresh out of jail, Kelly rode his friend Isaiah Wright's horse into Greta town, only to discover that the horse had been stolen. After a scuffle with police constable Hall, Kelly was arrested for the theft of the horse, and sentenced to three years in Melbourne's Pentridge Prison. (Wright, the actual thief, received just eighteen months.)

Following his release in the mid-1870s, Kelly – as he would later claim in his famous letters – took to stealing horses and cattle with his stepfather George King in response to the way rich landowners would impound their poorer neighbours' stock. Police also suspected his younger brothers Jim and Dan Kelly to be involved in the pair's criminal activities, and on 15 April 1878 police constable **Alexander Fitzpatrick** was assaulted by members of the Kelly family at their home while trying to arrest Dan. Fitzpatrick claimed that Kelly's mother Ellen hit him over the head with a shovel and Ned shot him in the wrist. For their part, the Kellys said that Ned wasn't even there, that Fitzpatrick had no arrest warrant and that the assault

only occurred after Fitzpatrick threatened to shoot Ellen unless Dan went with him.

The next day, **Ellen Kelly**, Ned's brother-in-law **Bill Skilling** and his friend **Bricky Williamson** were arrested and later jailed for the attempted murder of Fitzpatrick. With a reward of £100 offered for their arrest, Dan and Ned went into hiding in Victoria's Wombat Ranges with accomplices Joe Byrne and Steve Hart.

On 25 October, Sergeant Kennedy, along with constables McIntyre, Lonigan and Scanlon, set off into the hills to track down the fugitives. But the Kelly Gang ambushed them near some log cabins at Stringybark Creek, Kelly shooting Lonigan and Byrne killing Scanlon. Kennedy was also killed in the exchange but McIntyre escaped on horseback. Ned Kelly later defended his actions, writing "I could not help shooting them, or else lie down and let them shoot me which they would have done". Incensed, the Victorian government placed a £2000 bounty on the heads of the gang of outlaws.

But the Kellys remained unbowed. On 10 December 1878 the gang descended on the small town of Euroa, locked half the population in the train station and robbed the National Bank of £2260. Ned left behind the "Euroa Letter", written in red ink, explaining his side of the events at Stringybark Creek, and promising dire consequences unless the government recognized the plight of poor landowners. The gang struck again on 8 February the next year, in an even more audacious escapade in which they locked two policemen in the cells at Jerilderie, stole their uniforms and then robbed the Jerilderie bank of another £2000. This time Ned left behind the "Jerilderie Letter" but – like the first – its contents were suppressed by the authorities.

The Kellys laid low over the next year, until Joe Byrne discovered that his longtime friend Aaron Sherritt had turned police informer, and shot him dead. The gang then decided to ambush a train carrying in police reinforcements, and so they rode to Glenrowan station on 27 June 1880. Here they pulled up the train tracks and took forty hostages at the Glenrowan hotel, standing them drinks on the house.

But during the evening Kelly released schoolteacher **Thomas Curnow**, who managed to warn the train before it ran off the rails. Around 3am some sixty police laid siege to the inn and riddled the building in a murderous crossfire, killing Byrne and several hostages. In the dawn, Ned emerged dressed in a suit of armour forged from old plough blades; he was gunned down but captured alive. The police finally

A depiction of Ned Kelly in his bullet-resistant iron suit, from the 1906 silent movie *The Story of the Kelly Gang*.

let the hostages leave the hotel and set it on fire. Dan and Hart's charred corpses were later found inside; witnesses reported that they had committed suicide earlier in the siege.

Despite a petition signed by thirty-two thousand people, Ned Kelly went to the gallows on 11 November 1880 for the murder of Constable Lonigan. Having told the trial judge that he'd soon see him in hell, the last words of this unrepentant rebel were "Such is life".

For further investigation

📖 **Ned Kelly** Euroa Letter and Jerilderie Letter **(1878)** Kelly's case in his own words.

📖 **J.J. Kenneally** The Inner History of the Kelly Gang **(1945)** A pro-Kelly viewpoint, written while several eyewitnesses were still alive to give their testimony.

Ⓦ **ironoutlaw.com** The facts and mythology surrounding the Kelly saga, including the latest archeological discoveries.

HEISTS AND ROBBERIES

Heists and robberies

Theft is as old as humankind. And ambitious thievery - in the form of the heist, the bank raid or the art-gallery robbery - has become one of the most romanticized of crimes. Reality has often proven stranger than fiction in the brazen schemes that have been reported over the years: the cracking of supposedly unbreakable safes; the lifting of ever more valuable artwork and jewels each year; and the daring raids committed in broad daylight under the very noses of security guards.

A successful high-end heist can net an ambitious thief millions in one fell swoop. There are even a lucky few that manage to offend time and time again: **Bill Mason**, once a master jewel thief, targeted the rich and famous in a career of successful burglaries that spanned three decades. But you might be surprised to learn that it is not money or jewels that provide thieves with the most profitable haul. According to Interpol, it is worldwide art theft that ranks as the top-grossing form of theft, ranking fourth among the most lucrative crimes (after drugs, money laundering, and arms sales).

Art theft

The astronomical prices commanded by works of art have led to the leading galleries in wealthy countries being regularly targeted by thieves; some thirty thousand artworks are listed as stolen in Interpol's database. The **FBI** estimates that the underground market for stolen art is as high as $6 billion annually. Cases drag on for years and often go unsolved. Thieves may wait decades before attempting to sell a piece of stolen art in the hope that it has lain low for long enough for its theft to have become a low priority. But, while thieves may be patient, so too are the investigators who probe the cases. Officers and agents from Interpol, Scotland Yard, and the FBI work for years and even decades pursuing leads for unsolved art heists. An underground network of art thieves, vendors and buyers thrives because of the law of supply and demand. Wealthy private collectors commission thieves to bolster their private collections and secret galleries.

VINCENZO PERUGIA AND THE MONA LISA

Considered to be the most famous art crime of the twentieth century, the theft of **Leonardo da Vinci**'s oil-on-poplar-wood masterpiece of the woman with a mysterious smile took place in 1911. It was a sensational robbery that would not be solved for two years.

The portrait of *Mona Lisa*, which was unsigned and classified simply as painting number 779, hung in the Louvre museum in Paris from 1804. The painting's official title is *Portrait of Lisa Gherardini, wife of Francesco del Giocondo*. A wealthy Florentine silk merchant, **Francesco del Giocondo** commissioned Leonardo to paint his wife in 1503, during the era of the Italian Renaissance; the painting was to hang in the couple's new home to celebrate the birth of Andrea, their second child. But Leonardo only completed the picture sixteen years later, in 1519, after he had moved to France. The subtle brush-strokes used to depict the square-jawed woman set the painting apart from others of its time. But it was its theft that made it infamous.

The *Mona Lisa* was discovered to be missing from the Louvre, France's most renowned and important storehouse for the artworks of the masters, on Monday 21 August 1911. On that summer day, a thief had walked into the Louvre's Salon Carré. He had lifted the painting off the wall, gone to a staircase and removed it from its frame, hidden the small painting (just thirty inches high and twenty-one inches wide) under his coat, and simply walked out. The museum had been closed that day for cleaning and around eight hundred employees, including workmen, cleaners, photographers, and museum executives, were at work at the time of the theft. None noticed anything out of the ordinary that day. Afterwards, Paris police blamed museum officials for inadequate security.

The theft of the *Mona Lisa,* already a noteworthy Italian Renaissance portrait, made it even more famous. People flocked to the museum, like mourners at a wake, to view the blank space on the wall where the *Mona Lisa* once hung.

The missing painting was not reported to police until the next day, because museum workers assumed wrongly that the work had been moved to the museum's studio to be photographed. As soon as staff members realized the painting was missing, they immediately informed the museum curator, who in turn notified Paris police. An army of sixty inspectors and more than a hundred police officers converged on the scene. The doors to the museum were locked and visitors inside were questioned. For a week, officers searched every floor and every room on the 49 acres of the Louvre property. Everyone who had ever worked at the museum was questioned.

Inspectors had very few clues to go on. While there was no obvious evidence pointing to a specific culprit, it was thought to be an inside job. Museum administrators at one point were accused of staging the theft to boost museum attendance, which increased substantially following the theft. No evidence, however, linked them. Bizarrely, both the avant-garde poet **Guillaume Apollinaire** and his friend, the famous painter, sculptor, and inventor **Pablo Picasso**, were suspected of being connected. Picasso was rumoured at the time to have purchased various pieces of stolen merchandise from a friend, among them the *Mona Lisa*. Apollinaire was arrested and taken in for questioning by police on 7 September. After being held for a week, he was released without charge.

For two years, the whereabouts of the *Mona Lisa* was unknown. In the meantime, the crime continued to make headlines around the world. While the case may not have been the biggest art theft of its time, it was certainly the best known. Newspaper cartoons, riddles, jokes, and even popular sheet-music songs all referenced and

The avant-garde poet Guillaume Apollinaire: an unlikely suspect to be fingered for the *Mona Lisa* job.

Vincenzo Perugia's rented room: this was for a while home to the world's most famous work of art.

Florence, Italy, offering to sell the painting for 500,000 lire (about $356,000 or €258,228). The motive was supposedly not money. Perugia hated France, and he felt that Italian masterpieces belonged in museums in Italy, so he removed the *Mona Lisa*, rescuing her from France, with the goal of returning her to her homeland.

When Geri asked to see the painting, Perugia arranged to meet him the next day at the Albergo Tripoli-Italia hotel (later renamed Hotel La Gioconda). According to an online account by PBS.org, Geri and Giovanni Poggi, the director of the Uffizi Gallery in Florence, met with Perugia as planned. To their surprise, Perugia produced the painting, which was rolled and stashed in the false bottom of a wooden cargo trunk. Under the guise of wanting to authenticate the painting before purchasing it, Geri and Poggi took the painting to a museum as Perugia waited for them in his hotel room. Once it was decided that the painting was in fact authentic, the men notified the police, and Perugia was arrested. As it turned out, the *Mona Lisa* had been hidden away for two years in the modest apartment where Perugia lived in France, just a few blocks from the Louvre from where the painting was stolen.

Police then learned the details surrounding the theft from Perugia. The idea to steal the painting hadn't been Perugia's. The plan had instead been masterminded by **Eduardo de Valfierno**, an Argentinian con man who'd hired Perugia to carry out the deed. A house painter and carpenter born in Italy,

mocked the theft. Then, more than two years later, on 10 December 1913, **Vincenzo Perugia**, an Italian immigrant using the alias of Leonardo Vincenzo, approached art dealer Alfredo Geri at his office in

POLICE LINE DO NOT CROSS

The *Madonna with the Yarnwinder* painting by Leonardo da Vinci, valued between £25 and £50 million, was stolen by two men in broad daylight. They joined a public tour, overpowered a guide, and lifted the painting from the Duke of Buccleuch's residence at Drumlanrig Castle in 2003. Police finally caught up with the thieves after four years, in 2007.

POLICE LINE DO NOT CROSS

Perugia had worked at the Louvre in 1908. While there, he had been contracted to make special glass-covered viewing boxes for the more prominent paintings in the museum, the *Mona Lisa* among them. When the theft was discovered, so was the discarded box, found in a stairwell, along with the painting's gilt wood frame.

Police also discovered that, following the theft being reported worldwide, Valfierno had sold six fake *Mona Lisa*s, duping several buyers into believing their painting was the real thing. Valfierno was only interested in selling fakes while the *Mona Lisa* was missing – he had no designs on ever acquiring the original – and did not contact him again. Perugia was convicted of the theft and given a lenient sentence – on patriotic grounds – of a year and two weeks in prison.

The *Mona Lisa*, which is owned by the French government, was eventually returned to the Louvre, where it is still exhibited today. After the incident, stricter security measures were put in place to ensure that a theft of the masterpiece never happened again. The mid-sized composition now hangs in a private alcove at the end of a large hall, cordoned off by velvet ropes, and protected by security glass in the museum's Salle des Etats hall – the same hall once used for legislative sessions presided over by Napoleon III.

Hotel La Gioconda has a reproduction of the *Mona Lisa* hanging above its reception desk, together with a small plaque commemorating the stolen painting's brief stay in the building, in room number twenty, together with its thief.

For further investigation

J. **Patrick Lewis** The Stolen Smile (2004) From the viewpoint of the thief and based on true events, this book describes how and why Vincenzo Perugia stole the Mona Lisa from the Louvre in 1911.

ⓦ news.bbc.co.uk/2/hi/entertainment/3590106.stm The BBC's list of the most famous art heists in history, complete with stories and descriptions.

ⓦ pbs.org/treasuresoftheworld/a_nav/mona_nav/main_monafrm PBS's in-depth coverage of the 1911 theft.

MASATSUGU KOGA & THE KUNSTHALLE BREMEN
Stolen masterpieces

A fax labelled "URGENT" marked the end of a five-decade hunt for $15 million worth of pilfered drawings. Sent from the German embassy in Tokyo to the Kunsthalle Bremen, it read, simply: "Dürer. Rembrandt. Van Ruisdael. Millet. Your art has surfaced." The missive referred to one of the most bizarre art heists of the twentieth century: a crime featuring twice-stolen masterpieces that involved the KGB, a Japanese businessman, an Azerbaijani wrestler, and an international sting operation.

The Kunsthalle Bremen once housed a large collection of prints and drawings; they had been stored there to protect them from the Allied bombing runs

The Kunsthalle Bremen, Germany: original home of the looted masterpieces that Koga tried to hawk.

with *Raised Hands*), two chalk landscapes by the Dutch master **Jacob van Ruisdael**, a black ink drawing by the Barbizon-school founder Jean-François Millet and a drawing by sixteenth-century Italian Baroque painter Annibale Carracci. The Rembrandt, said to depict the artist's wife Saskia, was worth $5 million alone.

Nothing was heard of them in the West again until after the Iron Curtain fell. The KGB had donated a number of works, including the drawings taken from Karnzow, to the Azerbaijan State Museum of Art in Baku and in 1993 German diplomats heard tell of an exhibition planned in

that pummelled Germany in World War II. In 1943, to further safeguard their treasures, the Kunsthalle moved the lot to the vaults of Karnzow Castle, north of Berlin. But soldiers of the Red Army plundered the castle during the chaotic aftermath of the war, taking nearly 1500 works back to Russia. Among the spoils were twelve drawings of particular distinction that would resurface some 45 years later.

The star of the twelve was **Albrecht Dürer**'s influential *Women's Bathhouse,* itself worth $10 million. The scene of voluptuous nudes rendered in black ink, dating from around 1496, was the first work of art to depict the naked body that was entirely unconnected to a religious or mythological theme. The dozen works also included another Dürer (*Sitting Mary with Child*), a **Rembrandt** ink drawing (*Woman Standing*

Baku that included the twelve missing drawings. In the midst of talks with Germany about repatriating the art to the Kunsthalle Bremen, the pieces were stolen again. *Studio International*, an art news service in London, described the fiasco as "a series of incidents that would put John le Carré's fiction in the shade". The artworks ended up in the hands of Japanese businessman **Masatsugu Koga**.

Four years passed before Koga, wearing bent wire-rimmed glasses, a rumpled gray flannel suit, and polished but worn shoes, walked into Tokyo's German embassy with photographs of the stolen drawings. Claiming they were family heirlooms, he offered to sell them back to their country of origin for $12 million. Keen-eyed embassy officials, however, recognized the distinctive Kunsthalle Bremen stamp on the drawings and informed Koga that the pieces were stolen. Koga, in a desperate move to elicit sympathy, said he needed the money for a kidney transplant (which was in fact true) and dropped the price to $6 million. He changed his story and told the officials that he'd purchased the paintings a few years earlier in Baku, the capital of Azerbaijan. The Germans, however, declined his offer and instead alerted Interpol.

Officials were able to connect Koga to the "**wrestling mafia**" – an organized crime syndicate set up by a group of former Russian professional wrestlers whose reach extended across three continents. Koga was a former wrestler himself, and was half-Russian on his mother's side. Aged sixty, he suffered from a kidney disease and had not earned any real money in years; he was in desperate need of cash. In Azerbaijan, he had been introduced to Natavan "Nata" Aleskerova, the ex-wife of Aydyn Ali Ibragimov, a 1964 Olympic heavyweight wrestling champion. Although Ibragimov was involved in the scheme to ransom the paintings to Germany, it was Aleskerova that was the true mastermind behind the plot. A well-known politico in her native Baku, "Nata", as she was nicknamed, held a position equivalent to a deputy attorney general (her own lawyers referred to her as the "Madeleine Albright of Azerbaijan").

After being turned away in Tokyo, Koga disappeared before resurfacing in New York a few months later, where he offered the drawings to the auction house Sotheby's. They declined on the basis that the art carried the Kunsthalle Bremen stamp. But Koga didn't give up. He was back on the map when Bremen museum officials, under the guise of authenticating the artwork, set up a clandestine meeting with him at the fashionable Midtown Manhattan Grand Hyatt hotel. There to meet Koga were Anne Roever-Kann, curator of the Bremen museum, as well as an undercover agent posing as Roever-Kann's associate. More agents were positioned in a surveillance van outside the hotel. Koga produced half of the twelve missing drawings, including the Dürers and the Rembrandt. Instead of a sale, the drawings were seized and Koga was arrested.

Aleskerova caught wind of the bust and immediately flew to New York to try to secure the remaining drawings. US agents tracked her down through customs and put a tail on her car, but she bolted, initiating a high-speed car chase around Manhattan's Washington Square Park that ended in her capture. Nata was found carrying three passports, but there were no clues as to the whereabouts of her former husband, Ibragimov.

Koga was prosecuted. With the condition of his kidneys having deteriorated to the point where he was forced to use a wheelchair, he was arraigned in US Federal Court and pleaded guilty to violating the National Stolen Property Act. After the arraignment, he told reporters he was merely trying to return the missing artwork to the Bremen museum as "an act of kindness and cooperation". In September of 1997, he pleaded guilty to conspiracy and possession of stolen property.

He cooperated with officials, providing crucial evidence against his former associate Aleskerova and leading the authorities to the remaining drawings, which were found a month later, unceremoniously stashed under a bed and in a closet inside an apartment rented by an Azerbaijani wrestler in Brooklyn's Little Odessa. In exchange for his cooperation, Koga was released from custody on a $250,000 personal

MUNCH'S *THE SCREAM*

In August 2004, two masked thieves, one of whom was armed, pulled the paintings *The Scream* and *Madonna* from the wall of Oslo's Munch Museum in broad daylight. Roughly fifty visitors stood and watched, paralysed with fear, as the gunman held his weapon to a female guard's head.

The pair of thieves, wearing black masks, used wire-cutters to cut through a security line attached to the frame, then fled with the paintings to a waiting black Audi A6. Though an alarm was sent as soon as the painting was lifted, police arrived fifteen minutes too late. The next morning, Norwegian newspaper *Aftenposten* ran the front-page headline "Verden Skrikene" ("The World Screams").

The heist, which was the first armed art theft in Norway, was characterized by Norwegian culture minister Valgerd Svarstad Haugland as "dreadful and shocking". She also expressed great concern over the safety of the paintings, of which *The Scream* alone was estimated to be worth more than $70 million, as it was painted in tempera on cardboard and considered extremely fragile. "We have not protected our cultural treasures adequately. We must learn the lessons", Haugland told the BBC.

It could have been pointed out that these lessons ought to have been learned a decade earlier, when another version – one of four of Munch's 1893 paintings of *The Scream*, and the one that has been deemed the most significant – was also stolen. In that instance, the painting had been lifted from the Norwegian National Gallery on 12 February, on the opening day of the 1994 Winter Olympics in Lillehammer. Thieves propped up a ladder against a second-storey window and used wire-cutters to remove the painting from the wall.

Ten days later, Norwegian government officials found four pieces of the painting's frame in Nittedal, a suburb north of Oslo, plus they received a message and what appeared to be a

recognizance bond, and, once home in Tokyo, he received dialysis treatment. He died before he could receive a kidney transplant.

As for Aleskerova, after a three-week trial, a US federal jury found her guilty of two counts of possession of stolen artwork and one count of conspiracy to possess and sell stolen artwork. She was sentenced to eleven months in prison and three years of supervised release. On appeal, she asked to apply for asylum in the United States, arguing that the president of Azerbaijan, who at the time was Heydar Alirza oglu Aliyev, would persecute her because of her employment under former Azerbaijani president Abülfaz Elçibay. Her application for asylum was accepted, and when Aleskerova was freed from a penitentiary on 10 April 2001, she was allowed to remain in the US. An international warrant is still active for her ex-husband, who is known to sometimes travel on a Chinese passport. He remains on Interpol's "Most Wanted" list.

While the art was recovered in the late 1990s, it was not until July 2001 that US treasury secretary **Paul O'Neill** handed over the drawings to the president of the Kunsthalle Bremen. At a ceremony at

ransom demand of $1 million. Because police did not receive proof that the people had the painting, they ignored the demand. Three months later, the painting was recovered undamaged from a hotel in Asgardstrand, forty miles south of Oslo. Two months later, three Norwegians were arrested and charged with the theft.

The Scream and Madonna were parts of Munch's Frieze of Life series, in which sickness, death, anxiety, and love were central themes. In the Madonna lithograph, the woman's half-closed eyes represent pain, while her position, with her hands above and behind her back, depict life and death shaking hands, linking the past to future generations.

Norwegian police recovered the two paintings two years later, on 30 August 2006. While the paintings had been damaged, police reported it was much less than had been expected. During a news conference, Norway police chief Iver Stensrud told reporters: "For two years and nine days we have been hunting systematically for these pictures. And now we've found them."

The thieves, Bjørn Hoen, Petter Tharaldsen (believed to be the getaway driver) and Petter Rosenvinge, all in their thirties, were tried and found guilty of stealing the paintings after a trial in May 2007. They were sentenced to between four and eight years in prison. Three other men, also charged with the crime, were acquitted in connection with the theft and released.

Besides prison sentences, the convicted men were also ordered to pay the Oslo Township restitution, compensation for the estimated worth of the paintings, because they were returned damaged and had to be restored (Madonna had a scratch and a small tear that left a hole in the canvas, and The Scream was slightly crumpled from moisture damage to a corner).

The Munch Museum has since installed metal detectors, along with new devices for mounting the paintings on walls. In addition, master paintings are now mounted behind bulletproof glass. Munch – Norway's best-known artist – died in 1944 at the age of eighty-one.

the US Customs House in New York City, Wolfgang Ischinger, Germany's ambassador to the United States, said: "Allow me to express the hope that the other pieces which disappeared in the course of the war or after the war will also find their way back to Bremen and to other places where they belong."

For further investigation

📖 Jane Campbell Hutchison Albrecht Dürer: A Guide to Research (2000) A biography including reprinted journal entries and personal letters penned by Dürer, as well as a comprehensive look into Dürer's drawings, including his twice-stolen works.

Ⓦ query.nytimes.com/gst/fullpage.html?res=9C02E0D71439F9 33A2575AC0A961958260 An in-depth piece from The New York Times concerning the recovery of the looted art.

Ⓦ lubbockonline.com/stories/072001/wor_0720010103.shtml An article describing the return of three of the art works.

SHOW ME THE MONET

Europe's biggest art theft

Half an hour before closing on Sunday, 10 February 2008, three men wearing ski masks and dark clothing stormed into the **E. G. Bührle Foundation** museum in Zurich, armed with handguns. One of the men forced terrified employees and more than a dozen visitors to the floor. His accomplices moved swiftly through the elegant townhouse to the four most valuable paintings on display. The thieves pulled them from the wall, left the museum and fled to a waiting white saloon car. They had been in and out of the museum in less than five minutes, carrying with them $164 million worth of Impressionist masterpieces. Investigators described the heist as "spectacular."

"We're talking about the biggest ever robbery carried out in Switzerland, even Europe," baffled Zurich police representative **Mario Cortesi** told reporters the day after the heist. The stolen paintings were Cézanne's *The Boy in the Red Vest* (1890) considered the most valuable in the entire collection; Degas' *Viscount Lepic and His Daughters* (1871); Monet's *Poppies Near Vétheuil* (1880); and Van Gogh's *Blossoming Chestnut Branches* (1890), which was especially valuable having been completed just over the last six weeks of the artist's life. The robbers passed over the collection's second-most valuable painting, another Cézanne, leading authorities to believe that while the thieves appeared experienced enough to know about the world of art, they chose those particular paintings because they were conveniently displayed in the same small room.

STOLEN STOLEN PAINTNGS?

Emil Georg Bührle, whose collection is housed at the Bührle Foundation, was a German-born arms magnate. He made his fortune as owner of the Oerlikon-Bührle munitions factory in Zurich, which provided arms to the forces of the Third Reich during World War II.

The billionaire industrialist collected some two hundred works between 1951 until his death in 1956. His paintings were bought after the Nazis passed a law in 1938 legalizing the sale of artworks from its state collections; they were highly controversial purchases, since many of these works of art had been stolen from their rightful owners during Hitler's leadership.

At least thirteen of the paintings Bührle bought were verified as having been confiscated from Jewish families by Nazis during the war. Those paintings, following an official order brought by an independent commission, were returned in the 1990s to Jewish families. In exchange for handing over the paintings to their rightful owners, Bührle's estate received compensation from the Swiss government.

The daylight robbery went off with barely a hitch. The thieves loaded the paintings into their vehicle and sped off unimpeded in a south-eastern direction, toward the suburb of Zollikon. Witnesses reported seeing one of the paintings sticking out of the back of the car as the robbers fled.

Eight days later, on Monday 18 February, two of the four paintings were discovered in an unlocked, white Opel Omega that had been abandoned in a parking lot outside the University of Zurich's psychiatric clinic, just a few hundred metres from where they were stolen. The paintings, by Van Gogh and Monet, were still framed and undamaged. Museum director Lukas Gloor said during a news conference that, fortunately, both the recovered paintings were in absolutely impeccable shape. However, the Degas and Cézanne, which had a total estimated worth of 180 million Swiss francs ($163 million), remained missing.

With no ransom note delivered, the authorities determined the works had most likely been stolen for a pre-arranged personal order. The uninjured staff, security guards, and patrons had told police that one of the robbers spoke German with a Slavic accent.

THE BIGGER THE ARTIST, THE BIGGER THE TARGET

One weekend in October 2007, burglars sneaked into a factory in Tuscany, Italy, and made off with seven bronze statues – including a ballerina, a sparrow, and a male nude. They were all pieces by the famed Latin American artist Fernando Botero.

Botero is one of the bestselling living artists in the world. In 2003, *Artreview* magazine ranked him number five on the top-seller list for making £35.7 million – some $69.2 million – for his artworks. In late 2007, a bronze sculpture of a voluptuous nude female figure lying face down and holding a cigarette, entitled *Smoking Woman*, garnered $1.6 million at Christie's auction house. It was the priciest Botero sculpture sold to date.

A painter and sculptor, Botero is best known for his out-of-proportion animal figures and portly humans. He had stirred up a minor controversy in 2005 when a special exhibition of political drawings and paintings went on display at the Palazzo Venezia in Rome. The eighty pieces, in the artist's private collection and not for sale, were inspired by photographs depicting the torture of prisoners at Abu Ghraib in Iraq at the hands of US soldiers.

Botero is no stranger to losing his pieces. A year earlier, a bronze rooster and a Colombian idol were stolen from Botero's home studio. The bronze figures each weighed in at more than 55 pounds. And back in 2002, thieves stole two paintings by Botero from the Museum of Antioquia in his home-town of Medellín, Colombia. Three museum employees and an outside associate were later arrested after the paintings were found abandoned in a Bogotá park near the airport.

The sculptures stolen in 2007 were worth $5 million in total but were not insured, as they were still inside the Mariani foundry where they were cast and manufactured. Botero was in New York at the time of the burglary. The thieves, who forced open the foundry's back door and then broke into a metal cupboard housing the statues, removed only Botero's pieces. Because other artists' works were also in the foundry at the time of the theft, authorities believe the works were stolen on commission for a personal collector. The alarm was not set that weekend, and it was not until Monday that the robbery was discovered.

For Botero, that theft in 2007 was the last straw. He asked that production of his works cease until the Italian factory could be better secured.

Investigators studied other cases and compared evidence to see if they could find any similarities.

The three bandits had stolen the paintings from the Bührle just a week after another high-profile art crime had occurred. Two Picassos, *Tête de Cheval*, from 1962, and *Verre et Pichet*, from 1944, had been stolen from a cultural centre near Zurich's wealthy Gold Coast lakeside district. The paintings, valued at several million francs, had been taken from a small exhibition hall. However, after a couple of weeks, any connection to the latest case was ruled out.

A museum spokesperson told reporters the paintings were so well known that it would be near impossible for a thief to try to sell them on the open market. The underground market, to a private investor, was much more likely. Still, even then, it's not easy unloading some of the world's most famous paintings. Selling art on the black market typically garners thieves a fraction of its true market value, and unloading world-famous masterpieces is nearly impossible. Unless there's a quick ransom demand, stolen masterpieces can become a form of underground currency for illicit transactions.

The FBI listed the two remaining missing paintings, with accompanying colour photos, on a page headlined "Top Ten Art Crimes" on their website, asking anyone with information into circumstances surrounding the case to either call or submit a tip online. The reality, however, according to the FBI, is that only about five percent of stolen masterpieces are ever recovered. It's likely, if the pieces weren't sold to a private investor, that they were instead sold into the black market, in which case it could take years for the art to surface.

For further investigation

Ⓦ curatorandcollector.com Specialist website for museum workers that has an invaluable archive of information about art heists.

Ⓦ deccanherald.com/Content/Mar302008/ finearts2008032960092 An article about the increasingly popular trend of art theft.

Ⓦ mndaily.com/articles/2008/02/29/72165881 Information about a course at the University of Minnesota focused on art robberies, old and new.

Cash money

THE GREAT BRINK'S ROBBERY

On a freezing cold January evening in 1950, a gang of eleven men pulled off a meticulously planned robbery at the headquarters of Brink's Security – the largest money transporter in the US – located in an industrial section of Boston, Massachusetts. The job was a classic, textbook heist. But, perfect as its execution was, the raid's success did not keep the crooks from eventually turning on each other.

The planning and practice had a military flair to it, and the attention to detail – including the copying of the uniforms of Brink's armoured car guards – was ingenious. The mastermind behind the heist was **Tony "Fats" Pino**, a habitual criminal and infamous underworld figure. He recruited a large, specialist burglary team that included his brother-in-law Vincent Costa, Joseph "Big Joe" McGinnis, Joseph "Specs" O'Keefe and Stanley "Gus" Gusciora.

For eighteen months, they cased the Brink's depot,

learning employees' schedules and, equally important, the times the money was dropped off and the days the vault was cash-heavy. They acquired the floor plan for the alarm system within the three-storey Brink's building, laid out the plan step-by-step, and carried out dry runs by going in and out of the building undetected. Finally it was time to put the plan into action.

On 17 January the thieves armed themselves with revolvers and donned their uniform-like clothing – woollen pea-coats, navy-blue chauffeur-style caps, black leather gloves, and rubber-soled shoes (so their footsteps couldn't be heard) – and topped off their disguises with superhero Halloween masks. Once within the building's grounds they moved as silently as possible until ready to strike. Bursting into the company's money-counting room, they surprised five Brink's employees. They forced them onto the floor at gunpoint, then tied their hands behind their backs and put waterproof adhesive tape over their mouths. The robbers confiscated four revolvers from the employees, and then shoved $2.7 million in cash, cheques, money orders, and securities into fourteen large burlap bags (the bags and money had a combined weight of more than half a ton). The operation took less than half an hour, and the robbers left little behind aside from the tape, the rope, and one cap. Waiting outside in the getaway truck, keeping the engine running, was Joseph Banfield, who was the driver. After they had made good their escape and driven to safety, the gang dismantled the stolen 1949 commercial truck using a welding torch, and then buried it.

At 7.27pm, a distraught Brink's employee called the Boston Police Department to report the crime. Employees were unable to identify any of the masked robbers, leaving police and FBI agents no alternative but to round up known gangsters and convicted burglars for questioning. During the dragnet, most of Pino's gang were questioned, but nobody was talking, and the authorities had nothing to go on. As time went on, the scale of the job and the lack of arrests turned the story into a national obsession. TV chat-show host **Ed Sullivan** joined in the game, lining up a group of masked men on his popular Sunday variety show and introducing them as the Brink's robbers.

At the time, the haul was touted as the biggest in American history. The authorities were to ultimately spend six years and $29 million trying to figure out who was behind the robbery. Were it not for the mistake made by two members of the gang, the **FBI** may never have solved the Brink's crime. It happened six months after the robbery, when O'Keefe and Gusciora were arrested in Towanda, Pennsylvania, for breaking in and stealing clothing from a department store. Found in their car were guns. When O'Keefe contacted fellow gang members to assist in the mounting costs of his defence, nobody stepped forward to help him.

In Baghdad in 2003, a gang of burglars broke into the Central Bank of Iraq, filled three tractor trailers with cash equivalent to $1 billion and sped away. Half of the booty was later found by US soldiers in the environs of Saddam Hussein's palace. No one has ever been arrested, and the other half of the money remains unaccounted for.

O'Keefe was sentenced to three years in a county jail and fined $3000 for violation of the federal **Uniform Firearms Act**. Gusciora was acquitted but was then tried for an additional unrelated burglary, for which he was sentenced to five years in prison.

After O'Keefe had served his time and been released, two attempts on his life were made – believed to have been ordered by Pino, though never proven. O'Keefe escaped uninjured, but FBI agents suspected O'Keefe must have been part of something big. They upped the pressure on him, and he eventually confessed to his role in the Brink's heist. He felt betrayed by his co-conspirators, and he gave them up. All eleven were indicted for armed robbery and kidnapping charges.

O'Keefe turned state's evidence and took a plea deal. By the time the cases came to trial, six years after the heist, two members of the gang of thieves had died. In 1956, eight of the gang stood in court. All eight were convicted and received prison sentences of twenty years to life. And, twenty years later, the eight convicted members finally actually confessed to playing a part in the Brink's heist. All were eventually released and all eventually died of natural causes.

A paltry $51,906 of the total Brink's haul was recovered. No one in the gang could – or *would* – account for the rest of the stolen cache.

Anthony Pino, mastermind of the Brink's heist, flanked by two officers of the law.

For further investigation

ⓦ fbi.gov/libref/historic/famcases/brinks/brinks The FBI's account of the Brink's planning, heist, investigation, and arrests.

NORTHERN BANK (BELFAST) ROBBERY

The largest ever all-cash robbery in British history took an insider's knowledge to plan and seven men to execute. The precisely organized, 24-hour-long robbery began on 19 December 2004, when three thugs disguised in police uniforms entered the homes of **Chris Ward** and **Kevin McMullan**, both senior executives at Northern Bank's Donegall Square headquarters in Belfast. (Northern Bank was then the second-largest bank in British territory.) McMullan's wife was abducted from her home in her own car and held at an unknown location. At the same time, various bank employees, under threat of violence upon their families, were taken to a bungalow and interrogated about the financial institution's procedures.

At noon the next day, on the Monday before Christmas, Ward and McMullan reported to work as usual, acting, under strict instructions from the robbers, as if nothing were amiss. Around 6pm the two executives sent the staff home early, telling them it was so they could shop for Christmas gifts. With the place cleared out, they let the robbers in. For two hours, the suspects stuffed cash and notes from the vault into boxes, and then loaded the boxes into a white van parked against the inconspicuous Wellington Street side entrance, opposite City Hall. A driver took the

full van away and returned an hour later to refill it. They had cleaned out the bank's central cash vault. The gang then fled in a caravan of several vehicles, including the van loaded with the second round of stolen cash. The driver turned the van onto Queen Street and then took a sharp turn toward the highway that leads out of the city.

At midnight, the gang released Ward and McMullan's family members. They also released McMullan's wife, driving her in her own car to a forest near Ballynahinch, a market town in County Down. She walked in soaking wet trainers to the nearest house, and contracted hypothermia from the cold. Her burned car was later found in the same area.

The gang of robbers got away with more than £26.5 million, including £5.5m of the bank's £10 notes. Taking the notes was a foolish move, because the bank recalled all of its outstanding banknotes in denominations of £10 or larger – a total of £300 million – following the robbery, rendering the stolen notes useless. Anyone trying to use the notes would arouse suspicion. Northern Bank later reissued the notes in new colours with new serial numbers and a fresh logo.

At a news conference the next day, police in Belfast revealed the facts of the operation: that the gang of thugs had entered McMullan's home by impersonating police officers and claiming that they were there to notify the family that a relative had been killed

In 1992 Bill Brennan, a sportsbook cashier (bookie), left the Stardust hotel-casino after his shift with a bag holding $500,000 in cash and chips. It was the largest Las Vegas casino theft ever. Now on the FBI's Most Wanted List, Brennan is still at large.

Brazil's biggest robbery took place on a weekend in August 2005: robbers had spent three months digging a 260-foot tunnel from a rented house near the Central Bank, and got away with 164 million reals (some £38 million) from a vault.

in a car accident. Once inside the home, a gun was placed against McMullan's head and he was tied up. The gang members had named the **Provisional Irish Republican Army** (IRA) as being responsible for the robbery, but the IRA denied any involvement.

Two months later, on 17 February, police arrested seven people, who did, as it happens, include a member of the IRA. They recovered more than £2 million, which included £60,000 in silver and notes. In that same month, £50,000 was found stashed behind a toilet at the police athletic association's Newforge Country Club. The money was confirmed to have been stolen from the bank.

Later still, in December 2005, Chris Ward, one of the Northern Bank employees whose family was held hostage, was charged with being an accessory in the robbery and with false imprisonment. He denied any involvement, accusing the police of harassment and of trying to frame him. In October 2007 he was acquitted of all charges.

For further investigation

Ⓦ guardian.co.uk/print/0,,5091489-103690,00 An article about the hunt for the bank robbers.

Diamonds & pearls

THE ANTWERP DIAMOND HEIST

In the winter of 2003, skilled burglars busted into the **Antwerp Diamond Centre** in the heart of the Belgian city's historic diamond district, rifled through more than 123 vaults, built into maximum-security cellars, and made off with $120 million in jewels, most of which have not surfaced since. Any gems that were traceable were dumped, strewn upon the floor amongst overturned tables and diamond-cutting tools.

The thieves thought themselves in the clear. But they had left behind an important clue. A week and a half after the 16 February heist, police found bags that were used during the theft in a ditch beside a road leading out of town. One included a partially eaten sandwich, positively brimming with DNA evidence, together with surveillance videotape and documents from the centre. Within weeks, four men who had shared office space in the enormous diamond centre from the start of 2000 were arrested. These suspects included **Leonardo Notarbartolo**, a diamond merchant familiar with the vaults. Notarbartolo's fate was sealed when the DNA left on the sandwich was found to be a match with his. After the arrest, it came to light that one of the arrested suspects, **Ferdinando Finotto**, was the brains behind the operation. Finotto's gang of thieves were all of Italian nationality and were known as the **School of Turin**.

Shortly after Notarbartolo began renting an office at the Diamond Center – home to 1,500 retail and wholesale diamond companies and four diamond exchanges – he went about obtaining copies of master keys and learning how the alarm system worked. Having assembled a group of conspirators and planned the heist, the group waited for the day to pull it off. The opportunity finally arose with the **Diamond Games tennis tournament** in February 2003.

Surveillance cameras cover the building, clearance passes are required to gain access, and guards protect the vaults 24 hours a day. Lifting the gems from a building that houses eighty percent of the world's rough diamonds and half of its polished diamonds was an incredible challenge.

While tennis star Venus Williams was playing a match, Finotto's men circumvented the alarm system. They replaced surveillance videotapes with previously recorded footage and took the elevator to the basement. Once there, they deactivated motion sensors, taped over surveillance camera lenses and light detectors, and used their master keys to open the vault doors.

The *coup de grâce* was getting past the vaults' twelve-inch-thick, bomb-proof doors, rigged with internal magnets attached to alarms. If the magnets moved away from one another, the alarm would blow their cover and they would be trapped down in the vault with security storming down at them from above. With utmost care, holes were drilled into the doors, and the magnets were taped together so they wouldn't separate. Once inside, the gang broke open the safety deposit boxes and snatched all they could carry.

Their Saturday night theft had gone so smoothly that it was entirely unnoticed until Monday morning, losing the authorities some precious investigative time. But because of the ease with which the thieves had bypassed the surveillance system and avoided security guards, the authorities believed, correctly, that it was an inside job. Their suspicions were further aroused by the forward-thinking of the thieves, who had also taken records of authenticity from the vault, which would make it easier to resell the jewels.

Notarbartolo was given a ten-year prison sentence and a $10,000 fine while the other three suspects – Ferdinando Finotto, Elio D'Onorio, and Pietro Tavano – each received five-year sentences and $8000 fines.

In May 2003, three months after the theft, Italian police managed to retreive some of the diamonds. Only seventeen of them, however, which they discovered in a safe inside a house in which one of the four accused thieves had been arrested.

For further investigation

📖 **Vincent Powell** The Legal Companion **(2005)** A look into legal stories that includes the Antwerp gem heist.

🌐 cnn.com/2003/WORLD/europe/02/27/belgium.diamonds.ap/ index.html An article that details the diamond centre heist.

DIAMONDS ARE A THIEF'S BEST FRIEND. OR ARE THEY?

The curse of the Hope Diamond

In the middle of the seventeenth century, a French merchant named Jean Baptiste Tavernier travelled to India, where he is said to have stolen a large blue diamond from a statue of the Hindu goddess Sita. The diamond's perfect quality, its large size at 112-3/16 carats, and its steely blue colour made it strikingly unique. But the removal of the stone supposedly brought about a curse – a legend that seemingly had some weight: Tavernier died while visiting Russia; he was torn apart by a pack of wild dogs. This was but the first of the terrible deaths attributed to the diamond's curse. Before Tavernier's untimely demise, he sold the stone to Louis XIV, who had the gem re-cut to enhance its brilliance. The French king did not have the most comfortable of deaths: he succumbed to the painful spread of gangrenous tissue ravaging his body.

Renamed the "Blue Diamond of the Crown", the gem was passed down through the French monarchy until it was stolen from Louis XVI and Marie Antoinette as they attempted to flee France during the revolution in 1791. Both king and queen were famously beheaded, of course, and those who believe in the diamond's curse attribute their violent demise to the stone.

The diamond disappeared for a number of years, though it is rumoured to have landed in the purse of George IV. When the king died, deeply in debt, the stone was sold into the private sector, where London banker Henry Philip Hope bought it for his already large collection. Henceforth known as the Hope Diamond, the stone continued to taint the lives of those it touched. Hope lost his only son in an accident, and when his grandson inherited the diamond, it wasn't long before he had to hock it to pay off the gambling debts that had erased his family's fortune. It changed hands several times after that, dragging along with it madness, suicide, murder and upheaval – Sultan Abdul Hamid II possessed the stone just long enough to lose control of the Ottoman Empire. Sometime around 1910, Washington socialite Evelyn Walsh McLean came into possession of the diamond through the jeweller Cartier. She wore it around her neck as a good luck charm for some thirty years, but when her nine-year-old son was killed in a car crash and her daughter committed suicide, the whispers started up again about the curse of the stone. McLean died in a mental institution, and the diamond was donated to the Smithsonian. In perhaps its final diabolical act before being safely placed into storage, the stone struck out at James Todd, the man who delivered it to the museum, who suffered a crushed leg, a head injury, and the loss of his home by fire over the rest of the course of his life.

The Florentine

The Florentine, a golden-yellow, 137.27-carat diamond, is considered to be Italy's most famous gem; it's unquestionably the country's most famous *missing* stone. It was rumoured that the diamond was brought into the US in the 1920s, where it was re-cut and sold, although it is still listed as stolen. Officials at the Kunsthistorisches Museum in Vienna, however, where the Florentine was on display before 1918, reported in 1964 to the Gemological Institute of America that they had no knowledge at that time of the stone's location. The present whereabouts of the 80-carat diamond remain a mystery. Its last rumoured setting was as part of a hat ornament.

The gem dates back to 1657, when it was one of the treasures of the grand duke of Tuscany. But it was passed down one generation with the marriage of Francis Stephen of Lorena and Austria's empress Mary Theresa. After the fall of the Austrian Empire during World War I, the imperial family took the Florentine into exile in Switzerland. A couple of black-and-white photos, along with a drawing, are all that remain of the diamond. As far as we know...

Le Régent

Considered to be one of the world's finest diamonds and weighing in at a hefty 143.2 carats, the nearly flawless Le Régent has a chequered history that has witnessed slavery, theft and murder. Working in the Partael mines on the Kistna River in India, a slave discovered the uncut diamond in 1698. With no one looking, he sliced open his own calf, hid the stone in the bandages, and at nightfall was able to escape the labour camp.

Making his way to port, he met an English sea captain who agreed to take him onboard for half the share of the diamond's sale. But greed got the better of the Englishman, who stole the diamond after killing the slave and throwing his body overboard. He sold the rough diamond for $5000 to an Indian trader named Jamchund at the next port and it is rumoured that this unnamed seaman spent the remainder of his short life drinking heavily before he eventually hanged himself in a fit of drunken depression.

The diamond fetched a heftier price when it was sold to Thomas Pitt, the governor of Madras (the capital of the Indian state of Tamil Nadu) for $100,000 in 1702. The governor sent it to England where it was given a brilliant cushion-shaped cut that lopped off over 250 carats from the rough stone – but the loss was considered well worth it for the creation of such a fine, large gem. With its new shape came a new name, the "Pitt".

Fifteen years later, Thomas Pitt, through an intermediary, sold the gem to Philippe II, duke of Orléans and regent of France, hence the name Le Régent. It was worn in the crown of Louis XV at his coronation in 1722, and was frequently worn two generations later by Marie Antoinette. It was stolen during the French revolution, along with the valuable French Blue, but was found some months later in Paris, behind a panel in the attic of a house. Five years on, it was used as security against a loan that aided Napoleon Bonaparte in his rise to power. For his coronation as self-appointed emperor in 1802, he had the stone fixed to the hilt of his sword.

When he was exiled in 1814, Napoleon's second wife, Marie Louisa, brought the stone to her father, the emperor of Austria, and it was he who returned it to the French aristocracy via Louis XVIII. In 1825, Charles X wore Le Régent at his coronation, and it remained in this crown until placed in a diadem for the Empress Eugenie, wife of Napoleon III. In 1887, almost all of the French crown jewels were sold at auction. Le Régent stayed in the possession of the French people, and was put on exhibition at the Louvre in Paris, where it remains today.

DAMIANI: JEWELLERS TO THE STARS TAKEN TO THE CLEANERS

In a daring robbery that played out like a Hollywood movie, seven crooks crawled through a small, hand-dug tunnel and busted into **Damiani International**'s 15,000-square-foot showroom in Milan's fashion district, making off with $20 million in jewellery and loose gems. It would have been more had it not been the same day as the 2008 Academy Awards where, some six thousand miles away, the most valuable pieces of the Damiani collection adorned the elegant limbs and digits of the Hollywood elite.

The thieves – dressed from head to foot in black clothing, dark glasses and vests to make it look like they were wearing official Italian financial police uniforms – tunnelled through concrete and brick to carry off bags full of gold, diamonds, emeralds and rubies in broad daylight. They took advantage of a noisy construction site next to the showroom, digging their three-foot-round tunnel through the four feet of solid wall while construction workers were on duty. Once inside the building, they took an internal staircase up from the cellar to Damiani's showroom, careful to avoid surveillance cameras and door alarms along the way.

The gang explained to employees, in southern Italian accents, that they were financial fraud officers there for a spot examination of accounts. They didn't carry guns – at least not visibly – which may have been because they were familiar with an Italian law that encouraged much harsher sentences for armed robberies. Once they had the employees where they wanted them, the bandits forced a manager to open a locked vault and the safety deposit boxes, while the others bound and gagged the other workers with duct tape and plastic ropes before locking them in the bathroom. They then emptied the boxes into bags and loaded the loot into a waiting van, parked at a side entrance. From the moment they entered the building until the time they drove away, only thirty minutes had passed. A neighbour did, in fact, call the police after becoming suspicious watching the men loading bags into the van. But the officers arrived much too late to do anything more than untie the employees and take statements.

The plot is thought to have taken at the very least a month to plan, and the execution was flawless. **Francesco Messina**, lead police investigator, told the press that the heist was "highly professional" and that the robbers left few clues behind. "It will be a long investigation," he noted. The thieves remain at large.

It was extremely fortuitous for Damiani that the Oscar night gala coincided with the robbery. Best actress in a supporting role winner **Tilda Swinton** was bejeweled in two one-of-a-kind 18-carat white gold Damiani pieces, including a large diamond-studded signature bracelet containing 1865 diamonds and weighing in at a combined 47 carats. There is little doubt that they would have been stolen had they been in the vault at the time of the theft.

A statement was issued by Damiani, a family-owned establishment run by Guido, Giorgio and Silvia Damiani. "No one was injured or hurt and we are most grateful," said Silvia Damiani, the company's vice president. "My Brother Giorgio and I were in Los Angeles with many of the Damiani Masterpiece collections for the Oscars and are happy that these one-of-a-kind pieces were with us and are not in the robbers' hands."

For further investigation

Ⓦ news.bbc.co.uk/2/hi/europe/7263600.stm The BBC's news account of the heist.

Ⓦ people.com/people/package/article/0,,20168756_20180444,00.html *People* magazine's take on the Oscar night theft.

Cat burglars & lone wolves

Cat burglars are notoriously difficult to catch. The cat burglar's method is predicated on stealth – sneaking into homes and then stealing away into the night. A patient cat burglar will sit for hours casing a home, waiting for the right moment to pounce. They enter in the dark, busting outdoor light bulbs so no one can see them. (For information on the psychology of the cat burglar, see the box on p.58.)

But the lone operator, whose working milieu is invariably the dead of night, is not solely a modern-day phenomenon. Burglary is a profession as old as the hills...

DEACON WILLIAM BRODIE

William Brodie, born into a respectable Edinburgh family in 1741, was a pillar of his Scottish community. He was deacon of the Guild of Wrights on the Edinburgh Town Council and a freeman of the city. But the man revered by the community led a double life.

A cabinet maker by trade, his respectability was a façade. He had two mistresses, with five illegitimate children between them and heavy gambling debts. To pay off his creditors, he resorted to burgling the very people who trusted him the most – the people who invited him into their homes to carry out woodworking and lock repair. But his thefts did not stop with private homes. At the time, it was customary for shopkeepers to hang their keys from nails on the back of doors. Brodie, who was regularly commissioned to do repair work in shops, secretly made clay impressions of the keys. He would simply return at night, unlock the doors, and steal the unattended goods, cash and valuables from his unsuspecting clients. As he became more ambitious, he hired **George Smith**, an English locksmith and grocer, to work as his accomplice. The pair of them pulled off a series of small burglaries over the next few years.

Brodie became more confident with every success. After doing some work in Edinburgh's Customs and Excise Office in the small town of Canongate, he schemed to relieve them of their collected taxes, housed in a locked cupboard. To commit the deed, Brodie hired two more accomplices: small-time burglars **John Brown**, a convicted robber, and **Andrew Ainslie**, a sometime shoemaker. The three men had all met each other at a tavern in Edinburgh. At midnight on 5 March 1788, Smith, Brown, Ainslie, and Brodie broke into the Excise office. With Smith and Brown standing guard outside, Brodie and Ainslie went into the office to retrieve the cash. But when Ainslie had a panic attack inside the office, they abandoned the pot of gold – worth £600 in the money of the day – and walked out instead with just £16.

Authorities on the case had been suspicious of Brodie for some time. The connection between

Scottish businessman and burglar William Brodie, sketched c.1788.

the places where he had worked and the burglaries was too strong to ignore, and the break-in at the Excise Office was too serious a crime to go unresolved. As the investigation heated up, Brown was interrogated and gave up information about Ainslie and Smith. Having been arrested and thrown in jail, Ainslie agreed to inform on Brodie and give evidence on the rest of the gang. Police showed up at Brodie's door, finding the tools he had used to perform his night-time job – duplicated keys, guns, and a disguise. Brodie, however, had got wind of the raid and instead fled on a boat to Amsterdam before police could close in on him. There, he paid his fare and prepared to sail to America, but he was arrested at the port and extradited to Scotland, where he stood trial.

It began on August 27, 1788, with Brodie turning up to court dressed in a tan silk shirt, a red vest, and a black velvet suit jacket with long coat tails, given to him by his father. Despite portraying himself as a gentleman and a working man, a jury found Brodie and his accomplice Smith guilty of burglary, and the pair were sentenced to be publicly hanged, using a gallows Brodie had, as a member of the town council, voted to fund the year before. On October 1, 1788, before a crowd of 40,000 Scottish residents, the punishment was meted out at the Tollbooth Jail.

Lore has it that Brodie convinced a doctor to put a bendable metal tube in his throat, in the hope that the noose would not break his neck. Yet another story suggests that he paid the hangman to slip the noose around small hooks attached to a harness which would give the vivid impression of being hanged, but would actually do little harm. Another story goes that, after the hanging, Brodie's body was supposedly taken to a doctor in an attempt to revive him, and rumours abounded that his grave was opened some months later and the coffin found to be empty. Tales soon circulated that Brodie had been seen walking down the street in Paris. Not much credence, however, is given to these rumours these days.

The story of Brodie's double life is said to have been one of the inspirations behind Robert Louis Stevenson's 1886 novel *The Strange Case of Dr Jekyll and Mr Hyde*.

For further investigation

John S. Gibson Deacon Brodie: Father to Jekyll and Hyde (1993) A novel about the supposed family man with the split personality.

Philip Saville Deacon Brodie (1997) A made-for-TV feature film romanticizing the deacon's double life.

historic-uk.com/HistoryUK/Scotland-History/ DeaconBrodie More information about the light-fingered William Brodie.

BILL MASON, MASTER THIEF

Over the course of a criminal career that spanned 25 years, **Bill Mason** maintained two lives: he stole from the rich and famous but all the time he maintained the appearance of an ordinary lifestyle. As a family man, he kept a low profile and as a criminal he readily took advantage of sub-quality security systems and easy-to-climb patio balconies.

Mason was born in 1940. Beginning his life of crime in the 1960s and ending in the late 1980s, he moonlighted as a jewel thief while working full-time during the day as a property investor. Dressed in respectable yet unpretentious clothing that would not draw attention to him, he targeted the houses of the Hollywood elite, and stole some of their most precious possessions.

He was a poor boy (his father was a maintenance worker) who went to school in a wealthy community. While still in high school, he committed his first crime – stealing from neighbours when they weren't home. While in school, he played on the football team and dated rich girls. He was handsome – and charming – with a dimple in his right cheek and dark eyes. After high school, he married his childhood sweetheart. They settled in a suburb of Cleveland, Ohio. Bill became increasingly savvy in the real estate world, and clients trusted him to scout vacation properties for them in Florida. Bill began investing his own money – both stolen and earned – in condominiums and apartment buildings. The more money he made, the more he was wanted. Brokering property deals on the coast of Florida, he was introduced to country-club types, who took him

STATUTES OF LIMITATIONS

Legally speaking, a statute of limitation sets the maximum period, after a crime, that legal proceedings based on the event may begin. Such statutes were put there to protect people from prejudicial memory lapses by witnesses because too much time has passed in stale cases.

The statutes are predicated on a notion of fairness. Prosecution is barred if not brought against a defendant within that statute of limitations. The time periods vary from US state to state. If the claim is not filed before the deadline, the right to make a claim is forever revoked. That goes for law enforcement's ability to file charges against individuals for crimes committed where the statutes of limitations have expired. The time limit begins to run the moment the crime is committed – not from the time the crime was discovered or the suspect was identified.

For minors, the period ends when they turn eighteen. Nearly everyone breaks the law at some point, according to Paul Bergman in his *Criminal Law Handbook*. "Whether it's flashing lights pulling you over to the side", he writes, "or an auditor looking grimly through your tax receipts." The moment the crime occurs, the clock starts ticking. Bergman's advice? "Know your rights."

Murder

In the US, there is no statute of limitation for murder, with cases remaining open until there are convictions. Ten, twenty, even thirty years down the road, if there's a new development in the case, the perpetrators can be arrested and prosecuted.

One example is the 1975 murder case of Martha Moxley, a teenager from Greenwich, Connecticut, who was beaten to death with a golf club. In 2002, Michael Skakel, a neighbour of Martha's, was convicted for the murder after evidence surfaced linking him to both the weapon and to the scene of the crime.

Terrorism

Terrorist crimes are considered actions against humanity and the US government says statutes of limitation do not apply. The US Patriot Act gives authority to the US federal government to take whatever means necessary in combating terrorism, which includes detaining suspects.

to expensive restaurants. It was there that he observed celebrities as they arrived in town, with their expensive cars and jewellery, and checked into their respective four-star hotels and high-rise penthouse suites.

Working alone, Mason single-handedly stole millions in high-end gems and jewellery from the wealthy celebrities of the era, including the author **Truman Capote**, comedian **Bob Hope**, *Tarzan* star **Johnny Weissmuller**, American industrialist **Armand Hammer**, comedian **Phyllis Diller**, singer **Robert Goulet** and even a Cleveland mob underboss named **Angelo "Big Ange" Lonardo** (whose personal safe Mason robbed).

As a property manager with access to keys, he had access to many individual units inside high-rise apartment buildings. But in the case of buildings he didn't

The suspected Taliban and al-Qaeda fighters held at the US naval base in Guantánamo Bay, Cuba, a prison camp, had no right of access to American courts. One of the detainees was Sami al-Haj, an Al Jazeera cameraman. He was held at Guantánamo Bay for more than five years, from the start of 2001 until his release in May 2008.

Conspiracy

For conspiracy, the US federal government has to prosecute within five years. One famous case is that of two highly decorated former New York City Police detectives, Louis Eppolito and Stephen Caraccappa. They were accused of being hired killers for the Mafia, but were not tried for murder. Instead, the pair, known as "mob cops", were tried for conspiracy to commit eight murders and conspiracy to racketeer.

They were convicted, but the case was appealed, claiming the five-year statute of limitations had expired on the racketeering charge. The appellate court agreed, and the case was thrown out. However, in September 2008, a US Circuit Court of Appeals restored the guilty verdicts, finding the men responsible for conspiracy to racketeer.

Rape

In Alabama, the crime of rape, as with homicide, has no statute of limitations. However, in other US states, the statute is anywhere from one to ten years. Victim advocates in New York are attempting to have the statute of limitations lifted. In the case of sexual offences against children there is no time limit to prosecute the perpetrators in most states.

Miscellaneous crimes and misdemeanours

For arson, US state laws vary from between two and ten years. For major art theft, the limit is twenty years. For lesser crimes in various US states, it's another story. For many misdemeanours, state statutes are usually two years. That means that even if police find evidence against a person, they can't charge them for that misdemeanour if the time specified by the statute has elapsed. By comparison, in Canada, a criminal-limitations period for less serious offenses is just six months. In Virginia, writing a bad cheque is a misdemeanour: a petit larceny, which carries a limit of five years.

When it comes to international law, there is no limitation period. Two notable examples of violations of international law are genocide and war crimes.

manage, he would do his own research by thumbing through phone books, before climbing onto balconies. Often, he found that the external sliding-glass doors had been simply left unlocked.

When he broke into Weissmuller's apartment at the Coral Ridge Golf Club in Fort Lauderdale, Florida, he maneuvred himself onto a ledge and gained entrance through a sliding-glass door from the patio in the three-storey building. The apartment faced the golf course, which was deserted and pitch-black at night. From Weissmuller's bedroom, Mason stole his Olympic gold medal (though he eventually mailed it back to the former swimming star).

Mason regarded Armand Hammer's place – a high-security, eighteenth-floor, beachfront apartment in Fort Lauderdale – as a challenge. He watched the

Hammers' building and, on a rainy night when the couple were out for the evening, he climbed up to a narrow ledge of the building just below the roofline. From there, he dropped onto the patio. The apartment alarms weren't set and he was able to simply walk into the apartment. He exited the building, with the stolen goods in hand, through the front door.

Such high-rise thefts were not uncommon for him. On one occasion, he found himself suspended for several minutes, hanging from a ledge, by his fingertips, thirty feet up a wall, while he waited for a security guard to finish a cigarette before he could descend unobserved.

Mason took jewellery from Phyllis Diller twice: once when she lived in Cleveland, Ohio, around 1969; and a second time in Ravenna, Italy, where she was performing. In the latter instance, he nabbed $65,000 worth of jewellery from her hotel suite. Yet the most significant item Mason snatched from Diller was her address book, which provided him with a treasure trove of addresses for other famous people; Mason later described it in his autobiography as being the size of "a paperback novel". Over ten years later, that address book led to Mason's arrest: unlisted addresses, handwritten in Diller's address book, linked Mason to other burglaries. When Mason was suspected in a home invasion in Chagrin Falls, Ohio – which he ultimately was not charged with, because the statute of limitations had expired – a police search of his house came up with the address book. He hung onto Diller's jewels for a decade before selling them to a jewellery store in Manhattan, New York. Two weeks later, a European collector bought them. (A couple of times, Mason managed to get his stolen goods auctioned at Christie's and Sotheby's prestigious auction houses.)

CRIME-FIGHTING GADGETRY

In Fairfield, Connecticut, police have found a way to catch cat burglars; putting an infrared camera to work. Cat burglars hiding behind bushes, picket fences, or cars can be detected by the body heat they give off.

The infrared device picks up their heat, whether it is night or day, a process that can also detect burglars standing between objects. If a suspect flees on foot, the camera can also pick up the footprints.

The photos taken with the camera can be used in court as evidence against the suspected thieves. Similar cameras have been used by hunters to track animals.

Not all of Mason's attempts were successful. At one point, Mason tried, and failed, to burgle a high-rise, beachfront penthouse owned by a wealthy resident on Marco Island on the Gulf of Mexico in southwest Florida, by attempting to position a ladder on a balcony. In Puerto Vallarta, he targeted the actresses **Elizabeth Taylor** and **Margaux Hemingway**, but they failed to arrive at their respective hotels, so Mason never had the chance to grab their jewels. When he successfully broke into the three adjoining hotel rooms of the **McGuire Sisters**, a popular 1960s singing trio, while they were performing in Canton, Ohio, he was disappointed with what he found. While he was able to get into Phyllis McGuire's hotel rooms, the jewellery she travelled with consisted of only costume pieces, so Mason left empty-handed.

To learn where Truman Capote lived, Mason tracked

him down in Key West. He followed the writer when he left the Chart Room Bar, a hangout of Capote and **Hunter S. Thompson**, to his nearby beach cottage. When Capote wasn't at home, Mason broke in. But he was only able to get a few pieces, because Capote, known for wearing gaudy gold jewellery that made a statement, wore most of what he owned.

As crafty and secretive as he was, Mason was eventually caught for petty theft in the mid-1970s, but he was released after just ninety days in jail. Then he skipped bail and went on the lam for five years, living under an assumed name. To catch him, police staged a sting operation at a Ramada Inn, and Mason fell for it. But the police had a problem: they had a witness who claimed to have seen Mason wiping clean the doorknob to the hotel room he was accused of having burgled. However, when police arrived, Mason was *inside* the door, not *outside* of it. Mason's lawyer tried to prove in court that police were lying. But the jury convicted Mason anyway.

The thief's children were seven and thirteen, and their father was facing serious prison time. Rather than go to trial, Mason pleaded guilty in exchange for less time. He was released on his own recognizance – that's to say, he was trusted to turn up to his trial without having to pay bail – pending a sentencing hearing. A month later, he was sentenced to twenty years in prison. He appealed and the case was overturned. In 1988, he was released from prison.

Today, Bill Mason is a free man and was last known to be living in New York City, selling costume jewellery from a business he owns. As soon as the statute of limitations ran out on his crimes, he penned a memoir about his colourful exploits.

It seems that, ultimately, Bill Mason has managed to endure serving a mere five years behind bars for crimes that earned him a reported $35 million. In 2004, he sold the film rights to the tell-all non fiction book, *Confessions of a Master Jewel Thief*, for half a million dollars to Paramount Pictures. The film is currently in production.

For further investigation

📖 **Bill Mason** Confessions of a Master Jewel Thief **(2004)** Mason's personal account of his life as a career criminal.

Ⓦ courttv.com A lengthy Q&A article with Bill Mason into his exploits as a thief.

JOHN SEYBOLD (A.K.A. FRANK HOHIMER)

John Seybold was a career criminal – a successful jewel thief and cat burglar who, for six months in 1969, was listed as number 303 on the FBI's Most Wanted Fugitives' list.

Born in 1919, he was removed from the FBI's list upon his arrest in December of 1969, in Greenwich, Connecticut, after a citizen tipped off authorities as to his whereabouts. He was sent down for a 30-year stretch, during which time he began writing a semi-autobiographical book about his life of crime.

In 1973, while still behind bars, he was accused of having been the man who stabbed and bludgeoned a young woman named **Valerie Jeanne Percy** to death. Police investigated the claim but did not find evidence to link Seybold to the murder. During the incident, jewellery and cash that had been left on the dresser was untouched, plus nothing was missing from her

PSYCHOLOGY OF THE BURGLAR

The legal definition of burglary is the unlawful entry or attempted entry of a structure with intent to commit a felony or theft. Burglary is the third most common crime in the United States, behind larceny and motor vehicle theft. Two out of three burglaries are residential and, contrary to popular belief, about half of all residential burglaries occur in the evening – when the occupants might well be at home. Only about fifteen percent of all burglaries are solved by law enforcement, meaning that, for the overwhelming majority of burglaries, an arrest is not made. Notwithstanding the pervasiveness of the crime, there has been very little scientific study of the problem from a forensic psychological perspective.

Most burglaries are gain-motivated, the result of social, environmental, or situational factors, rather than an outgrowth of psychogenesis. Semi-professional and professional burglars – who steal because it is their job – fall into this category, in as much as their conduct is largely a product of the values of a subculture. The professional burglar has much *less* of a psychopathology than the semi-professional, and takes his occupation of burglary very seriously. Some professional burglars in the US are so sophisticated that they operate in multiple states and target only those locations where they are certain that

valuables will be present. Some even specialize in stealing different types of objects – such as expensive jewellery or power tools found at construction sites.

Law enforcement has always recognized a sub-group of burglars frequently referred to as cat burglars, who differ in criminal technique and motivation from the vast majority of burglars. Cat burglars frequently burgle as a result of a combination of gain-oriented as well as psychological motives, and frequently obtain a psychological thrill from entering the dwelling when the occupants are home.

Recent research has also identified another more dangerous sub-group of burglars, who are motivated by sexual drives. In fact, some researchers have found the basic personality structure of the sexual burglar to be closer to that of the rapist than any other type of offender. Individuals who burgle as a result of sexual motives have been known to achieve orgasm at the moment of entering a window or breaking a locked door. And sexual burglary has been connected to some cases of sexual homicide.

There are two types of sexual burglars: fetish burglars and voyeuristic burglars. Fetish burglars often steal various types of fetishistic objects like female underwear. The case of William Heirens (famous for writing on the wall of a victim's home: "For Heaven's sakes catch me before I kill more, I cannot control myself") was a fetish burglar who committed hundreds of burglaries in the Chicago area in the late 1940s. He subsequently killed two women

home. Seybold denied any involvement in Valerie's death.

Once Seybold was released from jail he scaled down, switching from armed robberies against people to tamer cat burglaries, after learning how to become a cat burglar from fellow inmates who were master thieves. His book took off. A titillating tell-all, *The Home Invaders: Confessions of a Cat Burglar*, was published in

1975 under the pen name **Frank Hohimer**. The movie rights were bought, and a film adaptation was shot by director **Michael Mann** in 1980, with Seybold on set as a technical advisor (despite being wanted by the FBI for several outstanding warrants). During his consultancy work on set, he provided actual burglary tools for the use of the actor **James Caan**, who played the character based on Frank. Some of Seybold's seasoned

during burglaries. He also murdered a six-year-old child, dismembered her, and disposed of the body parts in sewers and drains. This individual developed a fetish for female underwear at the age of nine, began to steal and collect female underwear, and then burgled to obtain them. He reported sexual excitement and an erection at the sight of an open window. The compulsion to burgle, in order to satisfy himself sexually, was so strong that if he resisted, he would sweat, tear his sheets at night, and try anything to distract himself before he finally submitted to his urges.

In voyeuristic burglary the sexual dynamics are not overt, but covert – expressed through looking. The sexual motivation of these offenders is not as obvious as a burglar who raids a residence for female underwear. Many voyeuristic burglars express a strong urge to look around and inspect drawers, and they often entertain a fantasy of seeing a naked woman. Albert DeSalvo, commonly known as the "Boston Strangler", had a history of voyeuristic burglaries before, and during, his killing of thirteen women over an eighteen-month period. His voyeuristic impulses began in adolescence and his burglaries started while he was in the military, stationed in Germany.

There was a common denominator in the crime-scenes in Albert DeSalvo's murders: the residences were ransacked but little of value was taken. This behaviour puzzled the investigators who, at that time, had little understanding of the significant relationship between voyeurism, burglary, and sexual homicide. Albert DeSalvo, like Heirens, was not apprehended for murder, but caught in the process of committing another burglary.

A full understanding of sexual burglary and its relationship to sexual murder is extremely important in conducting an investigation. Recent research has found that if a woman is killed or abducted from her home, the likelihood that the offender has a history of burglary in his background is about 65 percent. Accordingly, in these cases law enforcement would be well advised to check the burglars in a particular jurisdiction, rather than to look for sex offenders (typically child molesters), who actually have little likelihood of committing a sexually motivated homicide.

Professor Louis B. Schlesinger

criminal associates taught Caan resourceful burglary techniques for escapades in which he quietly went into homes and businesses without being detected.

Seybold's book didn't depict all of his crimes in a strictly accurate light. Unlike the burglar of the book, who relied on stealth alone, Seybold carried a handgun, and often terrified his victims by robbing them at gunpoint inside their own homes. The crimes,

according to the FBI, were not committed alone. Seybold, they claimed, worked with a band of under-world thieves.

After a couple of years, he was arrested once again. Seybold, federal inmate number 01881-089, was once more incarcerated, this time beginning on 21 May 1995, in the South Woods State Prison in Bridgeton, New Jersey. At one point he had the somewhat

The actor James Caan played a character based on Hohimer in Michael Mann's *Thief*, an adaptation of Seybold's book, *The Home Invaders*.

depressing distinction of being the oldest living prison inmate in the US, while housed in South Woods' emergency care unit. In an article published by APBnews.com (a now-defunct crime news site based in New York) in April 1999, the Wisconsin-based jewel thief claimed to be working on a second novel.

On 2 November 2001 he was paroled once again. He had given information to the FBI about various crimes of the Chicago mob, and entered the US Witness Protection Program. His old identities were replaced with a new one and he was sent to a city where he would not be recognized. He was said to have died of natural causes a couple of years after going into the program, but that has never been confirmed.

For further investigation

Frank Hohimer The Home Invaders: Confessions of a Cat Burglar (1975) The inside track on breaking and entering, straight from the horse's mouth.

NORMAN SINCLAIR

Dubbed by tabloids as "Britain's most prolific burglar," **Norman Sinclair** was responsible for thousands of break-ins, netting some £5 million over a thirty-year crime spree. It was especially noteworthy that Sinclair had pulled off so many burglaries while operating completely alone.

Sinclair did at one point confess to having committed over 2500 burglaries. Later, however, he recanted his admission, claiming his life had been far too chaotic and confusing to have remembered the details or number of the crimes he had committed. It was only after police began putting the pieces together that they realized Sinclair was a major serial burglar who had committed a staggering number of offenses.

At the time of his final arrest, Sinclair had twenty previous convictions for forty offences, twenty-one of which were for burglaries in residential neighbourhoods. Most of the jewellery, cash, and credit cards he had stolen had been to pay for his expensive drug habit, though he regularly paid for the services of prostitutes, to whom he gave generous gifts. Wimbledon police reported that Sinclair single-handedly carried out 303 burglaries between 2000 and 2006 alone. Tabloid newspapers dubbed him "Britain's most prolific burglar".

The Jamaican-born Sinclair used to don a business suit, so as to look as if he fitted in, as he carried out his one-man slew of burglaries across London, often concentrating on upscale areas. Sinclair told the judge that he often targeted the houses where affluent Asian, Chinese, and Jewish residents lived, as he found they had the most ample caches of jewellery and large sums of money stashed inside. He told of one burglary which alone had netted him somewhere in the region of £100,000. At one address, where he had noticed a crucifix on a wall, he had had enough of a momentary pang of guilt to leave a note with the word "sorry" written on it. To cover up his crimes, he pawned the loot and would occasionally donate it to various charities, such as London's Homerton Hospital.

Sinclair's arrest came after he was placed on Scotland Yard's most wanted list. In 2003, the police had gathered enough forensic evidence to establish that a large number of burglaries occurring in the Greater London area were being committed by the same one man. CCTV footage of Sinclair in a pawn shop, together with his photograph, were featured on *Crime Watch*, a BBC television programme. He realized the game was up, and decided to flee the country. Port authority officers caught Sinclair in Dover, in the county of Kent, England, as Sinclair attempted to drive onto a cross-channel ferry to France to flee the country. (Sinclair's lawyer later claimed that his client was on his way to Jerusalem, as part of a pilgrimage.)

Following his arrest, he told police he regularly used crack cocaine and heroin and needed £1000 a day to fund his habit. He also told police that his drug use had led to him contracting HIV in 2000. As part of the subsequent investigation, a search for evidence led detectives to thousands of addresses across thirteen boroughs Sinclair admitted to have burgled. He was also charged with using a fake British passport after he was stopped at Dover while trying to flee the country, for which he served a twelve-month prison sentence.

Despite his long list of burglaries, he pleaded guilty to just thirteen burglaries, claiming a lapse in memory was preventing him to admitting to more. Even then, at the last minute, the notorious defendant attempted to withdraw his guilty pleas. But the court refused his request.

At his sentencing hearing at Harrow Crown Court in West London, the prosecuting lawyer told the court that the authorities deemed him "the most wanted burglar in London." Then the judge, Nic Madge, described Sinclair as "the worst kind of criminal". He looked directly at Sinclair when he said: "You have, to use the words of the Court of Appeal, behaved as a predator preying on your fellow citizens."

Ultimately, the unemployed thief was convicted of just thirteen of his crimes, having made a plea bargain regarding his lesser offences for less prison time. He was jailed for six years.

For further investigation

Ⓦ news.bbc.co.uk/2/hi/uk_news/england/london/6091544.
stm The BBC's October 2006 article covering Norman Sinclair's sentencing hearing.

Bungled heists

FOOLISH ROBBERIES FROM AROUND THE WORLD

It was a matter of mistaking bread for dough, as the headlines put it. On April Fool's Day 2007 (appropriately enough), two robbers walked out of a bakery with a bag they thought was stuffed with bills totaling $30,000. The joke was on them: they had left with nothing more than a bag full of bread rolls.

The pair were apprehended and brought to trial. Benjamin Jorgensen and his accomplice Donna Hayes, both in their thirties, each pleaded guilty to having robbed employees at the Cuckoo Restaurant in the southern Australian city of Melbourne on April Fool's Day, 2007. During the hold-up, Jorgensen grabbed what he believed was a bag containing cash, not knowing that an employee had filled it with bread rolls. In the course of the caper, Jorgensen accidentally fired his gun, shooting his accomplice in her buttocks.

Judge Roland Williams handed down their sentences, but not before telling the robbers in open court that they were a "pair of fools." He gave Hayes an eight-year sentence, and gave Jorgensen seven.

One of the most ineptly handled robberies in US law enforcement history was carried out by thieves that were later described as "the gang that couldn't steal straight". Even though the crime got off to a promising start – a huge heist in terms of dollars – it soon became a joke with law enforcement officers and federal agents. The Discovery Channel, in a television special, referred to the caper as "The Unperfect Crime."

It all started on the night of October 4, 1997, when **David Scott Ghantt** succeeded in removing $18 million from the armoured car warehouse of a security firm in Charlotte, North Carolina. Ghantt, a driver for Loomis, Fargo and Co, loaded the loot into a van and fled. The problem was, everybody knew Ghantt was the one who had taken it, because Ghantt had forgotten to turn off the security cameras in and around the warehouse. The FBI had him on tape stealing the money. Ghantt, aged 27 at the time, disappeared the Saturday after the theft. He relied on his friends to help hide the money. One of them, **Steve Chambers** aided him in packing up the money from the van. To save space, they left the one- and five-dollar bills behind, not realizing that those bills added up to a hefty $3 million. Ghantt fled to Mexico with $25,000. He left the rest behind with his friends.

Within a month of the robbery, Chambers and his wife moved from a mobile home they owed money on to a $635,000 house, which they paid for in cash. Then they filled their new home with tens of thousands of dollars worth of furnishings. When FBI agents later raided the house, they recovered more than $720,000 in cash from an office desk and 68 pieces of expensive jewellery.

In March 1998, five months after the theft, Ghantt himself was arrested at Playa de Carmen, Mexico, near the island resort of Cozume. In the end, over 24 defendants were arrested and most of the take was recovered. Seventeen people were convicted in connection with the robbery.

While there are plenty of stupid criminals out there, there are equally some burglaries that simply defy explanation. In Burjassot, a small town near the community of Valencia, Spain, police reported in March 2008 that they had arrested an unnamed burglar who had broken into a funeral parlour. They had been called to the home in the middle of the night, after neighbours had heard the front door of Crespo Funeral parlour being broken into.

The burglar, after hearing officers arrive, tried to hide. He lay, pretending to be dead, in a glassed-in chamber used for viewings of deceased people during wakes. But he was caught when officers noticed that the corpse in the chamber was breathing. He was also wearing work clothes rather than the dressier attire usually chosen for burial. "The custom here is for dead people to be dressed in suits, in nice clothes that look presentable," a police official told the press. "This guy was in everyday clothes that were wrinkled and dirty."

The 23-year-old suspect had served jail time in the past for a robbery conviction. Police never did find out his motive. There was absolutely nothing there of value.

For further investigation

📖 **Jeff Diamant** Heist!: the $17 million Loomis Fargo theft (2005) The full story is told in this book about the warehouse employee who made off with millions of dollars – and how surveillance videotape doomed him from the start.

Ⓦ **dumbguide.com** A portal for stories about dumb crimes committed round the world.

Ⓦ **newsoftheweird.com** "News of the Weird" column and website, compiled weekly by syndicated columnist Chuck Shepherd.

THE DOME ROBBERY

It was a plot which, as the newspapers never tired of reminding their readers, could have come straight out of a Bond film. Now a successful music venue – then a vast government vanity project – the Millennium Dome opened in Greenwich, southeast London in the final days of 1999. At its heart was the **Millennium Star**, one of the largest and highest quality diamonds in the world – 203.4 carats of shimmering wealth. As the year 2000 hit, laser beams were fired through it, to glitter on the walls. The guests at the invitation-only jamboree were doubtless very impressed. As were a group of gangsters and robbers, who saw a chance to steal £300 million worth of precious stones, including the diamond, the Millenium jewels and twelve blue diamonds. Their plan was to smash into the Dome with a JCB digger, distract the guards with smoke grenades and escape along the Thames via speedboat.

With hindsight, much about the case seems rather comical, from plotter **Robert Adams**'s "Bob the Builder" nickname to the Catherine wheel the robbers for some reason took with their kit. On their way, according to some sources, they accidentally dropped a bottle of ammonia, which left their eyes steaming. Yet both the thieves – career criminals who had buyers set up in Spain – and the police, who had trailed them for months and eventually manned the Dome with ninety armed officers – took it very seriously indeed.

The five-strong gang consisted of Adams, communications expert **Aldo Ciarrocchi**, speedboat driver **Kevin Meredith** and organisers **Raymond Betson** and **William Cockram**. The planning began in summer 2000. The JCB the gang used was customized, trimming off unnecessary weight to maximize its speed. Betson and Cockram visited the Dome in September and by November the crew were ready to make their move.

The police were already onto them, having watched and filmed the known criminals Betson and Cockram on their September visit. Scores of policemen, disguised as cleaners, guards and maintenance workers, were moved into the building and its surroundings. The plotters had set the 6th November as the date of their heist, but unhelpful tides forced them to delay until the next day. Watched by the police from their control room, the masked men arrived in a white van and the converted JCB, which smashed through the perimeter gate and into the dome. They made their way into the diamond vault. Betson shot the glass with a nail gun and Adams took a sledgehammer to the cabinets.

Finally, the police swooped. "I was twelve inches from payday," Adams later commented. "It would have been a blinding Christmas. I cannot believe how easily the glass went – I only hit it twice. Then that fucking mob of a hundred policemen came in and jumped on us." Adams was not quite as close as he thought – the owners of the diamonds, De Beers, had already switched the diamonds with replicas.

If the gang had been successful, they would have accomplished the biggest robbery the world has ever seen. The Millenium Diamond alone was valued at over £200 million, making the £74 million stolen from a Paris boutique in December 2008 (believed to be the biggest gem theft in history) seem almost small-time. Instead, they ended up in court, with Adams, Betson, Cockram and Ciarrocchi getting between fifteen and eighteen years in jail, and Meredith five.

Audacious, dramatic and doomed almost from the word go, the robbery had enough romantic appeal to capture the attention of press and public, while the police's expensive sting operation netted a beleaguered force some invaluable positive PR. Yet the underworld connections of the failed heist ran deep: the financier of the operation is believed to still be at large.

For further investigation

Kris Hollington Diamond Geezers: The Inside Story of the Crime of the Millennium (2004) A journalist interviews the gang members, explores the police operation and examines the diamond trade. Paints the robbers themselves as harmless opportunists, and a shady "Mr Big" as the sinister mastermind, untouched by the trial.

Jon Shatford and William Doyle Dome Raiders – How Scotland Yard Foiled the Greatest Robbery of All Time (2004) The detective central to cracking the case gives the police's side of the story.

They'll never catch us, gem gang boasted

THE GANGSTER
Cockram was in top 50 villains

THE SIDEKICK
Ciarrocchi was baby of gang

THE DOME HEIST

By JEFF EDWARDS, Chief Crime Correspondent, and ADRIAN SHAW

THE £200million Dome raid would have gone down in history as the Robbery of the Millennium – the biggest and most audacious ever – if it had succeeded.

The gang who smashed their way into the Millennium Dome in a JCB to try to snatch the De Beers diamonds arrogantly boasted they would never be caught, priding themselves on their months of meticulous planning and preparation "down to the last detail".

They were armed with gas masks, smoke grenades, ammonia, sledgehammers and a nail gun to shatter the supposedly "impenetrable" glass around the world's rarest gems.

They had a getaway speedboat on the Thames and a van waiting on the other side of the river to collect their haul.

But their professionalism was matched by a sophisticated police operation – undercover detectives were shadowing their every move from the start.

Scores of officers moved in to catch the gang redhanded as they struck.

The raiders could not believe they had been outmanoeuvred by the Flying Squad and not "grassed up".

And one gang member told the court he believed there was only a billion to one chance they would be caught.

But yesterday five men were jailed for what a judge called a "wicked plan".

Gang leaders William Cockram, 49, of Catford, South East London, and Ray Betson, 40, of no fixed address, were given 18 years.

Aldo Ciarrocchi, 32, of Bermondsey, South East London, and Robert Adams, 57, of no fixed address, were sentenced to 15 years.

All admitted conspiracy to steal but denied more serious charges of conspiracy to rob.

But they were convicted by 10-2 verdicts after the jury deliberated for 35 hours at the end of the three-month trial.

Kevin Meredith, 35, of Brighton – who drove the speedboat – was given five years. He denied both charges but was unanimously convicted of conspiracy to steal.

Judge Michael Coombe told the court his defence that he

THE HARDMAN
Adams was impossible to quiz

THE BOSS Betson swanned around like a star

Kidnapped!

During the 1920s and 30s, a series of kidnappings for ransom terrified the American public. The most famous is probably that of aviator Charles Lindbergh's baby in 1932. The following year, eight high-profile abduction cases made international headlines, including that of Brooke Hart, the son of a wealthy department store owner. Six-year-old Bobby Greenlease, also the son of wealthy parents, was abducted in 1953. All three of these cases ended in murder, and the subsequent execution of the killers - in one case by public lynching, the last of its kind in California.

But not all kidnapping cases turn deadly. Fast-forward to the 1970s and the case of media heiress **Patty Hearst**, who was kidnapped by members of the Symbionese Liberation Army and held for ransom.

Notoriously, Hearst not only survived her ordeal, but joined with her abductors in an armed bank robbery.

In the US, ransom cases are typically handled by the **FBI**, but the authorities aren't always called, as for example in the case of Kevyn Wynn, whose wealthy casino-owning father didn't trust the police's ability to return his daughter alive, and so took matters into his own hands.

THE LINDBERGH BABY

Pioneering aviator **Charles "Lucky Lindy" Lindbergh** had achieved an ideal life. He had a loving family, and his piloting of the first nonstop solo flight across the Atlantic Ocean had brought him both fame and fortune. But his life went into a tailspin when his twenty-month-old son Charlie was taken from his nursery after dinner on 1 March 1932. The usually hyperactive family dog – a terrier named Wagoosh – had not barked an alert, and the blond, curly-haired boy disappeared into the night without a trace.

Charles and his wife Anne had not intended to spend the night at their new estate in Hopewell, New Jersey – a weekend home – but because Charlie had come down with a cold they decided to break from their routine and stay over. At about 7.30pm they put the boy to bed, and he quickly fell asleep, wearing an undershirt and sleeping jumper. His nanny, Betty Gow, checked on him at 8pm and again at 10pm. That's when she discovered he was missing from his crib. Just two months earlier, Lindbergh had played a prank on his household, claiming his son had been kidnapped. This time it was no prank. After the family and staff had frantically searched the house and property – Lindbergh carrying a loaded rifle – at 10.25pm a groundskeeper phoned the Hopewell Police to inform them of the boy's disappearance. Within thirty minutes, police roadblocks and check-points were in place and hospitals had been notified that the toddler was missing.

Meanwhile, police searched for clues. They found a broken ladder, tyre tracks and a carpenter's chisel. But they made mistakes too. State police helping with the investigation discovered traces of mud on the nursery floor and footprints on the wet ground beneath the nursery window, yet they failed to make plaster casts of the footprints or even to take measurements. The *Hunterdon County Democrat* reported that officers ignored police protocol in their panic to find the missing boy and catch his abductor.

The biggest clue, left in an envelope on the windowsill inside the boy's room, was a ransom note, demanding $50,000. No usable fingerprints were found on the note, in the nursery, near the window or on the ladder. In fact, no fingerprints were found at all – not even those of the Lindberghs and their staff – leading investigators to believe the room had been wiped clean. Handwritten on a single sheet of paper in blue ink and using poor English, the ransom note read:

"Dear Sir! Have 50,000$ redy 25,000$ in 20$ bills 15,000$ in 10$ bills and 10,000$ in 5$ bills. After 2–4 days we will inform you were to deliver the money. We warn you for making anyding public or for notify the Police. The child is in gut care. Indication for all letters are singnature and 3 holes."

The crime sent shockwaves not only across New Jersey but around the world. The latest in a long line of ransom kidnappings, it prompted everyday people to worry whether their babies were safe in their own beds. On reading of the kidnapping, retired teacher **John F. Condon** wrote an open letter to the kidnappers, published in the *Bronx Home News*, volunteering to act as a go-between. He soon received a letter from the kidnappers accepting his offer, and the Lindberghs also agreed to his proposal. After a series of exchanges, including the sending of Charlie's sleeping suit as proof that the correspondent was truly the kidnapper,

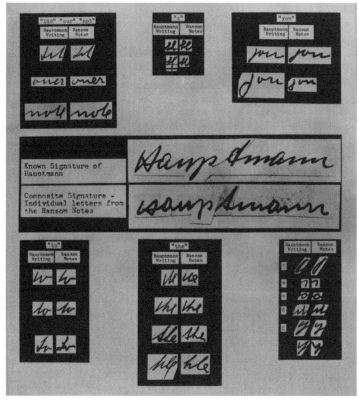

The evidence: Hauptmann's signature, compared to the handwriting of the ransom notes.

been kidnapped, the body of an infant, face down, covered with leaves, decomposing in a shallow grave, was discovered by a truck driver in the woods on Mount Rose Hill in Hopewell Township, two miles from the Lindberghs' 390-acre estate. Staff at nearby St Michael's Orphanage said the body was not one of their children. The boy's father and nursemaid identified the remains as those of Charlie, through a deformed toe and a hand-sewn flannel undershirt. A number of public officials were present during the identification, and the coroner's office concurred, before determining the cause of death to have been a massive fracture to the skull. Almost immediately, Charles Lindbergh had the remains cremated. This raised eyebrows: what was the hurry? Some went so far as to question whether the body actually was that of the Lindbergh baby. Because of advanced decomposition, the sex of the body could not be determined. Adding even more suspicion was the height discrepancy: a "Missing" poster had described Charlie as being 29 inches tall, but the remains were 33 inches long.

The discovery of the body stoked the fires of what was already sensational media interest in the case, with journalist **H.L. Mencken** describing it as "the biggest story since the Resurrection". The public's

a meeting was set up in St Raymond's Cemetery in the Bronx and the ransom money was handed over. In exchange, Condon was given a note which claimed the baby was to be found in a boat anchored near Martha's Vineyard; but after repeatedly flying over the area Lindbergh was forced to accept that this was a lie.

On 12 May 1932, about ten weeks after Charlie had

concern and sympathy was demonstrated by the one hundred thousand letters and telegrams that were sent to the family, including messages from President and Mrs Herbert Hoover and the Prince of Wales. Congress rushed through new legislation – the Federal Kidnapping Act – which enabled the Bureau of Investigations (what is now the FBI) to aid the pursuit of the killer. This act, which is still in force, makes kidnapping a federal offence and allows FBI agents to step in and pursue a kidnapper if a victim is taken across state lines or the mail service is used for ransom demands.

Under pressure from the continuing publicity and the concerns of local residents, the police were eager to make an arrest. But it was not until 1934, two years after Charlie's disappearance, that they were able to do so. In September of that year, police arrested **Bruno Richard Hauptmann**, a carpenter, and charged him with the murder. He proclaimed his innocence from the start and never wavered. But the evidence, although mostly circumstantial, was damning. He caught the police's attention when he used one of the ransom money bills to pay for petrol (the serial numbers had been logged), and after raiding his house they found over $14,000 of the ransom money in his garage. In addition, handwriting experts hired by the prosecution compared samples of Hauptmann's writing to that of the ransom notes and claimed similarities in grammar, spelling and penmanship. These experts testified against Hauptmann at trial. Witnesses also testified that they saw Hauptmann in his car near the Lindbergh estate.

The trial began on 2 January 1935, in **Flemington**, the county seat. As crowds poured into town, hoping to get a place in the packed courthouse, mob mentality took over. According to the *Hunterdon County Democrat*, state troopers were unable to control the throng of people. The *American Mercury* magazine reported that "for two months the world went mad and the center of the universe shifted to the sleepy town of Flemington. All sense of proportion and much of the sense of decency was lost." The trial lasted more than six weeks and ended in a unanimous guilty verdict from the jury. Hauptmann was sentenced to death, and in 1936 he was executed in an electric chair at Trenton State Prison.

In subsequent decades, many have argued that Hauptmann was wrongly convicted. **Lloyd Fisher**, who was a member of Hauptmann's defence team, called the trial and verdict "the greatest tragedy in the history of New Jersey". Several theories have been offered, including that the infant body found was not that of the Lindbergh baby. Scottish nursemaid Betty Gow has also been accused of being a party to the crime. After grilling by investigators, Gow left the US and returned to Glasgow, Scotland. In fact, police had initially suspected household staff, including Oliver Whatley, the butler and chauffeur, his wife, who was the cook and housekeeper, and Gow. But formal charges against them were never handed down. During Hauptmann's trial, Gow testified that she "might" have told her boyfriend Henry "Red"

The Lindbergh abduction was the inspiration for the Agatha Christie novel *Murder on the Orient Express*. The book's plot centres on the murder of an American passenger who turns out to be a renowned child kidnapper.

The convicted Hauptmann is escorted to his execution by electric chair.

Johnson, a Norwegian seaman, about the family's extended stay at the estate. For a short time, Johnson was considered a suspect. It has never been revealed what became of that piece of the investigation or how deeply police investigated Johnson.

Even after the trial was concluded, the Lindberghs had to contend with constant hounding from the press and hordes of onlookers drawn to the area. And so, in

December 1935, Charles, Anne and their three-year-old son Jon (with whom Anne had been pregnant at the time of his brother's kidnapping) sailed to Europe to seek privacy and safety and attempt to resume their lives. In the US, photographers had followed them wherever they went. In Europe, away from the media spotlight, they lived quiet lives.

For further investigation

A. Scott Berg *Lindbergh* (1998) A sympathetic biography of Charles Lindbergh.

Lloyd C. Gardner *The Case That Never Dies: The Lindbergh Kidnapping* (2004) The intricacies of the criminal case, and continuing questions surrounding Bruno Hauptmann's guilt or innocence.

Thomas Fensch *FBI Files on the Lindbergh Baby Kidnapping* (2001) Includes complete, previously never-released FBI files on the Lindbergh kidnapping.

nj.com/lindbergh A compilation of articles about the case.

BROOKE HART

Handsome, popular and wealthy, 22-year-old Brooke Hart was the most eligible bachelor in San José. But that very good fortune made him a target for those seeking a shortcut to riches. Less than two years after the Lindbergh abduction – and while the perpetrator of that crime was still on the loose – Brooke became

KIDNAPPING IN OLD HOLLYWOOD

The stars of the early film industry in Hollywood were obvious targets for kidnappers hoping to extort large sums from the super-rich. In 1925, police foiled a plot to kidnap silent film legend Mary Pickford. Three men – two truck drivers and a car salesman – were arrested in Los Angeles for conspiring to kidnap Pickford, along with Polish film actress Pola Negri (one of the great *femmes fatales* of the silent era) and child actor Jackie Coogan.

At the would-be kidnappers' trial, Pickford – visibly struggling to maintain her composure – glared at the defendants while she testified and called their lawyer "an insignificant pipsqueak". The judge had to silence Pickford by hammering his gavel and threatening to jail her for contempt of court. Two of

the men were convicted and sentenced to ten years in prison. The third was acquitted.

After the trial, Pickford was secreted away to Cape Cod and later told *Liberty* magazine: "If anyone has the idea they can get me, they are wrong. I am surrounded by watchers and friends, am never alone and am amply taken care of." But, of course, the kidnapping attempt only added to the public's fascination with her. *The New York World* recognized the publicity value of such an incident, publishing an editorial which warned. "There is danger that the thing will become epidemic. That is, enterprising press agents, now that the jewel-theft scheme has pretty well worn out, may try to fake kidnapping plots and in that way get their employers' names in the paper. Let us hope no such epidemic breaks out."

the latest victim of the epidemic of kidnappings for ransom that was sweeping the US. This time, however, the public wouldn't wait for justice to be served: within hours of the discovery of Brooke's body, the suspected killers – **Jack Holmes** and **Thomas Harold Thurmond** – were hanged by an angry crowd in what would be the last public lynching in California.

The Harts were one of the foremost families in San José. Brooke's grandfather had founded Hart's Department Store in 1866, and under his son Alex it had become a local institution: it provided employment to hundreds, and almost every family in the city shopped there. Brooke was Alex's eldest son; he had worked in the store throughout his childhood, and was expected one day to step into his father's shoes and run the business. Soon after he graduated from Santa Clara University, his father appointed him junior vice president of the store and began grooming him to eventually take over the day-to-day operations. He also presented him with a light-green 1933 Studebaker President roadster.

It was as he drove his new roadster out of a car park near the store, on 9 November 1933, that Brooke was kidnapped. His captors drove him ten miles out of town in his own car, then abandoned the Studebaker for a Chevy, shoved Brooke into the back seat and drove to the San Mateo Bridge. Here, they ordered Brooke out of the car and hit him over the head with a concrete block, knocking him unconscious. They bound his hands and feet with wire and tied two blocks to his feet before pushing him into the chilly waters of San Francisco Bay. The tide was out, and there was just a few feet of water at the base of the bridge. The fall didn't kill Brooke, who regained consciousness and thrashed about in the shallow water, yelling "Help". To finish him off, Thurmond shot at Brooke with a pistol until he stopped struggling.

Brooke's disappearance was noticed almost immediately. He'd left the store five minutes before closing, at 5.55pm, telling his father he'd be back directly with the car, ready to drive him to a dinner party. The car park lot was only half a block from the store. By 6.15pm, when Brooke still hadn't shown up, it was obvious to his father that something was amiss. It wasn't like Brooke to ignore an appointment. The family called Brooke's friends and co-workers. No one knew where he was.

At 9.45 that night, the kidnappers called the Hart home and spoke to Brooke's younger sister. According to court transcripts, the caller said: "We have your brother. He is safe, but it will cost you $40,000 to get him back. If you ever want to see him alive again, keep away from the police. We will phone further instructions tomorrow." The family notified police, and an all-points bulletin was issued, instructing all law enforcement officers to be on the lookout for the Studebaker. Meanwhile, Hart's employees scoured the streets in a desperate search for Brooke's car. Later that evening, Perry Belshaw, manager of the San José Country Club where Brooke and his father were to have attended a dinner meeting that night, spotted a Studebaker parked at an awkward angle on the shoulder of a rural road with its headlights left on. No one was inside. He went home and telephoned the county sheriff's department to report the abandoned car. The sheriff himself responded to the call and confirmed that the car's plate was registered to Brooke Hart.

The family waited anxiously for further instructions from the kidnappers. On Wednesday 15 November, six days after Brooke's abduction, Alex received a letter, telling him to take the ransom money and drive alone towards LA in the Studebaker. Alex was willing to cooperate, but had never learned to drive, so he had a large sign placed in the window of the department store reading "I cannot drive". That evening the kidnappers phoned. Alex spoke to them, and managed to keep the caller on the phone long enough for police to trace the call to a phone booth in downtown San José. Officers swooped down on the location and arrested Thomas H. Thurmond as

he left the booth. After some intense questioning, he opened up and described the murder, giving details of his accomplice. Early the next morning, Thurmond led police to a hotel where Jack Holmes, caught by surprise and wearing only his underpants, was holed up. He, too, confessed to the crime. The men, who were both from San José, were booked into the downtown county jail behind the court-house on First Street.

Then, two weeks after Brooke Hart went missing, his

The body of Thomas H. Thurmond, lynched by an angry mob.

body was discovered by duck hunters in San Francisco Bay, three miles south of the San Mateo Bridge where his killers had thrown him into the water.

When they learned details of Brooke's fate from the radio and newspapers, the public were outraged. The *San Francisco Chronicle* reported: "The temper of San José citizens is still at white heat." People wanted justice, and they weren't willing to wait for a trial, especially since rumours were circulating that the men might get off on the grounds of insanity. The evening after Brooke's body was found, an angry, hysterical throng of five thousand gathered outside the county jail. Armed with a battering ram and a garden hose – used to douse tear gas canisters that police threw at the crowd – the mob broke into the jail and dragged Holmes and Thurmond across the street to St James Park. The terrified suspects were stripped, strung up and hanged from trees: Thurmond from a mulberry tree, and Holmes from an elm.

The feeling in the community was that the kidnappers had got what they deserved, and this was reflected, the next day, in Oakland's *Post Enquirer*, which prominently featured photos of the two men's nude bodies hanging from the trees. The governor of California James Rolph earned himself the nickname "Governor Lynch" when he declared publicly that if it were up to him, he would release all kidnappers and murderers incarcerated at San Quentin and Folsom prisons in Northern California and deliver them to the "patriotic San José citizens who know how to handle such a situation". However, across the rest of the country newspapers reacted with horror to this extreme act of "vigilante justice", describing the mob as "bloodthirsty", "crazy" and "savage". Seven men were eventually arrested and charged in connection

with the mob violence, but no one was ever convicted. Since the lynchings, some have claimed the accused men were innocent, but no credible proof has ever been presented providing any reasonable doubt, and the case remains closed.

For further investigation

Harry Farrell *Swift Justice: Murder and Vengeance in a California Town* (1992) Written sixty years later by a newspaper reporter, this account includes reproduced newspaper articles and lays out the case in a suspenseful but factual narrative.

tinyurl.com/amedg9 An article in the *San Francisco Chronicle* about a film inspired by the case, which questions whether Holmes and Thurmond were forced to take the rap for a crime they didn't commit.

BOBBY GREENLEASE

A chance meeting between two grifters in a saloon in St Joseph, Missouri, in May 1953 led to one of the most publicized crimes of the decade: the heinous murder of a wealthy businessman's young son as part of a bungled kidnap plot.

The deadly saga began when Carl Hall, a newly released convict, sat down on a bar stool next to Bonnie Heady at the Pony Express saloon in St Joseph, an hour north of Kansas City. Middle-aged and frumpy, with a round face and a misshapen dark bob, Heady was a regular patron at the bar – a hardened alcoholic, in fact. Hall, also an alcoholic, had drunk away a large inheritance, then turned to crime to support his habit. He and Heady had two things in common: they enjoyed drinking and didn't like drinking alone. The pair struck up a conversation and, after a couple of hours, left the bar together.

The new lovers moved in together and in no time at all hatched an ill-gotten plan to make quick money. They would kidnap six-year-old Bobby Greenlease, then extort a ransom from the boy's millionaire father, who owned a series of Cadillac dealerships in Kansas City and the surrounding area.

On the morning of Monday 28 September 1953, soon after term had begun, Heady took a cab to Bobby's school, the exclusive Notre Dame de Sion Catholic School. The image of respectability, right down to her modest hat and white gloves, Bonnie told a nun that she was Bobby's aunt and that his mother had had a heart attack. She was aided in her deception by Bobby's docility: had he shown any hesitation in accompanying this strange woman, the nun's suspicions might have been roused. But he did not. Heady walked Bobby to the waiting cab and asked the driver to take them to a nearby car park lot. Here they met Carl, who was in a Plymouth station wagon.

Carl drove to a remote farm, where he attempted to strangle the boy with a piece of clothesline. When that failed, he bashed in the boy's top teeth with the butt of a revolver, then finished him off with a .38 calibre bullet. Carl later told police the boy had been cooperative and didn't appear frightened. According to the FBI file, the plan had always been to kill the boy: "he considered the boy evidence, and … decided to destroy the evidence."

With Bobby's body still in the car, the couple stopped off at a bar before heading back to St Joseph. When they reached home, Carl carried the boy's body to a hole he'd dug earlier in the back yard. He dropped the body in the grave and covered it with lime and dirt. Bonnie planted chrysanthemums in the freshly tilled earth. Carl then grabbed a ransom note Bonnie had written earlier and took it to the post office. He mailed it special delivery to Robert Greenlease Sr, who called police as soon as he received the letter. The letter read:

"*Your boy has been kidnapped get $600,000 in $20's – $10's – Fed. Res. notes from all twelve districts we realize it takes a few days to get that amount. Boy will be in good hands – when you have money ready put ad in K.C. Star. M – will meet you in Chicago next Sunday – signed Mr. G.*

Do not call police or try to use chemicals on bills or take numbers. Do not try to use any radio to catch us or boy dies. If you try to trip us your wife and your child and yourself will be killed you will be watched all of the time. You will be told later how to contact us with money. When you get this note let us know by driving up and down main St. between 39 and 29 for twenty minutes with white rag on car aerial.

If you do exactly as we say and try no tricks, your boy will be back safe within 24 hrs after we check money.

Deliver money in army duffel bag. Be ready to deliver at once on contact.

M.

$400,000 in 20's
$200,000 in 10's"

Greenlease gathered the cash, with the help of some banking associates. FBI agents recorded the serial numbers of all the bills, and an ad was placed in the newspaper, as the note instructed, letting the kidnappers know the money was available. But even though the Greenleases had carefully followed the note's instructions, Carl sent them a second letter, which began "You must not of got our first letter". The envelope also contained Bobby's Jerusalem medal, which Carl had removed from the boy's body. To let the kidnappers know he was cooperating and following their instructions, Greenlease spoke to reporters outside the front door of his home: "We think they are trying to make contact", he said. "All I want is my boy back."

Finally, two full days after Bobby was kidnapped, Carl called the Greenleases. He told them to be prepared to pay the ransom the following night, a Thursday, and said he would call back with the location for the drop. But he didn't call again until 6.30pm on the Friday, and still did not give a location. A friend of the family who answered the phone asked if Bobby was okay. The kidnapper replied, "He is fine, but homesick."

It wasn't until the early hours of Saturday morning that Hall called to give the Greenleases a location where they could find a note. They found the note, but its description of the location for the ransom drop was confusing; Hall had to give them new instructions for yet another location. That Sunday, two of Greenlease's friends set a duffel bag stuffed with cash on the side of a remote road on the outskirts of Kansas City. At 4.30am, Carl Hall

Bonnie Heady and Carl Hall.

called the Greenlease home to tell them he couldn't find the money. The Greenleases' friends retrieved the bag, then dropped it again, in a heavily wooded area at the end of a bridge ten miles east of Kansas City. This time, Hall got the cash. He made a final call to the Greenleases, telling them the boy would be back with his mother in 24 hours.

The cash stowed in a rented station wagon, Carl and Bonnie headed 240 miles east to St Louis, where they went barhopping. Afterwards, they dumped the station wagon, which was in Bonnie's name, and took a cab to an apartment Hall had rented, where Bonnie passed out in a drunken stupor. Carl left in the same cab after leaving Bonnie with $2400 in cash. The cab driver, Johnny Hager, stuck with Hall because of the $20 tips he was giving him. He dropped him off at a hotel, then returned to his office and told his boss about the fares he was getting and the cash Carl was keeping in a large suitcase. Hager and his boss, mob associate Joe Costello, saw an easy mark. Costello called a dirty cop, Lieutenant Louis Shoulders, and they agreed to squeeze Hall for half the cash, which they assumed was dodgy but didn't yet know was the Greenlease ransom money. Shoulders and another police officer, Elmer Dolan, arrested Hall in his hotel room, while Costello waited outside. But before taking him down to the police station for booking, they removed half the money from the suitcase. When they turned in the suitcase as evidence, it contained only $288,000. While questioning Carl, the officers learned he was the Greenlease

kidnapper. Carl admitted to planning and executing the kidnapping, but initially denied killing the boy. He gave police the address of the apartment where Bonnie was staying and she too was arrested. Once in custody, Bonnie confessed in full, and Carl then admitted he'd killed the boy.

The following morning, 7 October, Bobby's body was dug up from beneath the bed of chrysanthemums, and Heady and Hall were charged with kidnap and murder. In an attempt to avoid the death penalty, they each pleaded guilty, but the judge still decided they should be executed. And so, on 18 December, just after midnight, Carl and Bonnie were walked to the gas chamber, where they sat in chairs and were blindfolded. "Are you doin' all right, honey?" Bonnie asked Carl. "Yes, mama", he said. Those were their last words, spoken just before they were gassed to death.

After the executions, Dolan and Shoulders were convicted of perjury in connection with the missing ransom money. Dolan was sentenced to two years in prison, Shoulders to three. Costello escaped indictment. Cab driver Hager cooperated with investigators and was not charged. He returned what was left of the $2500 Hall had given him.

For further investigation

Ⓦ crimemagazine.com/greenlea.htm Lays out details of the Greenlease case.

Ⓦ fbi.gov/libref/historic/famcases/greenlease The FBI's own account of the case.

GARY KRIST: THE "EINSTEIN OF CRIME"

Before he reached the legal driving age of sixteen, Gary Krist had been caught stealing cars on three separate occasions. But being charged as a minor didn't deter him; over the next few years this self-proclaimed "Einstein of crime" dabbled in a variety of illegal activities, including additional car theft and a prison escape. In 1968, when he was still just 23, he set out to commit what he would later call the "perfect crime". Except it didn't turn out so well; Albert Einstein, Krist definitely was not.

It was 16 December, just before the start of the Christmas break. Emory University student Barbara Jane Mackle had taken ill with the flu, and her mother went to Emory to pick her up. The two planned to drive the nearly seven hundred miles to the family's rambling mansion in Coral Gables, Florida, but that night they only made it a few miles down the road, to a motel in Decatur, Georgia, where they intended to stay the night.

At 4am the following morning, Krist knocked on their hotel room door, saying he was a police officer and that a friend of Mackle's had been injured in a car crash. Once inside the room, Krist and his girlfriend Ruth Eisemann-Schier (disguised as a man) used chloroform to render Mackle's mother unconscious, then bound and gagged her, and left her in the motel room. They hustled twenty-year-old Barbara Jane outside at gunpoint, and forced her into the back of their car, telling her she was being kidnapped.

Mackle was driven to a remote pine forest near Duluth in Gwinnett County, some twenty miles from the motel. There, she was stuffed into a coffin-sized box and buried alive, though not before Krist took a photo of her inside the box holding a sign that read "Kidnapped". Mackle had begged her abductors not to put her in the ground, but after they chloroformed her she was powerless to resist. The box was ventilated with two snorkel-like plastic tubes, and equipped with a battery-powered lamp. Also included was some food, sedative-laced water, and a note from Krist telling Barbara Jane that she would soon be released.

Once Krist's buried treasure was secure in the woods, he telephoned Barbara Jane's father, Robert, and demanded $500,000 in a cash ransom. A Florida property magnate and friend of then-president-elect Richard Nixon, Robert Mackle could easily afford that sum, and responded with alacrity, in the hope of getting his daughter home alive. However, the first drop attempt failed as Krist panicked when he spotted two police officers in a patrol car who coincidentally happened to be passing by the drop location. He and Eisemann-Schier fled on foot, leaving their own car behind. FBI agents who searched the car found documents that included Krist's and Eisemann-Schier's names, plus the photo of Barbara Jane in her box. A hunt for the kidnappers ensued, using addresses and other leads found on the documents, but to no avail. So a second ransom drop was set up. This time, it was successful. Afterwards, Krist called an FBI switchboard and gave sketchy directions for the remote location where Barbara Jane was buried alive.

More than a hundred law enforcement agents and officers scoured the area, using their hands to dig in the dirt in search of the live grave. Finally, they located

Barbara Jane eighteen inches underground. She was alive but dehydrated after her 83-hour ordeal.

Meanwhile, Krist headed to West Palm Beach, where he bought a speedboat. He paid with cash, which he was carrying in a brown paper bag. It was suspicious enough for the boat dealer to notify the authorities, who closed in on Krist. Pursued by a police helicopter, Krist ran aground in his new boat on Hog Island, a dense jungle of mangroves off western Florida and, after a night-time chase through the crocodile-infested

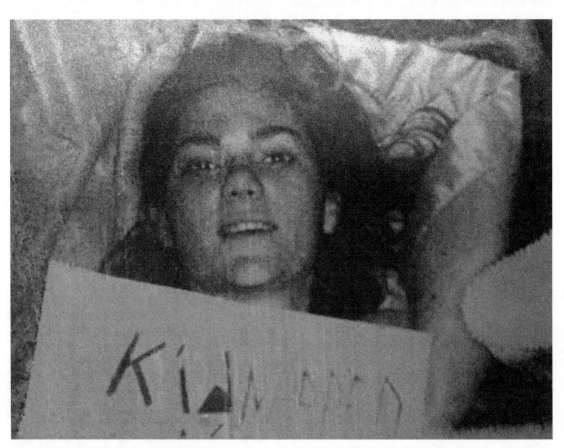

Barbara Mackle, as photographed by kidnapper Gary Krist, lying in the box in which he buried her.

waters, he was apprehended.

Eisemann-Schier eluded capture for a further two and a half months, during which time she became the first woman ever to be included on the FBI's Ten Most Wanted list. But the law finally caught up with her; she was convicted and served seven years in a federal penitentiary. On her release, she was deported to her native country of Honduras. Krist, too, was convicted, and sent to prison "for life". But he was paroled after serving just ten years when he convinced a prison board that he was rehabilitated and was planning to become a missionary.

In the years following his release, Krist trained as a medical doctor (abroad, since US medical schools bar felons), and repeatedly sought to practise medicine in the States. But no one would employ him once they knew of his history, and in 2003 his medical licence was revoked for a minor infraction. After that, Krist returned to crime: in March 2006, at the age of 60, he was arrested on a sailing boat in Mobile Bay, Alabama, when authorities discovered 38 pounds of cocaine on board, as well as 4 illegal aliens who had paid Krist for passage to the US. Krist pleaded guilty to narcotics smuggling and was sentenced to more than five years in prison.

For further investigation

📖 **Barbara Jane Mackle and Gene Miller** *83 Hours 'Til Dawn* (1971) A memoir by the victim about her kidnapping ordeal.

🌐 tinyurl.com/djmeyf Special Deputy Milton Buffington tells journalist Lindsey Williams about the kidnapping and the manhunt at Hog Island, in which he played a key role.

PATTY HEARST

On 4 February 1974, in a stunning crime committed in broad daylight, the granddaughter of American publishing tycoon William Randolph Hearst was dragged screaming from her Benvenue Avenue apartment in Berkeley, California, where she lived with her fiancé Steven Weed. Two men and a woman burst into the small apartment firing cyanide-laced bullets, beat Weed, and abducted the young woman. Hearst, just nineteen at the time and heiress to a substantial fortune, was blindfolded, bound, then dragged from her apartment and driven by her captors to a rented safe house, where she was thrown into a dark, narrow closet.

The Symbionese Liberation Army, a small, violent left-wing urban guerilla group, took credit for the abduction, declaring Hearst to be a "prisoner of war" in their fight against oppression and injustice. Previously little known, the group was led by escaped convict Donald De Freeze, who also went by the name Cinque, in honour of the rebellion leader who took over the slave ship *Amistad* in 1839. Originally, the group planned to trade Hearst for SLA members Russ Little and Joe Remiro, who had been jailed for the murder of Marcus Foster, the caretaker of a school in Oakland, California. But, in accordance with standard practice in such cases, the authorities ignored the release demand. So the SLA changed tack. Eight days after Patty's abduction they released an audiotape with an new set of demands. Her parents, Randolph and Catherine Hearst, were asked to use their wealth and power to distribute $70 worth of food to every needy person in California. They were also to use their publishing empire to print SLA propaganda. Tacked on to the tape was a message from Patty to her parents. "Mom, Dad," she said in a monotone voice, "I'm OK. I'm with a combat unit that is armed with automatic weapons … I want to get out of here … and I just hope you'll do what they say."

Patty's parents complied with her captors' demands, distributing millions of dollars' worth of food to the poor and printing the group's manifesto, titled "Symbionese Liberation Army Declaration of Revolutionary War & the Symbionese Program". But the good faith effort

STOCKHOLM SYNDROME

Although she received little sympathy from the courts at the time, Patty Hearst is now widely considered to have been a victim of Stockholm syndrome, a condition in which a hostage becomes emotionally attached to their captor.

The condition takes its name from a botched bank robbery in Stockholm, Sweden. On a summer morning in 1973, Jan Erik Olsson stormed into a branch of the Swedish bank Kreditbanken toting a sub-machine-gun and barking at terrified employees, "The party has just begun!" Together with an accomplice, he took four of the bank's employees hostage. For six days, the employees – three women and one man – shared a three-by-fifteen-metre vault with one of their captors, before the standoff ended and the robbers were taken into custody. During their 131 hours in captivity, the robbers put nooses around the hostages' necks and told them that if police tossed gas into the bank they would each be hanged. They were also deprived of sleep for three days. However, once their ordeal was over, in a move that shocked prosecutors, the hostages all refused to testify against their captors. One of the hostages even raised money towards the suspects' legal defence. Even though they had feared for their lives during the crisis, the hostages had emotionally bonded with their captors.

Similar behaviour has been seen amongst concentration camp prisoners, cult members, prisoners of war, incest victims, battered women, and women and underage girls forced into prostitution. Although rare, the condition seems to arise when a number of key factors – isolation from the outside world, a perceived inability to escape, physical and psychological threats, and total dependence on their abusers – are combined with small kindnesses on the part of those abusers. The victims begin to sympathize and identify with their captors.

Bonding to one's captor in this way appears to be a survival strategy subconsciously adopted under conditions of extreme stress. However, it is by no means an inevitable response to such conditions. Take, for example, the hijacking of Trans World Airlines Flight 847 by Islamist terrorists in 1985. On the morning of 14 June two armed men hijacked the flight shortly after it took off from Athens. After forcing the pilot to land in Beirut, Lebanon, the hijackers released the majority of passengers but held the remainder hostage for seventeen days. After the ordeal ended, one of the hostages demonstrated a degree of Stockholm syndrome, telling reporters, "They weren't bad people. They let me eat, they let me sleep, they gave me my life." However, the vast majority of the hostages felt quite differently about their captors, and related their terror at the prospect of being killed by them.

turned into a fiasco when riots broke out and mob-like groups grabbed the food to sell for profit. Immediately afterwards, instead of releasing the heiress, the SLA demanded another food giveaway, and negotiations broke down.

The most shocking twist in the tale came next, when CCTV images were published across the globe which showed Hearst as a seemingly willing participant in a robbery at the Hibernia Bank in the Sunset district of San Francisco, just two months after her abduction. At 9.40am on 15 April 1974, one man and four women, including Hearst, walked into the bank and yelled, "It's a hold-up! Down on the floor! On your faces, you motherfuckers!" Four minutes later, they walked out with about $10,000. Before the group fled in a getaway car, one of the SLA members shot and wounded two bystanders. The public had anxiously followed the story of Hearst's kidnapping, but when the images emerged of Hearst participating in the robbery, yelling commands at customers while toting an M1 Carbine assault rifle, sympathy for her waned. The FBI issued a warrant for her arrest as a "material witness", but it soon became clear they considered her to be more than a mere witness when they published a

Patty Hearst, captured on CCTV, carrying out a bank raid.

"Wanted" poster with her name and photo appearing beneath the words "Bank Robbery". Then an audiotape was distributed to radio stations in which Patty denounced her parents and her capitalist roots and rejected her fiancé, whom she called "a pig". She announced she was now going by the name of "Tania". Even more shocking, she said she had joined the SLA

PRINCESS ANNE

In what may have been a copycat crime, a month and a half after Patty Hearst's abduction a well-dressed man named Ian Ball made a failed attempt at kidnapping British princess Anne, then aged 23. It was the first time in recent history that anyone had made a serious stab at kidnapping a member of the British royal family. The attack took place as the princess's limousine left a charity event and headed back towards Buckingham Palace. The princess was accompanied by her husband, Lieutenant Mark Phillips, personal bodyguard Inspector James Beaton and chauffeur Alex Callender. As the vehicle made its way along Pall Mall, a car swerved to block it from moving. The car's driver, later identified by police as Ball, stepped out and fired six shots, hitting both the inspector and the chauffeur. Ball then ran to the limousine and ordered the princess out, but she refused, replying "Not bloody likely!", and he fled the scene on foot. A police officer chased him down, wrestled him to the ground, arrested and later charged him with attempted murder and attempted kidnap. Ball later pleaded guilty to both charges and was taken to Broadmoor Hospital, a high-security psychiatric institution.

as a soldier and had been a willing participant in the bank robbery. Despite this, Patty's parents continued to insist their daughter could not have been acting of her own free will during the heist.

About a month after the bank robbery, more than four hundred law enforcement officers stormed a bungalow in South Central Los Angeles in which SLA members were hiding, and a shootout ensued. During the gun battle the bungalow caught fire, and it burned to the ground with six SLA members – the majority of its tiny membership – perishing inside. The whole siege was broadcast live on TV. Patty and a couple of other SLA members had left the house before the shooting started, and for the next seventeen months she was shuttled between safe houses in Los Angeles and San Francisco. But on 18 September 1975 she was finally arrested in the top-floor apartment of a house in San Francisco and charged with armed robbery. Initially, Hearst maintained her allegiance to the SLA, stating her occupation as "urban guerilla" when she was booked in. But she soon changed her position, telling authorities she had been raped and kept in a state of sensory deprivation as a means of brainwashing her. She also said she was ordered to become part of the SLA or be killed.

Hearst's trial took place in the spring of 1976. It was dubbed the "trial of the century", the first time that term had been used with any seriousness since the Lindbergh trial in the 1930s. Hearst's defence, presented by renowned criminal lawyer F. Lee Bailey (who would go on to become a member of O.J. Simpson's "Dream Team" in his trial for the murder of Nicole Brown Simpson and Ron Goldman), was that she had participated only under duress and had been brainwashed. However, the brainwash defence was not recognized by US law, and anyway the jury did not buy the claim. On 20 March they convicted Hearst of bank robbery in what was considered one of Bailey's worst defeats. Critics at the time suggested that Bailey could have won the case, because there was ample evidence that Patty had been tortured, abused and threatened with death by SLA members, backing up the claim of brainwashing. His closing argument was short and rambling, and during it he knocked over a glass of water, which splashed on his crotch, giving the appearance that he had wet his pants. It's widely believed that, more than anything else, Bailey's weak closing was what sealed Patty's fate. She was sentenced to seven years and imprisoned at the Federal Correctional Institute in Pleasanton, California.

While serving her time, Hearst met bodyguard **Bernard Shaw**, who later become her husband and the father of her two children. In 1979, after Hearst had spent 22 months in prison, President Jimmy Carter commuted her sentence and she was immediately released from custody. In January 2001, Bill Clinton included Hearst among the 140 people he pardoned in the final hours of his presidency.

"Frankly", Hearst told CNN's Larry King in 2002, "I don't think I got my mind back until after I was released from jail, when I was out on bail pending appeal and I could get back with my family and get in a normal environment."

For further investigation

📖 **Patricia Hearst Shaw** *Every Secret Thing* (1982) Patricia Hearst's memoir, which includes details of her kidnapping.

Ⓦ tinyurl.com/cfqdms Transcript of Patricia Hearst's interview with talk show host Larry King following her presidential pardon.

THE CHOWCHILLA BUSNAPPING

In 1976 **Fred Woods** and brothers **James** and **Richard Schoenfeld** were in their early twenties, still living with their parents in the wealthy suburbs of the San Francisco Peninsula and enjoying the privileged lifestyle of the upper middle classes. But on 15 July of that year, at 4.15 in the afternoon, they threw all that away when they kidnapped a bus full of school-children from the small town of Chowchilla in the California Central Valley. The 26 summer-school children and their driver were heading home after a day spent swimming. They became the single biggest group of people to be kidnapped in US history.

The kidnappers had planned to extort a $5 million ransom for the hostages' release, then have them safely home within 24 hours. But before they were able to make their ransom demand, the bus driver, Edward Ray, and the children managed to dig their way out of their underground cell. Their ordeal had lasted thirty hours.

The saga began when Ray, driving his Dairyland Union School bus down a country lane, slowed to pass what appeared to be a broken-down van on the side of the road. As he approached, a man carrying a shotgun and wearing a nylon stocking stretched over his head stopped the bus. Two more men jumped out from behind the van and boarded the bus. One of the men ordered Ray out of the driver's seat and took his place, while an accomplice got into the van and followed the school bus as it was driven a few minutes further down the road to a storm-drain channel. Here, the men ordered half of the children out of the bus

The cargo van that was buried, with driver Edward Ray and 26 schoolchildren within, in a rock and gravel quarry.

and into the rear of the van, which they locked from the outside. Then a second van appeared and Ray and the remaining children were ushered into it. They were driven around for eleven hours before the vans finally stopped in the middle of the night at a rock quarry in Livermore, a hundred miles from Chowchilla and just thirty-five miles east of San Francisco. It was here that the kidnappers had buried a large cargo van in a cave to act as a holding cell. The masked men forced Ray and the children, ranging in age from five to fourteen, down a ladder in a small tunnel and into the buried eight-metre-long van. The kidnappers had provided limited food and water in the underground prison and equipped it with fans and crude air vents.

By 7.30 that night, the authorities had issued an all-points bulletin, alerting law enforcement officers in the area to the children's disappearance. By 8pm, the abandoned school bus had been discovered. No evidence of foul play was found: the children and their driver had simply disappeared.

Meanwhile, Ray began a plan of escape. He and the two oldest children piled mattresses, left for them by the kidnappers, to the top of the van, where they pushed on the roof, broke through and then dug themselves out. Sixteen hours after they'd been hustled underground, Ray and the children re-emerged, to find themselves at the California Rock and Gravel Quarry. Workers at the site recognized them from news reports and called the police. An Alameda County Sheriff's Department bus arrived and the children were driven to a rehabilitation centre, where they were cleaned up, and given fresh clothes and something to eat and drink.

At first, investigators had very little to go on. However, an examination of the logs that recorded vehicles going in and out of the quarry site provided a lead: Fred Woods, the son of the quarry's owner, was identified as driving onto the site in a large van, but never driving it out. Then, a search on the licence plates of the buried van showed that a man named "Fred" had paid cash for it at auction. As police began investigating Fred, two further suspects were identified: his best friends James and Richard Schoenfeld, who appeared to have dropped out of sight.

Shortly before dawn a few days later, a 25-car caravan stormed the estate of Fred's father, Frederick N. Woods. Sixty-two county sheriff's deputies and US federal agents armed with riot gear and tear-gas canisters emerged from the vehicles. The wanted men were not there. On 23 July Richard Schoenfeld, accompanied by his father and lawyer, turned himself in. Six days after that, Fred Woods was captured in Vancouver, British Columbia, after he wrote a letter from there to a friend who turned it in to the FBI. The same day, James Schoenfeld was arrested in Menlo Park, California, about a mile from his family home, after a resident recognized him and called the police. All three were sentenced to life imprisonment.

For further investigation

📖 **Jack Baugh** *Why Have They Taken Our Children* (**1979**) A behind-the-scenes account penned by a sheriff's deputy who helped investigate the kidnappings.

Ⓦ pleasantonweekly.com/story.php?story_id=994 An account, thirty years later, of the crime and its lasting effects on the rural community's residents.

ETAN PATZ

What happened to Etan Patz? This was the question on every New Yorker's mind after the six-year-old boy disappeared on his way to school one sunny May morning in 1979. Stanley and Julie Patz lived in a loft on tree-lined Prince Street in Manhattan with their three children, Shira, then aged eight, Etan, and Ari, aged two. Etan had begged his mother to let him walk alone to the school bus stop in their SoHo neighbourhood that day, and she eventually conceded. Carrying an oversized book bag, Etan left his apartment building and walked the two blocks west from where he lived. From their apartment's balcony, Etan's mother could see a small group of his classmates gathered at the bus stop, but she never saw Etan's head of shaggy blond hair. He had vanished in broad daylight, only yards from the bus stop on a busy street. He never got on the bus and he did not show up at school. His teacher did not report his absence. His parents did not learn about their son's disappearance until that afternoon, at which point they immediately called the police.

The search for the boy, which began the evening of his disappearance, consumed New York. Bloodhounds were brought in the next morning.

Julie Patz, Etan's mother.

A temporary command post was set up in the Patzs' apartment. Police, carrying photographs of Etan, combed the neighbourhood with loud hailers, asking, "Has anyone seen this boy?" Etan's father Stanley, a professional photographer, plastered his son's photo everywhere and provided it to police and news outlets, but to no avail.

It was not until 1982, three years after Etan's kidnapping, that police got their first real lead. Known paedophile **Jose Antonio Ramos**, who was in New York at the time of Etan's disappearance, was picked up by Bronx police for questioning and taken to the station. He was suspected of trying to lure young boys into a drainage tunnel in which he'd been living. A number of photographs of young boys, mostly blonde like Etan, were found in the tunnel. During the police interrogation Ramos at first denied any knowledge of Etan, but then admitted he knew a woman who used to look after Etan. He also let slip that in 1979, the year of Etan's disappearance, he had been hearing voices, which "would try to force me to get violent". However, there wasn't enough evidence to charge Ramos with a crime, and he was released.

Years later, Ramos was questioned again about Etan Patz. This time, he admitted that he had taken a boy to his apartment the day Etan disappeared. He said he gave the boy a glass of juice, and then picked him up and held him against his body. But he didn't confess to molesting the boy, and insisted he then let the boy go home.

Officials have described Ramos as an "unstable vagabond" with a long history of molesting children throughout the US. Without a confession, however, police could not charge Ramos with Etan's disappearance. Instead, they got him on another case of molestation, and he was sent to a Pennsylvania prison, where he is serving a twenty-year sentence for sexual abuse of an eight-year-old boy. If Ramos serves out his maximum sentence, he'll be released in 2012.

As the years passed, the Patz family remained in their Prince Street loft, and kept the same phone number – a number Etan had memorized – in the hope that one day he would return home. However, in 2001, more than twenty years after his disappearance, Etan was officially declared dead. His parents had sought the declaration so that they could sue Ramos for wrongful death, and in May 2004, a Manhattan judge ruled that Ramos was indeed responsible for Etan's disappearance and presumed death, ordering him to pay Stanley and Julie Patz $2 million compensation. During the hearing, it was claimed that Ramos had once confided to a cellmate, "Etan is dead. There is no body, and there will never be a body." However, the burden of proof required for a criminal conviction is much greater than that required in civil cases, and prosecutors have said they still do not have enough evidence to charge Ramos with Etan's abduction. But the New York police have not closed the case, and it is now the oldest open missing child case on the department's books.

Etan's case spurred the missing children cause, and was the impetus, in part, for printing missing children's photos on milk cartons and flyers. In Etan's honour, then-US president Ronald Reagan declared the day of his disappearance, 25 May, as Missing Children's Day. Brian O'Dwyer, a lawyer for the Patz family, told CNN: "The disappearance of Etan Patz was the end of innocence for many parents. They no longer believed it was safe to have your children walk around alone, because suddenly there could be somebody out there."

For further investigation

Ⓦ tinyurl.com/abx3k8 A comprehensive piece about the case by CBS News, including interviews with Etan's father and the family's attorney.

KEVYN WYNN

On 26 July 1993, two men surprised 26-year-old Kevyn Wynn, daughter of hotel tycoon Steve Wynn, in the garage of her townhouse in Spanish Trail, an affluent gated community in Las Vegas. They taped her eyes shut and put sunglasses on her, bound her hands and legs, and made her pose naked for photographs, threatening to release them to the media if she or her father went to the police. They then forced her to call her father, the owner of the Mirage, at that time the most expensive and lavish hotel-casino on the

In the film *Ocean's Eleven*, casino owner Terry Benedict (played by Andy Garcia) makes reference to the Wynn abduction when he cautions one of his employees, "If you should be picked up buying a $100,000 sports car in Newport Beach, I'm going to be extremely disappointed."

THE DAVID LETTERMAN PLOT

In 2005, Kelly Allen Frank, a painter and handyman, was hired to work on talk show host David Letterman's sprawling ranch in northwestern Montana. Frank was given a key to Letterman's house, and became familiar with the family's schedule. Soon he was boasting to an acquaintance of a plot to kidnap Letterman's young son, Harry Joseph, in order to extort a $5 million ransom. That acquaintance promptly informed FBI agents and Frank was arrested before the plot could be carried out.

Frank, who had a previous conviction for stalking and intimidating a woman, uttered two words during his arraignment: "not guilty". His lawyer insisted that the talk of kidnapping had been "light-hearted conversation", not intended to be taken seriously. The kidnapping allegations – the most serious – were eventually dropped in exchange for his pleading guilty to three other charges: felony theft for overcharging Letterman for the work he did on the ranch, obstruction of justice, and possession of illegally killed wildlife. Teton County attorney Joe Coble said he agreed to the deal because "Kelly Frank needed to go to prison. This gets that done."

Frank was sentenced to ten years behind bars. But on 8 June 2007, he and fellow convict William J. Willcutt, a 22-year-old serving time for theft and burglary, escaped from the Montana State Prison while on a work crew that was moving irrigation pipes at the prison's ranch. A Black Hawk helicopter, all-terrain vehicles and a K-9 officer and dog were involved in the search and, after six days on the run, the two men were apprehended and returned to prison. Frank would have been eligible for parole in three months' time. Because of the escape, more time was added to his sentence and parole was denied.

Las Vegas Strip. Kevyn later testified that her father thought she was playing a prank until she began to cry. "Don't worry, honey. I'm going to take care of this", he told her. Then, one of the kidnappers got on the phone, demanding a ransom of $1.45 million, and warning Wynn that he needed to cooperate "if you want to see her alive again".

Steve Wynn did not contact the authorities. Instead, he took the advice of his security chief, **Jim Powers**, who was a former head of the Las Vegas FBI's Field Office and had worked directly under J. Edgar Hoover. Wynn and Powers went to the Mirage's casino cage and withdrew the ransom sum, and then Powers coached Wynn as he made arrangements to deliver the money to the kidnappers. In Nevada, it's a crime for casino owners to personally withdraw cash from casino cages, but considering the circumstances, the Nevada Gaming Commission chose not to prosecute Wynn for the withdrawal.

The kidnappers instructed Wynn to drop the money off at Sonny's Saloon, a block from the Mirage, telling him that he would be contacted again after the money was received. Once they had picked up the ransom money and confirmed the amount was correct, Kevyn's abductors bundled her into the boot of her own car, a 1991 Audi, and drove her to an outdoor car park lot at McCarran International Airport, four miles from her home. They left her there in the car and informed Wynn of her location. Wynn had one of his casino drivers take him to the airport. He later testified: "Whatever I was going to find in the car, it was going to be me doing it. But after three steps, I couldn't do it … I called her name, 'Kevyn.' " She replied: "Dad, is that really you?" One of the people with Wynn opened the boot. His daughter was inside, shaken but unharmed. Two and a half hours after she had been abducted, it was all over.

It wasn't until Wynn opened the boot of the car and found that his daughter was alive that he called the FBI to inform them of what had just happened. Once the media caught wind of the story, coverage focused on Wynn's apparent lack of trust in the authorities to handle the situation for him and return his daughter unharmed. But whatever the rights and wrongs of the matter, the simple truth was that, unlike so many ransom abductions, this one did not end in murder; in fact it went off without a hitch.

Once they were brought in, FBI agents and Las Vegas police worked intensely to trace the kidnappers. Records of calls made from pay phones near Kevyn's house and at the drop location threw up some early leads, and within days, police had identified three suspects: cousins **Anthony Watkins** and **Jacob Sherwood**, and **Ray Cuddy**, the operation's ringleader. On 1 August, six days after Kevyn's abduction, Cuddy was arrested for a stupid mistake: trying to pay cash for a $200,000 Ferrari in Newport Beach, California. The car dealership called police and learned that Cuddy was a wanted man. **Sherwood** and **Watkins** were arrested on 20 September. The FBI named Cuddy and Sherwood as the men who'd grabbed Kevyn from her home, while Watkins acted as lookout.

A total of $1 million was recovered and returned to Steve Wynn. Cuddy and Sherwood rejected plea bargain offers of twelve-year sentences and instead went to trial in 1994. Each was found guilty and convicted of conspiracy, money laundering, extortion and the use of a firearm during a crime of violence. Cuddy was sentenced to 25 years in prison, Sherwood to 19 years. Watkins, who testified against his co-defendants, was sentenced to six years, and in 2001 he was released from prison. In September 1997, a court rejected appeals from Cuddy and Sherwood, noting that threatening the life of a family member during the course of an extortion made the crime an especially egregious one.

For further investigation

Ⓦ tinyurl.com/chy7c3 An article from the *Las Vegas Review-Journal* about how Wynn's kidnappers were tracked down and convicted.

WHITE-COLLAR
CRIME

GENUINE LEATHER

White-collar crime

The phrase "white-collar crime" was first used in a 1939 speech by the American sociologist Edwin H. Sutherland in a speech to the American Sociological Association. Sutherland explained that white-collar crime is "committed by a person of respectability and high social status in the course of his occupation".

Offences that do not involve physical violence, and which relate in the main to financial matters are the crimes conventionally termed "white-collar".

While thousands of people may be affected by the actions of white-collar criminals, these upper echelon lawbreakers usually end up in minimum-security prisons – which in England are called open prisons and which, in the US, have been scornfully dubbed "Club feds". Once their prison stints are over, many white-collar convicts return to society rested and ready to continue making money in the business world – with the fortunes that they secreted away before their incarcerations awaiting them.

Much has been written about sophisticated white-collar offenders, but the most famous of recent years is probably **Martha Stewart**, once listed as one of the most powerful women in the US. Also noteworthy is **J. Tony Serra**, an infamous radical lawyer from San Francisco who has been evading taxes for significant parts of his working life, and who has twice served time in a federal work camp. While in a US federal pen, the colourful lawyer practised law by helping the cases of his fellow inmates, who he referred to as "[his] people".

No one can forget, however, the scandalous misdeeds of top executives at the energy corporation **Enron**, a debacle that rocked Wall Street, and resulted in losses of hundreds of thousands of dollars to stakeholders. This chapter covers these cases and more, and looks into what these white-collar miscreants are doing today.

MARTHA STEWART

In 2001, Martha Stewart, a billionaire lifestyle guru, was described by *Ladies Home Journal* as being the third most powerful woman in the US. Following her rise to fame and fortune through the 1980s and 90s, Stewart was at the top of her game. Known throughout the world, she was welcomed into living rooms through her syndicated daytime TV show. Over a period of two decades, she had transformed herself from a housewife to a billionaire CEO.

The next year, however, Stewart fell dramatically from grace, and her reputation and credibility were badly damaged when she was accused of insider trading. Her popular TV show, *Martha Stewart Living*, was cancelled, and her business empire, which had taken her years to build, began to crumble. The usually stoic Stewart publicly apologized, saying she was "heartsick" and "deeply sorry for the pain and difficulties [the scandal] has caused employees". But there was nothing more that the once-powerful Stewart could do. The feds came down on her like a ton of bricks; the government returning a damning 9-count, 41-page indictment against Stewart, which painted a picture of a cover-up in which she and broker **Peter Bacanovic** made false statements and obstructed justice.

Stewart had grown a catering business and built a large reputation as an expert in old-fashioned, DIY living. Her first book, *Entertaining*, was such a success that it led to television appearances, a gig as a Kmart spokeswoman, and more books. In 1990, her magazine *Martha Stewart Living* was launched, followed closely by the release of her book *Martha Stewart Weddings*. In the 1990s, Martha had her own syndicated TV show and a line of home products. She was at her peak.

Having been a Wall Street stockbroker with business acumen, she understood the risks associated with the stock market, and knew all about the penalties for securities fraud. Exactly how, then, did Stewart, a woman who had enough business savvy to turn her own image into a household name, find herself the focus of an insider trading scandal?

Stewart owned shares in a pharmaceuticals company called **ImClone**. It had developed a drug called Erbitux, an experimental monoclonal

In 1992, Leona Helmsley, nicknamed the "Queen of mean", was one of the first high-profile women entrepreneurs to be sent to prison for white-collar crimes. She pulled off a billing scheme to cover $1.5 million in renovations of her Connecticut mansion and charge, by using phony invoices, interior decorating to her husband's business enterprises.

DAIMLERCHRYSLER

During a routine investigation of its own business in 2005, irregularities were discovered at the DaimlerChrysler Evo-Bus unit, the world's largest bus and van manufacturer.

The two-year in-house probe looked into secret bank accounts used to bribe government officials. Juergen Schiefer, a former manager for the auto-making giant, was charged in November 2006 after prosecutors in Stuttgart, Germany, accused him of filing fake invoices between 2000 and 2005 for work that was never done. Three employees who worked for Schiefer were each charged as accessories.

The US Securities and Exchange Commission and Department of Justice investigated whether the car manufacturer, at the time ranked number five in the world, had violated US anti-bribery laws. Two whistle-blower cases were settled out of court after former employees claimed that they were fired for complaining to superiors about secret bank accounts kept by the company's Mercedes unit.

In late 2006, the firm hired ex-FBI director Louis Freeh as an independent monitor of DaimlerChrysler's internal investigation, as the probe wound down.

antibody, which unexpectedly failed to win the necessary approval from the FDA (the US Food and Drug Administration). ImClone's share price subsequently fell dramatically towards the end of 2001: by the close of the next trading day – Monday 31 December 2001 – the price of ImClone stock tanked, dropping sixteen percent to $46. Ironically, the FDA later reversed their decision.

It was later discovered that many of ImClone's senior executives had sold their shares just before prices took their tumble. The company's founder, **Samuel D. Waksal**, was the most prominent, and was arrested in 2002 for attempting to sell his stock; various members of his family had sold theirs. He was convicted and then sentenced to more than seven years in a federal penitentiary.

Martha Stewart, it came to light, had sold four thousand shares in ImClone – worth $230,000 – on 27 December a day before the FDA announced its decision. Stewart's then-stockbroker, **Peter Bacanovic** of Merrill Lynch, was indicted the same day as Stewart. The US government stated that Stewart had received an unlawful tip from Bacanovic, prompting her to unload her stock to avoid a loss.

By selling when she did, Stewart avoided a loss of $45,673. The government claimed that Stewart and Bacanovic's alibi was false: the pair claimed that they had agreed earlier that she would sell if the price fell below $60 a share.

After being charged, Stewart said "not guilty" five times, speaking quietly and nodding as she entered the plea to five criminal counts in connection with her sale of four thousand shares of ImClone stock. Outside the courtroom, supporters wore "Save Martha" chef's hats and aprons.

From the start of the investigation to the end, controversy followed Stewart. She was publicly condemned by the animal rights group **PETA** – People for the Ethical Treatment of Animals – for allegedly wearing fur. "Martha may not get the electric chair, but the same can't be said for the chinchillas who were genitally electrocuted just so she could wear a frumpy scarf on the day of her conviction", the group wrote in a news release. As it happened, PETA's allegations turned out to be false. To viewers in an interview with television broadcaster Barbara Walters, Stewart, who has chinchillas as pets, countered the accusation. "That was faux fur", Stewart told Walters. PETA apologized and removed Stewart's name from its annual name-and-shame list.

Martha Stewart arrives at the Federal Court House in Manhattan to face charges of securities fraud and obstruction of justice, 4 February 2004.

The jury did not buy Stewart's innocence plea. On 5 March 2004, she was convicted of conspiracy, obstruction of justice, and making false statements. On 16 July 2004, Stewart stood before a US magistrate facing a possible sixteen years in custody. Instead, she was sentenced to five months in prison, five months of home confinement and two years of probation. She was also ordered to pay a $30,000 fine.

Stewart subsequently resigned as chairwoman and CEO of Martha Stewart Living Omnimedia, though she remained on the board. Public opinion polls at the time showed that many Americans believed Stewart should serve prison time; a minority thought overaggressive prosecutors had unfairly targeted Stewart, because of her celebrity status as a powerful businesswoman.

After her conviction, the price of her media company stock fell to $10.86 a share. At its highest point, it traded at $37.25. Stewart wanted to put the mess behind her. She requested – and was granted – to begin immediately serving her time. She also asked to do her time in Danbury, Connecticut, to be closer to her then-ninety-year-old mother. The court denied her request, and on 8 October 2004, Stewart was sent to a federal prison for women – a low-security facility in the West Virginia mountains dubbed "Camp Cupcake".

Her prison sentence, fines and the penalties levied against her suggested that she would never be heard from again. She was forbidden from ever serving again on a public company board of directors and wasn't allowed to work in certain executive capacities for five years. She was forced to permanently step down from her lofty position as CEO of Martha Stewart Living Omnimedia, a company she had built from the ground up. Her future was uncertain. Much speculation circulated about what she would do after her release from prison.

Five months later, wearing an electronic surveillance ankle bracelet to monitor her whereabouts and a poncho hand-knitted by a fellow inmate, Stewart emerged from the prison to begin house arrest on her 153-acre estate in Bedford, about 45 miles north of New York City. Fans cheered her return, and the media closely followed her homecoming. Pundits focused on the poncho, suggesting that Stewart, despite her wealth, could relate to everyday people, including women prisoners. In a statement released to the media, Stewart said that she "will never forget the friends I met here, all that they have done to help me over these five months, their children, and the stories they have told me".

Then the tide changed. The resilient Martha Stewart was back. Her book, *The Martha Rules*, written after the ImClone scandal, was a *New York Times* bestseller. She was even invited to speak before Congress in April 2008, addressing a Senate committee about the care-giving crisis for 78 million baby-boomers as they turn age 65.

Since Stewart's release from prison, stock in her company has nearly tripled, and the Martha Stewart brand appears to have more than survived her temporary fall from grace. In 2005, she was back on TV with *The Martha Stewart Show*, a syndicated American daytime talk show. In November 2007, the show's contract was renewed for a fourth season.

For further investigation

📖 **Christopher M. Byron** Martha Inc: The Incredible Story of Martha Stewart Living Omnimedia **(2002)** An informative look at Martha Stewart and her company.

Ⓦ **sec.gov** Click on "Press Releases" on this site and learn what the US Securities and Exchange Commission had to say about Martha Stewart and the timing of the sale of her stocks.

Ⓦ **usatoday.com/money/perfi/columnist/krantz/2005-07-28 -martha-stewart_x.htm** A comprehensive look at the stock value of Martha Stewart Living Omnimedia after she was sent to prison.

ENRON AND KENNETH LAY

The energy giant Enron Corp. collapsed in December 2001 in one of the biggest ever American corporate history scandals, causing Wall Street to all but fall to its knees. At the head of the brouhaha were founder and chairman **Kenneth Lay**, a grandfatherly type who held an economics doctorate from the University of Houston, and chief executive officer **Jeffrey Skilling**. Lay's name became synonymous with Enron and its misdeeds – and, more specifically, with massive corporate fraud and the looting of corporate coffers for personal gain. His eleven-count indictment was the centrepiece of a federal crackdown on scandals that rocked the corporate US.

The Enron Corporation was formed in 1985 when Kenneth Lay merged two natural gas companies, InterNorth and Houston Natural Gas, to create one giant multinational. In 1986, Lay was given a $731,000 bonus, making him one of the US's highest-paid executives. In 1990, he personally earned $1.5 million, along with millions in bonuses paid to him in shares of Enron stock. The son of a Missouri farmer who was also a part-time preacher, Lay played golf with President Clinton and was close friends with Barbara and George W. Bush, who affectionately referred to

Enron Corp. founder Kenneth Lay, right, and his wife, Linda, walk to the federal courthouse for the third day of his banking fraud trial, as the jury continues to deliberate in his fraud and conspiracy trial, 23 May 2006.

rich, powerful and well connected. Life was good for Kenneth Lay – until the US Justice Department launched an investigation into his firm's financial fine print, that is.

In its heyday, the Houston-based energy giant of Enron employed roughly 22,000 people and was one of the world's leading electricity, natural gas, pulp and paper, and communications companies, with reported revenues of $111 billion in 2000. It was ranked the seventh-largest company in the US, and *Fortune* magazine named Enron "America's Most Innovative Company" for six consecutive years. But when reports surfaced in 2001 that Enron was failing, the company's stock went from $90 a share to just pennies in a single day, with shareholders collectively losing billions. The Enron collapse put 4000 employees out on the street, and billions of dollars went missing. Enron became the largest corporation, at that time, in US history to declare bankruptcy.

The indictments against Skilling and Lay were brought after a two-year investigation by a special team named the **Enron Task Force**. Lay was accused of lying to his employees, investors, and analysts about the true, dire financial condition of Enron. Skilling, for his part, was accused of financial trickery in manipulating figures to defraud investors. His lawyer, on Skilling's behalf, said his client "did not steal, did not lie, did not take anyone's money". Still, the US Justice Department called the case "one of the most challenging and complicated matters" the department had ever handled.

Lay as "Kenny Boy". When their son George W. Bush became president, it was Lay that flew the senior Bushes to the inauguration in a private Enron jet. After spending $100 million to have Enron's name appear on a new baseball stadium, he invited the Bushes to watch him throw the first pitch. He was

FRAUD AND EMBEZZLEMENT - HOW THEY WORK

To commit a fraud is to deliberately practise deception for personal, unlawful gain. To embezzle is to misappropriate someone else's property (usually money). Together, they are the bread and butter of the white-collar criminal. Statistics suggest that two thirds of these offenders are between the ages of thirty-one and fifty, though perps in their sixties are common and they are responsible for the largest losses. The numbers also show that the higher the level of education obtained, the larger the amount these criminals tend to steal. And 75 percent of embezzlers – 60 percent of whom are men – work in sales, customer service and accounting, with the average fraud scheme lasting some 18 months before it is detected.

Fraudulent cash disbursements including billing schemes, payroll schemes, expense reimbursements, cheque tampering, wire transfers, and register disbursements – taking control of someone else's possessions – are all considered larceny. Many of these are much less complicated than you might think. In a billing scheme, for instance, an employee creates a "shell" company and bills an employer for nonexistent services, hoping the accounts department don't check up.

Cheque tampering is another simple favourite, easily accomplished by lifting a blank company cheque and making it out to oneself or an accomplice. Payroll fraud ups the ante a bit, with employees claiming overtime for unworked hours, or managers adding ghost employees to the payroll and then collecting the money personally. At higher levels, with corporate embezzlers directing more sophisticated schemes for large amounts, financial statements are intentionally misstated or altered, with money flowing to offshore accounts instead of into company coffers.

Embezzlement differs from larceny. In embezzlement, the property is already in the wrongdoer's possession, because it is entrusted to them for some purpose which isn't their own; in embezzling it, they wrangle it away for their own use. Embezzlement, in a nutshell, is a breach of the fiduciary responsibilities placed upon a person. For example, cashiers handling money can embezzle cash from their employers, just as lawyers and financial advisors who've been given access by their clients can embezzle funds from bank accounts. According to a 2006 Wells Report released by the Association of Certified Fraud Examiners, it was in the US's banking and financial sectors that fraud was most rife, with 148 cases; government and public administration had 119; and manufacturing had 101. In 315 cases, company officials chose not to prosecute the scammers. The most common reason company executives and owners gave for not prosecuting was the fear of bad publicity. Still, if prosecuted, most offenders are convicted.

It wished to send a clear message: nobody, not even the wealthiest of Americans, was above the law. After Kenneth Lay turned himself him in to the FBI office in Houston, Texas, he was led away, with his hands cuffed behind his back, by federal agents.

In May 2006, after a four-month trial in which Lay refused to testify, citing his rights under the Fifth Amendment to the US Constitution, he was found guilty of conspiring to inflate the energy company's stock price and misleading its investors.

Six weeks after his conviction, and three months before he was to be sentenced, Lay died of congestive heart failure while vacationing at a rental property in Aspen, Colorado, at the age of 64. Until his death, he had protested his innocence, while at the same time accepting responsibility. Six days before Lay's death, federal prosecutors sought to seize $6.3 million they claimed Lay was about to collect from an investment in a limited partnership fund. The government also wanted at least $1.5 million that Lay had borrowed from Enron to pay off the mortgage on a high-rise luxury condominium in Houston where Lay and his wife lived. Following Lay's death, a federal judge threw out the former US naval officer's convictions of fraud and conspiracy. The decision prevented the US government from attempting to seize more than $43.5 million in assets from Lay's estate.

Skilling, convicted on nineteen counts of fraud, conspiracy, insider trading, and lying to auditors, was sentenced to 24 years in prison. Two months before he began serving his sentence, he was ticketed for public intoxication, a misdemeanor. In December 2006, Skilling, 55 at the time, entered the minimum-security federal correctional institution for men in Waseca, Minnesota, about 75 miles south of Minneapolis. All inmates are required to work prison labour jobs that pay 12 to 40 cents an hour – a far cry from Skilling's former $850,000 yearly salary and $5.6 million annual bonus when he was a top executive at Enron. For leisure activities, inmates at Waseca have access to a basketball court, a running track, and a ping-pong table.

Since the convictions, Enron's victims have been paid restitution to the tune of a $1.7 billion payout in 2008 that settled a class-action lawsuit against the firm.

For further investigation

📖 **Bethany McLean and Peter Elkind** The Smartest Guys in the Room: The Amazing Rise and Scandalous Fall of Enron **(2004)** Two *Fortune* magazine writers chronicle the rise and fall of Enron as some top executives get creative with the books in a ploy to make themselves rich.

Ⓦ cbsnews.com/stories/2005/03/11/60minutes/main679706. shtml A rare interview with Kenneth Lay, after his indictment.

ABSCAM

In the late 1970s and early 1980s, an extensive, high-level US federal undercover operation was launched investigating corruption, trafficking in stolen property, and organized crime. Codenamed Abscam, the headline-grabbing sting investigation enticed members of the US 96th Congress into accepting bribes from a fictitious Arab sheik (Abscam is in fact shorthand for the crass full title Abdul-Scam), and ended in the arrests and convictions of 31 people, including a US senator, 6 US Congressional representatives, members of the Philadelphia City Council, and an inspector with the Immigration and Naturalization Service.

Abscam started in 1978 as an elaborate undercover investigation of New York City gangsters from **La Cosa Nostra** who were dealing in stolen art. Agents set up the operation with the goal of taking them down, but when they discovered, through wiretaps and surveillance, that government officials were involved with the mob, the focus of the probe switched to politicians.

The investigation led first to possible corrupt politicians in New Jersey, and then advanced to Washington, DC. To get the ultimate results they wanted, federal agents set up a sting operation. Posing as Middle Eastern businessmen, they offered members of the US Congress $50,000 in cash in exchange for legislative favours for a fictional Arab sheik they claimed to be lobbying for. Meetings with elected officials and undercover agents were set up on a yacht in Florida, hotel rooms in Pennsylvania and New Jersey, and a house in Washington, DC.

During the influence-peddling investigation, the FBI moved to a Long Island office under the fake name of Abdul Enterprises. The sting included agents posing as Middle Eastern businessmen, who offered money to politicians in return for political favours for a nonexistent Arab sheik. Undercover informant Melvin Weinberg acted as the representative to the mysterious sheik, named "Kambir Abdul Rahman". Weinberg was working for the feds in exchange for a lesser sentence in an unrelated wire fraud case.

One Congressman who met with the undercover agents but was never charged was **John Murtha** of Pennsylvania. When the scandal became public, six lawmakers fell, but Murtha, a Vietnam veteran, was not one of them. Murtha repeatedly maintained his innocence, saying he met with undercover agents only to discuss possible Arab investment in his district. Justice Department officials announced in 1980 that Murtha would not face prosecution.

The first elected official to fall was **Angelo Errichetti**, then-mayor of Camden, New Jersey. FBI surveillance video captured Errichetti making a deal with agents, purportedly representing the sheik, for a licence for a casino in Atlantic City the phony sheik planned to build. Errichetti took $25,000 in cash as a down payment for his service to fast-track the permit. In 1981, Errichetti was convicted and served nearly three years in prison. After his conviction, he resigned his mayoral post. Then, after Errichetti was released from prison, he ran for office. Surprisingly, despite the Abscam scandal, he won a seat on the New Jersey state legislature.

But it was Senator **Harrison A. Williams** who was the biggest casualty of Abscam. He had the unenviable distinction of being the first US senator in eighty years to be jailed. Before his fall from grace, Williams, a popular champion of organized labour, was described as New Jersey's "senator for life" because of his high approval rating over a twenty-year incumbency.

A 1990s insurance scam perpetrated by Martin Frankel, a former financier, brought about changes for tighter US insurance regulation. Frankel bought numerous insurance companies, along with their reserves, and used the money to fund a lavish lifestyle to the tune of $200 million. He was convicted in 2002, after being caught hiding in Germany, and sentenced to sixteen years.

John Murtha (centre) walks away from federal court on 21 November 1980, after testifying in the Abscam trial of Frank Thompson and John Murphy.

His political career ended after he was charged and convicted of nine counts in the Abscam prosecutions. Also convicted were five members of the House of Representatives – John Jenrette, Richard Kelly, Raymond Lederer, Michael "Ozzie" Myers, and Frank Thompson, all of whom were convicted in separate trials of bribery and conspiracy.

One politician – a congressman – who met with undercover Abscam agents refused the bribe. He was Senator **Larry Pressler**. On the surveillance videotape, his reaction was unlike that of the others. "Wait a minute. What you are suggesting may be illegal," he told undercover agents, and then he promptly reported the attempted bribe to the FBI – which is what US federal law mandates public officials to do. When veteran American broadcaster **Walter Cronkite** called Pressler a hero during a televised interview with the congressman, Pressler told Cronkite: "I do not consider myself a hero ... What have we come to if turning down a bribe is heroic?"

Richard Kelly's conviction was overturned when a judge ruled that the sting operation was a blatant example of illegal entrapment. But a higher court in 1984 upheld the conviction and sentenced Kelly to thirteen months in prison. Kelly's actions were difficult to explain away. After all, he was captured on videotape stuffing his pockets with cash, then asking the undercover agents, "Does it show?" All charges in the other defendants' cases stuck.

In the end, Abscam generated controversy and heated discussions over the government's undercover operations regarding strategies of entrapment of high-level elected officials. A 1983 special Senate committee looked into the government's handling of the case. And while committee members absolved the FBI of political persecution, at the same time they rebuked investigators' tactics in the case. Other than strong words, however, nothing more came out of that probe. The use of sting operations continues today, but Abscam was the last sting detail that tried to catch lawmakers in the act of committing corruption.

For further investigation

📖 **Robert W. Greene** The Sting Man Inside Abscam (1981)
Author Robert Greene offers intrinsic details of the FBI's undercover sting operation.

Ⓦ spectator.org/dsp_article.asp?art_id=10427 An illuminating story in *The American Spectator* that released for the first time information about Congressman John Murtha's meeting with undercover FBI agents in the midst of the Abscam sting.

LEWIS "SCOOTER" LIBBY

In March 2008, **Lewis "Scooter" Libby**, a lawyer and former chief of staff to US vice president **Dick Cheney**, was stripped of his licence and banned from practising law inside the nation's capital – his punishment for leaking the name of a US Central Intelligence Agency operative to the press, and then lying about it.

The CIA, operative in question was a **Valerie Plame Wilson**, an undercover agent who had worked for a number of CIA front companies overseas. It was revealed during Libby's trial that top officials in the administration wanted to discredit her husband, former US ambassador **Joseph Wilson**, by targeting his wife: Wilson had accused the administration of doctoring pre-war intelligence on Iraq. During the investigation into the leak, former deputy secretary of state **Richard Armitage** and **Karl Rove**, Bush's top political adviser, were found to be the two "senior administration officials" that the columnist and CNN contributor Robert Novak quoted when he outed Plame as a CIA operative. The pair were, however, never charged.

Joseph Wilson had hands-on experience in Iraq (and in Africa) from having been posted there. His experience more than qualified him to pen the now-famous opinion piece published in *The New York*

Times four months after the invasion of Iraq. Entitled "What I Didn't Find in Africa", the editorial heavily criticized the George W. Bush administration for its baseless escalation to war, and explained that, during an official fact-finding mission to Niger, Wilson had found no evidence for the White House's claim that Iraq had been attempting to buy yellowcake uranium in Africa. One week after the op-ed item appeared in the paper, conservative commentator and journalist Robert Novak reported in a syndicated column in the *Washington Post* entitled "Mission to Niger", that Wilson's wife was a classified covert CIA operative. The *coup de grâce* came when, in the same well-read column, he identified Valerie Plame by name.

Wilson responded publicly, saying his wife's identity was covert. He accused the Bush administration of releasing her name in retaliation for his op-ed piece. Furthermore, Plame's lawyer said that outing her put her life at risk, not to mention destabilizing sensitive CIA operations.

The CIA requested an immediate investigation into who leaked Plame's name to the press. The Department of Justice and the FBI responded in October 2003 by launching a criminal investigation into the possible unauthorized disclosure of classified information concerning Valerie Plame's CIA affiliation. Libby was called to testify before a federal grand jury. Afterward, he was accused of lying to FBI agents and the grand jury about conversations Libby had had with

Former White House aide I. Lewis "Scooter" Libby, right, is escorted to a waiting vehicle with his lawyer, Theodore Well, centre, outside federal court in Washington, on Thursday 14 June 2007.

reporters Tim Russert of NBC News and Matt Cooper of *Time* magazine.

After a 22-month investigation, Lewis Libby was indicted. He resigned from his government post just hours after the indictment was handed down, on 28 October 2005, charging him with obstruction of justice in connection with the Plame case, perjury, and impeding the grand jury's investigation.

In a twist in the case, former *New York Times* reporter **Judith Miller** refused to testify before the grand jury, so as not to reveal a conversation she had with a source in the case. She was held in contempt of court and sent to jail for 85 days. After Libby granted her authorization, releasing her from confidentiality, Miller was released from jail and later testified before a grand jury.

Libby was convicted in 2007 of obstruction of justice, making false statements to the FBI, and perjury – offences the Board on Professional Responsibility later found amounted to "crimes that involve moral turpitude". He was sentenced to thirty months in a federal penitentiary, the verdict concluding a nearly four-year investigation.

However, in July 2007, then-president George Bush commuted Libby's prison term, which meant Libby slipped out of spending even one day behind bars. The president stopped short of a pardon, however, meaning Libby's convictions remain, and his law licence is void.

For further investigation

D.M. Brown The Indictment of I. Lewis "Scooter" Libby: The Grand Jury Indictment with Documents Showing the White House Response to the CIA Leak Scandal **(2005)** This book details the legal case against Scooter Libby: one of the biggest scandals of the G.W. Bush administration.

ⓦ huffingtonpost.com/2008/03/20/scooter-libby-disbarred_n _92559.htm A roundup of stories about Libby on the Huffington Post blog.

ⓦ wmsnbc.msn.com/id/17479718/ MSNBC's article about the conviction of Lewis Libby.

JACK ABRAMOFF

Jack Abramoff's Republican lobbying empire fell apart in a swirl of controversy and scandal. He was accused of bribing lawmakers and their aides in exchange for legislative favours. Once powerful and extremely well connected, Abramoff has seen his name, as *Mother Jones* magazine once reported, "become a synonym for corruption".

Abramoff was a man who always had high ambitions. In college, he turned his work with a social organization into the $12,000-a-year chairmanship of the College Republicans, a multi-college lobbying group founded in 1892. He had a ten-year stint working as a producer in Hollywood before joining the lobbying firms of Preston Gates & Ellis and Greenberg Traurig. It was when he started working as a powerhouse Washington lobbyist that things began to go awry.

In 1995, Abramoff began representing Indian tribes with gambling interests. One of Abramoff's first acts as a tribal gaming lobbyist was to defeat a Congressional bill to tax Indian casinos, and, according to *Washington Business Forward*, a lobbying trade magazine: "Tom DeLay was a major factor in those victories, and the fight helped cement the alliance between the two men." DeLay was a senior Republican of considerable interest and House Majority Leader of the US House of Representatives from 2003 until 2005.

The most egregious of Abramoff's crimes was the pilfering of an estimated $86 million from Native American tribes, including the Saginaw Chippewa, owners of the Soaring Eagle casino and resort in Michigan, California's Agua Caliente, the Mississippi Choctaws, and the Louisiana Coushattas over a three-year span.

Federal investigators were seeking to verify whether legislative favours were granted in Congress to Abramoff in exchange for tribal campaign contributions. They found what they were looking for, according to court documents.

The favours done for Abramoff by the former press aide **Michael Scanlon**, who had worked with Abramoff in a scheme in which Abramoff directed tribes to hire Scanlon's public relations firm without telling the tribal leaders that Scanlon was kicking back half of the profits to Abramoff. He was also charging his clients absurd amounts of money for access to influential politicians.

In 2004, the firm of Greenberg Traurig fired Abramoff, who was at one point the company's top moneymaking lobbyist, when it began cooperating with federal investigators in the case against him.

Abramoff was about to become the main character in a massive public corruption investigation. It involved the FBI, the Justice Department's public integrity section, and the Interior Department inspector general working together. Agents focused on tribal clients that had paid $66 million between 2001 and 2003 to Abramoff and PR consultant Michael Scanlon, who'd been a spokesman in Tom DeLay's Congressional office, according to the *Washington Post*.

Abramoff pleaded guilty on 3 January 2006 to three criminal felony counts of mail fraud, tax evasion, and conspiracy to bribe public officials. The next day, he pleaded guilty in a Florida federal court to two felony charges of conspiracy and wire fraud in an unrelated case stemming from his purchase of SunCruz Casinos boat line in 2000. In the plea agreement in Florida, his home state, Abramoff signed a document admitting he was guilty of lying to lenders to help him qualify for a $60 million loan to purchase a $147.5 million fleet.

The 3 January plea deals required Abramoff to rat on his high-placed friends and provide evidence against certain members of Congress – the same lawmakers whom Abramoff had previously lavished with gifts, including campaign contributions, exotic vacations and golf junkets, sporting event tickets, and expensive meals at upscale restaurants.

During the hearing, senators expressed their disgust, including **John McCain**, who said: "What sets this tale apart, what makes it truly extraordinary, is the extent and degree of the apparent exploitation and deceit. Even in this town, where huge sums are routinely paid as the price of political access, the figures are astonishing."

It was the contents of his email messages that strongly contributed to Abramoff's fall. They were released at a public hearing before the US Senate Committee on Indian Affairs. The missives, seized by the feds from Abramoff's personal computer, outlined clandestine kickbacks and political payoffs. But it was the disparaging language used by Abramoff, a devout Orthodox Jew, in his descriptions of tribal officials that appeared to outrage some lawmakers. In emails presented as evidence in federal court files, Abramoff wrote to Michael Scanlon, calling tribal officials "monkeys" and "idiots". About one tribal client, Abramoff wrote: "These mofos are the stupidest idiots in the land for sure." In another, he wrote: "We need to get some dollars from those monkeys!"

The government sought to lessen his time served. Scanlon, as part of his plea agreement, was ordered to pay $19.6 million restitution to his former Choctaw Indian tribe clients. The plea agreement did not spare Abramoff from going to a federal penitentiary, where he was sent with an expected release in 2012.

All told, Abramoff's forced cooperation led to the conviction of White House officials J. Steven Griles and David Safavian, Representative Bob Ney, and nine lobbyists and Congressional aides. While other top-level officials, like Tom DeLay, who once described Abramoff as "one of my closest and dearest friends", were expected to be indicted as well, they were not prosecuted. For his part, Michael Scanlon pleaded guilty in 2005 to conspiring to bribe a member of Congress and other public officials in exchange for his assistance with the prosecution of others allegedly involved in the scandal.

For further investigation

Peter H. Stone Heist: Superlobbyist Jack Abramoff, His Republican Allies, and the Buying of Washington (2006) A colourful portrait of cosy business deals between lobbyists and officials in Washington, DC.

wslate.com/id/2116389/ A lengthy piece and biographical account of the rise and fall of Jack Abramoff.

washingtonpost.com/wp-dyn/content/linkset/2005/06/22 /LI2005062200936.html A Washington Post special report on the background of the Abramoff case and the political players surrounding it.

J. TONY SERRA: "THE PEOPLE'S LAWYER"

In 2006, the famed criminal defence lawyer J. Tony Serra began a ten-month prison sentence, at the age of 71, for tax evasion. It was almost thirty years to the day from his first prison stint, in the same federal facility, for the same offence.

Serra is a nonconformist to the extreme. He has described himself as a "radical lawyer", "civil rights lawyer", and "the people's lawyer". He took a vow of poverty when he received his law degree in the 1950s and became famous for his cases against government institutions on behalf of the little guy. In court, he typically wears thrift-store suits with colourful,

IRAQ AND CORPORATE GREED

In another high-profile corruption case, involving car-makers DaimlerChrysler, Siemens, Volvo, and more than two thousand other companies, corporate officials paid illicit kickbacks to the Iraqi government to win business from an aid programme designed to allow Saddam Hussein to sell oil to buy food and medicine, according to a US Federal Reserve report. The companies sold electric-utility equipment and vehicles to Iraq through the United Nations-sanctioned oil-for-food programme. Roughly sixty percent of companies involved in the programme also paid kickbacks on humanitarian goods for Iraq, totalling $1.8 billion for Saddam Hussein.

cartoonish ties and worn shoes, and he drives broken-down cars costing him no more than $500.

Until 2001, Serra's law firm – Serra, Lichter, Daar, Bustamante, Michael & Wilson – was located on Pier 5 at the Embarcadero in San Francisco. Today, his office is in North Beach, near Serra's modest rented apartment, which he has leased for $400 a month for years for when he's in court. It's the same neighbourhood in which Beat poets Jack Kerouac and Allen Ginsberg came of age. When not in court, Serra lives in the sleepy and remote Northern California beach town of Bolinas.

Paulette Frankl, a courtroom artist who for a decade followed Serra from defence table to defence table, said she learned more about Serra by observing and sketching him than through any conversation with him. "Tony long ago took a vow of personal poverty and vowed never to make money for the purpose of law practice", Frankl said in a telephone interview. "He vowed never to buy anything new. He has no watch and no fancy clothes." Serra was once a star athlete at northern California's Stanford University, and is six-foot-two. His jackets are often too short for his long arms.

"His courtroom attire is often a mockery of the high-priced designer suits of his peers", Frankl said. "He wears shirts with the cuffs stapled shut, pants torn at the knee and mended from the inside with coloured duck tape. The clothes rarely fit and are usually a size too small. His prized possessions are a mountainous soap collection from motels, in cities where he had trials, and an ever-expanding collection of noteworthy ties. They hang from crisscrossed lines in Serra's apartment like objects in an art exhibit. He has insisted, 'It's not what you wear that counts. It's who you are.' "

As a radical pony-tailed criminal and civil-rights San Francisco native who has admittedly smoked dope on a daily basis since the 1960s, he has passionately fought – and won – some of the most high-profile cases in the US, including two notorious death-row cases. His clients have included Black Panther leader **Huey Newton**, members of the Hells Angels and the New World Liberation Front and **Sara Jane Olson**, a Symbionese Liberation Army member who was on the lam for twenty years after being accused of a car bombing. During his representation of several Hells Angels members, Serra came down hard on a prosecutor by calling him, in open court, a "lying dog". Serra is also credited with being the first criminal defence lawyer to get a convicted felon off Death Row.

This was the case of **Patrick "Hooty" Croy**, a Native American sentenced to death for killing a police officer in a 1978 gun battle. It happened on the night of 17 July when dozens of police officers gave chase to a car of containing three Northern Californian Native Americans, who a shopkeeper had accused of shoplifting. The police had opened fire, and pursued them onto a reservation. There, Patrick Croy was shot in attempting to flee, and returned fire with a .22 hunting rifle, killing a police officer. All in all, more than a hundred shots were fired. Croy was granted a retrial. His new defence team, headed by Tony Serra, argued that Croy acted in self-defence. Serra also offered evidence of the genocide against California Indians that has continued since the 1850s. The strategy, known as a cultural defense, was used to explain why Croy feared for his life when he returned fire. The jury returned a "not guilty" verdict and Croy was released from prison.

Serra also managed to win a second death-row

case – that of **Chol Soo Lee**, a Korean American immigrant who was convicted for the 1973 killing of a San Francisco Chinatown gang leader, then subsequently sentenced to death for the self-defence killing of another prisoner. Soo Lee's first lawyers had tried to overturn the original conviction that sent him to prison, but they were unsuccessful. Serra took the case on in 1982 and proved to a jury that police had relied on faulty ballistics tests and witnesses whom, he said in court at the time, "could not tell a Korean from a Chinese from a Japanese from a Filipino". A jury acquitted Soo Lee. Although earlier convicted of second-degree murder in the prison case, Soo Lee was credited with time served and was released from prison.

In 2008, Serra represented Zachary Running Wolf Brown, a Native American activist and one of two people arrested for tree-sitting in protest at the planned destruction of a grove to make way for a $125 million gymnasium in Berkeley, California. Brown had ascended a redwood and taken up residence high above the branches. Serra, who represented Brown, spoke during a December 2007 rally at the grove about the actions of the police, whom protestors accused of cutting ropes used to pull food and water to the tree-sitters. "To litigate properly in an adversarial system, one must postulate an enemy", Serra said at the news conference. "Narcs are my enemies, informants are my enemies, overzealous, brutal police officers are my enemies. Prosecutors especially are my enemies, because so many of them are sick and twisted people who abuse their positions. Mostly they become cynical and contemptuous over time, but the worst are the 'true believers', because they feel they're entitled to go to

Tony Serra leaves the Federal Building after Humboldt County and Eureka law enforcement officers were found liable of using excessive force when they swabbed pepper spray on the eyes of logging protesters in April 2005.

NON-PAYMENT OF BILLS - IS IT A CRIME?

While it may be unethical not to pay bills, it is not a crime. Legally, however, bill collectors have rights and can sue in civil court. Consumers have rights too. In the US, bill collectors are mandated by the Fair Debt Collections Practices Act – or FDCPA – to follow specific rules. Even so, a growing group of debt collectors are using aggressive tactics to collect old debts.

Recent years have seen, junk debt buyers – investors, lawyers, and speculators – purchase old debts still on the books that credit card companies and department stores have long given up trying to collect.

Here's how it works. The original lenders sell the debt to buyers at a knockdown price. Many of those accounts, according to consumer reports, are open-end debt and mandated by statutes of limitation, which means there's a specific period of time as to how long the debt can be legally collected before it expires. If the statute of limitations is up, it means the debts are no longer collectable. But that doesn't stop some companies from attempting to collect on the debts anyway.

The debts – which are also referred to as zombie debts – are aggressively collected by agencies and lawyers who doggedly and sometimes aggressively pursue private individuals in their attempts to collect. Some debts are sold two or three times. According to lawyer Ellen Day in a blog. "An example of an old, or zombie debt, would be a bank or finance company, who sells an old account with a balance of $5000 to the junk debt buyer for $100. The 'scavenger' then pursues the unwitting consumer for the full amount of the so-called debt."

Such junkdebt buying is a multibillion dollar fast-expanding industry. Problems arise when the collectors go to extremes to find and pursue the debtors.

"The players in this 'junk debt' market range from fly-by-night outfits to well-established companies funded by Wall Street investors", wrote Liz Pulliam Weston in an article for Moneycentral.msn.com. The US Federal Trade Commission received more complaints against third-party debt collectors than about any other industry in 2005.

The junk debt buyers inundate individuals with letters and phone calls offering to settle the debt. Then, when individuals don't pay or make payment arrangements, the junk debt collectors file civil lawsuits against them.

Many people, who don't know their rights, ignore court summons and complaints and don't show up in court. That's what the debt collectors are banking on, according to hundreds of websites on the Internet offering advice to those being pursued by junk debt collectors.

If people don't show up in court, then judgements for the plaintiffs – the debt collectors – are issued and a person's wages can be pillaged to collect on the court-ordered judgement.

Many law firms advertise online, asking victims of abusive debt collectors to contact them offering to sue collectors on behalf of the victims.

any lengths to put somebody away."

Despite, or perhaps because of, his marching to the beat of a different drummer, Serra's successes have not gone unnoticed by his peers. He has been acclaimed by *California Lawyer Magazine* as one of the eight best criminal defence lawyers of the twentieth century – along with Clarence Darrow, Thurgood Marshall, and William Kunstler. In 2003, the Trial Lawyers for Public Justice handed him a Lawyer of the Year Award for his $4.4 million victory against the FBI in an Earth First car-bombing case. And *American Lawyer* magazine once ranked Serra as the second-best criminal defence lawyer in the country for both his handling of the Soo Lee trial and another murder case earlier the same year.

While he has preferred to go to trial rather than have his clients plead out to lesser crimes and serve time, when it came to his own tax evasion case, Serra accepted the plea bargain, admitting guilt and accepting his sentence. A parade of supporters from the San Francisco Bay Area's legal community argued for leniency, saying Serra had spent his life representing the downtrodden, mostly at no charge. Justice Department lawyer Blake Stamm, however, countered, telling the US magistrate that Serra was a "chronic and disdainful tax offender" and that he "has plainly not learned his lesson that he has to follow the Tax Code." At the end of the two-hour sentencing hearing, Magistrate Joseph Spero praised Serra's work: saying, "You're an exception to the rule of law." But because he had failed to comply with income tax laws for 21 years, Spero had no choice but to assign him time behind bars. In July 2005, Serra was sent to a federal minimum-security work camp in central California and fined $100,000, which his friends – all mostly fellow lawyers – paid for him.

In various interviews before his incarceration, Serra said he looked forward to prison, because "people in custody are far more interesting than the bourgeois people who populate society". Shortly after his February 2007 release, Serra filed a class-action lawsuit seeking minimum wages for him and other inmates, citing what he described as the "slave wages" received while working in prison as unconstitutional. He held a news conference slamming the government and claiming the prison pay scale was in violation of the Fifth and Thirteenth Amendments of the US Constitution.

For further investigation

Yves Lavigne *Hells Angels: Into the Abyss* (1997) A history of the Hells Angels, which includes segments of Tony Serra's representation in court of three of the gang's members.

sfgate.com A good site to search archived articles about Tony Serra, his IRS problems, his famous civil rights cases, and his prison stints.

sanfranmag.com Includes a story titled "The Believer Behind Bars" that's a comprehensive biographical portrait of Serra.

november.org/stayinfo/breaking07/TonySerra.html The California lawyer published a "Letter from Prison", in which Serra likens US prison work to "slave labour" programmes where federal inmates are paid pennies per hour to work for the government eight hours a day, five days a week.

FEI YE AND MING ZHONG

On 23 November 2001, two computer engineers – Fei Ye and Ming Zhong – were moments away from boarding a flight to China at the San Francisco International Airport when they were apprehended by FBI agents. Opening their luggage, agents were shocked by the scope of what they saw: thousands of pages of trade secrets and at least $10,000 in equipment stolen from four Silicon Valley companies – Transmeta Corp., Sun Microsystems, NEC Electronics Corp., and Trident Microsystems Inc. The suitcases also included microchip blueprints, design scripts, and other closely guarded tech secrets.

More documents, seized during a search of the two men's homes, revealed an extensive plot to smuggle US trade secrets to China with the purpose of starting a microprocessor company. The company was backed by the municipal government of the Chinese city of Hangzhou, as well as by the provincial government of Zhejiang province, long considered to be China's capitalist heartland. The microprocessors were to be manufactured and marketed by Supervision Inc., a company the pair had founded, and Supervision was to share profits from the sale of the pirated chips with its governmental backers.

Further implicating the Chinese government, a corporate charter found by US federal agents at Ye's home said the enterprise would "raise China's ability to develop super-integrated circuit design and form a powerful capability to compete with worldwide leaders' core development technology and products in the field of integrated circuit design". Supervision, also known as Hangzhou Zhongtian Microsystems Company Ltd, had applied for funding for their company from the National High Technology Research and Development Programme of China. But the pair, who had attempted to recruit others, including engineers, to their scheme, were arrested before it was approved. One of the people they tried to recruit tipped off the authorities. The resulting investigation was the first in a string of US probes headed by the **Computer Hacking and Intellectual Property** (CHIP) Unit of the United States Attorney's Office into counterintelligence efforts involving Chinese economic espionage.

A federal grand jury indicted Ye, a US citizen, and Zhong, a permanent US resident, and they were each charged with ten counts that included conspiracy, economic espionage, possession of stolen trade secrets, and foreign transportation of stolen property. To win a conviction, the US government had to prove that the men stole trade secrets with the intent of benefiting China. But as the January 2007 trial date approached – five years after their arrests – Ye and Zhong each pleaded guilty to the rare charge of economic espionage to benefit a foreign nation.

It was the first conviction of its kind. "These guilty pleas represent the first convictions in the country under this section of the Economic Espionage Act of 1996, a law that was enacted by Congress against a backdrop of increasing threats to corporate security and a rising tide of international and domestic economic espionage", US Attorney Kevin V. Ryan said in a news release. "Today's landmark convictions represent a significant victory in the fight to protect our Nation's critical intellectual property."

Ye and Zhong – who remained free on a combined $700,000 bail and lived with their respective families in the San Francisco Bay area during the five-year wait for their trial – each faced the possibility of a maximum thirty-year sentence and $1.5 million fines. Prosecutors, however, granted leniency because they cooperated with investigators and they were sentenced to a year each in prison.

Much of the case record, except for small portions of the plea and settlement agreement, remains under court-ordered seal, including the sentencing. Whether the Chinese government officials Ye and Zhong were working with knew that the trade secrets were stolen from US companies is information that has not been released. Prosecutors never accused the Chinese government of any wrongdoing.

In December 2006, after the plea agreement, US Attorney **Kevin Ryan** noted: "We know our [US] technology is sought all over the world. There are a lot of individuals who want to get it, and there's a lot of money being thrown at them to get it."

For further investigation

Ⓦ sanfrancisco.fbi.gov/dojpressrel/2006/sf121406a.htm The Department of Justice's press release about the investigation and arrests of Fei Ye and Ming Zhong.

Ⓦ usdoj.gov/criminal/cybercrime/yeIndict.htm The US government's case against Fei Ye and Ming Zhong is laid out on this site.

Ⓦ usatoday.com/tech/news/computersecurity/2004-12-18 -corp-spy_x.htm *USA Today*'s story about the sentencing of the pair.

SCANDAL AT SIEMENS

The investigation into corporate corruption began innocently enough, with an internal audit that German manufacturing giant Siemens began voluntarily. Nobody could have guessed that the audit would uncover more than a billion euros in suspicious payments to an outside company. Nor would anyone have believed that two former Siemens officials would subsequently be convicted in German state court at Darmstadt of bribing two managers at Enel, Italy's largest utilities company. The public backlash began as confidence waned – the high-profile case was a classic example of poor stewardship over publicly traded funds, not to mention one of bribing public officials.

Siemens' employees Andreas Kley, a former finance chief, and Horst Vigener, a former employee-consultant, admitted to providing up to $7.9 million dollars between 1999 and 2002 to secure gas turbine contracts for Siemens. Kley and Vigener also claimed they acted independently of Siemens and that it was the Italian managers at Enel who initiated the bribery scheme. Still, the court ordered Siemens to forfeit $51.5 million in profits from deals with Enel.

ROBERT PHILLIP HANSSEN

"Sad day for all of us, Bob." These were the words the arresting agent, who had been one of his co-workers, apologetically said to Robert Hanssen as he took him into custody. It was indeed a sad day: it hadn't been easy finding the person behind what has been referred to as one of the worst breaches in US intelligence history. So the FBI assigned **Eric O'Neill** to go undercover to catch the perpetrator in the act, under the guise of working as Hanssen's assistant. Hanssen, a senior FBI special agent who had been using the code name Ramon Garcia for more than two decades, was the mole they were looking for: he had spied against his country for the Soviet Union and Russia for 22 years. In the course of his espionage, Hanssen, as a double agent, had betrayed at least fifty sources.

The full extent of the damage done to US federal cases – just how wide the breach of intelligence leaked to the Soviets and Russians was – has never completely been made public. But the paperwork that the FBI released was voluminous and shocking. The case, the FBI wrote in a news release at the time, involved the "most traitorous actions imaginable against a country governed by the Rule of Law".

Hanssen – a devout member of the conservative **Opus Dei** Catholic organization – was a trusted government agent. Some speculated that Hanssen may have considered himself a patriot – or even that he'd wanted to prove how lax American security was. As with other potential special agents, Robert Hanssen had to pass an extensive background check when he became an agent in 1976 to qualify for top-secret security clearance. Once deemed to be clean, he was put through an intensive, seventeen-week training programme at the FBI Academy in Quantico, Virginia, that tested both body and mind. At the end of the programme, Hanssen was put out in the field, with limited occasional background checks and random drug tests required to maintain his eligibility for top-secret security clearance. No red flags ever turned up. Nothing ever remotely suggested that Hanssen's espionage activities would one day be classified as the worst in the FBI's existence. In 1979, three years after joining the FBI, he was transferred to the FBI's counterintelligence unit, where his job was to compile a database of Soviet intelligence. It was then that Hanssen began his clandestine career as a spy for the Soviets.

As the years went by, the seemingly loyal Hanssen was passed over for promotion, never making it past the rank of senior special agent in charge, despite his number of years served. He began feeling more and more underappreciated, which, according to David Vise – author of *The Bureau and the Mole* – may have been his motivation for betraying not only the agency he worked for, but his country as well. Hanssen, wrote Vise, felt like an outsider. He also, according to his profile, felt he was smarter than everyone else and that his talents weren't being utilized.

As part of his job, Hanssen was assigned to different national security posts that provided him with access to classified information relating to the former Soviet Union. From those assignments within the bureau, Hanssen gained access to some of the most sensitive and highly classified information within the US government. Perhaps out of frustration, in October 1985, while stationed at the FBI field office in New York City, Hanssen sent an anonymous letter to the KGB asking for $100,000 in cash in exchange for his espionage services and the handing over of intelligence gathered through radar, underwater hydrophones, spy satellites, and signal intercepts, which he continued until his 1991 arrest.

All appeared normal from the outside. Hanssen was a patriotic family man, attending church with his wife and six children. But inside was a completely different picture. Besides selling classified information, Hanssen's personal life was a little strange, to say the least. He installed hidden cameras in his bedroom and recorded intimate moments with his wife, who was unaware their sex life was being recorded. This was not for his own gratification. "Hanssen", wrote Vise, "put a secret camera in the bedroom in his home so that his best friend Jack could sit in the den and watch on the big TV screen while Robert Hanssen had sex with his wife Bonnie."

Once the FBI gradually came to the conclusion that one of its own agents was a mole for the KGB, it launched an inside probe. Still unaware that Hanssen was the culprit and trusting him as a fellow agent with an unblemished record, they put him in charge of the investigation. Ferreting out the traitor was particularly difficult, because Hanssen made a point of never having face-to-face contacts with his Russian handlers, and he never revealed to them his true identity or where he worked. He never took any foreign travel to meet with the Russians. And his lifestyle never changed, despite the fact that he received large sums of unexplained cash.

Eventually Hanssen began to arouse the FBI's suspicions. They placed Eric O'Neill, an undercover operative, in as Hanssen's aide. Hanssen's big mistake was in leaving telltale fingerprints on the plastic rubbish bags in which he wrapped government documents. In September 2000, a former KGB agent sold their mole's file to an undercover US agent. The FBI lab then could match the bags used by Hanssen, with his prints all over them, to the file. Even more damaging to Hanssen, however, was a voice recording of the spy with the code name Ramon Garcia. Agents were not expecting to hear the voice of a fellow agent. Hanssen's fate was sealed.

For his part, Hanssen had been getting increasingly nervous; his car radio was making crackling sounds and he suspected it was bugged. He was right, and his phone was bugged too. Still, his suspicions didn't dissuade him from continuing his extracurricular espionage activities. Then, on Sunday 18 February 2001, five weeks before his mandatory retirement from the FBI at age fifty-seven, Hanssen was arrested by a team of surveillance agents who'd followed him to Foxstone Park near Vienna, Virginia. Under a footbridge over Wolftrap Creek, Hanssen had stashed documents, wrapped in a heavy-duty rubbish bag. He walked to a nearby utility pole and tacked a small piece of cloth to the pole, signalling he'd made a drop. That's when agents surrounded him and took him into custody. Two days later, at a news conference, FBI director Louis J. Freeh told reporters: "Regrettably, I stand here today both saddened and outraged. An FBI agent ... has been charged today with violating [his] oath in the most egregious and reprehensible manner imaginable."

"The FBI", Freeh continued, "entrusted him with some of the most sensitive secrets of the United States government and instead of being humbled by this honour, Hanssen has allegedly abused and betrayed that trust. The crimes alleged are an affront not only to his fellow FBI employees but to the American people, not to mention the pain and suffering he has brought upon his family."

In the instances the feds were able to track, Hanssen on twenty occasions clandestinely left packages for the KGB, and the SVR, its successor agency, at drop sites in the Washington area. He also provided more than two dozen computer disks holding additional information. In those drops, Hanssen gave the KGB and SVR roughly six thousand pages of security-sensitive documentary material.

It has taken computer forensic analysis, substantial covert surveillance, court authorized searches and other sensitive techniques to piece together the story. In exchange for diamonds and cash worth more than $600,000 in total, Hanssen gave away highly classified US national security and counterintelligence information and secrets. He was charged with espionage and conspiracy to commit espionage, violations carrying a possible punishment of life, and, under certain circumstances, the death penalty.

Following his arrest, FBI agents searched Hanssen's residence, cars, and workspace for more evidence. On 6 July 2001, six months after his arrest, Robert Phillip Hanssen pleaded guilty, admitting to fifteen instances of espionage and conspiracy – in exchange

for federal prosecutors agreeing not to seek the death penalty. Hanssen, then 58, was sentenced on 10 May 2002 to life in prison without the possibility of parole. Afterwards, Hanssen said "Can you imagine sitting in a room with a bunch of your colleagues and everybody in the room trying to figure out the identity of a mole, and all along it's you?"

Hanssen is currently serving his prison sentence at the US Penitentiary Administrative Maximum Facility, or ADX, on 37 acres in Florence, Colorado, in the foothills of the Rocky Mountains next to the Arkansas River. The 490-bed facility houses inmates deemed the most dangerous and in need of the tightest control. Twenty-three hours a day, Hanssen is in solitary confinement at the prison, which has been called the "Alcatraz of the Rockies". He is given three meals a day through food ports and is under constant surveillance by CCTV cameras. He is allowed letters to and from his family and periodic non-contact visits – through tempered glass – from his wife, six children, and his many grandchildren.

For further investigation

David Wise Spy: The Inside Story of How the FBI's Robert Hanssen Betrayed America (2003) The spy author penetrates the case and dissects how Robert Hanssen was able to pull off selling secrets to the KGB for more than two decades.

fbi.gov/pressrel/pressrel01/affidavit.pdf The complete hundred-page affidavit, which goes into great detail about Robert Hanssen's clandestine espionage activities against the US government.

DECEPTION:
ART OF THE CON

Deception: art of the con

Scams, frauds, swindles, bunkos, grifts, and flimflams – all are names for the street tricks of the con artist, and the list is long. What these cons have in common is that they're perpetrated by sleights-of-hand – both literal and metaphorical – on small or grand scales.

The names of the games may vary, but the lure is always the same: easy money. Some frauds are relatively innocuous, such as losing a fiver on a shell game – the classic "guess which thimble the pea is under" street-corner scam. Others can bleed savings and ruin lives. Despite the warnings, skilled con artists are able to dupe people who are trusting into falling for cons as old as the hills.

Some tried-and-tested frauds from the past, however, can no longer be pulled off. Such is the case with cheque fraud. Because of today's electronic banking, with bank tellers requiring identification cards or a signature match before cashing cheques, yesterday's fraudsters have had to let old modus operandi go by the wayside. But where one fraud disappears, another replaces it: technology may have made in-person fraud harder to pull off, but the Internet has given the con artist a whole new playground.

Criminals go to great lengths to pull off swindles, and their methods become more sophisticated with time. Such was the case with the creative con jobs pulled off by **Frank Abagnale**, a teenager who impersonated everybody from FBI agents to airline pilots and was a master cheque forger. Frank served time in prison, but wound up on the FBI's payroll, helping agents catch criminals like him. Though, in truth, there were no criminals quite like him, and his extraordinary story was eventually turned into a movie, starring Leonardo DiCaprio and directed by Steven Spielberg.

But however ingenious, imaginative or sophisticated the scam, all are at base games of confidence, where the swindler wins the trust of his victims and then cheats them.

The many types of con

A HARD DAY'S GRIFT: LINGO OF THE CON

Confidence tricks of petty swindling are almost as old as humankind, and the con artist is often known as a 'grifter'. The scams are in turn often referred to as games – this has far more to do with the element of challenge facing the swindler than any pleasure they take in the con. While no common socioeconomic denominator defines the grifter, a shared behavioural trait appears to be the con man's natural ability to manipulate and lie to people – and be believed. To be a successful grifter, you need to be confident and inspire confidence: this is where the word "con" derives from.

Swindles, hustles, scams, or grifts also depend upon the greed of the **mark** – the victim – to lure

THE WIRE, THE PAY-OFF AND THE RAG

The wire con involves an inside man convincing the mark he can delay the horse-racing results going to the bookmakers long enough for the mark to place a bet after the race has run. The pay-off allows the mark to win money as part of a fraudulent racing syndicate, encouraging him to contribute increasing amounts to it until eventually the grifters pull the plug, making off with the cash. Usually this was effected by the syndicate "losing" a really big bet (which was never, of course, placed) financed by the mark.

The rag is a highly elaborate con, but is based around the setup of a fake stock exchange. It flourished in the US back in the 1920s, when investing in companies was a lot more like today's gambling on sports events, conducted in high-street premises. The con had a big cast – the staff and clientele of the show stock exchange, for one thing – but also required a "roper" and a "spieler". This pair of grifters would insinuate themselves with the mark, playing the roles of good-natured companion and investment expert: the former would encourage the faux-reluctant latter to share his knowledge and insider tips on the mark's behalf. Once in their clutches, and through the door of the fake stock exchange, the mark is confronted by a series of increasingly elaborate and confusing machinations: all are geared towards making the sucker believe he has not risked a penny of his own money, and is not liable for anything. He could not, of course, be more wrong...

money and valuables from them. (There's a lot of truth to the maxim "You can't cheat an honest man".) Back when the carnies (carnivals) toured the US – filled with rigged games and the like – the resident grifters would surreptitiously place a chalk mark on the back or shoulders of an intended victim known to be carrying a wad of cash, and the term has stuck to this day.

The Conjurer, attributed to Hieronymus Bosch, shows a "thimblerig" game: a guess which cup the pea is under con.

The **short** – or street – con is an opportunistic scam to take the mark for all the money on his person at the time. They usually happen quickly, in public places and for relatively small amounts of cash. One of the most common forms of the short con is the **pigeon drop**. This usually requires two grifters working together. The first, who is called "the catch", approaches the pigeon (another name for the mark) with a bag or other package containing a large amount of cash. The catch claims to have found it and enlists the mark's help in deciding what to do with it. Upon inspection of the cash, there is usually some kind of indication that it's the product of illegal activity and it is made to appear unlikely that it will ever be claimed. At that juncture in the pigeon drop, the second grifter – **the shill** – pretends to have overheard the conversation. The shill offers his assistance. He usually claims to know someone, often a lawyer, who will advise them what to do with the money. A phone call is made, and the mark is told they can split the money three ways,

BYTE 'N' SWITCH: PCS, EMAILS AND BIG BUSINESS

In a highly publicized accusation of bait and switch against a company, plaintiffs accused Dell computers of luring them in to buy an inexpensive computer, then selling them a higher-priced one. According to the suit, the allegation was that Dell was advertising low prices for its computers, but people who tried to purchase a machine for the advertised ticket price found that it was no longer available.

The suit, filed in San Francisco County Superior Court in February 2005, sought class-action status in California and accused Dell of bait-and-switch practices, false advertising, fraud, and deceit in sales and advertising, and breach of contract.

Then, in May 2007, New York attorney general Andrew Cuomo filed a civil suit against Dell after the state attorney general's office received seven hundred complaints. The suit alleged that Dell was offering no-interest financing, then switching to a higher rate when customers made a purchase. The former suit was dismissed, but a New York State Supreme Court ruled in favour of Cuomo's suit in May 2008.

Email subscribers have also been the targets of bait-and-switch scammers. A federal judge in Nevada in April 2002 granted a temporary restraining order to the Federal Trade Commission against BTV Industries, in an alleged email swindle.

In a mass email, BTV told recipients they had won free Sony PlayStation 2s and other prizes, purportedly sponsored by Yahoo! Instead, the email routed potential customers to an adult pornography site through their modem connection, that charged $3.99 a minute.

The alleged bait-and-switch email scheme landed in court because of an international task force – dubbed Netforce – comprising agents and officers with the FTC, eight US state law enforcers and four Canadian agencies. An FTC news release described Netforce as an "initiative targeting deceptive spam and Internet fraud". The FTC argued that the defendants' practices were deceptive and designed to mislead consumers; it asked that the defendants be barred from continuing the alleged scam. In the end, the FTC won, with a restraining order.

but they cannot spend it for a certain period while the lawyer attempts to find the rightful owner. The pigeon is asked to contribute some money towards paying the costs as a show of good faith. The grifters pretend to add the same amount of cash to the pot. The pigeon is then, as they say in the business, "dropped". The crooks walk away with the victim's cash. An alternative variant on the process involves the contributed money of all three being entrusted to the pigeon, who invariably decides to make off with the money. What the pigeon doesn't know is that there's been a bag-swap: the catch and shill have switched the bag of money for a bag stuffed with newspaper (or the like). Thus the pigeon ends up running away from his own cash.

The **long con**, big con or pay-off con is so named because it takes longer to commit the crimes: the scams target one person for an extended time. It's geared to steal a substantial amount of the mark's net worth. Long-con artists employ techniques similar to those used by salespeople – good listening skills, never appearing to ask personal questions, and agreeing with the intended victim's opinions. One classic, ancient long con was known as the **Spanish Prisoner**. It's a con thought to have originated in the UK during the sixteenth century, and involves a grifter convincing a mark that he is a retainer of a wealthy lord or member of a royal family held prisoner abroad. There is the promise of great riches – or perhaps marriage to his beautiful daughter – if the mark can stump up the funds to secure the lord's release. Depending on its success, and how far the mark's gullibility could be pushed, this long con could be milked for further and further demands on the mark's wallet. To give the mark the brushoff – and terrify him into silence at the same time – a convenient murder could be staged, in which a "Spanish spy" would kill the grifter in front of the mark's eyes.

For further investigation

Ⓦ loststudies.com/1.2/art_of_grift The Art of the Grift offers classic cases of how cons are successfully executed.

Ⓦ moneycentral.msn.com/content/p41488 An article on MSN.com about corporate-style grifters and their scams.

Ⓦ bbc.co.uk/drama/hustle/con_jargon Definitions by BBC.com of scam jargon used in the 1961 American film *The Hustler* about a pool game con man. The scam is in baiting, taunting, and deceiving potential opponents and side betters.

A SEMI-LEGAL CON: THE BAIT & SWITCH

Bait and switch, a form of fraud, is a deceptive sales tactic perpetrated by unethical salespeople merchants to attract customers by advertising exceptionally low-priced items. That's the **bait**. Then, when unwary customers arrive to buy the items, they're encouraged instead to purchase higher-priced merchandise, because they're told the store has sold out of the product, or the salespeople will convince them the pricier version is a better deal. That's called the **switch**. Customers often fall for the ploy. This practice, referred to as "switch selling" in Britain, is illegal in many US states under consumer protection laws. The US Federal Trade Commission regularly prosecutes merchants who engage in it.

The bait-and-switch scam is one of the oldest in the book; the term was first used back in the 1920s. It has long been a favourite tactic among unscrupulous car salesmen, estate agents, and electrical goods sellers but it is nothing if not adaptable, and a great deal of air travel advertising sails very close to being a bait-and-switch ploy. Lawmakers too have been accused over the years of using the trick in politics. Bills that propose minor changes in law with anodyne-sounding titles ("the bait") are introduced to the legislature with the objective of later substantially changing the wording ("the switch") to try to smoothly – and slyly – pass a controversial major amendment. Rule changes are also proposed (the bait) to meet legal requirements for public notice and mandated public hearings, then different rules are proposed at the final meeting (the switch), thereby bypassing the usually required public notice and subsequent public discussion on the actual measure voted upon. While legal, the political objective is to get rules passed without subjecting them to possible negative review from the community – which flies in the face of elected officials representing their constituents' wishes for the good of the community.

CLASSIC MOVIES, CLASSIC CONS

History has shown that filmgoers love a good con game. Many classic movies have made famous the capers played out on the city streets.

Paper Moon is one such con flick. The setting is in the Midwestern United States during the Great Depression, around 1936. The story, adapted from the novel *Addie Pray* by Joe David Brown, revolves around the growing affection between Moses, a small-time short-con artist, and Addie Loggins, a precocious nine-year-old girl who may or may not be Moses's illegitimate daughter. It stars Ryan O'Neal and his real-life daughter Tatum.

Passing himself off as a travelling salesman working for the "Kansas Bible Company", in one scam Moses delivers unordered Bibles in rural areas to bereaved widows, whose names he lifts from newspaper obituaries. He knocks on their doors and tells unsuspecting wives that their husbands ordered Bibles as gifts for them, but hadn't finished paying for them. He feigns surprise when they tell him their husbands have died. Addie jumps in during the transactions and sets the price of the balance due, making it higher than even Moses would dare charge – the nicer the home, the higher the price of the Bible. In another scam, when Addie and Moses stop in a small town, Addie berates a cashier in a department store, insisting when he gives her change that she gave him a $20 bill when it was actually a five. She wins, and walks out of the store with a profit.

Paper Moon was based on the film *Little Miss Marker*, released in 1934. It told the tale of Marky, played by Shirley Temple, and her gambler father. He gives his daughter to a gangster-run gambling operation as a marker, or collateral, for a bet he places. When her father loses his bet and commits suicide, the gangsters are left with the girl. They decide to use her to help pull off one of their fixed races, naming her the owner of the horse in the race. Like Addie, Marky begins using gambling terminology and slang, looking and sounding like a small con artist. These are Hollywood movies, of course, and are big on sentiment, with a suitably chastening moral ending to the tale. Addie's gangster associates become fond of her as well and fill the roles of her extended family. At the end of *Paper Moon*, Addie and Moses learn a lesson after Moses is

Robert Redford runs through the classic street-corner hustles in *The Sting*.

scammed at his own game when a con backfires and he's beaten and robbed of his money.

Faster and looser is *Dirty Rotten Scoundrels*, a 1988 caper film adapted from the comedy *Bedtime Story*, released in 1964 and starring David Niven and Marlon Brando. It concerns two con men who meet on a train and then attempt to work together. One, British con Lawrence Jameson, is suave and sophisticated; the other, Freddy Benson, is a small-time crook. They make a wager: the first one who is able to bilk $50,000 from a young heiress named Christine Colgate is the winner, and the loser has to leave town. Thus begins a series of double-crosses, schemes, and masquerades that spiral out of control on the French Riviera.

The film makes a strong statement by implying that, because the would-be victim's money was ill-gotten, she deserves to be cheated. Of course, it wouldn't be a caper if it didn't get more complicated than that, with a few unexpected twists…

Another classic caper film features a successful elaborate fraud committed as an act of revenge. Set in 1930s Chicago, 1973's *The Sting* (which won seven Academy Awards) concerns a pair of crooked operators, played by Paul Newman and Robert Redford, who plan a complicated sting operation against a powerful crime lord who murdered their friend. They team up to cheat a fortune from (fictional) Chicago mob boss Doyle Lonnegan and his gang of murdering thugs. The movie holds its cards close to its chest – the pieces of the puzzle only fall together on the morning the high-stakes sting is to take place. The story was inspired by real-life con games perpetrated by brothers Fred and Charley Gondorf, who pull off three long cons – the wire, the rag, and the pay-off.

The title of the film refers to the moment when the play, or con, is complete and the grifter successfully takes the mark's money; sting operations have been regularly used by law enforcement (notably the FBI), to catch criminals in the act.

For further investigation

David Maurer *The Big Con: The Story of the Confidence Man* (1999) Originally published in the 1940s, *The Big Con* is a compilation of anecdotes pulled off by the Gondorf brothers. Shady characters in the book are named Devil's Island Eddie, Limehouse Chappie, the Honey Grove Kid, and the Hashhouse Kid.

Ⓦ movies.msn.com/movies/article.aspx?news=256593 A roundup analysis of con-game movies.

Con artists and fraudsters

FRANK WILLIAM ABAGNALE JR

For five years during the 1960s, Frank Abagnale lived under at least eight different identities and passed bad cheques worth more than $2.5 million in fifty states and twenty-six countries – and all before he reached the age of twenty one. His life of crime and multiple false identities began just after his parents divorced, when a judge asked Frank to choose between living with his mother or father. Instead of living with one or the other, he ran away. Because he was only sixteen, he had difficulty finding work. Nevertheless, the industrious, intelligent, and confident teenager began passing himself off as being older. His hair had turned prematurely grey and he was tall for his age; he also started forging ID cards, giving himself the documentation he needed.

Frank Abagnale's remarkable ability – and probably his greatest talent – was to create and make use of false identities. He was a master at forging personalized cheques with his name(s) printed on them. It enabled him to get away with con after con and simultaneously elude capture; by the time federal agents were on to him, he had already changed his identity and moved on to another scheme. He was one of the most creative con men, forgers, imposters, and escape artists in history – all the more extraordinary, given his youth.

One famous trick Abagnale used was to print his bank account number on blank deposit slips and then add them to the stack of real blank slips inside the bank. Deposits written on those slips by bank customers would then end up going into Abagnale's account instead of the customers'. He collected more than $40,000 using the method before he was discovered. By the time the bank began looking into his case, Abagnale had collected all the money and had changed his identity to a new one.

However, his most famous stunt was masquerading as a Pan Am pilot – Frank Williams – for two years. He didn't actually fly any planes, but was able to use the perk of the job: free airfares around the world.

Leonardo Di Caprio played Frank Abagnale in the 2002 Steven Spielberg movie *Catch Me If You Can*. Abagnale got away with impersonating a pilot, travelling the world and living off forged cheques.

He "deadheaded" – taking the courtesy flights to the destination that a pilot's next flight is departing from. Everything from food, airline tickets, and lodgings was billed to Pan Am. To pull it off, all he needed was an ID card and a uniform. For the ID, he made a counterfeit card (using stickers from a toy plane for the logo). For the uniform, he contacted Pan Am headquarters and made up a story about how dry-cleaners had lost his suit, and that he needed one to fly. He forged a degree from Embry-Riddle Aeronautical University. The media dubbed him "Skyway Man" and the "James Bond of the Sky".

His pilot's licence wasn't the only qualification he faked. He also counterfeited a Harvard law diploma, impersonated a paediatrician and faked his way into a temporary position as resident supervisor at a Georgia hospital. Abagnale, a high school dropout, once taught college-level sociology for one semester at Brigham Young University, using his false Columbia University degree, and even masqueraded as an FBI agent. He conned his way into a role at a state attorney general's office, but legitimately passed the Bar exam, by studying.

In 1969 he was eventually caught after an Air France flight attendant recognized him from a "Wanted" poster in France. When the French police apprehended him, all 26 of the countries in which he'd committed fraud wanted him to be extradited. Abagnale initially served a one-year prison sentence that was reduced to six months at Perpignan's House of Arrest in France. During his stay there, he nearly died from malnutrition and pneumonia. It left him fearful of spending more time behind bars, and determined to escape. He was transferred from Perpignan to a low-security prison in Sweden while he waited extradition to the United States. Frank was escorted onto a plane bound for New York, where officers on the ground were waiting to take him into custody. Ten minutes before it was to land, Frank went to the plane's restroom. He knew the underbelly of the plane. He removed the toilet and made his way under the plane, hanging onto the underbelly. He jumped from the plane just as it approached the ground. Then, in the darkness of the night, he ran from the landing strip.

Once in New York, Frank made his way to an old acquaintance's house where he kept a stash of clothes and money. He stayed there only briefly before he left for Montreal, where a safe deposit box with thousands of dollars awaited him. Frank intended to use the money to buy a non stop ticket to Brazil, a place where the extradition of criminals was not practised. Abagnale made his way to Canada, where he had sent money to a friend for safekeeping. While

If you're going to try to cash a forged cheque, why not go for broke? That is what 21-year-old Charles Ray Fuller did in May 2008 when he matter-of-factly presented a check for $360 billion to a bank teller in Fort Worth, Texas, expecting it to be cashed. Fuller told the teller the cheque was given to him by his girlfriend's mother so he could start a record company. The teller notified authorities, and Fuller was arrested on the spot. He was charged with forgery and illegally possessing a weapon (in his pocket was a .25-calibre handgun and cartridge, along with less than two ounces of marijuana).

awaiting a flight to Brazil, Frank was recognized and arrested by Canadian police. He was released into the custody of the FBI, who made sure that this time Frank was securely delivered to a federal detention centre. Several months later, he was transferred to a prison in Georgia to await trial. Once again, Frank attempted another bold escape. This time, he enlisted the help of an ex-girlfriend, who, posing as a journalist, did a mock interview with an inspector at the US Bureau of Prisons in Washington, DC. The inspector gave her his business card, which she passed on to Abagnale, who persuaded prison guards that he was actually an undercover agent. He showed them the card and told them that he was a prison inspector, working undercover. The particular federal detention centre he was imprisoned in was vulnerable on this count, as it had already had two bad experiences with undercover prison inspections. The guards fell for it and released him from prison. Frank went to Washington (via New York), where he was arrested by two police detectives, who were in an unmarked car.

Over his criminal career, Abagnale managed to forge and cash cheques totalling $2.5 million. In 1974, after serving less than five years of his sentence, the United States federal government released him on the condition that he work without pay helping federal authorities against fraud and scam artists. After he fulfilled his end of the bargain, he tried various small jobs that did not work out. He then approached a bank, offering to talk to their staff about tricks of the fraud trade. Slowly, he began to piece together a legitimate life as a security consultant.

Today, Frank Abagnale advises businesses on fraud and lectures as a motivational speaker. On his personal website, Abagnale describes himself as "one of the world's most respected authorities on the subjects of forgery, embezzlement and secure documents". He is called upon professionally to help companies with security issues, and the FBI also continues to use him as a lecturer to the law-enforcement elite at its academy in Quantico, Virginia.

For further investigation

📖 **Catch Me If You Can (1980; 2001)** Frank W. Abagnale The true story of Abagnale and his cons.

🎞 **Catch Me If You Can (2002)** Steven Spielberg The serendipitous saga of Frank Abagnale's international life of crime was the source of inspiration for this feature film, based on the autobiography of the same name.

Ⓦ **abagnale.com/index2.asp** Frank Abagnale's personal website.

Ⓦ **abc.net.au/rn/talks/lm/stories/s111098.htm** A lengthy Q&A by Norman Swan, with ABC radio in Australia, talks to Frank Abagnale about his life as a fraudster and imposter.

THE WRITE STUFF... AND THE WRONG STUFF

Mention forgery and we tend to think of artworks and cheques. But there's long been a chequered history of chancers attempting to make a mint from forged letters, forged documents and forged books.

The autobiography of Howard Hughes

One of the most ambitious literary forgeries ever attempted made the headlines during the 1970s when the critically acclaimed author Clifford

Clifford Irving and his wife, Edith, leave the hotel where they were staying during their 1972 fraud trial.

Irving, desperate for a bestseller, manufactured an autobiography he said was written by Howard Hughes. By this time Hughes – an aviator, philanthropist, and one of the wealthiest people in the world – had become a recluse, and Irving was banking on Hughes' unwillingness to appear in public.

Irving forged letters and a signature in Hughes' handwriting in order to secure a hefty publishing advance, which was deposited in a Swiss bank account. He was eventually caught when Hughes' lawyers exposed the fraud, and served a seventeen-month jail sentence. Ironically, several of the books Irving wrote following his later release did indeed become

bestsellers, and a retitled version of the book – *Howard Hughes: My Story* – was published as a novel.

The Bixby letter

Perhaps the longest running debate about an artefact's authenticity is that over the infamous Bixby letter. The letter has been routinely cited as a remarkable piece of prose writing; a valuable historical artefact that demonstrates President Abraham Lincoln's eloquence and humanity. It crops up as a staple part of the history syllabus for American schoolchildren, was an inspiration for the Steven Spielberg film *Saving Private Ryan* and has been put on show in museums across the US for decades. Countless handwriting experts, scholars, and historians have pored over it. No concrete evidence has been found to prove either way whether it was written by Lincoln or whether it's simply the work of a forger.

The letter, purportedly written by Lincoln in the autumn of 1864, was addressed to Lydia Bixby, a Bostonian widow and mother of five sons. It was believed that all of Mrs Bixby's sons were killed in action for the Union cause during the American Civil War. Upon her son's deaths, the grieving widow received a letter of condolence from Lincoln, in which he attempted to console her for her tragic loss. The letter has been treated with much scepticism because of several major historical inaccuracies, most of which relate to the actual fate of Mrs Bixby's sons. There is evidence that two, not five, of Mrs Bixby's sons died in battle during the war. According to a brief article on Abraham Lincoln Online, one of the boys "deserted the army, one was honourably discharged and another deserted or died a prisoner of war".

Other details concerning Mrs Bixby herself led many to doubt the letter. An article in *U.S. News and World Report* stated that she was not only a liar, but also a Confederate sympathizer, the madam of a brothel, and had political views in direct opposition to Lincoln's. If true, it would make it less likely that Lincoln would have risked his reputation and political position by writing the letter.

Furthermore, there are two letters written in 1909 between Abraham Lincoln's son Robert T. Lincoln and Dr James Canfield, a librarian at Columbia University, that cast doubt on the letter's provenance. In the first, Robert T. Lincoln inquired about the Bixby letter, which he'd seen exhibited at New York's Huber Museum and inquired whether the letter was an original "or a very clever forgery". Dr Canfield responded to Robert T. Lincoln that, after receiving his letter, he retrieved the Bixby document from the Huber Museum and examined it. After careful analysis, Canfield discovered the letter was a lithograph (or a copy). It was suggested that it had been made from the original document, which was believed to have been at the Huber Museum in 1909.

Some historians believe that John Hay, Lincoln's secretary, may have authored the famous letter to Mrs Bixby. According to the *U.S. News and World Report* article, Professor **Michael Burlingame**, a Lincoln biographer who has studied the Bixby letter, is a strong proponent of this theory. He stated that, when analyzing the document, he found syntactical similarities between letters written by Hay and the Bixby letter.

However, he could not find any similarities between Lincoln's grammatical style and the letter of condolence. Moreover, the author of the book *Great Forgeries and Famous Fakes,* Charles Hamilton, further supported this theory by asserting that Hay actually claimed to have written the document.

There have been many documents circulated that have been passed off as original texts by Lincoln, which have been found to be forgeries. Still, there are those who refute the premise that Hay was the one who wrote the letter to Mrs Bixby. In one article Lauristan Bullard asserted that no one, as far as he was concerned, "has offered any letter or document written by Hay in what looked like Lincoln's script".

For further investigation

Ⓦ sciencedaily.com/releases/2007/07/070718001516 A July 2007 article in *Science Daily* about the Midwest Forensics Resource Center at Iowa State University and its library of ink

FORGERY FORENSICS

Determining the authenticity of an object involves questioning where the object came from, who owned it, what its purpose was, and where it has been. The physical characteristics are pinpointed – which often reveals anachronisms in the composition, as well as subjective information like content and style. Today's forensic technologies allow us to determine an object's age with an unprecedented degree of accuracy.

In the past, authentification has been subjective rather than scientific. Experts often relied on intuition and minute physical examination to identify discrepancies, such as unnatural *craquelure* – the fine pattern of cracks – in oil paintings, the absence of staining, or signs of wear in bound documents. One American art expert, Bernard Berenson, was famous in the early 1900s for smelling and licking paintings, a technique that worked because the paint on some masters' works was often barely dry. Even though his techniques were unorthodox, Berenson was widely regarded as the pre-eminent authority on the authenticity of Renaissance art.

In the last fifty years, however, the detection of frauds and forgeries has moved from the library to the laboratory. Laboratory analysis of pigments and inks, and chemical analysis of paper and canvas, can provide an indication of the age of an item, be it painting or document. Paper made from different material – such as grass, timber fibre, linen, and materials treated or coated with chemicals or whiteners – can point to different eras, when chemicals are detected using analyses.

In 2006, scholars at the International Foundation for Art Research, together with Dartmouth College, developed a software technique, using a high-resolution digital scan, that was capable of analysing drawings by Pieter Bruegel and successfully distinguishing between real and fake pieces by the master.

On the financial side of fake documents, the Xerox Corporation has jumped into the fray by developing technology with its Anti-Counterfeit Detection devices. The devices are used to prevent the unauthorized reproduction, transmission, and display of paper currency (money) and documents, such as stock warrants, certificates, and bonds.

profiles to help forensic scientists identify fraudulent documents.

ⓦ lincolnherald.com/1989article%20Bixby A site that includes all things Lincoln also provides details of the authentification of the Bixby letter. It includes a 1989 article written by Joe Nickell, which is a study of the authenticity of the widely disputed letter.

THE PORTUGUESE BANKNOTE CRISIS

Not many fraudsters make enough cash to attempt a buyout of their national bank. **Artur Virgilio Alves Reis** was nothing if not bold, producing so many fake notes that one per cent of Portugal's entire GDP was estimated to have come through his elaborate scam – one which arguably helped precipitate a coup that ushered in half a century of right-wing dictatorship.

Born in 1898 to a struggling undertaker father, Reis failed to finish his degree, married a rich woman and emigrated to the Portuguese colony of Angola in 1916 in an attempt to improve his fortunes. His lack of qualifications proved no barrier. With a chutzpah that was to define him, the young man copied a Portuguese university diploma, had it notarized and decorated with fake seals and ended up with a qualification from Oxford University's "Polytechnic School of Engineering". By all accounts, Reis's work in Angola – helping in the repair and construction of railways and sewers – was of a high standard. But his financially acquisitive sights were set a lot higher than public sanitation and transport. A few years after emigrating, he used a fraudulent cheque to buy a significant proportion of the **Transafrican Railways of Angola**.

Reis grew rich on the proceeds and set about expanding his empire, moving back to Lisbon in 1922, buying a US car dealership and forging more cheques, this time to buy a company called Ambaca. Once he had access to Ambaca's funds, he took over the **Angola Mining Company**. But he had reached too far too fast, and was arrested in Porto in 1924 for embezzlement and arms dealing. Reis only served 54 days, getting out on a technicality. It had been enough time for him to concoct his biggest idea.

European finances had been highly unstable in the years following World War I. By 1923, Germany was in the grip of a vicious circle of hyperinflation, flooded with notes issued by the government of increasingly ludicrous value (the highest denomina-

Artur Virgilio Alves Reis.

tion was DM100 trillion). Sniffing an opportunity, Reis did some research on the Bank of Portugal, which produced the nation's notes, yet did not appear to inform the government of all its printings or keep consistent records. It did not even have a department responsible for preventing the duplication of banknote numbers.

After his release in August 1924, Reis gathered a number of conspirators around him, including **José Bandeira**, whose brother António was the Portuguese minister to The Hague. He set himself up as an agent of the Bank of Portugal, claiming he'd been tasked with arranging a financing operation in cash-strapped Angola. Once he had Bandeira's signature, he forged other signatures around it, acquired certificates from various foreign embassies and approached Waterlow & Sons, a London printers who had handled previous printings of Portuguese notes.

Luck was on Reis's side – a letter from **Sir William Waterlow** to the governor of the Bank of Portugal was lost in the post. Elsewhere, he was able to keep the deal from being publicized by claiming it was a loan that had divided the bank's directors and had to be kept secret – the British took this as evidence of "typical" Portuguese corruption, rather than anything genuinely sinister. Waterlow & Sons printed 200,000 banknotes, using existing serial numbers, all of 500 Portuguese escudos – meaning almost half of all 500 escudo notes in circulation were false.

Because of the number of accomplices he had to pay off, Reis only received 25 percent of the proceeds, which were laundered into smaller notes in Portugal. But by 1925, he was rich enough to create the Bank of Angola and Metropole and buy what is now the British Council's headquarters in Lisbon, alongside three farms, a taxi fleet and vast amounts of clothes and jewellery. He tried, and failed, to buy a newspaper, but continued to move towards his ultimate aim – buying the Bank of Portugal itself.

By autumn 1925, he had gained a quarter of the company. Rumours about fake banknotes were growing, but since the notes were (save for their duplicate serial numbers) entirely correct, no action was taken. Eventually, Reis's rapid rise itself gave him away. In November *O Século* (*The Century*), Portugal's leading newspaper, began to investigate how the Bank of Angola and Metropole could offer low-interest loans without requiring significant deposits. Meanwhile, agents from the Bank of Portugal noticed the huge deposits made by Reis's bank, all in 500 escudo notes.

Reis's fraud was so well-established, and his documents so convincing, that the ensuing investigations took five years. At one point, the judge of the trial arrested the man in the witness stand – the governor of the Bank of Portugal – suspecting him of involvement in the conspiracy. Eventually Reis was sent to prison for twenty years, where he got religion and converted to an obscure Protestant sect.

His scheme had far-reaching effects. Reis introduced around £1 million worth of escudos, £44 million in today's terms, into the Portuguese economy. The resulting blow to the economy, and its results – a plunging international reputation, press anger and a salary devaluation which hit army officers hard – have all been held up as contributing factors in the success of the 1926 military coup, which deposed the First Republic and led to the dictatorship of **Prime Minister Salazar**, who ruled from 1932 to 1968. Reis was released from jail in 1945, and was soon facing another charge of fraud – this time over coffee beans. He died in poverty in 1955.

For further investigation

📖 **Teigh Bloom The Man Who Stole Portugal (1966)** Rounded and readable account of Reis's life.

📖 **Henry Wigan The Effects of the 1925 Portuguese Bank Note Crisis (2004)** An academic paper detailing the mechanics of the scheme and its destabilizing aftermath, which can be read at lse.ac.uk/collections/economicHistory.

📖 **Thomas Gifford The Man from Lisbon (1977)** Novelistic, sensationally packaged vision of Reis and the scandal from an American thriller writer.

HOMICIDE

Homicide

Murder is often gruesome and outlandish, an obscene spectacle of rage and brutality, whether it is the drive-by killing, a gangland execution or a robbery gone wrong, or a lovers' quarrel or family feud that has escalated beyond the point of no return. Such violent deaths are commonly the results of gang rivalry, conflict in families, lust and sexual jealousy.

Often these crimes seem like they belong to another world, like scenes from a movie, but homicides do not just take place in inner cities or seedy motels. Killings happen in respectable homes and upscale neighbourhoods, behind net curtains and wicker fences as well as by the light of neon signs.

One question always surfaces. Why? The answers are not always easy to take. When the perpetrators are hardened criminals, social misfits or dropouts from society, such acts seem less shocking – they are an inevitable part of a shadowy world that is separate from normal life. But what about when the victim is, like the elderly **Bertha Pippin**, killed in cold blood by

local teenagers with no apparent motive? Or when the alleged killer is, like **O.J. Simpson**, a celebrity with a glamorous lifestyle? In such cases, as with the murder of parents by their offspring, the problem of motive comes much closer to home. It can't just be put down to an underworld culture of violence.

What sets one murderer apart from another? Are there ever any circumstances in which homicide can be justified? Such questions are furiously debated, especially in the US, where the death penalty is widely carried out (though Bertha Pippin's killers were not executed). The issue becomes especially difficult in the case of victims of domestic violence who kill their abusive spouses.

As the O.J. Simpson case proved, there is an almost insatiable media appetite for stories of real-life homicide. Sometimes the interest lasts for decades, with murders passing into folklore. In the information age, that process is intensified by the Internet and wall-to-wall news. But the endings of these stories are not always neat: some killings are never solved, remaining shrouded in mystery and mythology.

Unsolved murders

Many killers remain at large, never identified let alone apprehended. Certain unsolved cases become legendary.

Even if an unsolved case remains open, in the hope that one day new leads might arise, investigators move on to other cases and the possibility of a solution recedes. In recent years, new achievements in forensic science – and especially **DNA** testing – mean that police have a powerful tool of identification which can be used retrospectively to clear up past cases. Technological advances mean that the techniques of crime-fighting changed beyond recognition during the twentieth century. The 1902 slaying of **Rose Harsent** in a sleepy English town might not have remained unsolved if scientists had been able to tell if blood found on a knife had come from the dead woman.

Yet although technology improves, society also changes in ways which mean that homicide happens in different ways in different places. The turn-of-the-century small-town settings of Harsent's death or the double murder of Andrew Jackson Borden and his wife Abby in Fall River, Massachusetts, are strikingly

different from killings that took place in more urban locales – such as the unexplained murder of Ginger Rios in Las Vegas or of mobster's daughter Susan Berman in suburban Los Angeles. Unsolved cases that linger in the imagination can often tell us something pertinent about changes in culture and society.

LIZZIE BORDEN

The 1893 trial of **Lizzie Andrew Borden** was a sensation. It ended in acquittal, despite significant evidence of guilt, and no other credible suspects ever emerged. The case gripped the imagination of the American public, heralding the modern age of murders scrutinized by the mass media.

Born in 1860, Lizzie was a plain-faced woman who, at the age of 32, was living an apparently quiet life in a spacious home in Fall River, Massachusetts. She lived with her father, **Andrew Jackson Borden**, and his second wife, **Abby Durfee Borden**. It seemed a solid, prosperous, unremarkable family. They employed a house cleaner, Bridget "Maggie" Sullivan, and on 4 August 1892 she was busy washing windows. It was a stiflingly hot summer day. Lizzie's older sister, Emma Lenore, was away from the home, as was her uncle, John Morse, who was at that time visiting the family. When Andrew took a short walk to town to run errands at the post office and the Union Saving Bank (of which he was president), he left his wife and Lizzie together in the house.

Abby was making up a bed in a second-floor guest bedroom when, according to accusers, Lizzie snuck up behind her, holding a hatchet. The weapon was

Lizzie Borden: was she a murderer?

When she was done, she leafed through a magazine.

Upon her father's return, Lizzie told him that Abby had received a note and then left the house to attend to a sick friend. His wife's apparent absence thus explained, Andrew retired upstairs, falling asleep on a sofa. By this time, Maggie the maid was also napping in her attic room. She was woken by the sound of Lizzie shouting. She "hollo'd so loud", Maggie said, "to come down quick. Father's dead! Someone came in and killed him!" Rushing downstairs, what Maggie found was grim. According to a subsequent account in the *Fall River Herald*, the crime scene was nauseating. "Over the left temple a wound six by four had been made as if he had been pounded with the dull edge of an axe", the reporter wrote. "The left eye had been dug out and a cut extended the length of the nose. The face was hacked to pieces and the blood had covered the man's shirt."

Lizzie sent Maggie to the neighbouring home of Dr. Seabury Bowen, the family's doctor. Shortly after he arrived, the maid discovered Abby's body upstairs. Dr Bowen notified the police. Afterwards, friends, neighbours, family members, and police went in and out of the home contaminating the crime scene. The newspaper reporter was able to walk freely throughout the house. By the afternoon, a whole convention of doctors huddled in consultation, all with bloodied hands from touching the bodies.

From the shed and property, police removed two axes, a claw-hammer hatchet, a hatchet with a plain head, and a hatchet with its handle missing. It was this last implement that would ultimately be exhibited in court as the probable murder weapon, but in fact there were no traces of blood or tissue linking it to the scene of the crime. It is likely that the actual murder weapon

used repeatedly and with great force. Nineteen blows of the hatchet fell on Abby, leaving a five-inch hole in her skull. The body was left where it dropped, in a bedroom that was otherwise neat and undisturbed. Ninety minutes elapsed before Andrew returned and in that time Lizzie got on with her daily chores, folding and carrying clothes upstairs from the cellar laundry, sewing a button on a dress, ironing handkerchiefs.

was never found and the murder investigation was poorly conducted throughout. Autopsies were not done on the dead couple for a week, by which time their bodies had badly decomposed.

In the days after the murders, there was talk of a "Portuguese labourer", to whom Andrew might have owed money. Lizzie did not initially arouse suspicion. Indeed the *Boston Herald* newspaper made a point of emphasizing her virtuous reputation. Other reports, however, suggested bad blood between daughter and stepmother. A decisive development came when Eli Bence, a clerk at S.R. Smith's drugstore in Fall River, revealed that Lizzie had attempted to buy ten-cents worth of prussic acid, or hydrogen cyanide, a poison. He refused to sell it without a prescription, even though she explained she needed it to clean and debug a sealskin coat.

On 9 August an inquest was held and Lizzie was questioned. Her answers were evasive and inconsistent. On 12 August, Lizzie was charged by Police Chief Hilliard with two counts of murder, based solely upon circumstantial evidence.

The following June, Lizzie's sometimes-dramatic, fourteen-day trial began. Visitors to the house the day of the killings testified that Lizzie was unemotional immediately following her parents' deaths. During the trial, however, Lizzie did react when her parents' skulls were introduced as evidence; she passed out in the courtroom.

A missing piece of the puzzle in the case against Lizzie was blood evidence. Had Lizzie committed the crimes, it is likely that she would have been covered in blood, and she would have had bruises and possibly cuts on her hands and arms from flinging the weapon enough to cause the multiple fatal blows. No physical evidence was submitted linking Lizzie to the scene of the crime. After deliberating just one hour, the all-male jury found Lizzie Borden not guilty of all counts.

Two weeks after the trial ended, Lizzie and her sister Emma moved into a large house on French Street, across town from the family estate. In 1905, after the sisters had a falling out, Emma relocated to New Hampshire, and Lizzie never saw her sister again. Lizzie passed away at her home, where she lived alone, on 1 June 1927. Nine days later, Emma died from injuries caused from a fall inside her house.

No one else was ever charged with the murders of Andrew and Abby Borden, and many continued to believe that Lizzie was their killer, leading to the once-popular playground verse: "Lizzie Borden took an axe / And gave her mother forty whacks / When she saw what she had done / She gave her father forty-one."

The Borden house at 92 Second Street where the murders occurred is said to be haunted. It was eventually turned into a bed and breakfast.

Neil Entwistle was considered likeable and successful, until his wife, Rachel, and baby daughter, Lillian Rose, were found dead in their Massachusetts home. An international manhunt led detectives to England, Entwistle's homeland, where he was captured while hiding out in his parents' Nottinghamshire home. He was convicted of murder in 2008 and sentenced to life imprisonment.

Stanford White, a world-famous architect, was fatally shot in the back in 1906 by the millionaire Harry Thaw at a rooftop theater at Madison Square Garden (a building White had designed). Thaw's young wife, actress Evelyn Nesbit, testified that White, who had a reputation as a womanizer, had sexually abused her and that Thaw had protected her from White. Thaw was found not guilty by reason of insanity and sent to a state hospital until 1915.

For further investigation

📖 **David Rehak** Did Lizzie Borden Axe for It? **(2008)** An updated edition, with more than seventy photos, researches and analyses the evidence and issues surrounding the double murder.

📖 **Rick Geary** The Borden Tragedy: A Memoir of the Infamous Double Murder at Fall River, Mass., 1892 **(1997)** A book of research into the case's investigation, trial, and the media blitz that followed. While the author lays out the intricacies of the case, he stops short of naming the killer.

🌐 **law.umkc.edu/faculty/projects/ftrials/LizzieBorden/ bordenaccount** An account of the proceedings by Doug Linder, a University of Missouri-Kansas law professor.

🌐 **lizzieandrewborden.com** A site devoted to everything pertaining to Lizzie Borden.

WILLIAM GARDINER

On the Sunday morning of 1 June 1902, the half-naked body of **Rose Harsent**, a live-in domestic servant aged 23, was found at the foot of the stairs near the kitchen of Providence House, the home of William and Georgeanna Crisp. The Crisps employed Harsent in their estate home in the Suffolk village of Peasenhall, England.

Harsent, wearing her maid's uniform, had been stabbed in the chest, her throat slit from ear to ear, and her upper body partially burnt. Doctors who arrived on the scene determined that the time of death was in the early hours of the morning. An examination of Harsent's body determined that the unmarried woman was six months pregnant.

When police went upstairs to Rose's bedroom, they found that the bed had not been slept in. A number of letters were discovered, one set of which included sexually explicit poems that were later attributed to a young local man, Fred Davis. Less flowery was another note, unsigned but obviously written by someone other than Davis: "I will try to see you tonight at 12 oclock at your Place if you Put a light in your window at 10 oclock for about 10 minutes and then you take it out again." Investigators linked the handwriting to that of William Gardiner, a foreman carpenter who lived with his wife and six children in a nearby cottage.

Gardiner, 35, and Harsent attended the same Primitive Methodist church, where Gardiner was the choirmaster and Sunday school teacher and Harsent sang in the choir. Harsent also took organ lessons from Gardiner. The pair had been the subject of a scandal the previous year after two teenage boys claimed that they had seen Gardiner and Harsent walking to a chapel in a field at Peasenhall, but a church inquiry cleared them of impropriety.

Several men emerged as suspects, including Harsent's former fiancé, a delivery boy, and a migrant farm worker. Though Gardiner denied any involvement, his pocket knife was found to have been recently cleaned of blood. Gardiner said he had been gutting

VIOLENT CRIME, PROFILING AND FORENSICS

Criminology has existed as a scientific discipline since the mid-1700s. Originally a branch of social philosophy related to law, in recent years (especially with the advent of DNA testing), criminology has become a highly sophisticated form of analysis, which can make or break cases. The smash-hit TV show *CSI: Crime Scene Investigation* and its spin-offs have exploited our fascination with the painstaking work of high-tech forensics. One of criminology's most notable techniques is "offender profiling" (made famous by the novel and film, *The Silence of the Lambs*). It is an attempt to assemble from available evidence a picture of the habitual behaviour and personality traits of a perpetrator whose identity remains unknown.

One of the earliest attempts at what we would now think of as offender profiling was undertaken by the police surgeon Dr Thomas Bond in 1888. Bond had helped conduct the autopsy of the murdered London prostitute Mary Kelly – thought to be the fifth and final victim of Jack the Ripper. Bond in his notes tried to deduce what kind of man was responsible for the slayings. He must have been physically powerful and audacious, Bond concluded, but not someone who would stand out in a crowd. He was probably an unemployed loner, neat but eccentric, probably middle-aged, and it

was likely that he went out at night wearing a cloak that would hide the signs of his bloody handiwork. Since the Ripper was never caught, there is no way of knowing how accurate Bond's picture was.

In the twentieth century, offender profiling evolved steadily into a sophisticated science. In 1956, the psychiatrist James A. Brussel, New York State's assistant commissioner of mental hygiene, successfully profiled a "mad bomber" who was terrorizing the city. Brussel was called in the press the "Sherlock Holmes of the Couch" and in 1968 he wrote a book, *Casebook of a Crime Psychiatrist*, which came to the attention of FBI agent Howard Teten. Teten adapted Brussel's techniques for use at the FBI's Behavioural Science Unit (which is depicted in *The Silence of the Lambs*) located on the huge military base at Quantico, Virginia.

Offender profiling has become a standard tool of law enforcement, though Brussel's success has not always been repeated. In the 1982 Tylenol poisoning case in Chicago, an unidentified assailant tainted bottles of the nonprescription painkiller with cyanide. Seven people died; an estimated 31 million bottles of the drug were withdrawn by the manufacturer. Profiling work was carried out, leading to the hypothesis that the perpetrator was a skilled shoplifter, probably in his early twenties,

rabbits but, just two days after the slaying, he was arrested and charged with the crime. Police accused Gardiner of killing Harsent because she was carrying his baby. There was circumstantial evidence. A local gardener claimed without corroboration to have seen, early that Saturday morning, bootprints leading from

Providence House back to the Gardiner home. The murder was a high-profile case and, according to accounts, England talked of nothing else for months.

During the trial, which began that November, Harsent was portrayed as an innocent virgin who was taken advantage of by an older married man. (Years later, it

a loner with a temper, possibly a drug user, who had difficulty holding down a job, and came from a troubled background. He knew the Chicago area and probably lived near where the tainted Tylenol bottles were planted. But did that profile help police find the killer? In this case, no.

Killers often leave behind crucial evidence at crime scenes. Forensic scientists are faced with the challenge of interpreting what's left behind. On 15 January 1978, Lisa Levy and Margaret Bowman were murdered while they slept in a sorority house on the campus of Florida State University, Tallahassee. Police found bite marks, which they photographed, on Levy's buttocks.

When Ted Bundy was convicted of these murders in June 1979, the marks were matched with plaster casts of Bundy's teeth. In a subsequent trial, for the murder of Kimberly Leach, fibres from the victim's clothing were found in Bundy's van. Bundy eventually admitted to killing as many as thirty women, bludgeoning and strangling them, then afterwards engaging in necrophilia. He was executed in the electric chair on 24 January 1989.

New criminal forensics procedures may one day allow on-site DNA testing in the field. DNA evidence has become a vital forensic technique to identify criminals when evidence is left behind at crime scenes, such as a strand of hair, saliva,

Dr Richard Souviron presents evidence at Ted Bundy's appeal trial.

urine, blood, or semen. DNA can be lifted and tested from chewed gum and even the back of a licked envelope. DNA testing can also help defence lawyers in proving their clients' innocence by ruling them out. DNA testing has already helped many people wrongly convicted of crimes.

was discovered that she'd had, in fact, many lovers.) A turning point came in the trial when the evidentiary value of the blood traces found on Gardiner's knife came to be discussed. In those days, forensic science was relatively limited. Human blood could not specifically be differentiated from that of other mammals.

The prosecution, led by **Henry Fielding Dickens** (a son of Charles Dickens) couldn't prove the blood was Rose Harsent's. On top of that, Gardiner had an alibi for the time of Harsent's murder. His lawyer, **Ernest Wild** – who would later have a distinguished career and be knighted, but was then inexperienced

For using his pick-up to intentionally kill a 12-year-old girl, 44-year-old George Ford Jr was sent to prison for second-degree murder in 2007. Ford had run down Shyanne Somers, a baby-sitter, in order to keep her quiet about having effectively kidnapped her for three hours behind an abandoned farmhouse.

– claimed Gardiner was at home in bed with his wife, Georgiana, at the time of the murder. She adamantly insisted during both trials that this was indeed where her husband had been that night.

A unanimous verdict was needed to convict, but the jury failed to reach a consensus. Gardiner was acquitted: one of the twelve jurors refused to join the others in declaring him guilty. A second trial, in January 1903, was held with the same "not guilty" outcome, except this time the majority was only ten in favour of convicting. A third trial was scheduled in the rural market town of Bury St Edmunds. But before it could begin, authorities decided not to go through with it. The court instead ruled the case *nolle prosequi*, which is Latin for "unwilling to pursue". Had Gardiner been convicted, he would have been hanged. He is listed as one of the few people in English history to be tried twice for murder with no verdict returned.

After the second trial, William Gardiner relocated with his family to Southall in London, where he ran a shop. The house where Harsent lived and was killed in is still standing.

Though no one else was ever tried for the murder, there is still speculation about the killer's identity. In his 2005 documentary about the case, the actor and writer **Julian Fellowes** concluded that it was Georgiana Gardiner who, in a jealous rage, killed Rose Harsent.

For further investigation

Richard Du Cann Art of the Advocate (**1999**) A book about the role of an advocate that examines new and old cases, including Rose Harsent's murder case.

Caroline Maughan & Julian Webb Lawyering Skills and the Legal Process (**2005**) Contains a short but incisive study of the case.

Dominic Santana Julian Fellowes Investigates: A Most Mysterious Murder – The Case of Rose Harsent (**2005**) A made-for-TV movie, released in 2005 in the UK, that's a re-enactment of the crime.

JIMMY HOFFA'S DISAPPEARANCE

When **James Riddle "Jimmy" Hoffa**, 62, disappeared on 30 July 1975, speculation about his fate was feverish. He was due to meet two Mafia bosses and had made many enemies in the course of a tumultuous union career, and it did not take long for him to be presumed dead. However, no body has ever been found.

Hoffa began organizing workers and challenging management while working in an Indiana food warehouse. After he was fired in 1932, he took a job as a full-time official of the truck drivers' union, the International Brotherhood of Teamsters, Local 299 (Detroit, Michigan). As the union president from 1957 to the mid-1960s, the labour leader wielded considerable influence and power. Hoffa maintained links with organized crime (when he was president, Teamster money was used to build several Las Vegas casinos) from early on. Union organizing was a dirty business then. Hoffa's predecessor Dave Beck went to prison for bribery and in 1964 Hoffa was sentenced to fifteen years for attempting to pay off a grand juror.

However, after serving a decade in prison, in December 1971, **President Richard Nixon** commuted Hoffa's sentence to time served. He was released on the condition that he not participate in union activities for ten years. Three and a half years later, Hoffa disappeared from a car park at the Machus Red Fox Restaurant in Bloomfield Hills, a suburb of Detroit. He was there for a meeting with Mafia capos Anthony "Tony Jack" Giacalone, from Detroit, and Anthony "Tony Pro" Provenzano, from Union City, New Jersey, and New York City.

The latest theory about the disappearance is to be found in a book by Charlie Brandt, a former prosecutor and chief deputy attorney general of Delaware. It tells the story of Wilmington Teamsters official and Mafia hit man Frank Sheeran – nicknamed "the Irishman" – and his connection with the presumed death. Sheeran learned to kill as a soldier in Europe during World War II, where he waded ashore in three amphibious invasions and marched from Sicily to Dachau, serving 411 days of active combat in what has been called General Patton's "killer division".

His combat duty prepared him for his future life of crime. After being released from the service and

James Hoffa, business agent for the Teamsters Union, in court, arraigned on an extortion warrant.

returning home, he married, became a truck driver, and met mob boss Russell Bufalino in 1955 in a chance meeting at a truck stop. To earn pocket change, Sheeran began running errands and doing odd jobs for Bufalino. That beginning led to a prominent position in the Teamsters and the Bufalino family. In a US federal suit using the Racketeer Influenced and Corrupt Organizations Act (RICO), then-US attorney Rudy Giuliani named him as one of only two non-Italians on a list of twenty-six top Mafia figures. When Bufalino ordered Sheeran to kill his friend and mentor, Jimmy Hoffa, Sheeran, in his confession (taped by Brandt), said he followed the order.

In the late 1990s, Sheeran had been represented by Brandt in an unrelated case. That's when he initially came close to confessing to killing Hoffa, according to Brandt: "He called me and we sat down. His soul wanted to tell the truth. [But] his body didn't want to go to jail." Both the FBI and Detroit police had already named Sheeran as one of a handful of suspects in Jimmy Hoffa's disappearance. The media, as a result, pursued Sheeran for years. "Frank said to me, 'I'm tired of being written about'," Brandt said. "I want to tell my side of it, and I want you to tell it for me." Finally, in 2003, the wise guy made a deathbed confession to Brandt that he was the assassin.

Brandt's book is called *I Heard You Paint Houses*. "To paint a house is to kill a man," Brandt explained during a book signing in Las Vegas. "The paint is the blood that splatters on the walls and floors." In the interview with Brandt, Sheeran described a professional hit: "Jimmy Hoffa got shot twice at decent range – not too close or the paint splatters back at you – in the back of the head, behind his right ear." He immediately dropped the gun and left the scene to "cleaners" (Mafia men who rid crime scenes of evidence) who put Hoffa's body in a bag. The corpse, Sheeran said to Brandt, was taken within minutes to a nearby mortuary and cremated – though what happened to the cremated remains was not explained.

Sheeran identified the cleaners as two brothers, whose names were listed by the FBI as suspects along with Sheeran. The two brothers in question have, however, never been charged in connection and always denied any involvement in Hoffa's disappearance. Sheeran was in and out of prison until his death in 2004, but was never charged with Hoffa's disappearance or murder.

On 17 May 2006, acting on a tip supplied by Donovan Wells (or so the *Detroit Free Press* reported – there was no official confirmation), a 75-year-old prisoner at the Federal Medical Center in Lexington, Kentucky, the FBI began digging for Hoffa's remains outside a barn on what is now the Hidden Dreams Farm in Milford Township, Michigan, where they surveyed the land and dug up sections of the 85-acre property. More than forty agents sectioned off a piece of the horse farm where they believed Hoffa's bones might be. The investigation team included forensic experts from the bureau's Washington laboratory and anthropologists, archaeologists, engineers and architects. A week later, on 24 May, FBI agents removed a large barn on the property to look under it for Hoffa's remains. Six days after that, on 30 May, agents ended their search for Hoffa's body without any remains being found at the Hidden Dreams Farm.

Officially, the Jimmy Hoffa mystery remains unsolved. And while the authorities have not closed the case, Dr Michael Baden, former chief medical examiner for the City of New York, has said that Charlie Brandt's book "is supported by the forensic evidence, is entirely credible, and solves the Hoffa mystery".

Jimmy's son, James Phillip Hoffa, became a Teamsters' president. His daughter, Barbara Ann Crancer, is an associate circuit court judge in St Louis County, Missouri.

For further investigation

📖 **Charles Brandt** I Heard You Paint Houses: Frank "the Irishman" Sheeran and the Inside Story of the Mafia, the Teamsters, and the Last Ride of Jimmy Hoffa (2005) Brandt's book is a personal account of the disappearance of Teamster union boss Jimmy Hoffa. This book includes Sheeran's confession that he's the one who pulled the trigger and killed Hoffa.

Ⓦ hoffasolved.com Author Charles Brandt's site that lays out his theory about who killed Jimmy Hoffa. It includes an NPR interview with the author, an audio interview with Frank "the Irishman" Sheeran, and book reviews of I Heard You Paint Houses.

"MAFIA PRINCESS" SUSAN BERMAN

The life of a journalist and author who spent her adult years writing about her mob roots ended dramatically, like a character in one of her books. **Susan Berman**, 55, was murdered in her Beverly Hills, California, home. She was shot execution-style by an unknown assailant, just as New York state police were scheduling an interview about a decades-old unsolved missing-person's case.

When she came of age, Susan was given a trust of $5.25 million – which, over the years, she squandered by spending too much and making bad investments. She purchased three homes and lost them all to foreclosure. Still, for years she kept up a façade and wished to be treated as if she had money. She was a wealthy Mafia daughter and a respected writer – but she ended up struggling and penniless, living in squalor while she waited for a big movie deal, until she was shot to death in the back of the head, her murderer never apprehended.

Berman's body was found on 24 December 2000 inside her rundown rented house in the woodsy Benedict Canyon neighbourhood, where she lived with her three dogs. The front door had been left wide open – there were no signs of a forced entry or struggle, no signs of a sexual assault, and no items had been stolen from the house.

Susan had lived what she once described as a perfect childhood, despite being the daughter of a Jewish mobster. In the 1930s and 40s, her father, **Davie Berman**, was part of the same crime syndicate as **Benjamin "Bugsy" Siegel** and mob kingpin **Meyer Lansky**. Working with Lansky, considered one of the shrewdest gangsters to ever walk the streets of twentieth-century New York, was an opportunity for Davie to learn from the mob's top echelon. After all, Lansky was known as Lucky Luciano's right-hand man and the mob's financial mastermind.

As a trio, Berman, Siegel and Lansky pioneered the development of Las Vegas from a sleepy desert cow town to a thriving gambling Mecca. Nevertheless, the gangsters soon found themselves in an uneasy alliance with the Italian Mafia, who moved in on the Jewish mob's territory. Davie, who co-owned the famous Flamingo Hotel and Casino with Siegel and Lansky, ran the place after Siegel was murdered in 1947 (in the Beverly Hills home of his mistress, Virginia Hill). Only in 1951, after the highly publicized and televised Kefauver Committee hearings of the US Senate's investigation into organized crime, did the public become aware of the extent of Jewish involvement in the underworld.

Susan knew nothing of her father's underworld dealings until she became an adult, but her Las Vegas childhood was not exactly normal. Her father had slot machines installed in Flamingo Hotel rooms so his daughter could pass the time gambling and ordering room service. Susan enjoyed the life of a spoiled, indulged child. She wanted for nothing. Elvis Presley, Frank Sinatra and Liberace performed at her birthday parties. Davie drove fancy new Cadillacs. To his Susie, he was the world. What Susan did not know then was that when mob families were feuding, her family was in danger. During times of mob unrest, Davie piloted Susan away to Los Angeles, flying out of McCarran Field to the Los Angeles airport, and then to the Beverly Wilshire Hotel for two or three days. He told Susan they were short vacations. Bodyguard **Lou**

Raskin, a mountain of a man, lived with the Bermans so he could watch over Davie's precious daughter. Susie remembered the trips as wonderful outings. She fell in love with Los Angeles.

The high-society lifestyle of the "Mafia Princess", as the media called her, came to an abrupt end in 1957, when she was twelve. That year her father died during intestinal surgery. Only a few months later her mother Gladys committed suicide by taking a barbiturate overdose. Her Nevada childhood would haunt Susan for the rest of her life.

In the ensuing years, what Berman wanted most was for her father to be remembered for his contributions

CRAIG JACOBSEN, A.K.A. JOHN FLOWERS

The kidnapping, rape and murder of Ginger Rios in the entertainment capital of the world was a bizarre, shocking crime, providing a glimpse of the dark side of Las Vegas. It was the American Dream meets the American Monster when Ginger, a vibrant singer with a bright future, had a chance fatal encounter with a madman.

Ginger was a young backing singer and dancer in a salsa band that had a regular gig at the Fiesta hotel casino in the north of the city. She dreamed of one day becoming Miss Las Vegas. But at the age of twenty, as her career was taking off, her life was violently cut short.

It happened on a sunny afternoon in April 1997, when Rios walked through the front door of the Spy Craft bookstore. Her husband, Mark Hollinger, waited outside in their car. Ginger never came out. Mark tried to persuade Las Vegas police to go to the Spy Craft store to look for his wife, but officers

told him it wasn't a crime for his wife to walk away.

Four months later it was learned that the store's owner, Craig Jacobsen, had raped and murdered Ginger, then driven her body 350 miles to a remote area of the Mojave Desert in Arizona, where he buried her in a shallow grave. Had police done a routine check of the store, as Ginger's husband had suggested, they may have caught Jacobsen in the act of cleaning up the bloody back room – the scene of the crime – and possibly found Ginger's body wrapped in a plastic rubbish bag in the rear of his van. In fact, according to a statement Jacobsen's wife eventually gave police, Ginger was still alive in the bag when she was placed in the van.

It was the killer's wife who eventually led deputies to the body of not one woman, but two. Arizona investigators also discovered the body of the second young woman buried in the desert floor not far from Ginger's grave. Days later, Craig Jacobsen,

to the development of Las Vegas. She wrote about Davie in two memoirs, 1981's critically acclaimed *Easy Street* and 1996's *Lady Las Vegas*. There was speculation after her death that perhaps digging into Davie's mob past was what got Susan killed. When police, responding to reports of dogs running loose, found Susan's lifeless body on the floor of her rented house, they also noticed a 1920s Chicago Police "WANTED" poster for her father. Combined with the cause of death – a single gunshot wound to the back of the head – it was not surprising that detectives wondered if Susan had been whacked by the Mafia. That notion was soon debunked when they realized the mobsters of her

father's era would be between ninety and one hundred years old. Moreover, nothing Susan was working on was anything she would be killed over.

No eyewitnesses to Susan's murder ever came forward. Susan's killer simply escaped into the night. At the scene, investigators found the casing of a spent bullet used in a 9mm handgun. It was the best evidence they had.

One person of interest to the police was Berman's University of California classmate **Bobby Durst**. Durst's wife, **Kathleen McCormack**, went missing in 1982; he was questioned about the disappearance but never charged with any crime. In 1999, Kathleen's

who went by the alias of John Flowers, was arrested in Los Angeles, where he awaited extradition to Florida on an unrelated parole violation. He was ultimately returned to Nevada where he faced a murder charge for killing Ginger.

In a strange twist to a gruesome case, after the second body was unearthed from its makeshift grave, a private company then re-buried it – but the company lost the records detailing exactly where the burial site was. Las Vegas police wanted to exhume the body, to get DNA from hair and to do a composite sketch based upon the skull. That is, until they learned the body was lost.

Jacobsen admitted to Las Vegas police that he killed the unidentified woman at the Lake Mead National Recreation Area and drove her body to Arizona. But once the remains were buried and the records misplaced, Las Vegas police and the district attorney dropped that case and concentrated their efforts on the Ginger Rios investigation.

Even though he was charged with first-degree murder, Jacobsen was offered a plea bargain by the district attorney, an agreement he accepted. He ended up pleading guilty while insane to Ginger's murder. However, in 2002, a judge reversed the plea of guilty but mentally ill, and Jacobsen was granted a new trial. Clark County district judge Michael Douglas, in his ruling, said he had no choice but to let Craig Jacobsen withdraw his plea, because he was obligated to do so given a Nevada Supreme Court ruling preventing the type of plea Jacobsen entered.

Then, in another unusual move, Jacobsen pleaded guilty a second time in yet another plea bargain with prosecutors, which meant he did not have to face a jury. Jacobsen was sentenced to twenty-plus years with the possibility of parole, with the first hearing in 2007. He was denied parole and remains incarcerated at the Ely State Prison, a maximum-security institution for violent male offenders in northern Nevada.

parents went to court and had their daughter declared dead, even though no body was ever found. It cleared the way for them to settle her estate. The Westchester County district attorney, had reopened the investigation into Durst's first wife's disappearance before Susan Berman's death.

Berman regularly referred to Bobby Durst as her brother and her best friend. They had much in common. Durst was a multimillionaire and the eldest son of a rich New York real estate tycoon family. Like Berman, Durst's mother had committed suicide when he was a child, falling from the roof of the family mansion while her son watched. Aged 57 at the time of Susan's death, Durst was interviewed once, but police never found evidence of a connection with her murder.

Rumours and speculation persisted. Three years later he was tried for killing Morris Black, an elderly neighbour of his in Galveston, Texas. At trial, Durst admitted the killing, but claimed self-defence. The jury acquitted him. After Durst was arrested in the Black case, police found a 9mm handgun in the boot of his car. LAPD investigators travelled to Texas and did ballistics tests on the gun to see if it matched the casing found at Berman's house. The tests were inconclusive. Durst all the time categorically denied any connection to his friend Susan Berman's death.

The Berman investigation, Case No. 000825485, is now a cold one at Parker Center on North Los Angeles Street, where the Los Angeles Police Department's Robbery-Homicide Division is housed. Berman's murder was one of 548 committed within the LAPD's jurisdiction in 2000.

For further investigation

📖 **Susan Berman** Lady Las Vegas: The Inside Story Behind America's Neon Oasis **(1998)** This memoir traces Susan's heritage as the daughter of a Jewish mob boss who grew up like royalty.

📖 **Miles Corwin** Homicide Special: On the Streets with the LAPD's Elite Detective Unit **(2004)** Corwin covered the homicide unit for a year, including when detectives landed the Susan Berman murder. Details of the case are included in this book.

📖 **Robert A. Rockaway** But He Was Good to His Mother: The Lives and Crimes of Jewish Gangsters **(2000)** Written by a historian and a member of the Department of Jewish History at Tel-Aviv University, the book begins in the early 1970s.

📖 **Cathy Scott** Murder of a Mafia Daughter: The Life and Tragic Death of Susan Berman **(2002)** An in-depth account of Susan Berman's life, written by the author of this book.

🌐 **courttv.com/trials/durst/keyplayers.html** A comprehensive list of players in both the Robert Durst and Susan Berman criminal cases.

🌐 **topics.nytimes.com/top/reference/timestopics/people/b/morris_black/index.html** Index of stories in The New York Times about Durst.

Louise Dimick prepared well for the 1920 Chicago murder of her young husband, nineteen-year-old Thomas Schweig, sixteen years her junior. Afraid that he would leave her, Dimick purchased a pistol, and, in a vacant lot, practiced shooting using one of Schweig's spare bowler hats as the target. As it turned out, their short marriage was not even legal, because they'd wed before Schweig's divorce from his first wife was finalized.

Women who kill

Women who kill their husbands often tell police that their spouses pushed them into doing it, or they did it because, as battered women, it was their only means of escape from violence.

San Diego socialite **Betty Broderick**, Canadian Army bride **Kimberley Kondejewski**, housewife **Donna Yaklich** of Colorado – each of their married lives began in city suburbs where they settled to begin family life with the sweetheart each one had married. But along the way, things started to go horribly wrong. These homes in which so much hope was invested became places of abuse and betrayal.

What causes women who have been victims themselves to use deadly force against their husbands? According to a 1991 study conducted by the Commonwealth Fund in New York, domestic violence is startlingly common. As many as seven percent of American women are physically abused by their partners.

Murder is overwhelmingly a male crime: according to a *Boston Globe* report, men commit 85 percent of all homicides. But when women do kill, their victims are family members – often the spouses who have battered them for years. When her abusive husband demanded that Kimberley Kondejewski commit suicide so that he could claim on her life insurance, she snapped. After the years of torment, the usually subdued Kimberley fought back – and took the ultimate revenge. Donna Yaklich also suffered abuse. Her solution was to hire two men to kill her steroid-using husband. But given that the murder was therefore premeditated rather than a desperate counter measure, would the argument of self-defence hold up in court?

It is not just husbands who abuse a marriage until it disintegrates in disaster. Susan Barber lived with her husband in an English seaside town in Essex. For years she waited for her husband Michael (who himself had a history of accusations of sexual assault) to go to work before meeting her lover. When Michael finally discovered the affair, he reacted violently. That was not the end of it; Susan took matters into her own hands by lacing her husband's meals with a deadly chemical.

In rare cases, a female murderer is every bit as ruthless as her male counterparts. Betty Broderick exhibited extreme narcissistic traits. She had an overwhelming need to be the centre of attention. Grandiose, ambitious, barely capable of empathy or sympathy, she was a control freak of the highest order. She pitilessly gunned down her husband and his new wife. She has never accepted responsibility for the murder, continuing to say that it was her husband's own fault.

SUSAN BARBER

Susan and Michael Barber were married in 1970. She was 17 and he was 24 at the time of the wedding. Michael, a labourer, already had a baby daughter from a previous relationship. The couple lived in Westcliff-on-Sea, Essex, but there was trouble on the horizon: in 1972, Michael was accused of molesting his six-year-old niece. Still, Susan stayed by his side and the two had three children.

Michael worked as a packer at a local cigarette factory while Susan stayed at home. What Michael didn't know was that his teenage bride had been involved from day one with another teenager, **Richard Collins**, who lived in the same terrace of houses. Richard would watch out for Michael's departure for work. When it was safe to do so, Richard would sneak in to join Susan.

It is perhaps a surprise that the affair remained undiscovered for so long. But on 31 March 1981, Michael returned home early from a fishing trip to find the secret lovers in bed. He attacked them both. The local doctor who treated Susan for her injuries offered to mediate to save the marriage. Susan cooperated, but she continued to contact Richard secretly by letter.

Three months later, Michael suffered a severe headache followed the next day by stomach cramps and vomiting. Soon he could hardly breathe. On Monday 15 June, he was admitted to the intensive care ward of Southend hospital; by the Wednesday he had been emergency transferred to Hammersmith Hospital, suffering from an acute renal condition which doctors had trouble understanding. They suspected poisoning but initial test results did not support the theory.

Michael died on 27 June. It turned out that the test results had been mixed up in the lab: he had indeed been poisoned – by what turned out to be Paraquat, a powerful herbicide.

The death proved lucrative for Susan: she received a £15,000 death benefit from Michael's employer as well as an annual payment of £3300 for each of her children. Initially Richard Collins moved into the house, but he was soon replaced by another live-in lover and Susan – whose CB radio call sign was "Nympho" – started hosting sex-and-booze parties.

Nine months after her husband's death, however, Susan Barber and Richard Collins were arrested. The lab results definitively proved the poisoning. Susan was charged with murder, conspiracy to murder, and administering poison with intent to injure. Richard was charged with conspiracy to murder.

Both denied guilt at their trial at Chelmsford Crown Court, which began on 1 November 1982. Though Susan admitted lacing her husband's food with herbicide, she said she didn't intend to kill him. Instead, she claimed, she wanted to make him ill so she could leave without him following her. Both Susan and Richard were found guilty. Susan Barber was sentenced to life imprisonment. Richard Collins was given a two-year prison sentence.

For further investigation

John Emsley Molecules of Murder (2008) A scientist explains how certain toxic molecules have been abused for murderous purposes.

BETTY BRODERICK

When Elizabeth Broderick received yet another letter in a series of missives from ex-husband Dan's lawyer about taking away visitation rights with her children, it threw her over the edge. The lengthy divorce battle between the two had dragged out for eight years, with Dan using his skills as a lawyer to play the system against Betty before and after the divorce was finalized. In the end, the bitterness metamorphosed into an out-of-control, full-on war, as Betty Broderick told it. Using colourful, often crude language, she took the stand in her own defence during a melodramatic homicide trial in which two of her children testified against her.

Elizabeth Anne Bisceglia had met Daniel T. Broderick

III at a Notre Dame American football game. Betty, a pretty blonde who was just seventeen, was taken by Dan's charm and good looks. In the early years, while Dan attended Harvard Law School, Betty worked two jobs to help pay for the student loans for both law and medical degrees. They had five children, but one son died in infancy.

Once qualified, Dan landed a position at a large law firm in San Diego, and half his income went to pay off the student loans. Dan bought expensive suits, earning him the nickname of "Dapper Dan," while Betty and the kids wore second-hand clothes because money was still tight. Slowly, the Brodericks paid off their debts and got back on their feet as the money started pouring in from Dan's increasing case load. Finally, they began living the good life. The kids attended an exclusive school for the privileged and the Brodericks made the A-list for all the best parties in San Diego.

At one of those high-society parties, Betty overheard Dan talking about **Linda Kolkena**, a young office worker from his firm. "Isn't she beautiful?" he commented to a colleague. Dan later hired Linda as his assistant. Later Betty accused Dan of having an affair with Linda. He denied it, telling Betty she was crazy.

Did he recognize that Betty was indeed sinking into insanity? Her behaviour became extreme. When he finally confirmed the affair, she ripped up all Dan's expensive clothes and piled them in the garden. As her distraught children looked on, she set the pile on fire. That night Dan moved out. He continued seeing Linda and soon the two were making the society pages of the local newspapers. To her children, Betty referred to the lovers as "the bastard and the bimbo" or "Mr and Mrs. Scum". For their part, Dan and Linda called Betty "the monster" and "the beast."

Once Dan filed for divorce, Betty's retaliation – and craziness – not only continued, but escalated. When Betty drove her SUV into Dan's front door, crashing through into the entryway, San Diego police arrived to take the screaming, kicking woman to the mental ward of a local hospital where she was straightjacketed for three days. Dan succeeded in having an emergency restraining order raised against Betty. Still, Dan paid Betty $9000 a month in support until their divorce was settled.

She was undeterred. "You pounded a hole with a hammer into the wall," a judge told her in court not long afterwards. "You broke the answering machine with the hammer. On another occasion, you broke the sliding glass doors. You spray-painted the wallpaper in several rooms, including the fireplace. You broke the television." Next she broke in to Dan and Linda's house over the Christmas holiday, smashing ornaments and ripping open every gift with Linda's name on it. For this act of destruction, Betty was briefly sent to jail.

Betty, who'd fired her lawyer, didn't show up at court for the crucial divorce hearing. When Betty subsequently started leaving obscene phone messages, Dan started taping the calls as well as phone conversations with their twelve-year-old son Danny. During one call, Danny begged his mother to stop screaming at his father. His plea went on deaf ears. "I was the best mommy in the whole world and the best wife in the whole world," she told the boy. "It's not my fault your father is such a fuckhead. I cared about my family enough to put up with him fucking Linda for two years." Her son, in turn, begged his mother to stop using "bad words."

After the divorce was granted, Betty ended up

getting a cash settlement of a mere $28,000 from the multi-millionaire husband she had helped put through college.

Three months later, when Dan and Linda announced their engagement, Betty took the news extremely hard. Her frustration caused her to leave even more obscene phone messages. She also went into Dan's house, this time to steal the mailing list for the wedding. Dan hauled her into court again, and a judge ordered Betty to return the list within 24 hours. When Betty ignored the order, she was again put in jail.

The final straw for Betty, however, came when she received notice of a pending custody hearing regarding the children. On the morning of 5 November 1989, Betty grabbed a Smith & Wesson .38 pistol she had recently purchased, put it in her purse, jumped in her white Suburban van, and drove from La Jolla, California, to her husband's fashionable house in the Mission Hills neighbourhood above downtown San Diego. Betty used her daughter's house key to enter the two-storey brick home through a back door. She quietly and carefully walked up the staircase to the master bedroom.

Dan and his new wife Linda were asleep in their double bed. Linda was woken by the sound of Betty coming in and hurriedly said to her husband, "Dan, call the police." Betty, in turn, yelled, "No, you don't!" and started firing. Dan, who was shot in the back, was still able to grab the phone from the side table, but Betty yanked it from him, ripping the cord from the wall, before he had a chance to dial for help. Before she was finished, Betty had fired off five rounds from her pistol, three of which fatally injured Dan and Linda. Then she ran out of the house and drove to La Jolla Shores, where she sat on the beach. From a payphone, she called her oldest daughter, Kim, and told her about the killings. Kim later testified that, whilst shocked and scared, there was a part of her that was not surprised. Then Betty called a male friend, who drove to Dan's house and discovered the bodies, confirming what her horrified friend had hoped would be just another crazy claim made by an unstable woman. A few hours later, Betty turned herself into police.

The televised murder trial of Elizabeth Broderick ended in a hung jury, but the district attorney's office tried the case again. This time, the jury panel returned a guilty verdict on two counts of murder. Betty is currently serving a 32-year sentence at Las Colinas Women's Detention Facility just south of San Diego. She will be eligible for parole in 2010. In interviews and on her website, she continues to say she was a victim of domestic violence and abuse.

Those claims of abuse, however, were not formally reported to police until she began to fight for her freedom, and they have never been substantiated. Broderick's twelve-year-old son Danny's taped phone conversations with his mother, in which he pleaded with her to stop verbally assaulting and screaming at his father, was used in court by the prosecution.

Betty Broderick is said to be writing a book in prison, although, by American law, she cannot earn money from anything having to do with the murders. She has shown no remorse for the killings. Also still in prison, Betty runs her own website, which she uses to rant about life behind bars and provide the latest on the status of her continual appeals. On the site, she continues to blame her dead husband for her own plight.

For further investigation

Bryna Taubman Hell Hath No Fury: A True Story of Wealth and Passion, Love and Envy, and a Woman Driven to the Ultimate Revenge (2004) A book that dissects the dysfunctional relationship between Dan and Betty that ultimately ended in a double murder.

ⓦ oprah.com/tows/vintage/past/vintage_past_20010810_b A 1992 interview by Oprah.

ⓦ bettybroderick.com Betty Broderick's personal site, which is maintained by her supporters but advertised as having been dictated from prison by Broderick.

CAROL ANN HUNTER

A millionaire businesswoman from Chiswick, London, Carol Ann Hunter, 50, could not accept that Colin Love, 59, her partner of 22 years and the father of her two teenage children, had cheated on her and fallen in love with someone else. Judith Crowshaw, 51, was Colin's former college sweetheart; their relationship was rekindled through the Friends Reunited website. Judith quickly moved in with Colin to the luxurious country home Hunter owned. Hunter, a former pharmaceuticals executive and baby goods entrepreneur, earned a much higher salary than her partner. When he sought a share of the £600,000 Bedfordshire cottage, Carol Ann began plotting retribution.

By this time she had also found a new lover, 54-year-old **Anton Lee**, a financial adviser who had helped Colin with his accounts. Carol Ann hired him to kill Colin and Judith. Anton asked a friend for help in finding a hit man, but instead of helping the friend went straight to the police, who sent an undercover officer to pose as the assassin. Carol Ann then changed her mind and decided instead that she just wanted the new wife permanently maimed by being blinded or put in a wheelchair. In secret surveillance conversations in 2005, authorities captured Lee on audiotape telling the undercover cop that Carol Ann "wants to kill Judith. She doesn't want Colin killed. Just take Judith out." Carol Ann handed over £5000 to the cop (promising a further £5000 after the job was done). It was enough to have her arrested along with Anton.

Carol Ann told police she'd been under enormous strain and that Anton had misunderstood her. She explained that she was afraid during meetings with the hit man, did not want to appear weak, but had planned to cancel the attack. Still, in an email dated August 2005 and later used as evidence against her, Carol Ann wrote to Colin about Judith: "You threw

Carol Ann Hunter, who attempted to have her husband and his girlfriend assassinated.

your family out and their love away after a year of us showing how much we loved you. The self-gratifying scum, parasitic whore. Her callous, calculating actions. Her cowardice, her grasping, scheming nature. Her total lack of remorse. The gutter is too good for her, she would destroy it."

During the subsequent trial, the jury heard hate-filled emails sent from Carol Ann to Colin. One particularly scathing missive was sent to Love in March 2005. It read: "I have no trust in you, only repulsion and derision for the whore, getting a meal ticket for life, lying on her back whispering sweet words. You carry the stench of the whore whenever you come to the house and see the kids."

After just eight hours' deliberation, in December 2006 a jury at the Old Bailey unanimously convicted Carol Ann and Anton. During sentencing, Hunter was told by Judge Brian Barker that she was callous and manipulative and used her new lover as a hit man, bringing disgrace upon herself and pain and

BERTHA LEE PIPPIN

On a rainy day in November 2000, Bertha Pippin, 85, was fatally beaten with a baseball bat inside the Oklahoma home where she lived alone. Frail Bertha was utterly incapable of defending herself against her teenage attackers, one of whom was a local girl, Amanda K. Lane. Bertha paid an appalling price for taking an interest in the welfare of this troubled teen.

Bertha was a grandmother. She talked about Amanda and how she regularly called her the "old lady". Despite that, Bertha expressed high hopes that by being kind to the teen, she could reform her. Bertha empathized with Amanda, because Bertha had gone through a lot when she was young too. She understood. Her mother had died giving birth to Bertha. Her sharecropper father told her she wasn't wanted. He shipped her off to her grandparents, simple farmers who had little money.

A few years later, Bertha went to live with an uncle she had never met. She attended a small Protestant church and met her future husband, the son of a Baptist preacher. They married and had four children. They lived a quiet life, while her husband made a meagre living. Bertha felt Amanda deserved a chance, but she didn't like the boys Amanda hung out with. She thought they were a bad influence, especially after Bertha learned that they had abused a pitbull that lived across the street. But Bertha insisted that her son Jerry not report the abuse to authorities. Bertha was afraid the boys would find out and retaliate against her. She had a good sense about people, and it turned out her feeling about the boys being trouble was right.

Bertha was comfortable living alone, especially as only a narrow alleyway separated her from her daughter Beverly Robertson's home. Bertha got involved in her neighbourhood. Between 9 and 10am on 3 November, Amanda and two of her friends – Gary Rightsell and Travis Phillips – carried a baseball bat to Bertha's house.

Amanda knocked on the door, telling Bertha she was locked out of her house and needed to use a phone. While Amanda pretended to call someone on the phone, Bertha went into the kitchen to get a

anguish to those who loved her: "You have the ability to control and get everything you want. You are a woman who can present two entirely different faces. You are capable of manipulation and callousness of the highest order."

To Anton, the judge said: "You had taken leave of your senses." He sentenced Carol Ann to eight years in prison for plotting to maim Judith, and Anton was sent to prison for four years for soliciting the hit.

For further investigation

Ⓦ news.bbc.co.uk/2/hi/uk_news/england/london/6201757.stm
The BBC's coverage of the guilty verdicts.

Ⓦ telegraph.co.uk/news/uknews/1536853/Emails-sent-by-Carol-Ann-Hunter-to-her-former-partner.html Graphic emails from Ann Hunter to Colin Love.

Ⓦ telegraph.co.uk/news/uknews/1536854/High-flier-hired-hit man-to-kill-her-former-lover-and-his-new-wife,-court-told. html An article in The Daily Telegraph that gives background information on the case.

glass of water for one of the boys. As Bertha was walking back to her living room, Gary hit her over the head with the bat. Bertha reeled and landed on the sofa. They asked her for money, and she told them to hang on, because her head hurt, and that she would get it for them and she wouldn't tell anyone. That's when Gary began hitting her repeatedly. Then the other teen took the bat and continued. Amanda later testified that she was ordered to hit Bertha too, otherwise the pair would kill Amanda's three-year-old daughter. So Amanda too took her turn. Bertha's body was discovered after Beverly sounded the alarm and called her husband and her brother, Jerry Pippin. There was blood everywhere. In Bertha's wallet, untouched, was $300 in cash.

One of the teens, Gary Rightsell, who weighed 200 pounds, admitted to helping kill Bertha using a baseball bat. He pleaded guilty in Muskogee District Court to two counts of accessory after the fact. Rightsell cooperated with the prosecution, as part of a plea bargain, and helped in the arrest of Amanda Lane. She was convicted of first-degree murder and robbery by force or fear. She is incarcerated at the Mabel Bassett Correctional Center in McLoud, Oklahoma, where is she serving out her life sentence.

Two months later, Judge James E. Edmondson sentenced Rightsell to thirty years in prison on both counts, ten of which were suspended. Rightsell could have received forty-five years of hard time in a maximum-security prison, but because of his cooperation, ten years from his sentence were suspended. He is serving time at the Howard McLeod Correctional Center in Atoka, Oklahoma. According to the prison's website, Gary's current release date is June 2016.

Travis Phillips, owner of the baseball bat used to bludgeon Bertha, received a year's probation after pleading guilty to a charge of obstructing a police officer in the course of the investigation. Today, Travis is a free man. A subpoena to testify was about to be served on the fourth suspect, Randy Hughart, when he was killed in 2001 during a street fight with a drug dealer. Hughart died from blunt trauma to his head, the same fate suffered by Bertha Pippin.

LINDA STEIN: "REALTOR TO THE STARS"

Two worlds collided when a quiet 26-year-old Afro-American woman named **Natavia Lowery**, went to work for powerful, outspoken 62-year-old **Linda Stein**, a white property broker to the rich and famous.

For years, the New York City media referred to Linda as the "realtor to the stars". Despite her toughness, people were drawn to her. Stein, a self-made woman who swore like a sailor and smoked pot like a hippie, could command a room equally with her wit and razor-sharp sarcasm. She had jumped head first into the music industry in the 1970s when she had co-managed the legendary punk band The Ramones. She had turned herself into a successful, fiercely independent businesswoman with big-name clients.

Natavia's working class upbringing was in stark contrast to Linda's upper-class life. She was an only child, the daughter of a housekeeper and maintenance man, and had been raised in the Grant projects on Amsterdam Avenue in Harlem. After her father's death, her mother eventually remarried and the family moved to Brooklyn. Natavia excelled both academically and in competitive sports. In high school, she was a star runner on the girl's track team. Upon her graduation from high school, she enrolled at North Carolina State University, where she was a member of the modelling troupe Black Finesse. She dropped out after just one semester to finish a business degree at Hunter College in Manhattan. Natavia's classmates remember her as being soft-spoken, but also sticking up for herself when she needed to.

The morning of 30 October 2007 started out like any other. Natavia Lowery showed up for work at her boss's Fifth Avenue penthouse on Manhattan's Upper East Side. Linda was in her bedroom doing yoga exercises while Natavia printed emails from Linda's personal computer. But as the day progressed, something went terribly wrong. By that night, Linda was dead and the police and paramedics were investigating the crime scene inside her spotless apartment, preparing to move her body to the morgue. Six days later, Linda was buried. Four days after that, Natavia was under arrest, charged with the murder of her boss. The case generated intense tabloid publicity and gossip.

According to a confession made by Natavia and released by the Manhattan district attorney's office, but which Lowery's lawyers are now challenging, Linda had walked to the desk in her living room, where Natavia was working on her emails, and asked what was taking so long. Linda started blowing marijuana smoke in Natavia's face and berating her at the same time.

"Get the fucking emails! How can you be so fucking slow?" Linda reportedly hollered. If that's what actually happened that midday, perhaps Stein's anger was born out of frustration: she could no longer open her own messages because her right hand and arm were numb from the after-effects of chemotherapy she'd had to fight breast cancer. Linda apparently smoked marijuana to ease the lingering pain. In addition, she was on prescription medication that caused mood swings. Verbally, Linda was a fighter; physically, she wasn't in shape to defend herself against physical attack.

Whatever it was that sparked the tirade that day, according to Natavia Lowery's reported account to police, Linda then waved a walking stick at Lowery as she continued berating her assistant. Then, at about

12.30pm, Linda returned and offered, as a way of making peace, to buy Natavia lunch.

"I've got my own money in a savings account. I don't need you to buy me lunch," said an indignant Natavia, who repeated the alleged conversation to detectives.

"Black people don't have any money," Linda purportedly responded. "C'mon, save your money. I'll buy you lunch."

Linda, petite at five-feet tall, with a reefer in one hand and her cane in the other, stood in front of Natavia, waiting for a response. Natavia apparently told Linda she was allergic to smoke, but Linda ignored her. That's when Natavia told police she snapped. Linda's body was found to have three crushed vertebrae and a fractured skull in five places. Police afterwards said the murder appeared to be an act of passion and not premeditated.

Published reports claimed that, following her crime Natavia went into the bathroom of the three-room home and cleaned herself up. She then pulled Linda's cashpoint card from her wallet. Natavia dialled her boss's yoga instructor to cancel Linda's training session, saying that Linda had a business engagement. After Natavia left the apartment, one of her first stops was a neighbourhood ATM machine. Using Linda's PIN, she withdrew $800. The transaction was captured on the bank's surveillance camera.

On 2 November, three days after her death, Linda's funeral drew a standing-room only gathering to Manhattan's Riverside Memorial Chapel. Attending the service were some of Stein's celebrity friends, including pop star Sting's wife, **Trudi Styler**, famed record producer **Clive Davis**, film director **Brett Ratner**, comedienne **Whoopi Goldberg**, bandleader **Paul Shaffer**, and rock'n'roll photographer **Bob Gruen**.

Natavia stood at the back of the chapel, crying.

Seven days later, Lowery was arrested after a twelve-hour interrogation that had ended in written and videotaped confessions. In the indictment against her, prosecutors contended that Lowery killed Stein and then stole money from her. The problem was that, as one of Lowery's duties as Stein's assistant was to withdraw cash for her boss, the defence could contend that Lowery was merely getting money from the account for her boss like she had many times before.

Police Commissioner **Ray Kelly** held a news conference following Natavia's arrest on 9 November 2007. Apparently, the personal assistant had said in her confession that she had snatched the walking stick from her boss and smashed Linda's head and neck half a dozen times. But Natavia's lawyer accused the detectives who had interrogated his client for more than twelve hours of coercing a confession. Lowery's family have defended her innocence, questioning the prosecution's heavy reliance on what they see as a forced confession, now retracted in its entirety.

Natavia was remanded in custody. But in March 2008, her lawyer, **Ron Kuby**, argued in a bail hearing that male DNA which had been found at the murder scene weakened the prosecution case. In front of more than 150 supporters from Natavia's church, Manhattan assistant district attorney Joan Illuzi-Orbon tried to rebut Kuby's argument, stating that all the DNA proved is that "a man may have touched Linda Stein's sink" at some time during her residence in the apartment. In November 2008 investigators then argued that the DNA had found itself on the sink because a cop had washed his hands at the scene, leaving behind a microscopic drop of blood.

The Linda Stein murder case is scheduled to play out in a New York courtroom later in 2009. Lowery will face charges of grand larceny and murder.

For further investigation

Steven Gaines Sky's the Limit: Passion and Property in Manhattan (2005) The book includes a chapter devoted to Linda Stein, her background, and her knack for selling million-dollar apartments in Manhattan to celebrities.

Monte A. Melnick & Frank Meyer On the Road with the Ramones (2007) This memoir is an inside view of the life and times of a roadie and Linda Stein's role as co-manager of the band.

abcnews.go.com/US/story?id=3845376&page=1 An account on ABCNews.com of the second-degree murder charge against Natavia Lowery.

www.nydailynews.com/topics/Natavia+Lowery Collection of New York Daily News stories about the case.

www.nytimes.com/2007/11/03/nyregion/03stein.html?ex =1351742400&en=644f78cda3eecd23&ei=5088&partner =rssnyt&emc=rss A lengthy article in the New York Times recounting Linda Stein's funeral.

DONNA YAKLICH

Dennis Yaklich was a narcotics detective in Pueblo, Colorado, with four children from a previous marriage, when he married again, to Donna (31 at the time). Donna gave birth to a son and the family lived a seemingly normal, comfortable life on a farm. But the appearances were deceptive. Dennis, six-foot-five-inches tall and weighing 280 pounds, was an obsessive weightlifter. He regularly took large doses of a steroid – the same kind speculated to have caused welterweight wrestling performer **Chris Benoit** in

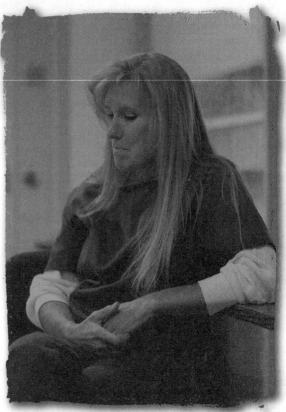

Donna Yaklich, whose conviction and sentence has proven controversial.

2007 to fly into a "roid rage" and kill his wife and young son. The drugs not only bulked up Dennis's muscles, but they also made him dangerously aggressive and verbally abusive toward his family. Afraid for herself and her children, Donna tried to leave, but Dennis refused to let her go. After futile attempts at escape, Donna took matters into her own hands.

On a December evening in 1985, Donna had Dennis killed. The hit was carried out by brothers Charles and Eddie Greenwell, armed with 12-gauge shotguns, who ambushed Dennis Yaklich in his own driveway. It looked like an execution and police did not initially suspect Donna. Investigators assumed that some crook with a grudge against the cop was responsible, but they had few leads. But a tip-off brought them to the young killers, who in turn pointed the finger at Donna. At the subsequent trial Charles Greenwell, who was sixteen at the time of the murder, was convicted and given a twenty-year term in prison. Eddie, nine years older than his brother, received a thirty-year sentence. He testified that Donna had promised him $45,000 payment from a $450,000 life insurance policy in exchange for killing her husband. But he was paid just $5000. In 2004, Charles was released from prison.

For her part, Donna, through her lawyers, argued that she was a battered wife and the murder was a last resort to end the physical abuse. But the self-defence claim was problematic because Donna had gone to the trouble of hiring others to carry out the killing. Consequently the prosecution threw the book at her, charging her with first-degree murder.

A first trial ended in a hung jury. After the second trial in 1988, while she was acquitted of first-degree murder, the jury convicted her on a conspiracy charge. The court found that her situation lacked the "imminence" of violence necessary for a self-defence claim. She was sentenced to forty years in prison with the possibility of parole. Some US states have allowed self-defence claims based on battered woman syndrome even if the husband was sleeping at the time of his killing. But no US state has yet to allow the self-defence claim where the battered wife hired contract killers. After Yaklich's conviction, she apologized for the crime.

Later the story took a completely unexpected turn. Donna claimed that, during her volatile marriage to Dennis, he often warned her to be careful, otherwise she'd end up like his first wife, Barbara, who died on Valentine's Day, 1977. He told Donna he could make it look like an accident. For 28 years the death of Barbara was officially considered accidental, caused by an overdose of prescription diet pills. But Barbara also had injuries from what her husband told police were "energetic" attempts on his part to revive his wife. After a Denver TV station hired two pathologists to review the autopsy reports in 2005, a new task force was formed and the case reopened. On 22 September 2005, an inquest began into the 1977 Valentine's Day death of Barbara. Pueblo County sheriff **Dan Corsentino** held a news conference announcing the task force's appointment. As a result, the death of Barbara was ruled "suspicious", with the cause of death listed as blunt force trauma to the abdomen. The case remains open and unsolved.

In 1994, Donna's story was turned into a made-for-TV movie titled *Cries Unheard: The Donna Yaklich Story,* starring Jaclyn Smith, known for her role in the 1970s TV series *Charlie's Angels*. Donna Yaklich was denied parole in 2003. But in October 2005, at the age of fifty, having served eighteen years of the forty-year sentence inside the walls of the high-security Colorado Women's Correctional Facility in Canon City, she was released to a nearby halfway house. In due course she relocated to the Denver metropolitan area. She is technically considered still incarcerated and wears a house-arrest electronic bracelet.

For further investigation

📖Angela Browne When Battered Women Kill (1989) The author takes a scholarly look at more than forty cases and what drove the women involved to kill their partners.

KIMBERLEY KONDEJEWSKI

On 15 May 1997, lying in wait for her husband John to return home from a rifle club meeting, **Kimberley Kondejewski** fatally shot him three times. Seventeen years earlier, the abuse began almost as soon as she married her childhood sweetheart. After the wedding, Kondejewski saw a completely different side to her husband, one she'd never seen before. John became controlling and seriously abusive. Still, she stayed with him. They had two children and settled down in Brandon, a city in southwestern Manitoba, Canada. But she faced her life with John a day at a time.

Kondejewski wasn't a violent woman, but she later claimed her husband gave her no choice. She testified that he was going to kill her. On that fateful day in May 1997, John went too far, she said, giving her an ultimatum that forced her to act in self-defence. Commit suicide before he returned from work that evening, he said, so he could collect on her life-insurance policy and become a rich man. "Do as I say", he told her, "or you will be dead and so will the kids."

His words sent the quiet housewife into a frenzy. To protect the children, Kim decided she'd have the final word this time, instead of her husband deciding. It was final, she told herself: John would die instead of her. After shooting John, she turned the gun on herself, but she recovered from her injuries.

Kimberley was arrested and charged with first-degree murder. Afterwards, a case study by the Canadian Association of Elizabeth Fry Societies (CAEFS) argued that Kimberley should not have been charged in the first place, let alone with first-degree murder, in light of the evidence of threats. At the most, CAEFS said, she should have been charged with manslaughter.

During her trial, she took the stand in her own defence, telling the jury her compelling story about her seventeen years of abuse at the hands of her husband. Her lawyer told the court that Kimberley suffered from battered wife syndrome and had no choice but to kill him. Kondejewski's lawyer declared that men cannot abuse women without suffering the consequences. The jury agreed. She faced a mandatory minimum life-in-prison sentence, if convicted. But moved by Kondejewski's blow-by-blow account of the lengthy abuse she underwent, the jury found her not guilty.

In 1998, after the verdict, Kimberley Kondejewski was released from custody. Today, she works as a library clerk at a community college in Canada.

For further investigation

🌐 inthesetimes.com/article/2422/bad_girls An article by Ilja J.A. Talvi about the Kondejewski case and similar ones.

🌐 elizabethfry.ca/Response/21.htm Both a case study of two murder cases, including Kimberley Kondejewski's, and am investigation into the reasons battered women should not be charged, under Canadian law, with first-degree murder.

Murder and the media

In the 1990s, the courtroom cameras that are allowed in many US trials combined with the phenomenon of rolling news broadcasts to make certain murder cases compulsive viewing for many people – almost like a soap opera, a form of constantly updated entertainment that dealt in life-and-death drama and spotlighted social issues that divided a nation. Court TV (now renamed TruTV and a subsidiary of Time Warner), launched in 1991, alternated live courtroom coverage with pundit analysis. Two murder trials above all became associated with this new kind of TV excitement. First was the trial of Erik and Lyle Menendez, indicted on 8 December 1992 for the shotgun murders of their parents. Then came the trial of O.J. Simpson, charged with killing his ex-wife and her friend, which began on 25 January 1995. Never before had murder trials received such high-profile coverage, allowing millions of people to argue about every detail and to take sides.

THE TRIAL(S) OF O.J. SIMPSON

Orenthal James Simpson was born in San Francisco in 1947 and was once best known for his feats on the American football field, earning a Heisman Trophy for his athletic achievements as a tailback for the University of Southern California. *The New York Times* said of him that he was "adored by college and professional football fans for the dazzling displays of speed, power and finesse that made him impossible to catch and even harder to bring down". In 1969, he began a stellar ten-year career in the National Football League, playing first for the Buffalo Bills and then for the San Francisco 49ers. Known as "The Juice", O.J. was the first running back in the league's history to gain two thousand yards in a single season (1973). He was a legend in the sport and, after he left it, an entertainment star. He was a TV football commentator, a frequent endorser of products and a successful actor, perhaps best known for comic turns in the *Naked Gun* trilogy of cop-show spoofs.

But in 1994, everything changed. Once again he was known for being hard to catch – only this time it wasn't a football game. Accused of murder, O.J. was supposed to turn himself in to Los Angeles police on 17 June 1994. He didn't show. An Orange County patrol car spotted his car driving south on Interstate 405. A TV news helicopter was called to cover the low-speed chase. All afternoon and into the evening, the car's progress was followed by TV audiences. NBC interrupted basketball coverage to broadcast the pursuit. By the time he pulled up at his home, twenty news helicopters were recording events as they unfolded. O.J. was soon in custody. He would go on trial accused of stabbing to death **Nicole Brown Simpson** (from whom he had divorced in 1992) and **Ronald Goldman**. The pair were found on the evening of 12 June 1994. Nicole had been brutally hacked and was almost decapitated. Ron was found with a series of wounds that police later agreed showed that his killer had taunted him before ending his life.

In what has been called the "Trial of the Century", the case against O.J. Simpson played out in front of millions in their living rooms on their TVs. The trial mesmerized viewers. Among other things, the public would learn that defence lawyers for ordinary citizens are quite different from those for the rich and famous. But this was a trial which divided the nation in many ways – and particularly in terms of race. As the trial continued, it became clear that while white Americans often believed O.J. to be guilty, black Americans thought him innocent. The case, the state of California versus Orenthal James Simpson, cost more than $20 million to try in Clark County District Court in downtown Las Vegas.

A COURTROOM RAMPAGE: BRIAN NICHOLS

Murder often hits the headlines when the scene of death is gruesome and shocking; when motivation suggests sexual perversity or a twisted family saga; or when a killing remains unsolved and mysterious. But in other cases, what catches media and public attention is a sudden eruption of violence in a usually safe environment. Sometimes the crime even takes place in a courtroom, as happened on 11 March 2005 at the Fulton County Courthouse in Atlanta, Georgia.

Brian Nichols, 33, was being retried on charges of rape. His original trial had ended in a hung jury. To get ready for court, Nichols changed from jailhouse scrubs into street clothes, then as Sheriff's Deputy Cynthia Hall accompanied him down a hallway toward the courtroom, Nichols, a 210-pound former college American football player skilled in martial arts, overpowered the deputy, stole her gun and fired it, grazing her head with a bullet. Nichols then entered the courtroom and shot and killed Judge Rowland W. Barnes. He shot court stenographer Julie Ann Brandau in the head at close range, ran out of the courtroom, and escaped down a stairwell to a door leading outside. Once on the pavement, Nichols fatally shot Sergeant Hoyt Teasley, who had followed Nichols outside. Nichols ran to a parking garage and stole a Honda from an *Atlanta Journal-Constitution* reporter.

Nichols became the object of a massive manhunt that covered Georgia, Alabama, Tennessee, and the Carolinas. Schools in the greater Atlanta area were on lockdown. During his first few hours of freedom, Nichols carjacked as many as five cars and murdered US Customs agent David Wilhelm, taking the off-duty agent's pick-up, badge and gun. Finally, Nichols held his ex-girlfriend hostage for seven hours in her apartment in the suburb of Duluth until she persuaded Nichols to surrender to the authorities. The woman called 911, officers and agents surrounded the apartment, and Nichols walked out of the apartment waving a white T-shirt to surrender. Twenty-six hours after the first shootings, Nichols was in custody again.

Paul L. Howard, Jr, the district attorney of Fulton County, announced that he would seek the death penalty against Nichols. Besides murder and attempted murder, he also faced charges pf sodomy, possession of a machine gun, possession of a handgun, and possession of a large quantity of marijuana from the earlier case. In all, 54 charges

The investigation of O.J. Simpson began just after midnight on 13 June 1994, when Nicole's howling Akita dog was pacing in front of her townhouse at 875 South Bundy Drive in the affluent Brentwood suburb of West Los Angeles. When neighbour Steven Schwab went outside to retrieve his mail from his box, the dog followed him home. He took her inside. Only then did Schwab notice that the dog's feet and belly were soaked in blood. He walked her back outside, and the distressed dog dragged him to Nicole's gate. When Schwab peered into the courtyard, he saw the bloody scene and the lifeless bodies of Nicole and Ron.

were filed against Nichols, who pleaded not guilty.

The murder case appeared to be open and shut, because the first two murders – of the judge and the court stenographer – occurred in front of several witnesses, plus Nichols confessed to all four of the killings in statements to police. But nearly three years later the case stalled and was caught up in a bitter dispute over funding.

After his lawyers were paid a collective $1.4 million from the state of Georgia, the state agency responsible for indigent defence ran out of money, and other cases were at risk of being delayed too. Jury selection, which began a year earlier, was not yet complete when the funds dried up. Then, after the presiding judge, Hilton Fuller, was quoted in *The New Yorker* magazine saying about the defendant, "everyone in the world knows he did it", he removed himself from the case and another judge was appointed.

In a letter that was made public giving the reasons for his voluntary recusal from the case, Judge Fuller wrote: "In light of recent media reports, I am no longer hopeful that I can provide a trial perceived to be fair to both the state and the accused." It was difficult to find a judge to preside over the case who didn't know the victims. The trial was in limbo. Then, causing further complications, the prosecution asked that the new judge, James Bodiford, be removed from the bench because he reportedly was friends with the murdered Judge Barnes. At a hearing to consider the motion, Judge Bodiford admitted he was shocked and saddened by the killings but that his feelings wouldn't interfere with his ability to remain impartial as the presiding judge over the trial.

The Nichols case was extremely costly. According to Stephen B. Bright, the senior counsel for the Southern Center for Human Rights in Atlanta, "We are just now starting to see the ripple effect of Nichols. The question now is whether the whole thing is going to come crashing down."

The case didn't fall apart. In the end, the legislature came through and provided further funds. Three and a half years after the slayings, Nichols' trial began in the Atlanta Municipal Court on 22 September 2008. His defence was an imaginative one: Nichols was delusional, his lawyers asserted, and believed himself to be a superhero leading an uprising. Comparing himself to Nat Turner, Nelson Mandela and Malcolm X, Nichols had told police: "I felt that possibly I could use talents to do something noble, and I thought a slave rebellion was noble." However the jury was unpersuaded by the claim of delusion and, having deliberated for twelve hours, on 7 November 2008 found Nichols guilty of all charges.

O.J. Simpson appears in court, trying on the infamous pair of gloves.

And while investigators almost immediately honed in on O.J., he was nowhere to be found. In fact, he was on a flight to Chicago to deliver a speech there. O.J.'s activities that night show that he had roughly an hour, from the time he and his live-in maintenance worker, Kato Katlin, arrived home from dinner to when a limo driver picked up O.J. just before 11.00pm that night. The timeline showed that O.J. was unaccounted for between 9.36pm and 10.54pm The prosecution argued that O.J. left a trail of evidence from the murder scene to his home.

The prosecution case received a blow early on. Two potentially important witnesses gave interviews to the tabloid press. Their stories were not good for O.J. Jill Shively claimed she had seen his car racing away from Nicole's house, while knife salesman Jose Camachio said he had sold O.J. a large knife less than a month before Nicole was hacked to death. These claims might have been important to the case against O.J., but because the stories had been sold, these witnesses were never called to give evidence in court.

Instead Los Angeles County prosecutor Christopher Darden painted a picture of O.J. as a wife-batterer. He played to the court a recording of an emergency call Nicole had made on New Year's Day 1989. In the background, O.J. could be heard shouting at his wife while she spoke of her fear that she was in danger. Having indicated a violent background, the prosecution mostly relied on forensic evidence, interpreted by expert witnesses. DNA tests were minutely scrutinized. Shoeprints were measured and analysed. The amount of evidence was significant. It was argued that blood found at the scene was likely to be O.J.'s – the odds of it having come from anybody else being one in 170 million. Blood on one of O.J.'s socks almost certainly belonged to Nicole. O.J.'s hair was found on Ron's shirt. A left-hand glove was found at the scene: blood on it was a mixture of O.J.'s, Nicole's and Ron's. O.J. testified that he did not own gloves of this kind, but photographs emerged showing him wearing a pair.

O.J.'s multimillion-dollar lawyers were called the "dream team" in the media. They shone a bright spotlight on the police investigation. They claimed that evidence had been planted by cops, that DNA evidence had been contaminated. O.J.'s lawyers zeroed in on one officer, Mark Fuhrman, accusing him of being a racist. He denied the accusation, but was later confronted with a writer's research tapes on which he could be heard repeatedly making racial slurs against black people. The defence successfully undermined Fuhrman's credibility as a witness. During the trial, he pleaded the Fifth Amendment to avoid further questioning about his use of racist epithets. He was later charged with perjury.

Critical evidence – drops of blood on Nicole's back – was not lifted by crime scene analysts or by the coroner. According to forensic pathologist Dr **Michael Baden**, who investigated the case for the defence, the blood splatter left by someone whose blood dripped on Nicole's back as her body lay on the ground could have either ruled in or ruled out O.J. as the murderer. In addition, the result of hair analysis found on the glove which was left at the scene was not introduced during the criminal trial. The results of testing pointed to the hair being similar to that of O.J. – a crucial omission that could have changed the outcome of the case. The glove, however, was admitted into evidence and became a dramatic centrepiece to the case, after the prosecution asked for permission for O.J. to try on the glove. The judge allowed it. So, while wearing a latex glove, O.J. attempted to put his hand into the wrinkled leather glove. But his hand did not fit. The ploy backfired on the prosecution when O.J. was only able to put his hand about three quarters of the way in. Defence lawyer Johnnie Cochran Jr. uttered the now-famous line, "If it doesn't fit, you must acquit", in an attempt to equate the prosecution's failed glove experiment with other evidence used against O.J.

O.J. Simpson was acquitted of both murder charges on Tuesday 3 October 1995. He sighed in relief, while team member **Johnnie Cochran** pumped his fist in the air and slapped him on the back. The Dream Team lawyers afterwards gathered in a victory huddle. From the court gallery Ron's sister, Kim Goldman, was heard crying. Ron's mother, Patti Goldman, exclaimed "Oh my God. Oh my God." It was estimated that 150 million watched on TV as the verdict was delivered. Interviewed afterwards, a few jurors said that they believed O.J. probably did murder Nicole and Ron, but that the prosecution case had been bungled.

It didn't end there. In 1997, the families of the victims sued the fallen football star in civil court. In this new trial, the arguments went in a different way, partly because the court ruled that allegations of racism were inflammatory and speculative. Certain evidence introduced during the civil trial had not been seen during the first trial – notably photographs of O.J. wearing shoes similar to the ones whose impressions were identified at the scene of the killings. Whereas O.J. hadn't taken the stand at his first trial, during this one he did, but without greatly swaying jurors in his favour. On this occasion, O.J. was found guilty by a jury that was predominantly white (whereas in the first trial most of the jury were black) and required only to deliver a majority verdict. The families of Nicole and Ron were awarded punitive damages of $33.5 million. The families, however, have not been able to get the damages from O.J. His $22,000-a-month NFL pension is protected by California law. Furthermore, by subsequently relocating to Miami, he was able to buy a residence that was protected by Florida law from being seized for the purposes of collecting a debt.

O.J. has continued to stay in the headlines ever since. In 2006, the **HarperCollins** publishing house announced the publication of a book, *If I Did It*, scheduled for release the next day, in which O.J. recounted how he hypothetically would have committed the murders. Publisher Judith Regan told the Associated Press: "This is an historic case, and I consider this his confession."

O.J., for his part, in an interview with Fox News promoting his book, said: "I don't think any two people could be murdered without everybody being covered in blood." The book was the lead story on TV and headlined in newspapers. In response to public outrage that O.J. stood to profit from the crimes, HarperCollins cancelled the book. The company later fired Judith Regan and News Corp., the parent company of HarperCollins eventually settled a breach of contract lawsuit brought by its former employee in 2008. In the meantime, the Goldman family quickly went to work, through the courts, trying to gain ownership of the book; they won, and the book was released by a different publisher in September 2007. When the book was released, it quickly soared to number one in sales on Amazon.com.

Then, in 2007, cane a bizarre twist in O.J.'s strange life. He was accused of leading an armed posse into a hotel room at the Palace Station hotel-casino in Las Vegas, to steal sports memorabilia related to his football career – including a photograph of him with the late FBI director **J. Edgar Hoover**. Once the story hit the media, O.J. called into CNN to give his side of the story. He explained that he had been tipped off that some of his personal items – memorabilia he hadn't seen in years – were for sale at the hotel. Among the items, he told CNN's Ted Rowlands, were photographs of his family, including of himself as a child, and photos and negatives taken by his ex-wife, Nicole. The photos were removed years earlier from O.J.'s trophy room and his mother's storage locker, he told the reporter. O.J. also said no guns were involved and that it wasn't a robbery. "I just wanted to get my stuff back", he told Rowlands. "What would you have done? I'm O.J. Simpson. Who am I going to rob?" It was vintage O.J. – his standard non-denial denial. Just as he'd said after Nicole was killed – "I wouldn't have killed her" – this time he said, "I wouldn't have robbed anybody."

A few days later, O.J. was arrested and charged with felony kidnapping, burglary, armed robbery, coercion, and assault with a deadly weapon. Bail was set at $125,000. O.J. was warned that a condition of bail was that he have no contact at all with any of his co-defendants. On 29 November 2007, he pleaded not guilty. At the beginning of 2008, O.J. was arrested in Florida and taken to Nevada accused of violating the no-contact order. Bail was consequently raised to $250,000. O.J.'s second lawyer, Yale Galanter, said outside the courthouse that his client had not committed a crime and was trying to reclaim family heirlooms. He also slammed the motives of others concerned in the trial. "I have never been in a case where every witness had a financial motive, where every witness had a credibility problem", Galanter said. The Palace Station hotel meeting had been arranged by Thomas Riccio, a memorabilia dealer who made a secret recording of O.J.'s hold-up. In the recording, which was played during the trial that started on 8 September 2008, O.J. could be heard shouting out, "Nobody leaves the room!" Riccio sold the recording to the media. He was paid more than $200,000.

The trial was presided over by Judge Jackie Glass, who on occasion spoke severely to O.J., berating him for "ignorance and arrogance". On 3 October, O.J. was found guilty of all charges. Associated Press reported that after conviction, he was held in solitary confinement in a seven-by-fourteen-foot jail cell, communicating with visitors using only a live closed-circuit video hook-up. His friend Tom Scotto said: "he sounds good. He is upbeat. He's looking forward to the sentencing so he can get on with the appeal." In December 2008, Simpson was sentenced – a possible maximum of 33 years at one end of the spectrum or a minimum of 9 years at the other – and Simpson is currently serving it at Lovelock Correctional Center in Nevada.

For further investigation

Jeffrey Toobin The Run of His Life: The People versus O.J. Simpson (1997) a comprehensive look at the criminal trial and behind the scenes machinations with the lawyers.

Mark Fuhrman Murder In Brentwood (1997) Written by one of the highest-profile detectives involved in the O.J. Simpson case.

The Goldman Family If I Did It: Confessions of the Killer (2007) The infamous and controversial so-called confession by O.J. Simpson.

abcnews.go.com/US/wireStory?id=3609365 An in-depth piece, posted on ABCnews.com, by Associated Press writer Ryan Nakashima about the alleged robbery case involving O.J. Simpson.

topics.nytimes.com/top/reference/timestopics/people/s/o_j_simpson/index.html Large archive of stories in *The New York Times* about O.J. Simpson, going back to 1983.

Offspring who kill

SEF GONZALEZ

At 11.45pm on 10 July 2001, a distraught **Sef Gonzalez** called emergency services to say that his sister **Clodine**, father **Teddy** and mother **Mary Loiva** had been murdered at their family home in North Ryde, Sydney. Police found that the three had been brutally beaten and stabbed with kitchen knives between around 4pm and 6pm that afternoon: eighteen-year-old Clodine, home from Melbourne for the school holidays, in her upstairs bedroom; Gonzalez's parents inside the front door as they had returned home separately from their work at Teddy's legal practice. Racist graffiti had been spray-painted on the living room wall – "Fuck off Asians KKK". But soon afterwards, police began to suspect twenty-year-old Sef Gonzalez himself.

He was born in 1980 at Baguio, 250 kilometres north of the Philippines' capital, Manila. His father owned a hotel there, which collapsed during an earthquake when Sef was ten – his dad had in fact rescued him from the rubble. The family subsequently moved to Australia, where his father set up a practice as an immigration lawyer. Gonzalez's parents were loving but strict, pushing him to succeed academically; they wanted him to become a doctor or join the family business. Sef did fairly badly at school, though he managed to get into Macquarie University. There he continued to struggle academically, and he skipped lectures and faked his exam results. His parents were planning to cut his allowance and take his car from him. Gonzalez's mother also disapproved of his girlfriend - four days before the murders, she had threatened to turn him out of the family home if he continued to see her.

In the aftermath of the killings Gonzalez appeared distraught and elicited a great deal of public sympathy. He sang a version of Mariah Carey's anthem "One Sweet Day" at his family's funeral and appealed to

SCIENCE AND UNSOLVED CRIMES

With the advent of ever-improving DNA testing and other forensics technology, many cold cases are being re-opened and prosecuted. One string of cold-case rapes was solved in June 2008 in Wooster, Ohio, when an prison inmate's DNA sample was taken. Jeffrey Humrichouser's sample was put into a national database and it came back matching forensics' evidence left at scenes of sexual assaults spanning eleven years, from 1996 to 2007. Humrichouser was serving a two-year prison sentence for an unrelated crime.

Police departments have opened entire units devoted to cold cases: their job is to re-examine unsolved old files using modern techniques. The re-opening of cases is not just a question of new developments in technology: witnesses come forward with new information, new suspects that were previously overlooked resurface, and alibi witnesses might affirm or recant their original stories.

A well-known cold case is the one of Judge Joseph Crater, who stepped into a cab in 1930 and subsequently became the "missingest man in New York." In April 2005, police revealed that they had found some evidence in the 1950s which was related to the case. It was a handwritten note from Crater's wife, inside an envelope that read "Do not open until my death". The note claimed to give the location of Crater's body. Human remains were found at the location, but because of the lack of technology such as genetic fingerprinting, police were unable to confirm the identity of the remains.

Some cases, however, defy any kind of resolution. One such cold case is the unofficially unsolved murder of Hollywood silent-film director and actor William Desmond Taylor, who was found murdered

the public for help in solving the crime. Yet within three days he was busy pestering his father's accountant about his A$1.5 million inheritance. He sold his parents' cars and his mother's watch, moved into a large apartment and put a deposit down on a Porsche – later changing it in favour of a Lexus SC430. He also faked death certificates to send to his extended family in the Philippines, hoping to speed up the processing of his parents' wills.

Over the next few months, Gonzalez's stories of where he'd been at the time of the killings began to unravel. Initially he had described leaving his part-time job at his father's legal practice at 4.30pm, driving around looking for a friend's house and then going clubbing at 8pm. However, a witness described having seen his distinctive green Ford Festiva with personalized number plates in the driveway of the family home at 4.15pm. He admitted the story was "a lot of lies" and claimed that he had actually parked his car at home and then caught a taxi to visit a prostitute that afternoon. When this was again disproved by cab records, he threw up a smokescreen, claiming to have received emails proving that a prominent Philippine businessman was behind the killings. It was all desperately thin. On 13 June 2002, the New South Wales police team "Strike Force Tawas" arrested Gonzalez,

in his home in 1922. In spite of several suspects and even a 1964 deathbed confession by actress Margaret Gibson, it is still considered an unsolved crime, because of a combination of poor crime-scene management and the disappearance of some of the physical evidence.

Unsolved cases of rape and murder against women – all believed to have been at the hands of one man – are still unsolved in four California coastal communities. Police are closer, however, to identifying the unknown serial killer because of new DNA evidence linking ten cases to a man dubbed the East Area Rapist. The crimes, committed between 1979 and 1986 in northern and southern California, spanned three counties and four law-enforcement jurisdictions. New DNA evidence in 2001 linked six murders to four other cases.

As suddenly as the murders had begun, they abruptly stopped. It's believed the perpetrator may have been sent to prison. His method of operation was the same in all the cases. Using new pairs of shoelaces, he tied his victims' hands so tightly behind their backs that their hands turned black. He was armed and usually wore a mask. So far, however, DNA matching that found at the scenes has not matched anyone in a large database. It's just a matter of time, however, before a computer match is found, according to law enforcement.

The most recent well-known cold cases involve the still-unsolved murders of hip-hop artists Tupac Shakur in September 1996 and the Notorious B.I.G. (a.k.a. Christopher Wallace and Biggie Smalls) six months later, in March 1997. Investigators in both cases faced refusal to cooperate from witnesses. Without willing witnesses, the cases stagnated. Theories abound, but none have been proven accurate.

committing him to Silverwater Correctional Centre.

At his trial in April 2004 it emerged that Gonzalez, despite being a seemingly likeable and genuine young man, was a persistent liar. Aside from his shaky alibis, he had, at one time or another, claimed to have cancer, be running a charitable foundation and to have a recording contract (he performed in an a cappella band called Definite Vibez).

Furthermore, police discovered, via Internet records, evidence that Gonzalez had made a previous murder attempt. In February 2001 he had searched the net looking for information about lethal plant toxins, and in June had ordered a batch of seeds from an Australian supplier. Immediately afterwards – just ten days before the killings – his mother was taken severely ill with suspected food poisoning. Liquid found inside a film canister in Gonzalez's bedroom was analysed and found to contain one of the poisons he had been looking for online.

Rejecting his alibis – including a story that he had ordered the poisonous seeds in order to commit suicide – and convinced of his presence at the murder scene by traces on his clothes of the paint used to spray the graffiti, the jury convicted Gonzalez of the murders in May 2004. He is currently serving three concurrent life sentences without parole in the maximum security wing of Goulburn Correctional Centre, Sydney.

For further investigation

📖 **Kara Lawrence** Unmasked: The Gonzalez Family Killer (2006) Detailed account of the whole Sef Gonzalez story, from his upbringing to possible motives behind the killings.

ⓦ geocities.com/TheTropics/Cabana/6795/dd2.html Sef Gonzalez's website tribute to himself.

THE MENENDEZ BROTHERS

It was like a nightmare version of the TV show *Beverly Hills 90210*, though the accused would later admit to being influenced by the 1987 TV movie starring Judd Nelson, *Billionaire Boys Club*, about a criminal gang of wealthy teens in Southern California. Handsome, athletic, pampered Erik and Lyle Menendez were suspects in the bloody 1989 slaying of their parents, who were found with multiple gunshot wounds at home in front of the TV. The case would have to be tried twice, first in 1993, then (after jurors failed to agree on a verdict) in 1994. When it came to the second trial, the judge banned cameras from the court. The previous year's proceedings had become cult viewing for many, who tuned into live broadcasts and pundit commentary on Court TV, the fledgling channel which had first aired in 1991 and came into its own with the trials of the Menendezes. (In 2007 the channel changed its name to TruTV.) According to a report in *Newsday* magazine on 26 November 1993, President Bill Clinton was so hooked on the brothers' first trial that, from time to time during the afternoons, he was in the habit of leaving the Oval Office to watch the unfolding saga of family debauchery.

By the time the first trial began on 21 July 1993, nearly four years after the crimes were committed, there was no longer any doubt that Lyle, 21 at the time of the deaths, and Erik, 18, had pulled the shotgun triggers again and again. The question was whether the jury would accept that the killings were excusable because the brothers had been tormented and sexually molested by their father, **Jose** (45 when he died). The brothers' defence team was led by the mercurial and often ferocious Leslie Abramson. Abramson had a track record of success in a similar case, having got a murder charge against teenage father-killer Arnel Salvatierra reduced to voluntary manslaughter on the grounds of persistent vicious abuse. She was a mesmeric courtroom performer. According to *Vanity Fair* correspondent Dominick Dunne who wrote lengthy articles about the Menendez case, "she knows how to play the Court TV camera as well as Barbara Streisand knows how to play to a movie camera." She did her job well, succeeding first time round in making the abuse argument stick sufficiently to get a hung jury.

Cuban-American Jose was an executive at Live Entertainment, a subsidiary of Carolco Pictures. He had a reputation for ruthlessness in business and for driving his sons hard. **Kitty**, his wife, came from Chicago, and had met her future husband at Southern Illinois University. Because their respective parents disapproved, the couple married secretly in 1963. The brothers' lawyers would later portray Kitty as a weak, hysterical woman with a nasty streak, who failed to protect her children from a tyrannical father. Jose was a car-rental executive at Hertz before breaking into the entertainment business at RCA's music division, where he signed up Eurythmics and Duran Duran. While at RCA, the Menendez family lived luxuriously in the university town of Princeton, New Jersey. The boys attended the exclusive Princeton Day School where they excelled at tennis and soccer. In 1986, Jose failed to get a promotion at RCA and clashed with a senior manager. He left the company and, despite Kitty's protests, took the family to Los Angeles, where he entered the video business, achieving great success

at Live Entertainment. "He had an incredible dedication to business," an associate said. "He believed that whatever had to be done should be done – with no heart, if necessary."

Jose wanted high-achieving sons. He dreamed of founding a dynasty like the Kennedys. But by the time of the move south problems were mounting. The brothers had been getting into trouble. In 1988, Lyle and Erik were involved in stealing more than $100,000 worth of property in burglaries of homes belonging to parents of their friends. When the theft was discovered, Erik took the fall. A juvenile with no record, he was sentenced to community service. Lyle's reputation was left intact and he was therefore free to take up a place at Princeton University, fulfilling a cherished dream of Jose's that his sons have Ivy League educations. But during his first semester in 1988, having already been disciplined for bad behaviour, Lyle was caught cheating in an exam and suspended. A gifted high-school actor, Erik hankered after the movie business as well as the pro tennis circuit. In 1988 he co-wrote a screenplay about a rich kid who murders his parents after he discovers he has been disinherited. And there were suggestions Jose had indeed begun to talk about changing his will. The family was in crisis. Kitty told her therapist she was scared of her sons and even feared that they were sociopaths with no conscience. The day before violence erupted, the Menendezes all went on a fishing trip, chartering the *Motion Picture Marine*. Its captain later commented on the frosty atmosphere: "there was not much interaction going on", he said. A day earlier, Lyle and Erik had gone to San Diego to buy shotguns.

On 20 August 1989, Jose was watching TV with Kitty

in the "family room" of their $4 million mansion in Beverly Hills. They were relaxing. Jose was wearing shorts when he died, Kitty sweatpants. Strawberries and ice cream were on the table in front of them. At around 10pm a neighbour heard what sounded like fireworks. Police arrived on the scene as a result of a call from Lyle. Distraught, weeping, he told the operator: "They shot and killed my parents!" Erik could be heard screaming in the background.

When police arrived at the scene they found carnage. Quoted by Dominick Dunne, Dan Stewart, an inves-tigator hired by the family, described it like this: "I've seen a lot of homicides, but nothing quite that brutal. Blood, flesh, skulls. It would be hard to describe Jose, as resembling a human that you would recognize." Jose had suffered six wounds from a 12-gauge shotgun. Ten rounds had hit Kitty. Defence lawyers later tried to keep the crime-scene photos out of court, arguing that they might prejudice jurors, but the judge allowed five to be shown. The couple had been shot at point-blank range. They had "contact wounds" caused by the gun muzzle being placed right against the skin when

MARRYING DEATH ROW INMATES

For men in prison – including those on death row – there's no shortage of suitors. Scott Peterson, convicted of murdering his wife Laci and their unborn child in 2002, had been on death row at California's San Quentin State Prison barely an hour when the first marriage proposal arrived. Peterson's main recreation inside is reading his mail – about 25 pieces a day, mostly from women – what prison officials refer to as "fan mail".

Prison weddings in California are regular occurrences. Roughly twenty inmates get married in ceremonies held on the first Friday of even-numbered months at San Quentin, and usually at least one condemned inmate is among them. Apparently the more notorious the murderer, the better his chances of getting betrothed. Convicted mass killer Richard Ramirez, the infamous Night Stalker, was married at the San Quentin prison in October 1996. As ABC News puts it: "Men serving time for some of the most notoriously heinous crimes apparently have enough sex appeal to turn death row into a sort of lovers' lane."

Two other notorious inmates who married are Erik and Lyle Menendez. They were first acquitted then convicted of the 1989 shotgun murders of their parents, Jose and Kitty Menendez, at home in Beverly Hills, California. The brothers became a sensation when the television show CourtTV News – whose host network had just been launched – broadcast the trial in 1993. Neither showed remorse during the trial and, instead, testified that the killings were committed because they were abused for most of their lives by their parents and sexually molested by their father. The brothers were each sentenced to life in prison without the possibility of parole.

Lyle, the older of the two brothers, was the first to celebrate his nuptials. He married pen pal and former model Anna Erikson on 2 July 1997, the day he was sentenced. The ceremony was a proxy one, taking place down a phone line. According to The New

it was fired. One of Kitty's eyes was missing when she was found dead at her husband's feet, in a pool of blood. Only one loose tooth was left in her mouth and her hair was standing up straight because of the shock of the gunshot impact.

Police at first wondered about a Mafia hit. The brothers were not suspects. So credible were Lyle and Erik when they told their story that they weren't even asked to take tests for gunpowder residue. Lyle hired bodyguards, saying he feared that his parents' killers would come after his brother

and him. Then Lyle and Erik went on a spending spree with their parents' life insurance. Two Rolex watches and money clips, clothing and accessories, a pool table, and entertainment centre, professional tennis coaching for Erik, vacations in Cancun and Aspen and the Lake Tahoe gambling resort, several cars, a restaurant, and luxurious property. Erik paid $40,000 to invest in a rock concert, but it was a con and he lost the money.

On 8 March 1990 Lyle was stopped by police at the entrance to the family home. In front of the neigh-

York Times, the brothers' lawyer Leslie Abramson was with Anna to place a ring on her finger on her client's behalf, while Erik joined his brother as best man. The marriage only lasted about a year, but Lyle married again at Mule Creek State Prison in 2003, when he was 35 – the bride was a local woman, Rebecca Sneed, 33, of Sacramento, California.

Erik was 28 when he married Tammi Ruth Saccoman, 37, in the waiting room of Folsom State Prison in June 1999. Tammi later self-published a book titled *They Said We'd Never Make It – My Life with Erik Menendez*. When it was released, she went on the talk-show circuit, including CNN's *Larry King Live* and MSNBC's *The Abrams Report*, discussing the pair's long-distance relationship. According to ABC News, the marriage has been successful. "Tammi says she's very happy. But she gave up a lot for Menendez. She felt scorn from family, friends and colleagues. She lost many friends. She was even fired from a volunteer job she dearly loved, working with animals."

The United States Ninth Circuit Court of Appeals

rejected Erik's latest appellate filing in 2006. In the meantime the two continue researching and working with lawyers to find possible technicalities in the court rulings. California law prohibits prison conjugal visits, but Erik and his wife continue to have non-conjugal visits on Saturdays and Sundays, from 9am to 3pm.

Marriages between condemned men in the US and women from Germany and the Scandinavian countries are the most common, according to *Death Penalty News*, a newsletter published by a death penalty opposition group. Ten women, the newsletter says, have wed men on Florida's death row since 1997. The interest from Europe, according to the *San Francisco Chronicle* newspaper, is probably rooted in opposition to the death penalty and sympathy for those subjected to it.

Whatever the reason – whether women are attracted to bad boys or they simply want to be married but don't want to be bothered having to live with their partners – death row inmates have no trouble attracting potential spouses.

bours he was searched before being arrested on suspicion of murder. In Israel for a tennis tournament, Erik was afraid of being detained in that country and he immediately flew back to Florida before turning himself over to Los Angeles police. Investigators had been informed of the existence of taped confessions made to the brothers' therapist, **Dr Jerome Oziel** – who had started to see Lyle and Erik after the burglary trouble. The confessions had been discovered and reported by Judalon Smyth, who was in a relationship with Jerome. The previous October, the therapist had asked her to listen outside the door of his consulting room while Erik was speaking inside. He wanted a witness. During the first trial, the brothers' defence strenuously argued that what went on between therapist and patient was confidential, but in mid-November 1993 the judge allowed the tape to be played as evidence, and jurors heard Lyle admitting his and Erik's guilt. In his testimony, Jerome gave further details of what the brothers had confessed. Their father died quickly from his wounds, but Kitty was resilient. Despite her numerous wounds, she moaned as she crawled on the floor – then Lyle fired a last, fatal shot.

"I think one of the big, biggest pains … is that you miss just having these people around," Lyle said on the tape. "I miss not having my dog around – if I can make such a gross analogy". Sexual abuse was the cornerstone of the brothers' defence. For twelve years, they claimed, Erik had been abused and raped by Jose; this was the dark secret of the family that, if you believed the brothers, was finally coming to light. In the brothers' account of it, the secret finally came out in a totally unexpected way. A week before the slayings, Kitty and Lyle argued angrily. Kitty grabbed at Lyle's hair and wrenched off the hairpiece that he wore. (Lyle was

prematurely bald and wore a wig. It was convincing enough to have fooled everyone in court: when Lyle arrived one day without it, the explanation that he had decided to shave his head was widely accepted.) Erik said this revelation of his brother's baldness caused a chain reaction of intimacy. Moved by his protective older sibling's vulnerability, Erik claimed he finally confided that their father had been molesting him since the age of six. Erik's advocate Abramson was blunt and detailed in making the allegation. It had begun, she told the court, with inappropriate caresses of the child and then "escalated in a carefully calculated pattern of grooming the child for his father's sexual gratification. This pattern included repeated acts of forcible oral copulation, sodomy, rape, and the intentional infliction of pain by the use of foreign objects upon Erik's person." In his testimony Erik described what he said Jose called "rough sex", which involved sticking drawing pins into Erik's thighs and buttocks. When Abramson closed the defence case, she dwelled on this by pushing pins into a photograph of Erik as a child, to illustrate the abuse.

The last incident of abuse occurred just a week before the killing, the brothers said, leading Lyle to confront his father about what was happening. Lyle claimed that Jose threatened to kill him and that this was the last straw: something drastic had to be done in self-protection. Although the defence case relied heavily on what had supposedly happened to Erik, the truly electrifying testimony came, reporters agreed, from Lyle in September 1993. There were rumours that Erik was gay and he was the more sensitive-seeming brother. As the first trial progressed, Erik became increasingly thin, pale and wan. Lyle was more tough and virile and so it came as a surprise when he was the one who seemed to crack and be overwhelmed. Breaking down in tears as he did so, Lyle said that when he was a child, he too had been raped by his father.

It was, according to the veteran reporter Dunne, "one of the most overwhelmingly emotional moments I have ever encountered in a courtroom". *The New York Times* reported that jurors, journalists and spectators wept. In spite of the prosecution's objections, Lyle's lawyer Jill Lansing was allowed to exhibit nude photographs that Jose had taken of his elder son as a child. The photos seemed to back up Lyle's testimony. Two weeks later, the prosecution cross-examination was predictably sustained and vigorous. Deputy District Attorney Pamela Bozanich asked Lyle at one point about his mother. "When you put the shotgun to her left cheek and pulled the trigger, did you love your mother?" But perhaps it was that testimony by Lyle that was decisive. For after extensive deliberation, the two juries (one for each brother) that were hearing the evidence could not reach a verdict. In January 1994, the prosecution of Lyle and Erik ended in a mistrial. It was suggested that women jurors had favoured the brothers' side of the story, with men more sympathetic to the prosecution. There was deadlock. But District Attorney Gil Garcetti immediately announced that there would be no plea bargain. "We have an ethical, professional moral responsibility to go forward with this case as

Lyle (left) and Erik (right), during their trial for the murder of their parents.

a first-degree murder case", he said. "This may cost $1 million. We are seeking justice and that is what we are going to do, and be damned with how much money it is going to cost."

The second trial, which began that October with no cameras allowed, received much less publicity.

CLASSIFYING AND PREDICTING MURDER

Since not all murder is alike, there are many ways to classify this crime. One method of homicide classification – specifically designed to help in offering predictions of future violence, a major issue in the criminal justice field – has been shown to be particularly useful to mental health professionals, members of law enforcement, the court, and others involved in the management and disposition of dangerous offenders. This system is based on an analysis of the dynamics of the anti-social act itself, which is viewed as falling on a motivational spectrum. On one end of the spectrum are externally (socially) motivated homicides, and on the extreme opposite end of the continuum are internally (psychologically) motivated homicides. Five different types of murder (social-environmental, situational, impulsive, catathymic, compulsive) can be differentiated, and fall on the spectrum according to this motivational approach. Those homicides which are due to a primary psychiatric condition form a group of their own, separate from the motivational spectrum.

Contrary to popular belief, only a small percentage of all homicides are a direct result of some type of psychiatric disorder. In those cases where murder is a direct result of a primary mental disorder, most are an outgrowth of an organic, toxic, or paranoid state. Epilepsy, brain tumours and brain injuries are common organic causes; toxic states commonly involve alcohol and various forms of drug abuse; paranoid disorders manifest themselves in delusions and hallucinations where the offender responds directly to these psychotic symptoms.

Environmental or socially stimulated homicides are a result of external factors such as social pressure, a weakening of social controls, and even the effects of political ideology. For example, Nazi killings, murder during times of war and social upheaval, gang-related homicides, cult murder, and terroristic killings would all fall in this category.

Situational murders are in essence a reaction to stressful situations, committed mostly by individuals with little or no psychopathology. About 65 percent of all murders would fall into this category, and they include domestic homicides, homicides triggered by arguments or carried out in the course of committing another felony, or romantic triangles.

Impulsive offenders who commit murder are distinguished from situational offenders by the multiplicity of anti-social acts in their backgrounds as well as their poor impulse control. Impulsive murderers have a loose and poorly structured personality, with a life pattern marked by lack of direction and unpredictability. Strong feelings of inadequacy and an inability to cope in the competitive world are common characteristics of such offenders. These individuals do not necessarily have a need to commit the murder; instead, they overreact to circumstances and have little ability to modulate their emotions.

The prosecution team was changed, David Conn and Carol Jane Najera replacing Pamela Bozanich and Lester Kuriyama. There were soon setbacks to the defence: in early March a judge refused Abramson's plea that her bill be picked up by the government. The defence had already cost Jose and Kitty's estate $1.5 million and she explained that after creditors had been paid there would be nothing left for further legal fees. The judge furthermore declined to allow extra government funds for co-counsel Marcia Morrissey. Abramson managed an acerbic quip: "So the court has now ruled that I have to work for free and I have no

Catathymia is a word literally meaning "in accordance with emotions"; catathymic murders involve an eruption of underlying emotionally charged (usually sexual) conflicts. These homicides are of two types – acute and chronic. The acute catathymic homicide is a sudden murder where underlying emotionally charged conflicts are triggered by a victim who has some symbolic significance to the offender. In these cases, hidden conflicts are suddenly brought to the surface by the victim's behaviour, such as an insult or put-down, typically sexual in nature. The victim is usually a stranger, the homicide is spontaneous and unplanned, and the method of attack is sudden, violent and excessive. There is typically a flattening of emotions following the homicide, and memory for the event is poor due to its explosive nature.

The chronic catathymic homicide, on the other hand, involves an incubation period that can be anything from several days to many months. During this time, the subject becomes obsessively preoccupied with the future victim and develops a fixed idea that the solution to his internal conflict – often involving sexual inadequacy – is through murder. The homicide is often planned and there is a feeling of relief once psychic tension is discharged through the violence. The victim is often an intimate or former intimate partner, but sometimes a stranger with whom the offender has become obsessed. In fact, many stalking homicides often involve catathymic dynamics.

The compulsive-repetitive murderer is on the extreme opposite end of the motivational spectrum (from the social-environmental homicides), and the act is determined entirely by internal psychological sources with little external influence. These are a different type of sexual murder than the catathymic. Compulsive homicides are not triggered by internal sexual conflicts; rather, by a sexual arousal pattern where there is a fusion of sex and aggression, so that the violent act itself is eroticized. Accordingly, compulsive offenders do not kill an intimate partner, but seek out a victim to kill (often a stranger) to satisfy their sexual drives. Such individuals often commit their murders in a repetitive-ritualistic manner and in serial fashion.

The main benefit of the motivational spectrum as a classification system is its usefulness in prediction of future violence. The best prognosis (i.e. the offender most likely not to repeat his crime) is the situational murderer; the worst prognosis is found in the compulsive offender. Catathymic offenders have a somewhat better outcome than the compulsive-repetitive murderer, but worse than the impulsive. Individuals who commit social or environmentally determined homicides may repeat their acts, depending upon the circumstances they return to once released from confinement. In those individuals whose homicides are a direct result of a psychiatric condition, the likelihood for repetition is dependent on how successfully the underlying disorder can be treated and contained.

Professor Louis B. Schlesinger

lawyer to help me?"

In mid-March 1996, the single jury's deliberations were abandoned after the forewoman and a pregnant juror were dismissed on medical grounds. Judge Weisberg told the reconstituted jury that they had to begin deliberating again from scratch, but the end was in sight. On 21 March, Lyle and Erik were convicted of murdering their parents. They might have received the death penalty, but this was rejected. On 2 July, both were sentenced to life imprisonment without the possibility of parole.

In a twist to the case, Leslie Abramson was accused

of professional misconduct for having cajoled a defence witness, psychiatrist Dr William Vicary, into deleting portions of his notes – a charge she adamantly denied. But in October 1997, it was announced that no criminal charges would be brought against the fiery lawyer who had made such an impact during the trial. So in 2004, she was hired by record producer Phil Spector, who had been charged with the second-degree murder of a Los Angeles nightclub hostess. In Spector's case too, a first trial ended in jury deadlock, with the second ending in a guilty verdict.

For further investigation

ⓦ crimelibrary.com/notorious_murders/famous/menendez/index_1.html Detailed account by Rachel Pergament, hosted by TruTV (formerly Court TV).

ⓦ topics.nytimes.com/top/reference/timestopics/people/m/lyle_menendez/index.html Archive of news stories from *The New York Times* about the case.

ⓦ vanityfair.com/search/query?keyword=Lyle+Menendez& Five lengthy articles, unsympathetic to the Menendez brothers, by *Vanity Fair* Special Correspondent Dominick Dunne.

ⓦ abcnews.go.com/2020/Story?id=123804&page=1 An interview with Tammi Menendez.

ⓦ courttv.com/trials/menendez/ A comprehensive summary of stories, posted on Courttv.com, about the trial.

ⓦ people.com/people/article/0,,1123260_1,00.html An extensive prison interview with Erik Menendez, who discusses his marriage and the status of his chances for appeal.

📖 **Tammi Menendez** They Said We'd Never Make It: My Life with Erik Menendez **(2005)** The wife of the youngest of the Menendez brothers not only lays out her husband's case, from his viewpoint, but she also writes about Erik's search for spiritual meaning and offers an inside look into the bleak realities of prison life and a marriage in which they can never live as man and wife.

SERIAL KILLERS

Serial killers

Murderers who kill repeatedly have existed for thousands of years. But the term "serial killer" is thought to have first been coined in the 1970s. Of all criminals, these murderers are the most disturbing - and the most disturbed. In the early 1970s the writers Thomas E. Gaddis and James O. Long authored a biography of Carl Panzram, one of the US's most brutal and unrepentant murderers, referring to Panzram as a serial killer.

The term stuck. While there is no specific "type", history has shown that these killers are typically white, heterosexual men in their twenties and thirties, and are often sexually dysfunctional, with low self-esteem. This chapter examines a variety of these serial offenders and their psychological make-up.

DAVID BERKOWITZ: THE SON OF SAM

For two years in the late 1970s, a psychopathic murderer who killed women in New York City with a .44-calibre handgun was so sought after by police that a special task force of 300 officers was formed to hunt him down. The task force – "Operation Omega" – was headed by Deputy Inspector Timothy Dowd, and went after the **Son of Sam** with a vengeance. The effort eventually worked. After a thirteen-month killing spree that began in the summer of 1976 in the New York metropolitan area, and after six people were dead and seven wounded, one David Berkowitz was arrested and eventually confessed to the crimes. He was sentenced in 1978 to 365 consecutive years in prison.

THE TYLENOL MURDERS – AND THEIR COPYCATS

In the autumn of 1982, someone put potassium cyanide in Extra-Strength Tylenol capsules. As a result, seven people in the Chicago area died that year from cyanide poisoning, between 29 September and 1 October, all after they had taken Extra-Strength Tylenol capsules. The Halloween killings prompted copycat attacks, setting off in the US what was referred to as the "Tylenol Scare". And scary it was.

Once the deaths of the five women and seven men were linked to Tylenol bottles, panic swept throughout Johnson & Johnson, the parent company of McNeil Consumer Products and the makers of Extra-Strength Tylenol. Chicago police drove through neighbourhoods blasting warnings over loudspeakers and bullhorns. News broadcasts spread the warning, causing alarm in households throughout the US. Stores removed Extra-Strength Tylenol from their shelves. Hospitals were flooded with calls, and emergency rooms were swamped with people fearful they had been poisoned. In response, the head of Seattle's Poison Control Center announced that if someone took a lethal dose they would not live long enough to make a phone call.

Meanwhile, a Cook County toxicologist discovered that each bottle contained contaminated capsules that had been emptied and refilled with about 65 milligrams of cyanide. Blood tests backed up the findings by confirming that at least one victim's blood was filled with deadly cyanide, ten thousand times the amount needed to kill. The Johnson & Johnson company, for its part, recalled all Tylenol capsules from the market. The recall included 31 million Tylenol bottles with a retail value of more than $100 million.

At the height of the scare, law enforcement did not have a clue as to who the culprit was. Years later, police and the FBI were still no closer to making an arrest in the case.

During their investigation, police sought links between the Tylenol murders and unsolved poisonings in Wyoming, Pennsylvania, and California. The cases were later determined to be copycat crimes where people other than the Tylenol killer put small, non-fatal doses of strychnine in Tylenol capsules. Between 1982 and 1987, eleven people died from swallowing headache and cold capsules laced with cyanide. A total of 270 cases

A year before Berkowitz was caught, he had complained in a letter to Jack Carr, a neighbour whose black labrador was proving a nuisance by, barking too much. When the problem wasn't resolved, Berkowitz sent a second letter dated 19 Aprilm 1977. Ten days later, when the dog continued howling and barking, Berkowitz eventually shot the dog. He later claimed that it was the dog who had made him kill people. "He told me to", was Berkowitz's blunt excuse.

On a dark July night in 1976, a pedestrian approached two women, **Donna Lauria** and **Jody Valenti**, as they sat talking in a parked car in front of Lauria's apartment building. He raised his gun and pumped five shots into the vehicle through the windshield. Lauria, who was hit in the neck, died instantly; Valenti suffered an injury to her thigh. The Son of Sam's reign of terror had begun. Police had little evidence to go on other than the weapon's spent bullets, which they identified

of suspected product tampering were reported in the months following the Chicago murders. In the years after the Tylenol scare, product tampering, some of which ended in fatalities, included mercuric chloride in Excedrin Extra-Strength capsules, acid in Sinex nasal spray and Visine eye drops, rat poison in Anacin, sodium hydroxide in chocolate milk, razor blades in hotdog franks, straight pins in candy bars, and poison in a tea bag from a supermarket.

With the actual Tylenol murders, and the copycat acts, the possibility that cyanide was inserted into the capsules during production was ruled out. Investigators surmised that a person had acquired bottles of the painkiller, tampered with the contents, and then randomly selected stores where one or two bottles were put back on the shelves. While investigators have had a short list of suspects, no one has ever been charged with the Tylenol murders. However, one man, James Lewis, was convicted of attempting to extort $1 million from McNeil Consumer Products after he was arrested and charged with sending an extortion letter to the company with the word "TYLENOL" written across the envelope. The letter demanded that the ransom money be delivered to a Chicago post office box. If

payment was not made, the letter threatened more deaths. James Lewis was caught and ultimately received a twenty-year sentence for extortion. While Lewis remains a suspect in the deaths, the authorities have been unable to produce evidence that he was the Tylenol killer. In October 1995, Lewis was released from an Oklahoma prison after spending more than twelve years behind bars. Lewis has always denied any guilt and the police never charged him in connection with the deaths.

Ten weeks after Johnson & Johnson pulled Tylenol bottles from store shelves, the company began putting them back, but with new triple-seal packaging. In May 1983, US Congress approved the Tylenol Bill that made it a federal offence to maliciously tamper with consumer products. In addition, the Food and Drug Administration in 1989 established a uniform requirement for tamper-resistant packaging of over-the-counter products. Tamper-proof packaging has now become the norm.

The Tylenol murder cases remain officially unsolved. A $100,000 reward offered by Johnson & Johnson for information leading to the arrest and conviction of the killer has never been claimed.

as belonging to a Bulldog – a .44-calibre, five-shot, double-action revolver manufactured by the now-defunct Charter Arms Company. They believed the murder to have either been a case of mistaken identity – possibly the work of the mob – or the revenge of a spurned lover of Donna Lauria.

Then, on 23 October of the same year, two more people – **Carl Denaro** and Rosemary Keenan – were shot at as they sat in a parked car outside a bar. Berkowitz walked behind the car and fired his Bulldog into the back window. Denaro was hit with a bullet in his head but both passengers survived. The spent slugs matched up with the Lauria murder; the police knew that a random serial killer was on the loose, preying on young couples.

The following month, on 26 November, two friends, **Donna DeMasi** and **Joanne Lomino**, were walking near Lomino's Queens home when they were approached by a stranger. He asked them for directions, then suddenly pulled a gun on them and fired. They both survived, but Lomino was left permanently paralysed. The murderer struck again on 30 January 1977, targeting a young couple, Christine Freund and her fiancé, John Diel, who were sat in a parked car. Berkovitz's three shots left Freund dead, though Diel escaped with minor injuries. The next of Berkowitz's motiveless executions took place on 8 March; he shot and killed Virginia Voskerichian, a nineteen-year-old Columbia University student, as she walked home after classes. It was the first time Berkowitz had targeted a single person, rather than a couple.

The next month, on 17 April, Berkowitz returned to his previous profile, murdering a couple in the Bronx, a few blocks away from the site of the Lauria and Valenti shooting. The pair were Alexander Esau and Valentina

TWENTY-TWO DISCIPLES OF HELL?

A few weeks after his arrest, David Berkowitz started to suggest that he had not been acting alone. Over the years, he has given more details – though nothing substantial – about a Satan-worshipping cult that he was part of. Its New York membership was referred to in the Breslin letter – the "22 disciples of hell". He has said that the cult had branches across the whole US, and was involved in organized crime, though he has not provided any hard facts due to his professed fear of reprisals against his family. A journalist named Maury Terry has thoroughly investigated Berkowitz's claims and believes that a branch of the so-called "Process Church" may have been responsible for some of Berkowitz's crimes. Nobody else, however, has ever been charged.

Suriani; Berkowitz shot each of the pair twice and left a handwritten letter near the scene, referring to himself as the "Son of Sam" and "Mr Monster". Its spelling was childlike and erratic, and was written largely in block capitals. "I am the 'Monster' – 'Beelzebub' – the chubby behemouth [sic]. I love to hunt", was just one among many sentences that made up a chilling mix of self-aggrandizement, boasts and contradictory threats and promises.

Despite one particular assertion in the letter – "I don't want to kill anymore" – the violence didn't stop. Two more couples were shot. The next attack occurred on 26 June, when Judy Placido and Sal Lupu were shot while leaving the Elephas disco in the Bayside area of Queens. Both survived, even though Placido was hit with three bullets. Then, on 31 July, Bobby Violante and Stacy Moskowitz were shot in a car while they were parked at a lover's lane in Brooklyn. Moskowitz died instantly from a gunshot wound to her head, while Violante lost all his vision in one eye and was reduced to only partial vision in the other.

With the gunman having averaged an assault every month and a half, police stepped up their search for the killer by forming the "Operation Omega" team of detectives dedicated to finding the Son of Sam. Two years later, in 1977, the FBI took into questioning the man who was referred to by the media as The ".44 Calibre Killer". During that interview, Berkowitz confessed to the shootings. He told

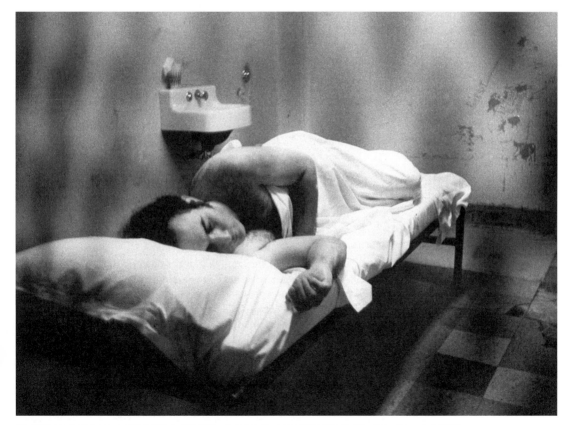

David Berkowitz, the accused Son of Sam serial killer, sleeps in his cell at Kings County Hospital prison ward, 1977.

the FBI he did it because he resented his overbearing mother and his failures with women. Between July 1976 and July 1977, Berkowitz killed six people and injured seven others.

David Berkowitz is currently serving six life terms in Attika state prison for the Son of Sam murders. Before his June 2002 parole hearing, Berkowitz, now a born-again Christian, declared that he did not want to be released.

For further investigation

Ⓦ nymag.com/news/crimelaw/20327/ Feature article in, *The New York Times Magazine* by Steve Fishman, profiling David Berkowitz in his first interview with the media in seven years.

Ⓦ forteantimes.com/features/articles/234/i_am_the_son_of _sam.html An article in *Fortean Times* questioning whether all of the murders linked to the Son of Sam killer were actually committed by Berkowitz.

JEROME HENRY BRUDOS

Also known as the "Lust Killer" and the "Shoe Fetish Slayer", **Jerome "Jerry" Brudos** was a serial killer and a sexual deviant who practised necrophilia. His grisly signature was the practice of cutting off a foot and often the breasts of his victims. He froze one of the feet he had removed from a victim, and periodically took it out of the freezer to dress it up in high-heeled shoes. The severity of his psychopathic tendencies has meant that Brudos has become archetypal: he is regularly cited by forensic psychiatrists as the quintessential case of the type of killer motivated by lust.

At the age of five, he was exhibiting early signs of a shoe fetish after his chance find of a pair of black patent leather, open-toe high-heels. They were nothing like the practical shoes his mother wore, and he took the shoes home and often played dressing-up in them. When his domineering mother caught him in the act, she burned the shoes. That's when his deep hatred for her appears to have set in.

Brudos' odd but harmless behaviour continued along similar lines. His fetish for women's shoes developed into an obsession with stilettos, as well as women's undergarments. By the age of sixteen, after his family moved to Oregon, he began stealing women's clothes from his neighbours' washing lines. The obsession took a violent turn when, at the age of seventeen, he held a woman hostage at knifepoint and ordered her to remove her clothes while he photographed her. He was arrested and committed for nearly a year to Oregon State Hospital's mental ward, and was diagnosed with an "early personality disorder".

Nevertheless, he managed to graduate from high school in 1957, and went on to college, where he studied electronics. He dropped out and joined the military service in March 1959, but was released seven months later on a medical discharge. He returned home, living in the family's tool shed behind their house. It wasn't long before he regressed back into his previous behaviour, and he began hit-and-run assaults upon women in the street, knocking them down, pulling their shoes off their feet and running off.

Despite his increasingly violent secret life, he was still just about grounded enough to find himself work as an electrician. In 1961 he married a seventeen-year-old girl, who he had got pregnant. The pair's domestic life was more than a little strange: he persuaded her to walk around the house nude – or, often, nude with high-heels on – while he paraded around in her undergarments. The couple had two children and settled in a Portland suburb.

Unknown to his wife, however, Brudos' crimes were escalating, and, around 1967, he began breaking into people's homes at night in order to steal women's shoes and underwear. During one of these burglaries, a woman awoke to find him ransacking her closets in her bedroom. Brudos choked her until she was unconscious, raped her, and then fled.

Not long after this, Brudos' acts turned fatal. His first killing was in January 1968. It happened when **Linda Slawson**, a nineteen-year-old girl working as an encyclopedia salesperson, knocked on the door of the Brudos home. Brudos led her to his garage workshop, where he bludgeoned her to death. He cut off one of her feet, which he froze, and periodically used to model his growing collection of spiked-heel shoes. He weighted her body and dumped it in the Long Tom River, near where he worked.

When Linda didn't arrive home that evening, her parents reported her missing. But because the company she worked for didn't keep records of the addresses she visited, police had very little to go on. A few weeks later, her car was found, abandoned, in the neighbourhood, but no clues inside the car could be found.

The second killing became apparent after sixteen-year-old **Stephanie Vikko** disappeared from Portland in July 1968. Her remains were discovered nine months later in a wooded area northwest of Forest Grove. Brudos' third victim, Jan Whitney, vanished in November 1968 on her way home from work. Her car had broken down; Brudos was driving past and stopped and offered to help. Once in his car, he strangled the 23-year-old. He then drove the body to his garage where he had necrophiliac sex with the corpse. He then cut off the right breast and made a plastic mould from it. He used a hook and pulley to hang the body from the rafters and kept it in his garage for a couple of days before dumping it in the same river where he'd deposited the body of Linda Slawson. Whitney's car was found abandoned on a main road in Albany, Oregon.

A few months later, **Karen Sprinkler**, a nineteen-year-old college student, vanished on 26 January 1968, during her two-hour drive from Eugene to McMinnville for a weekend break. Her car turned up abandoned north of Albany, Oregon. Her mother, who was to meet her daughter at a restaurant, reported her missing when Karen didn't show up. Jerry Brudos, instead, had abducted Karen, and raped her before strangling her and cutting off both her breasts. He took photos of the body after he dressed it up like a life-sized doll in a variety of frilly underwear from his private collection. Before taking Karen's body to the river for disposal, he performed a necrophiliac sex act

In 1987, the male driver of a van was seen dumping a woman's body into a South Central Los Angeles alley. Twenty-two years later, police are looking anew for the witness who reported it. They're hoping to learn more about the man they've dubbed the "grim sleeper" – a serial killer who is preying on African-American women in the inner city. Eleven killings later, the perpetrator remains at large.

The home of Jerry Brudos, Salem, Oregon, June 1969.

on the corpse.

Brudos' fifth and final killing was a month later. Posing as a police officer by flashing a phoney law-enforcement badge, he lured 22-year-old **Linda Salee** from a shopping mall to his car. He drove her to his garage workshop, where he killed her after shocking her with an electrical cord. Linda had gone shopping for a birthday present for her boyfriend and had arranged to meet him afterward. She didn't show up and was never seen again.

Three weeks after Linda had been reported missing, a fisherman in the Long Tom River in western Oregon hooked onto something large. He took a closer look and discovered, to his horror, a body. The corpse had been weighted down with a transmission box from a car. An autopsy determined that the cause of death was strangulation. Dental records identified the body as that of Linda Salee.

A few days later, a second body was discovered in the same river. This time the body was weighted down with an engine block and tied in the same manner as the first corpse. It body was fully clothed and matched the description of Karen Sprinkler. The body had also been wearing a black bra stuffed with paper. Both breasts from the body were gone.

In April 1969, **Sharon Wood**, a 24-year-old secretary, entered the basement level of her company's parking garage when a tall, pudgy man approached her from behind. He was holding a gun and told her not to scream. Sharon, who was wearing high heels, kicked him and ran to safety. Shortly after that, witnesses reported sightings of a large man dressed in women's clothing loitering in the parking garage.

Because of the young age of the women, police looked for a lead by contacting students. One told them she had dated a man who seemed overly interested in the cases of the murdered women. She arranged to meet him again, and this time police were waiting for him. It was Jerry Brudos. Officers put him under surveillance and, five days later, in May 1969, Brudos was taken into custody. They were only able to hold him for a few days, and he was eventually released.

But after a woman came forward and identified Brudos in a photo line-up as the man who'd recently tried to drag her into his car, Brudos was once again arrested and taken to police headquarters. A body search revealed that Brudos was wearing women's underwear. When questioned, he immediately confessed to the murders. Investigators searched his garage and discovered nylon rope exactly like the rope that had been used to tie weighted car parts to the women's bodies.

Besides the confession and the rope, evidence against Brudos included a particularly damning photo of one of his victims that also showed his own reflection in a mirror.

On 4 June 1969, Brudos was arraigned. He pleaded insanity. His lawyers revealed to the court that Brudos had an overbearing mother and that he'd had an accident as a child and suffered a head injury. Through it all, Brudos showed no signs of remorse toward his victims. When it became clear the insanity defence was not going to work, Brudos pleaded guilty to the first-degree murders of Jan Whitney, Karen Sprinkler and Linda Salee, who were all from Salem, Oregon. Brudos was sentenced to three life sentences to be served consecutively. At the time, Oregon did not have a death penalty in place.

Brudos' wife, Darcie, was arrested too and tried as her husband's accomplice. But because there was no evidence that Darcie knew about, let alone participated in any of her husband's crimes, a jury acquitted her. She ended her eight-year marriage to Brudos in 1970, changed her name, and moved with their children to an unknown location.

The Oregon Court of Appeals turned down all attempts by Brudos to reverse his guilty pleas and seek a new trial. After 37 years in prison, Jerome Brudos was the longest-serving inmate in Oregon, housed at the Oregon State Penitentiary, until 28 March 2006, when he was found dead from natural causes in his cell.

The only explanation Brudos ever gave investigators as to why he killed was the characteristically blank and uninformative admission that it was just his way of "letting off steam".

For further investigation

Ann Rule Lust Killer (1983) Author Ann Rule's account of the Jerry Brudos's trial and events surrounding it.

Ⓦ newsregister.com/news/story_print.cfm?story_no=206036
A clip from a 1969 article in the News Register in McMinnville, Oregon, about the arrest of Jerome Brudos and a more recent story about the killer's death.

JEFFREY DAHMER

On 27 May 1991, a fourteen-year-old boy stumbled out of apartment 213 at the Oxford Apartments at 924 North 25th Street in Milwaukee, Wisconsin. He'd managed to escape and had wandered into the streets with Dahmer in pursuit. Two police officers stopped them both. Dahmer, calm and composed, told the officers that the youth was his nineteen-year-old boyfriend and that the pair had merely had a lovers' quarrel. The police report that the officers filed stated: "Intoxicated Asian, naked male. Was returned to his sober boyfriend." Months later, the officers would learn the truth. After they had left, Dahmer had raped and killed the fourteen-year-old boy.

Two months later, at midnight on 22 July, a terrified young man wearing handcuffs on one hand fled the same apartment. Two Milwaukee police officers were sitting in their patrol car in the high-crime area near Marquette University and noticed the man, later identified as **Tracy Edwards**. They stopped, and the victim told the officers his incredible tale of terror. The two policemen went back with Edwards to the apartment. Jeffrey Dahmer answered the door, and told the officers he'd lost his job and had become angry with his friend in a drunken stupor. One officer went inside, and immediately noticed an incredibly revolting stench. Polaroid photos of dismembered bodies and skulls covered the refrigerator door. The officer opened it, and shouted to his partner, "There's a goddamn head in here!" But there was more – the body parts of at least fifteen men, in fact. There were further severed heads in the refrigerator, torsos stuffed into a barrel, and skulls, boiled clean, in a filing cabinet. The 31-year-old Jeffrey Dahmer was immediately arrested.

After his arrest, the pale, sandy-haired Dahmer confessed to eleven murders. But investigators would later learn that Dahmer was responsible for more than that: between 1978 and 1991, Jeffrey Dahmer had killed seventeen men.

Author **Don Davis** has pointed out that neighbours had suspected that something strange was afoot, but that nothing in their wildest imaginations could have led them them to guess what it actually was. "They smelled the foul odours. They heard the power-saw buzzing in the dead of night. But neighbours never imagined the horrors happening right next door."

Dahmer's life story was one of bizarre sexual encounters, mutilation, and cannibalism: one of history's most appalling true crime cases. The question that demanded answering was what had turned a handsome, former tennis-player – the son of hardworking, middle-class parents – into a perverted serial killer whose unthinkable acts shocked the world.

Jeffrey's early childhood started much like any other boy in the 1960s. He had two parents who took good care of him and his brother. While in grade school, his chemist father, Lionel, worked long hours at his job in a laboratory, while his mother, Joyce, worked as a teletype machine instructor. His parents separated; his mother took his brother to live with her, while Jeffrey stayed with his father. The breakdown of his parents' relationship profoundly affected Jeffrey. He vowed never to marry. Still a child, the first manifestations of his homicidal tendencies became apparent: he began killing neighbourhood animals and impaling their heads on sticks in his back garden. The picture of his childhood at this point is unclear: the fact that Dahmer's bizarre chemistry experiments in the basement – strip-

Serial killer Jeffrey Dahmer is seen here in a 1982 Milwaukee county sheriff's department mugshot.

ping dead animals of their flesh using acid – went unchecked is unusual to say the least. It is rumoured that Dahmer was once molested by a neighbour while a boy. In his teens, Dahmer was a loner, and became an alcoholic.

In 1978, at the age of eighteen, Dahmer committed his first murder, in Bath Township, Ohio. After giving a lift to a hitchhiker named Stephen Hicks, Dahmer invited him back to his apartment. There he killed him with a barbell and hammer, after the young man said he wanted to leave. It was not until many years later that the crime was to be solved: Dahmer had got away with murder. He enrolled at Ohio State University and did not kill again for nine years. He didn't do well academically, dropped out, and joined the US military service, but he received a dishonour-

Killer John Joseph Joubert left his male victims for dead in their underwear after holding them in bondage, then biting, slashing and ultimately strangling them. Joubert was found guilty of three murders – two in Nebraska and one in Maine between 1982 and 1983 – and was executed by electrocution in 1996 at the age of 33.

able discharge for repeated drunkenness. He moved to Wisconsin and eventually got a job as a factory worker. It was at a gay bar in Milwaukee in 1987 that Dahmer befriended the man who was to be his second victim, 24-year-old **Steven Toumi**. The following year, Dahmer was arrested for molesting a thirteen-year-old boy and served ten months in jail. The court ordered him to register as a sex offender. After Dahmer was released from jail, he killed again. By 1991, he had murdered fifteen more men, mostly from around his neighbourhood.

The modus operandi Dahmer used was always the same. He frequented local gay bars where he would pick up young men, offering to pay them money to pose for photographs, or simply to watch videos and drink beer in his apartment. He would drug them by spiking their drinks before strangling or stabbing them to death. Dahmer often practised necrophilia on their corpses, and dismembered the bodies, frequently keeping body parts as gruesome souvenirs. By the summer of 1991, Dahmer was murdering approximately one person each week. He killed Matt Turner on 30 June, Jeremiah Weinberger on 5 July, Oliver Lacy on 12 July, and Joseph Brandehoft on 18 July.

On 17 February 1992, Jeffrey Dahmer was sentenced to fifteen consecutive life terms – one for each of his victims – for murder. He was transferred from the county jail to Columbia Correctional Institution, a male-only maximum-security correctional facility in Portage, Wisconsin, and incarcerated in cell number 648 in unit 6 – or what inmates called the "Smurf Unit". Dahmer was not to live long enough to serve out the sentence.

On 28 November 1994, Dahmer was assigned with two other inmates to clean the prison gymnasium. Twenty minutes later, prison officers found Dahmer on the floor, severely beaten. He died in the ambulance on the way to Divine Savior Hospital. A second inmate who'd also been beaten, was left in a critical condition and later died. Fellow inmate Christopher Scarver, who was in prison for murder, was found guilty of the deaths of both Dahmer and Jesse Anderson. In court, Scarver described the murder of Dahmer as "the work of God".

A wrecking ball brought down the Oxford Apartments where, in apartment 213, Dahmer is believed to have committed most of his crimes in November 1992.

For further investigation

📖 **Richard Tithecott** Of Men and Monsters: Jeffrey Dahmer and the Construction of the Serial Killer **(1999)**

📖 **Donald A. Davis** The Jeffrey Dahmer Story: An American Nightmare **(1991)**
Two of the best accounts of the chillling and inexplicable life of Jeffrey Dahmer.

Ⓦ time.com/time/magazine/article/0,9171,973550,00.html
Time magazine's article, by Alex Prud'homme, detailing what the magazine titled "The Little Flat of Horrors".

JOHN GLOVER: THE GRANNY KILLER

When **John Wayne Glover** hanged himself in his cell at Lithgow Jail, New South Wales, in September 2005, he had served fourteen years of a life sentence for the brutal murders of six women in Sydney during a thirteen-month period between 1989 and 1990. The women, all over sixty, were beaten and strangled by Glover in apparently motiveless attacks, for which he became known as the "Granny Killer". At the time of his death he was also suspected of at least five other similar killings.

Born in Britain in 1932, Glover migrated to Australia in 1956 as a **"Ten Pound Pom"** – one of the UK citizens who took advantage of an assisted passage scheme for preferential migration to Australia, with his fare largely paid by the Australian government. He settled in Melbourne and worked as a TV engineer. But in 1962 he received five years' probation for theft, indecent exposure and several violent attacks on women. In 1968, however, he married and moved to Mosman in Sydney, passing the next twenty years quietly raising two children and working as a meat pie salesman.

All this changed when, on the afternoon of 11 January 1989, Glover assaulted the 84-year-old Margaret Todhunter in a Mosman street, punching her in the face and stealing her handbag containing over $200. She was able to give a description of her grey-haired attacker to the police. Then on 1 March Glover followed Gwendoline Mitchelhill into the lobby of her apartment building, battered her in the head with a claw hammer and ran off with $100. She was found unconscious by two boys but died before reaching hospital.

Two months later Glover killed again, setting a pattern he would repeat. On 9 May, he followed an elderly lady named Winfreda Ashton into her home, assaulted her with a hammer and then bashed her head against the floor of the garbage recess until she passed out. In what police believe was an attempt to make the murders appear sexually motivated, he then strangled her with her tights and arranged her body suggestively. He stole another $100, spending it – as he had spent his earlier thefts – on poker machines at the local RSL (Returned Servicemen's League) club. Police linked the two murders together, but did not tie them to the earlier assault, and they thought they were looking for a youth.

Between June and October, Glover cased local nursing homes, indecently assaulting at least three women patients, one of whom was blind, after posing as a doctor, and severely assaulting 86-year-old Doris Cox in the stairwell of her retirement home. On 2 November he killed for a third time, beating 85-year-old Margaret Pahud to death with a

In December 2007, Robert Pickton, a Canadian pig farmer, was found guilty of the second-degree murders of six women after the longest trial – and, at $1 million, one of the most expensive–in Canada's history. Pickton preyed upon prostitutes and runaways and is believed to have killed some sixty women. He is serving out a 25-year prison sentence while his convictions are on appeal.

Westley Allen Dodd began exposing himself to children passing by his house at the age of thirteen. His perverse behaviour escalated, and he began molesting his young cousins. Then, when he was in his late twenties, he molested and stabbed two brothers, ten-year-old Billy Neer and eleven-year-old Cole. Next, Dodd lured Lee Iseli, aged four, from a school playground and the boy suffered a similar fate as the Neer brothers. Dodd was captured, convicted and sentenced to death in 1990.

hammer, leaving her body in an alley and stealing $300. He struck again the next day, killing Olive Cleveland after having befriended her in a park by beating her head against the pavement in a nearby lane. He once more tied her tights around her neck and stole $60 from her purse. In almost exactly the same way, he killed the 92-year-old Muriel Falconer – his oldest victim – on 23 November, stalking her to her home, beating and strangling her, then robbing the corpse. A boot print found at the scene was later confirmed to have been Glover's; it was virtually the only forensic evidence he had left that could link him to any of his crimes.

Glover made his first serious mistake exactly a year after he began his violent spree. On 11 January 1990, he indecently assaulted 82-year-old Daisy Roberts at Greenwich Hospital. Roberts called for help and Glover ran off, but hospital staff wrote down the numberplate and called police.

They did not connect the assault to the killings but requested Glover come in for questioning. When he failed to appear, the police learned that he had attempted suicide and was recovering in hospital. Hospital staff found a note in Glover's handwriting which read "no more grannies". After a two-week delay the note was handed to the task force investigating the serial killings, who immediately placed Glover under surveillance.

Police were therefore watching when, at 10am on 19 March, Glover was let into the home of his friend Joan Sinclair, a middle-aged lady it is thought that he might have been having a relationship with. At 6pm, having had no sign of him in the interim, police broke into the house. They found Joan Sinclair lying in a pool of blood, stripped from the waist down, her head smashed in and strangled with her underwear. Glover was unconscious in a bathtub, having slashed his wrists and taken an overdose of Valium with a bottle of whisky.

His suicide attempt was not successful, however. He was arrested and his case reached court the following year. Glover pleaded not guilty through diminished responsibility. But told of the way he had stalked his victims and waited for a suitable moment to carry out his crimes, the jury rejected his plea and Glover went to jail for life. He was to later say that he never cared who his victims were or why he killed them, and that he was powerless to stop himself. In September 2005 Glover committed suicide – his body was found in his cell after he had hanged himself.

For further investigation

Larry Writer Garden of Evil: The Granny Killer's Reign of Terror (1992)

Ⓦ trutv.com/library/crime/serial_killers/predators/glover /killer_11.html A tabloid-style interview with Glover by journalist Paul Kidd.

THE MOORS MURDERS

Ian Brady and **Myra Hindley** appeared before Hyde Magistrates Court in 1965. They had been charged with murdering five children in a case that has become known as the Moors Murders, so named because four of the victims were buried on Saddleworth Moor near Oldham, Lancashire.

No one knows for certain what caused Brady and Hindley, who met in 1961 while they both worked at a chemical factory in Manchester, to take a murderous path. Brady had grown up in the slums of Glasgow after his father – a journalist on a newspaper – died when Brady was a baby. His mother supported her son by working as a waitress, and often left him alone. When Brady was four months old, she gave her son to a couple who already had four children. His mother visited regularly, but he was never told she was his mother and, at the same time, he never felt he belonged in his family. He grew increasingly distant and emotionally disconnected. Hindley was believed to have been physically abused by her father, who was an alcoholic. Hindley had gone through a sad period in her life and

IAN BRADY

Three concurrent sentences of life imprisonment for what the judge called "three calculated, cruel, cold-blooded murders."

MYRA HINDLEY

Two concurrent sentences of life imprisonment for what the judge called "two equally horrible murders" ... and seven years as an accessory.

Daily Mirror

4d. Saturday, May 7, 1966   No. 19,399

3.38

'Calculated, cruel murders,' says judge

BRADY AND HINDLEY GO TO JAIL FOR LIFE

By MIRROR REPORTERS

PARTNERS in murder Ian Brady and Myra Hindley were both jailed for life at the end of the Bodies on the Moors trial yesterday.

Brady, 28, was found guilty of three murders — which meant three life sentences. Hindley, 23, was convicted of two murders — which brought her two life sentences.

A Home Office spokesman said last night: "A person sentenced to life imprisonment is liable to be detained for the whole of his or her natural life.

"But the Home Secretary has powers to release such a person on licence."

The all-male jury at Chester Assizes brought in these verdicts after a retirement of two hours, fourteen minutes.

BRADY: Guilty of the murders of 17-year-old Edward Evans, ten-year-old Lesley Ann Downey and 12-year-old John Kilbride.

HINDLEY: Guilty of the murders of Edward Evans and Lesley Ann Downey, but not guilty of the Kilbride murder. She was found guilty of harbouring Brady knowing he had murdered John Kilbride.

Edward Evans was found dead at the couple's home in Wardle Brook-avenue, Hattersley, Hyde, Cheshire. Lesley Ann Downey and John Kilbride were found in moorland graves after they had vanished.

Impassive

After the jury's verdicts the judge, Mr. Justice Fenton Atkinson said to Brady: "Ian Brady, these were three calculated, cruel, cold blooded murders."

He added: "In your case, I pass the only sentence which the law now allows, which is three concurrent sentences of life imprisonment."

Brady, impassive, then left the dock ... leaving Myra Hindley to hear her sentence.

"The judge said to her "In your case, Hindley, you have been found guilty of the jury of two equally horrible murders and, in the third, as an accessory after the fact of murder

Boos

"On the two murders she sentence is two concurrent sentences of life imprisonment. On the accessory charge, a concurrent sentence of seven years' imprisonment."

As she was sentenced, Hindley swayed forward and looked down. Then she left the dock.

Later, Brady and Hindley were escorted from the court building to a police van. As the van swung out from the Chester Castle courtyard, a crowd of about 200 people pressed forward and cheers.

This was the the couple to a "ended centre."

Today they will be taken to the prisons in which they will serve their sentences.

The Final Hours—See Page 9.

Watery beer upsets an MP

AN M.P. hit out last night against brewers who, he claimed, were steadily "watering down" their beer.

Mr. Geoffrey Rhodes, Labour M.P. for Newcastle East, told the Commons that tests on many beers showed a big fall in the "original gravity"—the measure of a beer's strength—over recent years.

Brewers are making bigger profits as a result, said Mr. Rhodes, who does not drink beer.

He suggested that a beer's strength should be shown on the container.

Promise

Agriculture Minister Fred Peart promised that beer strength would be considered when the whole question of food labelling was reviewed.

A spokesman for the Brewers' Society said last night: "The quality of beer does not rest on its potency. If you judge a drink on that, then methylated spirits would be the best drink on the market."

He added that the average beer was now nearly 10 per cent. stronger than it was twenty years ago.

her family had worried about her state of mind when, as a teenager, she was inconsolable after a thirteen-year-old boy, who was her closest friend, had drowned in a reservoir. But nobody could have predicted that the events of Hindley's and Brady's respective childhoods could have left them so warped that they would commit such terrible crimes.

Soon after Brady and Hindley met, they became romantically involved. Brady encouraged Hindley to obtain a weapons permit and learn to shoot a gun – he had a half-baked notion that the pair would rob banks together. But they never robbed a bank. Instead, in the mid 1960s, they raped, tortured, and murdered several children between the ages of ten and seventeen.

Their first victim was the sixteen-year-old Pauline Reade, who was a neighbour of Hindley's. She disappeared on her way to a party in July 1963. After raping the teen, Brady, using a shovel, smashed the side of her head and slit her throat with a knife while Hindley stood by watching. Reade's body would not be discovered for twenty years.

The remains of the youngest victim, **Lesley Ann Downey**, aged ten, were found buried in peat on the Yorkshire moors in a treacherously misty area of bogs. She'd disappeared from a fairground on Boxing Day in December 1964. In an eerie tape recording made by the accused, the terrified and bewildered girl pleaded with Brady and Hindley to take their hands off her. In one of nine photographs taken by the couple, the girl was seen lying naked, face down on a bed, her hands bound, a scarf tied around her mouth and her eyes bulging. Upon her death, Brady carried Downey's naked, limp body to a bathroom, rinsed the blood off her, wrapped her in a sheet with her clothing, then drove her to the moors, where the couple buried Downey in a shallow grave. After her remains were uncovered, it was found that her head had also been smashed in. Their voyeuristic documentation was

used a damning evidence that helped send the pair to prison for life.

Other known victims of the couple included **John Kilbride**, aged twelve, who disappeared without a trace from a in November 1963. His body was found two years later, in October 1965, on the moors. His throat had been slit with a serrated six-inch knife and his jeans and underpants had been pulled down to his knees.

Keith Bennett vanished in June 1964 while walking the mile to his grandmother's house to spend the night with her. He had turned twelve just four days earlier. He was lured by Brady into a ravine, where he was raped, tortured, and strangled with a piece of string. The body was buried near where the boy was killed. Hindley and Brady had taken photographs of Bennett's ordeal, but Hindley destroyed the evidence after Brady was arrested. Again, as in the other cases, Hindley stood by and watched the murder as it took place. The boy's body has never been recovered.

Edward Evans was the oldest victim, aged seventeen. He was murdered in 1965 after Brady, using an axe, cracked the boy's head and finished him off by strangling him. Hindley's eighteen-year-old brother-in-law, David Smith, witnessed the scene and saw the boy's body just after he'd been murdered. Afterwards, when Smith returned home, he told his wife, Maureen, who was Hindley's sister, what had taken place, and they called the police.

When Brady was arrested in 1965, it was for Evans's murder. Upon questioning by police, Brady admitted killing the boy, but he also claimed Smith had been involved. (Smith later testified at trial against the couple.) Brady and Hindley were each eventually charged with the other murders as well; during their trial, the pair repeatedly attempted to implicate Smith in the murders, protesting their innocence despite overwhelming evidence to the contrary. Brady was convicted on three murder charges and sentenced to three concurrent terms of life imprisonment. Hindley was convicted of murdering Edward Evans and Lesley Ann Downey and received two life sentences. Despite this, the judge stated his belief that, with the removal of Brady's presence and his influence over her, she might indeed be capable of a measure of rehabilitation. The pair were sent to prison, where Hindley died in 2002 aged sixty. Brady had been described by the judge as "wicked beyond belief" and "beyond hope of redemption", suggesting that he should never be released. He spent nineteen years in prison before he was declared insane and sent to a mental institution.

For further investigation

Ian Brady The Gates of Janus: Serial Killing and Its Analysis (2001) A book that caused, upon its release, heavy criticism of its publisher, because it was written by the killer. It includes court transcripts and grisly, first-hand details of the Moors Murders.

TED KACZYNSKI:
THE UNABOMBER

It took nearly two decades of investigations before **Theodore John Kaczynski**, a Montana resident who lived a hermit-like existence, was identified as the Unabomber. Through the US postal system, he waged a bombing campaign, killing three people and wounding twenty-three. His reign of terror

Former child prodigy, maths genius and woodsman mail terrorist Theodore Kaczynski, a.k.a. the Unabomber.

continued for more than eighteen years, stumping investigators.

Kaczynski was a former professor of mathematics at the **University of California** at Berkeley; he had given up a promising academic career in the early 1970s and dropped out of society. He traded academia for a secluded, solitary life in the woods by moving into a tiny, one-room, primitive cabin tucked away on one and a half acres in the heavily timbered Western Montana valley on the edge of the Lolo National Forest. He lived as a recluse. Eighty-foot high lodge-pole pine and Douglas-fir trees stretched to the sky, helping shelter him from the outside world. To get to the twelve-by-ten-foot primitive cabin that was four miles from the town of Lincoln, visitors had to climb a sixty-degree slope of winding trails. From his property, Kaczynski designed carefully crafted, homemade letter bombs, tested them in the Montana wilderness, packaged them, and mailed the devices to unsuspecting victims.

Kaczynski carried out sixteen attacks between 1978 and 1995. It was mostly universities and airlines that he attacked, terrorizing his targets. The locations prompted FBI agents to give the unknown terrorist the moniker "Unabomber", shorthand for "UNIversity" and airline "BOMber." The first explosive parcel was sent in May 1978, and the last – which killed Forestry Association president **Gilbert Murray** – in April 1996. The Unabomber had hinted at the bombing, without naming any particular people or locations. In a 1995 letter, the Unabomber, who often identified himself as "FC", warned that he intended to kill or injure university scientists and engineers. He detested certain academic studies, including philosophy, and referred to them as "bullshit subjects".

On 24 April 1995, Kaczynski sent a letter to *The New York Times* saying he would "desist from terrorism" if it would publish his manifesto. *The Washington Post* also published the manifesto. In it, Kaczynski unknowingly left evidence that would point to him. Although the Unabomber investigation was one of the most expensive and expansive in the FBI's history, it was ultimately Kaczynski's sister-in-law, **Linda Patrik**, married to Ted's brother, who discovered the Unabomber's identity. She recognized similarities in Ted's writings and philosophy to those of the Unabomber's manifesto.

Some of the more idiosyncratic, strident points made by the Unabomber had caught Patrik's eye. A philosophy professor at Union College in Schenectady, New York, and a counsellor at a shelter for runaway teens, she joined the dots from what she'd learned about her husband's brother – the profile of the Unabomber portrayed by the media seemed eerily familiar. She told reporters it took at least a month to convince her

husband that his brother could be the Unabomber. The FBI, who suspected the killer might be in academia, had released more details about the Unabomber, including the fact that he was an expert woodworker. That information also matched Ted's profile.

The Kaczynski family, however, was in denial at that time, according to David, about his brother's mental illness, believing that Ted – a graduate of Harvard University who had also received a doctorate from the University of Michigan – was simply a bit different to other people. Ted's sister-in-law, however, strongly disagreed. She had a gut feeling and a nagging suspicion about Ted, despite the fact that she'd never met him. "I couldn't get this thought of Ted being the Unabomber out of my mind. I was obsessed, and I couldn't tell if it was a realistic obsession or a fantasy obsession", Patrik, in a 1998 interview, told a Kansas daily newspaper.

Linda convinced David to read the Unabomber's published manifesto and decide for himself. David compared the manifesto with letters sent from Ted to their mother, to match the writing style. He noticed the term "cool-headed logicians"; his brother Ted had used those words. From the comparison, David believed there was a fifty-fifty chance his older brother could be the Unabomber. He and his wife then took the letters to a handwriting analyst, who agreed, and, in 1996, David and Linda went to the FBI and turned over their evidence. Afterwards, Ted's mother allowed her house to be searched by agents, who turned up more evidence that pointed to Ted being the Unabomber.

Investigators searched Ted's cabin, where they found supplies for bomb making and 22,000 journal pages of manic writings and ramblings that matched the writings of the Unabomber. After his arrest, a prison psychiatrist diagnosed Ted as a paranoid schizophrenic. An interesting aside in the case is that the FBI felt sure that Ted did not fully appreciate the harm he was inflicting on others. In the end, the government did not seek the death penalty against Ted Kaczynski, perhaps as a show of gratitude to the Kaczynskis for turning in their relative. Ted Kaczynski avoided the death penalty by accepting a plea agreement with US federal prosecutors in exchange for a sentence of life in prison with no possibility of parole.

Soon afterwards, Kaczynski tried to commit suicide. In a 1999 interview, the former Unabomber told *Time* magazine that he couldn't tolerate being called a "nut", "lunatic", or "sicko" – and that he only pleaded guilty to stop his lawyers from arguing that he was a paranoid schizophrenic.

Today, Ted Kaczynski, inmate number 04475-046, who in 2008 turned 66, is incarcerated at the Florence Federal Correctional Complex, a maximum federal penitentiary, in Florence, Colorado, that houses offenders who require the tightest of controls. He lives on what prisoners have dubbed "Celebrity Row" – a group of eight cells separated from the prison's general population. Also living on his row at one time were Ramzi Yousef, one of the planners of the 1993 World Trade Center bombing, and Timothy McVeigh, co-conspirator of the Oklahoma City bombing. Ted spends his days writing and preparing legal papers, and also reading the *Los Angeles Times*, the *New York Review of Books*, and *New Yorker* and *National Geographic* magazines, all gift subscriptions. Inmates on that row are permitted a ninety-minute recreation period when contact with fellow prisoners of the row is allowed.

David Kaczynski, along with his wife Linda, received a $1 million federal reward for turning in his brother. In 1999, the Kaczynski family donated $500,000, from the reward to victims of crimes committed by paranoid schizophrenics. The family's hope was that the Unabomber's victims would apply for and receive the funds.

Then, also in 1999, David and Linda received the highest honour – the Justice Award – for non-lawyers from the New York State Bar Association. "It's in the name of justice", David told the Associated Press at the time, "so we're particularly pleased and grateful."

For further information

📖 **Don Foster** Author Unknown: On the Trail of Anonymous **(2000)** The author, an expert at identifying anonymous writers, recounts his involvement in the search for the Unabomber.

📖 **Chris Waits and Dave Shors** Unabomber: The Secret Life of Ted Kaczynski **(1999)** Co-written by Kaczynski's neighbour of 25 years, this book covers the Unabomber's life in the mountains as he was then perceived: as a seemingly harmless hermit.

📽 **A&E Biography** Ted Kaczynski: The Unabomber **(2007)** An Arts and Entertainment television documentary that examines the life of the infamous man who launched an eighteen-year campaign of terror against the corporate US.

Ⓦ salon.com/news/1997/11/14news.html A Salon Q&A piece by Ros Davidson, with Jack Levin, director of a study on violence at Northeastern University, questioning just how crazy – or not – Kaczynski really was.

Ⓦ cnn.com/SPECIALS/1997/unabomb A chronology and archived list of articles on CNN.com before, during, and after the Unabomber trial.

RICHARD "THE ICEMAN" KUKLINSKI

One of the most cold-blooded serial killers in history, Richard "The Iceman" Kuklinski, worked on contract for the mob. During a lengthy interview with HBO, when the interviewer referred to him as an assassin, Kuklinski responded: "Assassin? That sounds so exotic ... I was just a murderer." Kuklinski the murderer, who without hesitation admitted to killing two hundred people, expressed no remorse for his crimes. Yet he once insisted to his accusers: "I'm the *niceman*, not the Iceman."

Kuklinski was of course anything but nice. He once described a "test murder" he had committed on the street: walking along in a crowd with a handkerchief over his nose and spraying a man with cyanide. The man collapsed and died, and everyone thought he had had a heart attack. "The best effect is to get 'em in the nose; they inhale it", he said. Killing by cyanide, although an admitted favourite, was not Kuklinski's only method of choice. He used lead, steel pipes, hammers, knives and guns to kill – whatever he had handy.

A powerful force at six-foot-five, weighing nearly 3002 pounds and wearing a size 14 shoe, he had a personal thing about "disrespect": one of his early victims was a man who Kuklinski said had insulted him in a bar. After Kuklinski discovered the man asleep in his car, Kuklinski apparently said to himself, "I am really gonna light your fire, you little sucker". And he did. He tossed a lit bottle of petrol into the man's car, causing it to explode. Kuklinski later said he could hear the man yelling and screaming in pain as he walked away into the night. He has also described having committed his first murder at the tender age of fourteen, exacting a bloody revenge on an older boy – the leader of a gang based in the same housing projects as Kuklinski, who had bullied and beaten him.

Kuklinski graduated from random, essentially motiveless murders to being a paid assassin for the Gambino crime family for some thirty years. In taped confessions to investigators, he revealed that he started out doing robberies and other assignments for the family, but soon his talent for killing was recognized, attracting the attention of the *Capo di tutti capi* – the family's boss. Over a thirty-year span, Kuklinski killed regularly for the Gambinos.

Initially nicknamed the "Polack" by his Italian associates because of his Polish heritage, Kuklinski claimed he earned the nickname "Iceman" due to his tactic of freezing the corpses of his victims in an industrial freezer in order to confuse the authorities by disguising the time of their death. Kuklinski also claimed he used a **Mister Softee** ice cream truck for that purpose, although the FBI is sceptical about it. (He has contradicted himself, telling author Philip Carlo that he got the idea to freeze his victims from another hit man, who drove a Mister Softee truck.) The authorities grew wise to Kuklinski's method when he failed to let one of his many victims adequately thaw before he disposed of the body. The coroner discovered the ploy when he found chunks of ice in the corpse's heart.

More grisly evidence of Kuklinski's killings came to light on 27 December 1982, when a decomposing body was found in a hotel room. The fourth couple to rent the room had complained to management of a terrible stench. After the mattress on the bed was lifted, beneath the bedsprings was found a bloated, blackened body, eventually identified as that of Gary Smith, who was an associate and partner-in-crime of Kuklinski's. Autopsy results showed Smith had been poisoned with cyanide and strangled. Later, Kuklinski confessed to having killed his erstwhile associate as the police had been turning up the heat on Smith, and, having moved him from motel to motel in New Jersey, the Iceman had decided to cut his losses, fearing that Smith would give him away.

At the same time as he was a career hit man, Kuklinski met and married **Barbara Petty** and fathered their children, none of whom had any idea their father was a hit man for the mob. They instead believed, like the Kuklinski's neighbours, that he was a successful businessman.

When Kuklinski was eventually caught in 1986, the case against him was based largely on the testimony of New Jersey State Police detective **Pat Kane**. An undercover agent, he had been investigating Kuklinski for

Richard Kuklinski, wearing sunglasses, is escorted by police from a court room in Hackensack, New Jersey, where he was charged with killing five people over a two-year period on 17 December 1986.

six years. The final part of the investigation involved a joint operation with the New Jersey Attorney General's office and the Bureau of Alcohol, Tobacco and Firearms; the Bureau began a joint operation with the NJ State Police. Detective Kane managed to recruit a close friend of Kuklinski, who introduced **Dominick Polifrone**, a special agent who had undercover experience specializing in Mafia cases, to the killer. Polifrone acted like he wanted to hire Kuklinski for a hit and recorded him speaking in detail about how he would pull off the killing. When state police and federal agents moved to take Kuklinski down, they blocked off his street and it took a dozen officers to arrest him.

Kuklinski was given two life sentences in 1988, specifying that he would not become eligible for parole until 2046, at which time he would have been 110 years old. In the event, he missed his unlikely shot at parole by some forty years. He died on 5 March 2006, of unknown causes, while behind bars at Trenton State Prison in New Jersey. He was seventy years old.

The timing of his death was considered suspicious by some, because he was scheduled to testify that he had killed a New Jersey police officer in the 1980s on the orders of former Gambino crime family underboss **Sammy Gravano**. A few days after Kuklinski's death, prosecutors dropped all charges against Gravano, saying that, without the hit man's testimony, the evidence would be insufficient to continue.

For further investigation

📖 **Philip Carlo** The Ice Man: Confessions of a Mafia Contract Killer (2006) Based on lengthy, taped interviews with Kuklinski, the book gives insights into what drove the killer into a life as a paid hit man.

ⓦ hbo.com/docs/programs/iceman Includes links to a series of lengthy interviews with Richard Kuklinski.

ⓦ philipcarlo.com/works/iceman/iceman.html Excerpts from a biography by author Philip Carlo.

BRUCE GEORGE PETER LEE

In December 1979, when a troubled nineteen-year-old arsonist set fire to the home of the Hastie family in the city of Hull, England, near the Yorkshire coast, his arrest led to the sobering realization that he had killed before. **Peter Dinsdale**, known as Bruce George Peter Lee, was eventually discovered to have been one of Britain's most prolific serial killers.

The Hasties weren't the most popular people in the area. For that reason, initially some thought the murders might have been some kind of act of neighbourhood retaliation – or a family quarrel gone horribly wrong. Thirty-four-year-old Edith Hastie was the mother of seven – three daughters and four sons. The family lived at 12 Selby Street, a run-down area, and locals referred to them as a one-family crime wave, with the boys and their father Tommy committing petty crimes on a regular basis. The police were called almost daily to one incident or another involving a Hastie male, whether it was throwing rocks at the elderly, robbing children of pocket money, vandalizing shops, or even urinating in mailboxes or defecating on porches. Despite all of this, Detective Superintendent **Ron Sagar** told the *Hull Daily Mail* the father was "a likeable rogue", noting that the Hastie boys "may have been somewhat mischievous at times, but they didn't deserve to die like this".

In the early morning hours of 4 December, Edith suddenly awoke. When she walked out of her room and onto the landing, flames were shooting up the stairs. Her three daughters were staying with friends and relatives, while her husband, Tommie, was in jail. But the boys – Charlie, 15, Paul, 12, Thomas, 9, and Peter, 8 – were all at home. She ran to Charlie's room and awoke him, then they both ran back to Edith's room, where Thomas, who had muscular dystrophy, was sleeping. They were pushed back by the flames and smoke and into another bedroom. That's when Charlie, to save his mother, threw her out of a second-floor window. She injured her foot falling fifteen feet to the ground. She yelled up, calling for Charlie to follow, but by the time firefighters arrived and rescued the boys, Paul, Peter, and Charlie had suffered burns over about eighty percent of their bodies. Within two weeks, three of the boys died from their injuries. Only Thomas, who had less serious burns, survived.

Firefighters discovered two burned matches and flammable fluid near the letterbox at the front door. The odour of paraffin was strong. The fire appeared to be the work of an experienced arsonist. Police had very few leads. No one seemed willing to help investigators, since there was so much animosity towards the family. Edith accused her neighbours. On 4 January 1980, the day of her boys' funeral, as the procession made its way down Selby Street, a local TV camera crew captured Edith screaming hysterically at onlookers. "It was one of you bastards!" she yelled. "One of you in the street is the murderer!"

Police received what appeared to be a break in the case in the form of a note, left months earlier in the Hasties' mail slot. Edith had saved it, and, after discovering it had survived the fire, turned the note over to investigators. The note, written on the back of a piece of cardboard cut from a Cornflakes cereal box, said this: "I'm not kidding but I promised you a bomb and by hell I'm not kidding. Why don't you just flit while you've got the chance. If we can't get you out normally then we'll bastard well bomb you out, and that's too good for you." Police had a thousand residents submit handwriting samples. Investigators narrowed it down to the handwriting of an elderly woman who had been terrorized by the Hastie boys; they did not believe, however, that she was the arsonist.

Several months later, acting on a tip-off that Charlie Hastie may have been a rent boy, police interviewed men who frequented a local gay bar. One of them, **Bruce George Peter Lee** (Peter Dinsdale had changed his name earlier that year in honour of his kung fu idol), told detectives he knew Charlie because they'd had sexual encounters.

Police took Lee to the station, read him his rights, and implied they thought he had committed the arson, hoping for a lead. They were floored when Lee confessed to not only the Hastie arson, but also a string of other killings. He went on to explain that he had set the fire to get back at Charlie, who had continually demanded money for sex that had initially been consensual. Detective Superintendent Sagar asked Lee if he enjoyed watching fires burn, and Lee responded with an admission: "I like fires, I do. I like fires. Yes, you are right. I killed a little baby once."

In January 1981, a court accepted Lee's plea of guilty on 26 counts of manslaughter and 11 of arson. Among his victims were children and the elderly. In 1983, a judge reviewed evidence against Lee in the case of a 1977 fire at Wensley Lodge old people's home, which resulted in the death of eleven retirees and these specific convictions were overturned. Lee remains incarcerated in a secure mental institution.

For further investigation

📖 **Carol Anne Davis** Children Who Kill: Profiles of Pre-teen and Teenage Killers (2004) A profile of thirteen killers, all of whom were aged between ten and seventeen when they killed. Bruce Lee (a.k.a. Peter George Dinsdale) is among them.

Ⓦ crimelibrary.com/notorious_murders/classics/bruce_lee/1 .html A history, written by Johnny Sharp and posted on truTV's Crime Library, gives details of the case and the background of the victims and killer.

BOBBY JOE LONG: THE MOTHER'S DAY KILLER

In 1980, **Bobby Joe Long** committed the first of a series of brutal rapes in Fort Lauderdale, Ocala, Miami and Dade County, Florida, that led to him being named the "Classified Ad Rapist". Long would answer classified ads in the newspapers with items for sale at the homes of women who lived alone, or arrange to come round when their husbands were at work.

The body of Long's first murder victim was discovered by teenagers at a construction site in Hillsborough County, lying face down with her wrists tied together loosely behind her back and a noose with a hangman's tied around her neck. It was Mother's Day 1984, and the victim had been dead for about three days. The cause of death was stran-

gulation, and the victim had been raped before she was killed. A missing person's report for a young Asian female matched the description of the victim. She was identified as **Ngeun Thi Long**, a twenty-year-old dancer at the Sly Fox Lounge in Tampa. The killer had left behind crucial evidence – tyre tracks from a truck – at the scene of the crime.

The body of a second victim was found two weeks later by a construction worker. The corpse had been dumped in a lover's lane near a rural area. Investigators noticed that the murder was similar to the one fourteen days earlier. The killer once again had left behind tyre marks from a truck. The cause of death was asphyxiation and severe injuries to the head. The victim was identified as a 22-year-old prostitute who'd only been in the area for a couple of days. This time, the killer left semen stains behind.

Based upon the evidence, police put together a profile of the killer, whom they believed to be a white man in his early twenties, probably with a criminal past. They were correct – Bobby Joe Long had been arrested and convicted of a rape earlier, in 1981. But the conviction had been subsequently overturned on appeal and Long had been released.

Police ultimately estimated the number of rapes Long committed as being as many as fifty. By November of 1984, he had murdered at least nine women. But he made a big mistake when one of his victims managed, by an incredible effort of self-control, to survive her 26-hour kidnapping ordeal, and convince Long to let her go. The woman immediately reported the attack to police, and, based upon her description and vehicle information, officers picked up Long about two weeks later. But it was too late for his tenth victim; Long killed again within the fortnight.

He was eventually caught during a routine traffic stop for driving too slowly. Long's address matched the area that police were searching for the killer. And the car's interior fitted a description the surviving victim had given to police. Police let Long go, and then put a tap on his phone and put him under surveillance. After accumulating enough evidence against him, detectives were granted search and arrest warrants. During a police interrogation, Long admitted to raping and killing one victim, then admitted to killings police had not yet connected to him. Long's signed confession was 45 pages long.

He was tried for nine murders and the rape of the lone survivor, all committed over a six-month period. During his first trial, long was convicted and given both life and death sentences. After the verdict, as he was escorted out of court by deputies, Long turned and laughed at the rape victim, who was in court for the verdict. Long appealed against the decision, and the Florida Supreme Court granted him two new trials, one for the murders and the second for rape. He was found guilty once again, in both trials, and in 1986 sentenced to death, one five-year sentence, four ninety-nine-year sentences, and twenty-eight life sentences.

Today, Bobby Joe Long is incarcerated on Union Correctional Institution's death row in Raiford, Florida.

For further investigation

Ⓦ groups.msn.com/murderscrime/bobbyjoelong.msnw A lengthy synopsis of the murders and legal decisions in the Bobby Joe Long murder and rape cases.

Ⓦ dc.state.fl.us/ActiveInmates/Detail.asp?Bookmark=1&From =list&SessionID=700691205 Florida Department of Corrections inmate information online page for Robert J. Long.

IVAN MILAT

On 20 September 1992, bushwalkers found a decayed corpse partially covered in undergrowth near a gorge known as "Executioners Drop" in Belangelo State Forest, New South Wales. A police search the next day located a second body, along with a small brick fireplace, cigarette butts and .22 gun cartridges. The remains were identified as those of **Caroline Clarke** and **Joanne Walters**, British backpackers last seen in Sydney in April 1991. They had clearly been murdered. Clarke had been shot in the head and stabbed, Walters stabbed nine times and possibly strangled. The knife attacks were so violent that they had severed the victims' spines.

Just over a year later, two more bodies were discovered in another part of the forest. The remains were incomplete, but dental records identified **James Gibson** and **Deborah Evereist** from Melbourne, who had been missing since 1989. The victims had again been stabbed through the spine, and a similar makeshift campfire nearby linked the murders together.

On 1 November 1993, forty officers of the investigating "Task Force Air" began a sweep through Belangelo. The team almost immediately discovered another skeleton, its skull still wearing a purple headband. It proved to be that of German backpacker **Simone Schmidt**, missing since January 1991. She had been stabbed to death in the same manner as the previous victims. Clothes belonging to missing German tourist **Anja Habschied** were also uncovered, along with another fireplace and more .22 shells. Two days later, the remains of Anja Habschied and her boyfriend **Gabor Neugebauer** were found buried nearby in shallow graves. Gabor had been strangled

Ivan Milat, in his suburban Sydney home, shows off his handgun and air-rifles.

and shot by the same weapon used in Caroline Clarke's murder; his body was concealed by a heavy log. Anja had been decapitated. All seven victims showed signs suggesting sexual molestation.

Police forensic psychiatrists believed the killer behind the "Backpacker Murders" to be a local man with a history of violence, who spent a good deal of time outdoors. They also speculated that he might not have worked alone, and was from a large family. Amongst the thousands of responses to appeals for information from the public, the name **Ivan Milat** began to surface as a man fitting their profile.

Milat had been born in 1944, one of fourteen children. While growing up he became fond of hunting and weapons, and when he was an adult he worked on road maintenance crews with his brother. Ivan had served time in prison for various offences. In 1971, he was accused of abducting and raping two female hitchhikers at knife-point, though the charges had been dismissed. When police dug deeper, they found Milat owned property near Belangelo, had been absent from work at the time of each killing, and had sold his 4WD immediately after the first bodies had been discovered. Tracing the vehicle, police found ammunition matching that used in the killings under a seat.

Then a man named **Paul Onions** contacted the investigation from his home in the UK. He described how, while hitching in Australia in 1990, he was given a lift in a 4WD by a man calling himself "Bill". Near the Belangelo turn-off, the man had pulled over, threatened Onions with a gun and tried to tie him up, but Onions had escaped and was picked up by passing motorist Joanne Berry. The police consequently flew Onions to Australia where, on 5 May 1994, he identified Milat in a video line-up as the man who gave him a lift.

On 22 May Milat was arrested during a dawn raid on his home in Campbelltown, New South Wales, for the 1990 assault. Searching his house, police found clothing and camping gear owned by the murdered backpackers, along with numerous weapons. One of these was a dismantled .22 Ruger rifle hidden in a wall. After forensics confirmed that this Ruger was the weapon used in the killings, Milat was charged with the Backpacker Murders on 30 May.

Delayed by legal complications, Milat's trial began in March 1996. He steadfastly protested his innocence, claiming he had been framed by his brothers. But on 27 July, after three days of deliberation, the jury found Milat guilty of the murders, along with the assault on Paul Onions. Justice David Hunt accepted that it was unlikely that Milat carried out the killings alone, but gave him seven life sentences.

Milat was imprisoned in New South Wales at Maitland Jail until he attempted to escape in 1997. He is currently serving his sentence under maximum security at Goulburn Jail, where all appeals against his sentence have been rejected. There is still debate over whether he acted alone, and even today Milat still vigorously protests his innocence.

For further investigation

📖 **Les Kennedy & Mark Whittaker** Sins of the Brother: The Definitive Story of Ivan Milat and the Backpacker Murders (2001) Meticulously researched account, including about the only published details concerning the unsettling Milat clan.

Ⓦ sydney.indymedia.org.au/node/37637 The other side of the tale: Ivan Milat is innocent and it's all a conspiracy.

GARY RIDGWAY: THE GREEN RIVER KILLER

For twenty long years, **Gary Leon Ridgway**, the Green River Killer, evaded police before he was named as the serial killer that had preyed on Seattle-area women. All his killings had taken place near the Green River in the Seattle suburb of Kent, Washington. Once caught, Ridgway confessed and pleaded guilty to more murders than any other serial killer in US history.

Many of Ridgway's victims were prostitutes, drug

users, or runaways who were vulnerable targets. Some were underage, and many of the victims knew each other. Their bodies were each found submerged in water, near the edge of the Green River, which is accessed by a two-lane, winding, country road twenty miles from Seattle, or in the tall grasses, thick reeds, and thorny blackberry vines on the riverbanks. One tattooed female body was discovered on a slip of sandbar in the river, covered in silt and burned by the sun. The victim on the sandbar was later identified as Debra Lynn Bonner, aged 24 years old. She had been arrested a few times for prostitution while using a variety of aliases. Despite just one road leading to and from the river, witnesses never saw the killer dump her body or any of the other victims' remains that turned up at the Green River.

Who exactly was the man the media called the Green River Killer? According to reports, he was "unremarkable". Gary Ridgway, born in Salt Lake City, Utah, grew up in McMicken Heights, in King County, Washington. Possibly one of the most significant things about his childhood was his mother, who was domineering and controlling. In grade school, Ridgway tested with a low IQ of 80. He got in trouble with the law for the first time at age sixteen when he stabbed and injured a six-year-old child.

During his confession to police, Ridgway, by then 54 years old, admitted to murdering 42 women whom police had identified as being victims of the Green River serial killer. But he also admitted to murdering six more women whose deaths previously were not known to be connected to the Green River killings. Then, in a move that attracted opprobrium from many local citizens, Ridgway avoided a death

THE G·R·K· DOSSIER

The Green River Task Force's internal investigative tool was a twelve-page FBI psychological profile of the Green River Killer, written by then-FBI special agent John Douglas with the Behavioral Science Unit in Quantico, Virginia. It was written in 1982, and revised in 1984. The profile has never officially been made public, but details were leaked to reporters over the years and printed in news stories. One new detail in the revised profile was the possibility that there was more than one Green River Killer. Details also appeared in the book *The Search for the Green River Killer*, written by a team of *Seattle Times* reporters. The original FBI profile was based on crime scene photos, as well as the first five victims, plus the bureau's studies of serial killers. Critics, however, questioned the validity of the profile, pointing out that it was so vague that the killer could have been half the men in King County, Washington, where the Green River Killer preyed upon unsuspecting women.

Once Ridgway confessed to being the Green River Killer, claiming responsibility for murdering 48 people between 1982 and 1998, his psychological profile was put aside and police stopped looking for the guilty party. While critics have questioned whether Ridgway was, in fact, the killer, he did lead the authorities to four separate remains, knowledge prosecutors said only the killer could have possessed.

sentence by instead accepting a plea agreement from prosecutors that allowed him to live out the rest of his life in prison.

In exchange for a prison sentence instead of a death penalty, Ridgway provided information that helped locate lost remains of victims who were abducted by Ridgway on a strip of Pacific Coast Highway South known to be frequented by prostitutes. The killer was the most prolific serial murderer in American history.

On 5 November 2003, Ridgway pleaded guilty to all charges. In his confession, he told police that strangling young women was his "career" and that he wanted to kill as many prostitutes as he could. He is serving out his 48 consecutive life terms in the Washington State Penitentiary in Walla Walla. Four years after Ridgway pleaded guilty, investigators publicly released photos of three victims whose faces were reconstructed, hoping someone would identify them. While Ridgway admitted killing them in 1983, he didn't know their names. They remain unidentified.

For further investigation

🕮 **David Reichert** Chasing the Devil: My Twenty-Year Quest to Capture the Green River Killer (2005) County Sheriff David Reichert tracked the Green River Killer for twenty years. This book covers his investigations into the murders.

🎞 **Norma Bailey** The Capture of the Green River Killer (2008) A Lifetime Movie Network four-hour, narrated film based on true events and including a re-creation of the crimes.

Ⓦ greenriverkiller.com/Nav.htm A comprehensive site that includes artist sketches of the suspect during his years'-long serial crime spree along with background information about Gary Ridgway.

DR HAROLD SHIPMAN

One of the most prolific serial killers in modern history, Harold "Fred" Shipman was a respected country doctor, with the public reputation of being a gentle man. He was convicted in 2000 on fifteen murder charges and sentenced to fifteen consecutive life sentences. Shipman, who had a practice in the Hyde area in Greater Manchester, England, was arrested after attempting to forge an elderly victim's will, worth £368,000. At the time of his capture, the authorities estimated he was killing at a rate of one patient every ten days. In most instances, the doctor's assassination method was poisoning: the administering of a dangerously large dose of a sedative drug. Many of his victims died after Shipman had paid them house calls, including at least seven who lived at the Ogden Court sheltered housing block, near where Shipman had his practice.

The investigation into suspected deaths at the hand of Dr Shipman began in 1998 when a dozen bodies, one by one, were exhumed from the Hyde Cemetery for further forensics examinations. For four months, bodies were removed from their graves and new evidence gathered. Toxicology test results showed that some of the victims had died from morphine overdoses, even though their medical records showed no prescriptions for morphine and they were not drug abusers. On their death certificates, Shipman had listed the cause as being heart attacks and strokes. It was also learned that Dr Shipman was the last person to see many of the victims alive. If relatives or friends were present as the victims were dying, Shipman would sometimes pretend to call for ambulances – but, of course, none ever came.

BURKE AND HARE: VICTORIAN SERIAL KILLERS

The Irish labourers William Burke and William Hare, who had both worked on the 1818–22 construction of the Union Canal in Scotland, shared a lodging house owned by Hare's common-law wife Margaret Laird in West Port, Edinburgh from November 1827. At the time, medical schools bought cadavers, often with no questions asked, for use in anatomy lessons and for student dissections. According to the testimony Hare would later give, when another resident of the lodging house died owing rent, the two men sold his corpse to Edinburgh Medical College where the unscrupulous Dr Robert Knox paid them the handsome sum of £7 for it.

Attracted by the ease with which they had made the money, they decided to go into business. For the next year Burke and Hare ferried further bodies to the dissection school, earning up to £10 each time. Their victims included a prostitute and two disabled youths. One of the reasons suspicions arose about the two men was that students recognized one of the youths, eighteen-year-old "Daft Jamie", who was mentally retarded.

When, after a dozen cadavers had been sold in this grisly trade, police caught up with the killers, they were faced with a lack of evidence. Apart from the fact that the corpses had been used for dissection, the two killers had used a killing technique that has since become known as "burking" – simultaneous smothering and compression of the torso, which leads to suffocation with few telltale signs. To get round the lack of evidence, Hare was offered immunity in return for his testimony. The trial of Burke began at 10am on Christmas Eve 1828, and lasted only until Boxing Day, when he was found guilty.

On 28 January 1829, Burke was hanged at Edinburgh's Lawn Market while a large crowd looked on. According to *The Scotsman's* report, "During the time of the wretched man's suspension, not a single indication of pity was observable among the vast crowd: on the contrary, every countenance wore the aspect of a gala-day, while puns and jokes were freely bandied about." The 1832 Anatomy Act was passed in order to make provision for cadavers to medical schools. Hare went into obscurity, though there are reports he was mobbed and buried in quicklime.

The Anatomy Museum of the Royal College of Surgeons of Edinburgh has Burke's death mask – a plaster cast made of his face following his death – and a wallet allegedly made of his skin. His skeleton is also on display in the medical school.

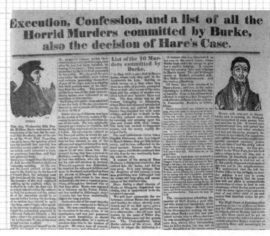

The results of an official investigation into Shipman's crimes were shocking. It concluded that between 1971 and 1998, Shipman had killed an estimated 250 people, 32 of whom were never positively identified. Most of his victims, the majority of them women, lived near the doctor's clinic. Shipman's youngest known victim was 44-year-old Konrad Robinson and the oldest was 92-year-old Hilda Couzens. The evidence police gathered and the forensic techniques they employed put an end to Shipman's two-and-a-half decade killing spree.

Shipman was not found guilty for all the murders that the police suspected him of, although what they did connect to him put him away for life: in January 2000, he was convicted by a jury at Preston Crown Court for killing fifteen female patients between 1995 and 1998 while he worked at a surgical clinic.

On 13 January 2004, Harold Shipman's body was discovered at 6.20 am in his cell at Wakefield Prison. He was pronounced dead nearly two hours later. An inquiry, while finding no wrongdoing on the part of the prison, made suggestions for improvement in procedures. Prison officials said the 57-year-old, using bed sheets, had hanged himself from prison window bars. He had recently been taken off the prison's suicide watch list.

That so many deaths had occurred in the ward of a then highly respected doctor without any questions being asked, for so many years, was scandalous. After Shipman's death, a new inquiry was opened to

DR DEATH

- **Guilty of killing 15 women patients**

- **Shipman faces 23 new murder charges**

- **Police have files on at least 100 more**

- **Coroner admits it could be up to 1,000**

FACE OF EVIL: A new picture of Shipman released by police yesterday

KILLER doctor Harold Shipman was locked away last night for murdering 15 of his patients – but the true toll could run into hundreds.

Shipman, 54, will die behind bars as Britain's worst mass murderer. Police believe the evil Dr Death from Hyde, Greater Manches-

By PATRICK MULCHRONE and IAN DISLEY

ter, could have poisoned at least 100 more and are ready to charge him with a further 23 murders.

But a coroner believes that over 30 years, the GP may have claimed up to ONE THOUSAND lives. The South Manchester coro-

TURN TO PAGE 2

BRITAIN'S BIGGEST MURDERER: PAGES 2-11 ● THE SHIPMAN STORY: 12-PAGE PULLOUT

look into how a doctor of his stature could have got away with it. Criticism of the coroner system and of the process of death certification featured strongly in a report by a select committee commissioned by the British government, revealing the failures in the system that allowed a doctor to enter false causes of death on official certificates.

During the inquiry it came to light that Shipman had robbed some of his victims of their jewellery. The robberies aside, it was never determined what Shipman's motives were. He continued, until his death, to protest his innocence. In July 2005,

at a gathering in Hyde Park, a memorial garden, called the Garden of Tranquillity, was dedicated to Shipman's victims.

For further investigation

📖 **Wensley Clarkson** The Good Doctor (2007) A biography that traces the early years of Harold Shipman's practice to discover what drove the doctor to murder his patients.

Ⓦ news.bbc.co.uk/2/hi/uk_news/england/manchester/4210581 .stm A compilation of stories about Harold Shipman and his victims, written by the BBC.

Ⓦ guardian.co.uk/uk/2006/aug/01/politics.shipman An article by Sarah Hall about a government-commissioned inquest into

SERIAL KILLERS: FACTS & MYTHS

There has been a dearth of scientific study of serial homicide – the killing of a number of individuals in a row, with some cooling-off period between murders – which is in striking contrast to the enormous interest this topic has received in film, print and television media. In fact, the curiosity of the lay-public has been so intense that many notorious serial killers have even become household names. But the Hollywood conception of the serial killer, depicted most notably by Thomas Harris' fictional Hannibal Lecter – a brilliant, sophisticated psychiatrist who was able to elude law enforcement for years – could not be further from the truth. And despite what is often portrayed in the media, serial murder is nither a twentieth-century phenomenon, nor an American one; and there is no evidence whatsoever that the number of such killings is increasing.

There are many types of serial killers, including contract killers, those who kill multiple people in response to a psychosis, cutt – inspried killers, those who operate in

medical facilities, spree killers, and various mixed cases. The type of serial killer that is best understood is the sexually motivated serial murderer – but even here, there has been minimal actual scientific research conducted. For example, in comparison to depression, or post-traumatic stress disorder (which respectively have had 72,000 and 18,000 research articles published over the past 30 years), the number of scientific publications on serial homicide has only been 79.

Serial killer myths are plentiful and most conform to Hollywood's depiction of this type of offender. But it is very rare that a serial sexual murderer is highly intelligent or has any unique ability to elude law enforcement. In fact, most of these individuals have below-average to average

the events surrounding Harold Shipman's actions and new procedures recommended to prevent anything similar from happening again.

THE YORKSHIRE RIPPER

After nearly six years, between 1975 and 1981, a frightening crime spree that gripped a community came to an end when **Peter William Sutcliffe**, a serial killer identified as the "Yorkshire Ripper", was arrested during a routine police stop in Sheffield, England. At

a hearing following his arrest, Sutcliffe, who once worked as a gravedigger, claimed he'd heard voices that directed him to hunt down and kill prostitutes. Sutcliffe was overheard in the courtroom telling his wife he was hoping to be pronounced insane. Instead, the majority of the jury believed that Sutcliffe was simply a sadistic murderer. They convicted him of killing thirteen women and injuring seven people. The judge handed down a sentence of life in prison, and he is serving it confined to a mental hospital.

Sutcliffe's first murder was committed in 1975. He had previously made several unsuccessful attempts, during which his intended victims managed to escape with

intelligence and are typically working-class or unemployed. Even those offenders who have eluded law enforcement for many years – and who have killed numerous victims – generally do so as a result of their own luck, as opposed to possessing any degree of criminal sophistication. Other serial murder myths are: that these killers are dysfunctional loners (most are quite social); that all are white males (they span all racial groups); that they travel and operate in different parts of the country (most stay in one geographical area); that they cannot stop killing (many stop killing for many years); that they are insane (most are not psychotic or overtly mentally ill); and that they want to get caught (most do not want to get caught but sometimes do things, like communicating with the police, that lead to their arrest).

Recent research has found that the popularized notion of serial sexual murderers engaging in the exact same ritualistic behaviour, or leaving unique signatures at every crime scene – such as placing butterflies in the mouths of victims – has little scientific basis. Although serial killers do engage in repetitive ritualistic conduct, the crime-scene behaviour of this group of offenders is complex and varied.

There are, however, a number of tendencies that lurk in the backgrounds of serial murderers that should be considered red flags for the development of such extraordinary acting-out: childhood abuse, the experience of inappropriate maternal sexual conduct, pathological lying and manipulation, sadistic fantasies with a compulsion to act, as well as animal cruelty, especially against cats.

These offenders typically also have a long-standing need to control and dominate others; they often engage in repetitive fire-starting, and they frequently have a history of voyeurism, fetishism, and sexual burglary. As children, adolescents, or young adults, such future offenders engage in unprovoked attacks on females, which are associated with generalized misogynous emotions. It is interesting to note that, as more and more scientific studies of the serial sexual murderer are carried out, more and more of the media's portrayals of this type of offender become unsupported.

Professor Louis B. Schlesinger

Detectives at the crime scene of another victim of the Yorkshire Ripper, in Roundhay Park, Leeds.

injuries. Sutcliffe hit, then repeatedly stabbed Wilma McCann, a 28-year-old mother of four. McCann's body was found by a milk delivery driver, lying face-up in the grass on a country road. The thirteenth, final victim of the Ripper – as the press described the killer – was nineteen-year-old Jacqueline Hill, a student at Leeds University, who was bludgeoned and left to die behind a campus building.

Sutcliffe came close to being caught after his murder of **Jean Jordan**, a twenty-year-old prostitute from

Manchester. He had paid a £5 note to the victim, which was traced back to an engineering firm in Bradshaw where Sutcliffe worked. It led police to his doorstep. After police interviewed Sutcliffe several times, co-workers jokingly called Sutcliffe "The Ripper", little realizing that it was in fact true. But police accepted Sutcliffe's explanation and he wasn't arrested.

Sutcliffe's killings continued unabated, and in January 1976 he stabbed to death **Emily Jackson**, a 42-year-old impoverished housewife, in the middle of a prostitution transaction. Jackson, unbeknownst to her family, had resorted to prostitution to help her family through financial hardship. Her murder was particularly violent. Sutcliffe, using a hammer, first bludgeoned Jackson over the head, then repeatedly stabbed her with a sharpened screwdriver in her neck, chest, and abdomen. Sutcliffe also stamped on her hip and thigh, leaving behind prominent boot imprints. After her murder was made public, neighbours and family members expressed shock at learning that Jackson had taken money in exchange for sex.

The randomness of the killings made it difficult for police to identify the murderer. Sutcliffe was one among thousands of people interviewed by the police. Eventually, a commander from Scotland Yard – the headquarters of the Metropolitan Police Service – oversaw the case for a month and left, satisfied that police had been thorough in their search. Police upped their presence in red-light areas and car licences were logged. On sixty occasions, Sutcliffe was observed driving through red-light districts. After several sightings of his car, Sutcliffe was questioned. Each time, however, his wife either gave him a plausible alibi or he had an explanation that made sense.

Under pressure by the public to solve the crimes, police stepped up their investigation by forming a special Super Squad – dubbed the Ripper Squad – making the manhunt for the Ripper one of the largest in British history. Police profiled the killer, surmising he was between twenty and fifty-five years old, white, having a size nine shoe or less, and with blood type B. Some 30,000 statements were taken.

When the sun went down in Leeds, the streets were empty because residents were too frightened to go out at night, and prostitutes were warned to stay off the streets. But after **Olivia Reivers**, a street prostitute, ventured out one night and got into a brown Rover with a man later identified as Sutcliffe, two officers followed the car; they were intending to make an arrest for soliciting. But the routine stop abruptly ended the Ripper's killing spree.

They pulled over the driver and ran the plates, which were suspiciously attached to the car with black tape. When the plates turned up as stolen, they arrested Sutcliffe and took him to the station. Upon further questioning, Sutcliffe eventually confessed to being the Yorkshire Ripper. It took fifteen hours for Sutcliffe to tell police his tale of terror. He also told police he'd targeted prostitutes because in his youth he'd been cheated by a prostitute out of £10.

On Friday 22 May 1981, Sutcliffe stood as the foreman declared the jury's decision that Peter William Sutcliffe was guilty of thirteen counts of murder and seven counts of attempted murder. After the jury convicted Sutcliffe, he walked out of the courtroom, flanked by courtroom officers. He showed no signs of remorse. Shortly after commencing his jail stint he was diagnosed with schizophrenia.

Despite the length of the sentence he received, Sutcliffe could in theory be released from prison should his parole board agree that he represents no danger to the public.

He has been attacked in prison at least three times and his release, should it ever happen, would be certain to cause considerable controversy.

For further investigation

Michael Bilton *Wicked Beyond Belief: The Hunt for the Yorkshire Ripper* (2003) A detailed and definitive account of the Ripper's reign of terror.

Ⓦ trutv.com/library/crime/serial_killers/predators/sutcliffe/ mask_1.html An in-depth portrayal of the killer and his prey in a chapter-by-chapter chronology.

ORGANIZED CRIME

Organized crime

Drugs, extortion, gambling, smuggling, hijacking, corrupt business deals, sex slavery, loan-sharking, money-laundering, and, arms trading are just some of the numerous illegal activities that take place in the ruthless black economy of organized crime.

The Mafia has a clan structure: hierarchical, with a boss at the top, then underbosses, then lieutenants, then soldiers. In this it resembles other traditional outfits – notably the Japanese **yakuza** and the Chinese **Triads**. All three organizations are bound by strict codes of loyalty and silence, of "honour among thieves". Members see themselves as outsiders and outlaws. They get their sense of belonging from the surrogate family that is the mob. Many such men tattoo themselves to proclaim their affiliations, or use other signs and marks to signal to those in the know that they are gangsters.

Though its exact origins are obscure, many think that the Sicilian Mafia – the **Cosa Nostra** ("our thing") – began as a resistance movement, a band of fighters rebelling against the island's foreign invaders. But it soon enough became a criminal conspiracy which today makes annual profits estimated to be well over $100 billion. From the small Mediterranean island off the "toe" of Italy, the web of the underworld extends across the globe. In the nineteenth century, the Mafia found a foothold in the US, where it would soon become entrenched, an integral factor in the country's pursuit of wealth. From Chicago mobster **Al Capone** in the 1920s to New York's "Dapper Don" **John Gotti** in the 1990s, the Mafia constitutes a significant chapter in the American story, mythologized in the *Godfather* films, in Martin Scorsese's *Casino* (about the Mafia in Las Vegas) and *Goodfellas* (set in New York) – and of course in the hit TV show about the New Jersey Mafia, *The Sopranos*.

The profits made in the black economy are staggering. **Pablo Escobar**'s Medellín Cartel's 1980s narcotics operation boosted the entire economy of Colombia before the cartel was smashed. Today, the Russian Mafia are thought to be the most powerful and ferocious organized-crime group, with tentacles stretching across the world.

There are of course smaller players in the underworld too, especially in the multicultural US. Here, it's not so much about money but about belonging – gangs that spring up on city streets and in prisons such as the Bloods and Crips, the Black Spades and Latin Kings, the Mongols MC and Aryan Brotherhood.

The US mob

AL CAPONE AND THE CHICAGO OUTFIT

Historian Robert Isham Randolph once told the Chicago Citizens Committee for the Prevention and Punishment of Crime, known informally as the "**Secret Six**", that "there is no business, not an industry in Chicago that is not paying tribute, directly or indirectly, to racketeers and gangsters". The Chicago mob got its start with perhaps the most notorious of all gangland kingpins, the scar-faced **Al Capone**. Violent Chicago bosses since then have all been descendants of the Al Capone mob in one way or another. Capone was the man who refashioned the feudal Italian criminal society into a modern American criminal enterprise.

Alphonse Capone was born in Brooklyn, New York,

to a quiet, law-abiding Italian-American family on 17 January 1899. Shortly after Al was born, the family moved to better lodgings in an apartment over his father's barbershop in Brooklyn. A few blocks from the Capone home was a small building that served as headquarters for **Johnny Torrio**, one of the most successful gangsters on the East Coast. He was a role model for neighbourhood boys. Capone, a scrappy kid, joined the South Brooklyn Rippers street gang, of which Torrio was the leader, and earned pocket money by running errands for Torrio. But in 1909, when Capone was ten, Torrio moved to Chicago. Al went on to join the Forty Thieves Juniors gang and then Manhattan's violent Five Point Juniors gang. He dropped out of education in 1913, having been expelled from his Catholic school, and took jobs in a candy store, a bowling alley and a book bindery. At his next job, at the Harvard Inn, owned by gangster Frankie Yale, Capone waited tables and worked as a bouncer. During his stint with Yale, he got his facial scars and the nickname Scarface when an aggrieved customer at the saloon, Frank Gallucio, slashed his left cheek three times. (Yale persuaded Capone to apologize to Gallucio – and Gallucio would later be employed by Capone as a bodyguard.) Serious violence became second nature to Capone at this time. He murdered two men – but a code of silence meant he was never prosecuted.

Around 1920, Capone moved with his wife Mae and young son Albert (nicknamed Sonny) to Chicago, perhaps because Al had hospitalized a rival gangster and been urged by Yale to get out of town, or perhaps because Torrio had invited him. He soon became Torrio's right-hand man and manager of the Four Deuces, a speakeasy and whorehouse. Torrio had muscled in on the Colosimo mob, whose boss **James "Big Jim" Colosimo** was subsequently murdered, and profited from gambling, prostitution, bars and bootlegging.

After being attacked and badly wounded by rival gangsters, Torrio gave it all up to move back to Italy, passing the crown on to Capone, still only 26. The outfit respected their new boss, calling him the Big

Scarface chomps on a cigar: Al Capone.

Fellow. Capone bribed city officials and over the rest of the decade he made a fortune from the rackets, while police turned a blind eye. But other Chicago hoods were not so accommodating, with North Side mobsters attempting to assassinate Capone. He fought back by building up a spy network in the city and ordering the killing of his enemies. Most famously – though Capone's direct involvement was never proved – there was the bloodbath at 2122 North Clark Street, which came to be known as the **St Valentine's Day Massacre**.

The SMC Cartage Co garage at that address was in reality the main booze stash of bootlegger **George "Bugs" Moran**'s North Side gang. Capone's men, two of them dressed as police, fired more than one hundred and fifty bullets from Thompson sub-machine-guns and shotguns into the six North Side heavies and one unfortunate companion, believed to be a local optometrist, who happened to be at the location. The murdered men were unrecognizable as a result of the fusillade, their bodies almost cut in two. Moran's deputies were among the dead and the North Side operation never recovered, though there were reprisals against the Capone outfit. The man presumed to have led the 14 February killers, Jack "Machine Gun" McGurn, was himself gunned down at a bowling alley on Valentine's Day 1930.

But the easy ride Capone had managed to enjoy before the massacre was now at an end. He was targeted by Prohibition Bureau agent **Eliot Ness**, who determined to take apart the Capone empire. In 1931, Capone was indicted for evasion of income tax. In 1931, he was convicted and sentenced to eleven years in federal prison, fined $50,000 and charged $7692 for court costs, plus $215,000 in back taxes and interest. The game was up. Capone was imprisoned at the US Penitentiary in Atlanta, Georgia, and became its most famous prisoner. Claims that he was living "like a king" were immediately reported. While they were exaggerated, he did indeed live better than the rest of the prisoners, with ample pairs of clean socks, underwear and sets of sheets and towels, as well as smuggled letters and messages. In the handle of his tennis racket Capone stashed several thousand dollars in cash, which he used to pay off guards.

It did not last, however. Capone was sent to Alcatraz, where his days of living in comfort were over. On top of that, the syphilis he had contracted as a young man progressed, and by 1938 he became seriously ill. In November 1939, he was released from prison. His family moved Capone to his Florida estate on Palm Island in Biscayne Bay near Miami. In 1946, his doctor and a psychiatrist concluded that Al Capone had the mental capabilities of a twelve-year-old. In January 1947, at age 48, Capone died from a stroke and pneumonia.

"In his 48 years, Capone had left his mark on the rackets and on Chicago, and more than anyone else he had demonstrated the folly of Prohibition ... in the process he also made a fortune", wrote biographer Laurence Bergreen. "Beyond that, he captured and held the imagination of the public as few public figures ever do."

For further investigation

📖 **Laurence Bergreen** Capone: The Man and the Era **(1994)** A biography of the gangster and study of his milieu.

🌐 chicagohs.org/history/capone.html An article about Al Capone on the Chicago History Museum's site.

JOHN GOTTI AND THE GAMBINO FAMILY

The Gambino family – one of the five families that controlled organized crime in New York City – became a household name when the flamboyant "Dapper Don" **John Gotti**, a former truck hijacker from Queens, burst onto the scene and positively revelled in the media attention he attracted. It happened soon after he took control of the gang, having orchestrated the murder of his predecessor, **Paul Castellano**, who was gunned down outside Sparks Steak House on 46th Street during the rush hour.

A few days later, the little-known Gotti showed up dressed to the nines for a previously scheduled court appearance. Asked by reporters if he was the new boss of the Gambino family, Gotti answered: "I'm the boss of my family – my wife and kids at home." With that remark, Gotti pushed his way through a gaggle of reporters on his way to becoming the most famous gangster since Al Capone.

Born in 1940, Gotti's rise to the top started out with the familiar apprenticeship in street fighting and robbery. He was a member of the Fulton-Rockaway Boys, a local teenage gang that stole cars, fenced stolen goods, and rolled drunks for cash. He moved into fencing in a more serious way, selling goods stolen from **Idlewild Airport** (now the John F. Kennedy International Airport) from a hunting club in Queens, the base for the Bergin Crew of the Gambino family. In 1968, Gotti was jailed for four years for hijacking, but despite being on probation he soon rejoined the crew, which became involved – against the code of the family – in heroin trafficking. The resulting dispute with Capo Castellano culminated in the steakhouse killing and Gotti's ascendancy.

Gotti married in 1962. He and Victoria had five children. A bad-tempered parent with a vicious streak, Gotti treated his family cruelly (as FBI surveillance tapes would later reveal). In 1980, aged twelve, Frank's son John was accidentally killed in an automobile accident. Gotti's neighbour John Favara had run his car into the boy's bike. Police filed no charges, but, soon after Favara was discharged from hospital – having been attacked with a baseball bat by Victoria – he disappeared. It is rumoured that Gotti himself cut Favara to pieces with a chainsaw.

As well as being known as the Dapper Don, people called Gotti the Teflon Don because 1980s assault and racketeering charges against him wouldn't stick. He was known to bribe or threaten jurors during several trials, but there was never sufficient evidence for prosecution. He was extremely popular in his Queens neighbourhood, where he organized free street parties and festivals and had a reputation for keeping street crime out of the immediate area. He also hosted an annual elaborate fireworks show on 4 July each year in Ozone Park.

Long having been under electronic surveillance, Gotti was eventually caught on tape by the FBI discussing a number of murders and other criminal activities. On 11 December 1990, FBI agents and New York Police Department detectives raided the Ravenite Social Club and arrested Gotti, Salvatore "Sammy the Bull"

Gravano, Frank Locascio and Thomas Gambino. Gotti was charged with the murders of **Paul Castellano**, **Thomas Bilotti** and eleven others. He was also charged with conspiracy to commit murder, illegal gambling, loan-sharking, tax evasion, racketeering and obstruction of justice. The evidence was insurmountable: not only had prosecutors caught Gotti on tape, but testimonies against Gotti were heard from several high-ranking rival Mafia members. He was tried in US District Court's Eastern District of New York before Judge I. Leo Glasser and in the spring of 1992, after just thirteen hours of deliberation, a jury found Gotti guilty as charged. He was sentenced to life in prison.

Gambino fortunes waned following Gotti's imprisonment and a string of other arrests. Gotti gave orders from prison, conveyed to a group of trusted lieutenants. One of them was his son John (known as Junior), who was himself jailed for six and a half years in 1998. On 10 June 2002, after nearly ten years of his life sentence, John Gotti, afflicted by throat cancer, died aged 68 at a federal prison hospital in Springfield, Missouri. The funeral at the Papavero Funeral Home in Queens was marked by a seventy-five-car motorcade, which included nineteen carloads of flowers.

Prominently missing at his service, however, were top members of the mob. None of the bosses of the four other New York crime families – Bonanno, Colombo, Genovese, and Lucchese – paid their last respects. Federal agents later speculated that the main reason for the boycott of Gotti's wake and

After Rudy Giuliani was appointed US attorney for the Southern District of New York in 1983, he vowed to fight organized crime and political corruption. "How, you may wonder", he said during an acceptance speech, "do we end corruption? By scaring the living shit out of the criminal – and their families if we have to." Two years later, he indicted the heads of New York's five crime families for murder, extortion, and racketeering.

Lawyer Bruce Cutler, left, gestures broadly during the arraignment of his client, Gambino crime boss John Gotti, right, in New York City in January 1989. Gotti and two associates were charged with first-degree assault in the May 1986 shooting of a New York City union leader.

funeral was that the Castellano hit had never been authorized.

After Gotti Sr's death, his brother Peter was briefly in charge before also being imprisoned in 2003. The power of the Gotti family was broken. In recent years, leadership is thought to have passed to others. But the gang has been hounded by federal investigators. In 2008 a four-year FBI investigation, **Operation Old Bridge**, into the drug-trafficking alliance between the Gambinos and Sicilian mobsters-in-exile, the Inzerillo ("runaway") family, was brought to fruition with sixty-two Gambino associates indicted.

For further investigation

Jerry Capeci Gotti: Rise and Fall **(1996)** Subsequently made into a movie for HBO, this is a comprehensive biography of John Gotti.

John Ernest Volkman Goombata: The Improbable Rise and Fall of John Gotti and His Gang **(1992)** A portrait of John Gotti along with details his trial.

ganglandnews.com This site features stories about Gotti and his rise to power within the Gambino crime family.

THE LOS ANGELES "MICKEY MOUSE MAFIA"

The Mafia moved out west to Hollywood shortly after movie studios began making films on Sunset Boulevard in 1911. But the mob in Southern California proved itself to be disorganized and often incompetent in comparison with their East Coast and Chicago counterparts, and even with the violent street gangs that have always been a feature of LA organized crime. It was the former LAPD chief **Daryl Gates** who coined the disparaging nickname "Mickey Mouse Mafia", neatly encapsulating the bungling habits of the local wiseguys with a reference to nearby Disneyland.

By 1947 (the year Benjamin "Bugsy" Siegel was assassinated in Beverly Hills), Anthony Rizzotti,

better known as **Jack Dragna** – who was rumoured to have ordered the hit on Siegel – controlled the Los Angeles bookmaking rackets. After Dragna was found dead in February 1956 in a motel room from an apparent suicide, **Frank DeSimone**, Dragna's second-in-command, took control of the Los Angeles Family. DeSimone was ruthless and vicious, a model for the psychopathic Tommy DeVito character played by Joe Pesci in Martin Scorsese's 1990 film *Goodfellas*. However, in more recent years the LA Mafia has thankfully gained a reputation for avoiding violence. Jack Dragna's nephew, Louis (nicknamed the "Reluctant Prince"), who was briefly acting boss in the mid-1970s, was noted for being timid about the use of brutal tactics.

In the early 1980s, power was passed on once more, this time to **Peter John Milano**, who was ably assisted by his brother Carmen. The Milano brothers were no strangers to the mob; their father was the potent Cleveland Mafia force **Tony "The Old Man" Milano**. They too have avoided old-school violence and were accordingly not regarded as a great threat to law and order. "We see the mob scratching and digging out here", was the derisive way Captain **Stuart Finck**, then head of LAPD's Organized Crime Intelligence Division, put it in 1987.

Then in 1997 **Herbert "Fat Herbie" Blitzstein**, Tony Spilotro's old 1970s comrade, was found dead from a head shot in his Las Vegas townhouse. In 1986 Blitzstein had been jailed for tax evasion. When he got out in 1991, he was in poor health (having suffered two heart attacks and had toes amputated as result of diabetes complications) and was often heard to say that he was retired. But investigators claim that he had persisted with loan-sharking and insurance racketeering behind a front business, Any Auto Repair. Because Blitzstein was an independent, not tied to any mob (nor paying tribute to one), he was always going to be a potential target for forceful advances from the competition. Blitzstein was involved in a planned con to sell a large diamond to a buyer but switch it for a fake when it came to deliver the goods – and this may have been the cause of his downfall. Quoted in the *LA Weekly*, Las Vegas FBI spokesman **Aurelio Flores** claimed that expansionist LA wiseguys targeted Blitzstein's operation for takeover. It was alleged that when the veteran mobster refused the demand to hand over his operation, he was killed.

A subsequent grand jury indictment accused two men of murder. Opening statements in the Blitzstein murder trial began on 27 April 1999. Prosecutors told the jury that Blitzstein had been murdered because he "had failed in his obligation to 'share the wealth' of his business activities with members of La Cosa Nostra". Because of that failure, mobsters who wanted to take over his loan-sharking operations in the Las Vegas Valley killed him. The prosecution claimed that top Los Angeles Mafia players had sanctioned the killing. The four-week trial featured testimony from paid snitches.

Of the seven Mafia-connected men that federal prosecutors claimed were involved in the plot to kill Herbert Blitzstein, four pleaded guilty in exchange for reduced sentences, one died in prison awaiting trial, and two went to trial and were acquitted. It was hardly a successful outcome for the prosecution. All were low-ranking members of the Los Angeles mob.

Peter Milano remains at large. The LA mafia is still active, if not so powerful these days. Nobody killed Herbert Blitzstein, according to the official record.

For further investigation

Peter Maas & Joseph Valachi The Valachi Papers (1968) A first-person account of a disgruntled soldier in New York's Genovese crime family in the 1960s.

Carl Sifakis The Mafia Encyclopedia (2005) Includes substantial information on the history of the Los Angeles Mafia.

laweekly.com/news/news/la-mob-does-vegas/7395 An overview in the *LA Weekly* newspaper of the Los Angeles mob's involvement in Las Vegas and the Herbie Blitzstein murder.

THE LUCCHESE FAMILY

Gaetano "Tom" Reina was, in the 1930s, the first boss to run the Long Island Mafia in New York. But the Lucchese mob syndicate took its name from loyal underboss Gaetano "Tommy Gunn" Lucchese, who finally became boss in 1953, after the death of Reina's successors Joseph "Fat Joe" Pinzolo and Gaetano "Tommy" Gagliano. The Luccheses were one of the "Five Families" that for two decades had a stranglehold on organized crime activities in New York.

In their heyday, the Luccheses ran most of the street rackets (loan-sharking, gambling, restaurant extortion, construction payoffs, and construction bid rigging) on Long Island and in New Jersey. Another sideline moneyspinner was the family's fleet of hotdog wagons and coffee trucks that doubled as bookmakers. Lucchese himself kept a low profile, gaining respect from fellow bosses for never being convicted of a crime. He was deft at infiltrating trucker unions, workers' co-ops and trade associations, and his organization successfully ran rackets out of Idlewild Airport. The Lucchese family became one of the most profitable of the East Coast mobs.

Tommy Lucchese died in 1967. By the 1970s, the gang was heavily involved in heroin trafficking and was implicated in the so-called "**French Connection**" – a Corsican-run smuggling ring based in Marseilles that smuggled drugs to the US in partnership with the Mafia. The Lucchese family also conspired with corrupt NYPD cops to get at heroin seized by the authorities. This tangled web of corruption and criminality was the source material not only for the *French Connection* films, but also for *Serpico*, the Al Pacino movie which deals with the crooked New York cops' drug dealings.

This period also saw the rise of **Anthony "Tony Ducks" Corallo**, head of the Lucchese family from 1973 to 1986. With great ingenuity, the FBI managed to bug Corallo's car (where he conducted most of his business). The recorded material was dynamite and led to the Mafia Commission Trial in which all the heads of the Five Families were prosecuted, Corallo being sentenced to life imprisonment. He died in jail in 2000.

Under subsequent Lucchese bosses, notably **Vittorio "Vic" Amuso**, violence and rivalry increased – there was particular animosity towards Gambino boss John Gotti. Amuso was imprisoned in 1992, but he is reputed to have remained nominally in command – albeit of a much-weakened organization.

On 1 July 2004, **Louis "Louie Bagels" Daidone**, the acting boss of the Lucchese crime family since 2001, was sentenced to life in prison on loan-sharking and racketeering charges. The charges were in connection with conspiracy to murder two men – Thomas Gilmore and Bruno Facciolo – one of whom was found with a dead canary stuffed in his mouth, which was meant as a warning to government informants that if they talked, they too would die. Testimony during Daidone's trial detailed him lying in wait

A December 1969 photograph of Anthony "Tony Ducks" Corallo, reputed head of the Lucchese family.

for Facciolo, ambushing him, fatally stabbing and shooting him, then leaving the body in the trunk of Facciolo's own car.

But it was not only Daidone's imprisonment that damaged the family. The year before, the crime family was seriously shaken by a massive three-year investigation into the Luccheses' involvement in the construction industry in New York City. The result was crippling. In September 2000, 38 people were indicted by the state of New York for racketeering. Named in the indictment were **Steven "Wonderboy" Crea**, the acting Lucchese boss at the time who was inducted into the family in the 1980s, and two Lucchese capos, Dominic Truscello and Joseph Tangorra. Also named were five Lucchese soldiers and three associates. Among the indicted were union officials and contractors suspected of benefiting from criminal enterprise. Based on the scope of the investigation and resulting indictment, the district attorney's office called it the decade's most significant case involving organized crime in the construction industry.

In a joint news conference, Manhattan district attorney Robert M. Morgenthau and New York City police commissioner Bernard B. Kerik laid out the specifics of the case against the alleged mobsters. The suspects were accused, the authorities said, of engaging in a criminal enterprise through "the Lucchese Construction Group" to commit "labour bribery, bid rigging", and other schemes to systematically siphon "millions of dollars from both public and private construction projects". The case involved eight different construction projects, including the renovation of the Park Central Hotel, the construction of the Doral Arrowwood Conference Center and the addition of five floors of apartments to a building on Broadway in Manhattan. The projects each enabled siphoning of $6 million directly to the Lucchese family.

In December 2007, among those arrested for promoting gambling, money-laundering, and racketeering were alleged capo **Ralph V. Perna** and his three sons, and **Joseph DiNapoli** and **Matthew Madonna**. The authorities touted the arrests as the "breaking up" of the crime family, but the parole of Wonderboy Crea,

who made a plea bargain in 2006, ended in 2009. It is thought that he might again take over the day-to-day running of the family.

For further investigation

Ⓦ query.nytimes.com/gst/fullpage.html?res=9800EFDA173FF9 3AA15750C0A9679C8B63 A story by Alan Feuer posted on the *New York Times* website about the Lucchese crime family.

Ⓦ wcbstv.com/local/lucchese.mob.family.2.613653.html Story on WCBS-TV about the 2007 busts of Lucchese crime family members for gambling-related charges.

Ⓦ thelaborers.net/newspapers/ny_times/nyt -2000-09-07.htm *New York Times* article, dated 7 September 2000, outlining the racketeering indictment of the Lucchese Construction Group.

TONY SPILOTRO, THE HOLE IN THE WALL GANG & THE LAS VEGAS MOB

In the 1970s Anthony "The Ant" Spilotro, a Chicago mobster, was mob overseer of the Las Vegas "skim" (illegal casino profits). In 1976, Spilotro formed a burglary ring with his top lieutenant Herbert "Fat Herbie" Blitzstein, utilizing ten associates as burglars. The crew became known as the **Hole in the Wall Gang** because they used industrial drilling equipment to gain access to the buildings they robbed.

Spilotro was targeted by law enforcement from early in his life. Born in 1938, Tony's parents ran Patsy's Restaurant in Chicago, a neighbourhood Italian eatery popular with mafiosi. Tony and three of his brothers were in trouble at a young age (though one of his brothers became a successful doctor) and by his early twenties, Tony was suspected of trying to bribe college sports players to fix games. After a mob informer claimed Spilotro was behind the 1963 torture and murder of a loan shark, he was tried in 1972 but acquitted.

Spilotro is thought to have taken over the "skim" in 1970, succeeding veteran hood Marshall Caifano. Spilotro was closely associated with casino boss and sports-betting legend **Frank "Lefty" Rosenthal**, who ran four casinos – notably the Stardust Hotel. Folklore has it that when Rosenthal arrived in the Nevada gambling Mecca, the local police chief told him: "You and your Chicago friends aren't welcome in this town." But the cop's warning to leave town was not heeded and throughout the 1970s Rosenthal managed the casinos while Spilotro acted as his enforcer. Eventually the two men would fall out after Rosenthal discovered that Spilotro was sleeping with his wife Geri – the three-way relationship which would form the basis of Martin Scorsese's 1995 film *Casino*.

From the mid-1970s, Spilotro and Fat Herbie were partners in the Gold Rush Jewelry Store just off the Las Vegas Strip. It was, in fact, the front for the Hole in the Wall Gang, who netted millions between 1976 and 1981 – when they were

Reputed mob boss Anthony Spilotro, left, and his brother, Michael, leave the federal building in Chicago after a bond hearing on 17 June 1986.

THE CONTRACT KILLER

The contract murderer is a person hired to take the life of another – usually someone the hit man has never met. The motivation of the contractor (i.e. the individual who hires the hit man) may be purely financial, exclusively personal, or a combination of the two. Although there are no US crime statistics on the number of contract murders, a number of factors suggest that this type of homicide occurs relatively frequently and may be increasing.

Examination of press accounts of identified cases of contract murder indicates an increase in this type of criminal activity over the past thirty years. Some crime analysts have concluded that more and more people are hiring strangers to kill their no-longer-loved ones, demonstrating the increasingly commonplace attitude towards contract killing. The publication of a technical manual on how to commit contract killing is one example of the intrusion of this form of homicide into our culture. In fact, as a result of the apparent increase in contract killings, a number of US jurisdictions have tightened laws to combat the problem. Even in the United Kingdom, there has been an increase in high-profile contract killings since the 1960s. And in Russia there has been such a dramatic rise in the number of contract killings – 500 documented cases in a single year – that some Russian teenagers have actually spoken of contract murder as an acceptable career choice.

Although contract killing has been referenced in novels, short stories, plays, and movies, there has been very little serious psychiatric or psychological study of the problem. One researcher has differentiated three types of contract murder: the amateur, semi-professional, and professional contract killing. Each of these three different types of contract killings vary in methods, crime-scene characteristics, typical target, contractor's motive, and personality organization of the hit man. For instance, the amateur is usually hired to eliminate a spouse, an intimate or formerly intimate partner. He acts for a gainful purpose, and often has a history of minor criminal conduct. Frequently, the amateur hit man leaves physical evidence behind, and the killing itself is often impulsive and not well planned.

The semi-professional contract killer has a more sophisticated homicide technique than the amateur, but less so than the professional. This individual has less personality instability than the amateur, and the target is not

caught trying to burgle Bertha's Household Products. Despite being apprehended at the scene in possession of burglary tools, Spilotro was not convicted of any crime. But Spilotro had become a high-profile figure, embarrassing the Chicago bosses. Shortly after a new kingpin, **Joseph Ferriola**, rose to prominence in Chicago, Tony and his older brother Michael disappeared. Rumour was that they were savagely beaten before being buried alive.

Nearly two decades later, in 2005, the FBI made arrests as a result of the Operation Family Secrets investigation into eighteen unsolved gangland murders. The details of the Spilotro brothers' deaths were finally revealed during the "Family Secrets" trial for murder and other crimes of Joey "The Clown" Lombardo, Frank Calabrese Sr, James Marcello, Paul

generally a spouse or intimate partner, but usually a business associate or someone involved in a criminal enterprise. Little physical evidence is left behind and the method of killing is more often planned, orderly, and systematic.

The professional hit man may be a direct participant in organized crime, performing his job out of loyalty to the organization; or he may be an independent contractor – essentially a freelance agent not connected to any particular crime group, who hires himself out for a fee.

Professional hit men usually have minimal overt personality disturbances. They typically target victims consistent with the crime organization's goals, leave little inculpatory physical evidence behind, and engage in elaborate body disposal and effective crime-scene staging, with a highly planned, orderly and systematic approach to the murder itself.

The well-known US case of Richard "The Iceman" Kuklinski is an example of a professional independent contract killer, the only hit man ever studied extensively from a psychological perspective. He is alleged to have killed over one hudred individuals and carried out his murders in a highly planned, methodical fashion, employing a number of techniques to kill,

including cyanide poisoning. This hit man had a background of poverty and childhood abuse that desensitized him to violence. Kuklinski had adept social judgement, personality traits of orderliness, control, and paranoid vigilance, and useful defence mechanisms of rationalization and reframing, as well as an exceptional capacity to encapsulate his emotions so that his feelings would not interfere with his work. He pursued a middle-class lifestyle and kept his family totally separate from his criminal career.

Many contract killers – particularly the semi-professional and professional – are able to elude law enforcement, because there is no direct connection between the victim and the offender. And even when these individuals are apprehended, they rarely receive detailed psychological assessment, since it is usually not part of their legal defence. And even if a hit man is referred for evaluation, they typically deny guilt and are uncooperative in revealing much about themselves or their work. The vast majority of contract murderers have no background of mental illness or psychosis, but instead have varying levels of anti-social or psychopathic traits.

Professor Louis B. Schlesinger

"The Indian" Schiro, and Anthony "Twan" Doyle.

In August 2005, Dr John Pless, a forensics pathologist, testified that there was no evidence leading him to believe the Spilotro brothers had been buried alive. Instead, he said, they were in all likelihood punched and kicked to death with bare fists, knees, and feet. Bruises on the backs of the Spilotros' hands suggested they had defensive wounds from attempts to shield themselves from the blows. On 27 September 2007, a jury convicted Marcello of the Spilotro murders.

For further investigation

📖 **Nicholas Pileggi** Casino: Love and Honor in Las Vegas **(1995)** The source material for Scorsese's film.

BREAKING THE CODE OF SILENCE: JOE VALACHI

Joseph "Joe Cago" Valachi was the first paid Mafia informant for the FBI. In the 1960s, the US Department of Justice extracted a deposition from Valachi concerning his life in a crime syndicate. The document detailed the inner workings and activities of members of the New York Mafia. The manuscript later became known as *The Valachi Papers*, when author Peter Maas turned it into a memoir of the same title.

Valachi testified about underworld crime before the US Senate. But despite the publicity surrounding his testimony, nothing he offered led directly to the arrests of any underworld figures. He did provide details filling in gaps for crimes that law enforcement already knew about. In that, his testimony for police was important. But in reality Valachi was a low-ranking member of the Mafia, functioning at the street level. He wasn't a "made" member – a soldier who killed – and he wasn't therefore privy to inside information. Probably the most important information Valachi provided was the identification of 371 members of the Mafia. Then-US attorney general Robert F. Kennedy described Valachi's testimony as "a significant addition to the broad picture. It gives meaning to much that we already know and brings the picture into sharper focus."

The media was impressed too. "Not since Frank Costello's fingers drummed the table during the Kefauver hearings has there been so fascinating a show", *The New York Times* opined.

Protecting Valachi during the time he was testifying before the US Senate were two hundred marshals. Valachi had violated the *omerta* code of strict silence – and a $100,000 assassination bounty was said to have been placed on his head. But gangland justice was never carried out. Valachi died of a heart attack in 1971.

The original document written by Joe Valachi is on display at the John F. Kennedy Presidential Library National Archives and Records Administration in Boston, Massachusetts. Maas's book was turned into a 1972 Charles Bronson movie, *The Valachi Papers*, and Valachi may also have been the model for the character of Frank Pentangeli in *The Godfather Part II*.

📖 **William F. Roemer Enforcer (1995)** Ex-FBI Special Agent William Roemer tells in graphic detail the Spilotro story from the FBI's standpoint.

Ⓦ **suntimes.com/news/mob/index.html** A roundup of stories about the Operation Family Secrets investigation and trial, posted on the *Chicago Sun-Times* site.

Two men and a woman were apprehended at the port of Sevastopol, Crimea, in March 1999 while attempting to sell two hundred Ukrainian women and girls into the transnational sex industry in Greece, Turkey, and Cyprus. The victims ranged in age from thirteen to twenty-five and were held in bondage under the guise of having to repay their travel expenses. The traffickers, police said, received $2000 for each victim.

Organized crime worldwide

ASIAN GANGS: YAKUZA, TRIADS & BIG CIRCLE BOYS

Asia has its own variants of the Mafia and the Colombian cartels. The most notorious organized gangs are the Japanese yakuza and the Chinese Triads, both of which have (like the Mafia) their outposts, strongholds and franchises in other parts of the world, especially the US.

With membership estimated at more than eighty-five-thousand the yakuza is one of the largest criminal gangs in the world. Like the Sicilian Cosa Nostra, the yakuza's history stretches back centuries, originating at a time when samurai warriors – mercenaries unaffiliated to any local shogun (lord) – roamed the feudal country. As Japanese society changed, with business and trading on the rise, such men became involved in smuggling and gambling, providing protection or getting involved in extortion. And so the modern yakuza was born. In the twentieth century, the group has been involved with politics, as well as simple illegal financial gain. In particular, before World War II, the **Black Dragon Society** was committed to an ultra-nationalist, right-wing agenda. Black Dragon members included government officials and military officers.

Like the Mafia, the yakuza is organized hierarchically. Outcasts and misfits are absorbed into the family-like structure, gaining a sense of order and belonging. Unlike the Mafia or the Triads, the yakuza is not secretive: members often advertise their affiliation openly. The groups have their own rituals and practices, such as *yubitsume* – the cutting off of a finger as a punishment. Yakuza gang member tattoos sometimes cover the whole body, a way of graphically affirming the group identity. The biggest yakuza group is the Yamaguchi-gumi, based in Kobe, which has 750 clans and which collectively makes up nearly half of all the Japanese gangsters. Like all organized-crime outfits, the yakuza's activities are diverse. There is significant yakuza involvement in prostitution and pornography, drug smuggling, blackmail and extortion (but not theft), property and banking, gambling and loan-sharking and even professional wrestling.

The Chinese Triads were first formed in the mid-1700s in opposition to the Qing Dynasty then in power. The name of the organization refers to the idea of the triple harmony of heaven, earth and humanity. After the 1949 Communist revolution, law enforcement was stepped up significantly and the Triads' power was considerably cut back as a result. The gangs moved to Hong Kong, parcelling up the city between the main groups.

Joining the Triads traditionally involves an elaborate initiation ceremony that typically involves an animal sacrifice. The initiate has to drink the blood of the sacrificed animal and then walk under an arch of swords. During the ceremony, elaborate oaths are sworn. One such oaths reads: "I will offer financial assistance to sworn brothers who are in trouble ... If I break this oath I will be killed by five thunderbolts."

As a result of migration, the Asian gangs have established a presence in many parts of the world. Triad activity is to be found in most cities which have witnessed substantial Chinese immigration, such as San Francisco, New York City, Philadelphia, Seattle, Chicago, Vancouver, Toronto, Cape Town and Buenos Aires. Recent reports suggest that Triads are becoming more active in Europe, especially in conjunction with people-smuggling. This issue hit the headlines in Britain in 2004, when 21 illegal Chinese immigrants were drowned while picking cockles in Morecambe Bay, Lancashire, northwest England. The so-called "gangmasters" involved in this kind of illegal work are reported to be closely connected to Triad and Snakehead (human-trafficking) gangs. In 2006 the UK government made an award of a Justice Shield to the task force who investigated the deaths of the cockle-pickers and the connection to Chinese gangs.

Other Asian gangs have also surfaced abroad. In the 1980s, a violent new gang known as the **Big Circle Boys** (or Dai Huen Jai), whose members are reported to include many former Red Guard soldiers from China – arrived in several North American Chinatowns, notably Toronto and San Francisco. As well as being a Snakehead gang transporting illegal aliens, the mob is involved in heroin distribution, prostitution, counterfeiting and credit card fraud.

There are also gangs in American cities whose members have roots in Vietnam, Laos, Cambodia and ethnic Hmong communities. Rather than tattooing themselves as yakuza members do, some of these Asian gangsters favour ritual branding and burning on the arms, hands and feet. There is some evidence however that new gang members prefer not to have distinguishing marks that can easily be identified by police.

For further investigation

Ko-lin Chin Chinatown Gangs: Extortion, Enterprise, and Ethnicity **(1997)** An ethnographic study of juvenile Chinese street gangs.

PABLO ESCOBAR AND THE MEDELLIN CARTEL

The notorious Colombian drug lord **Pablo Emilio Escobar Gaviria** was one of the most brutally ruthless, ambitious, and powerful criminals in history. Escobar was so wealthy from his profits in the drug trade that in 1989 *Forbes* magazine listed him as the seventh-richest man in the world. The drug lord had become one of the narcotic trade's first billionaires. One law enforcement agent interviewed for a PBS documentary, *The*

When a Tel Aviv court convicted nine men in 2009 of extortion and other crimes, it was the first time that a verdict had been rendered under a 2003 Israeli law against syndicated crime. The defendants were convicted of crimes ranging from being a member of a crime organization to money-laundering, carrying firearms, and deliberate injury to persons. The companies the men worked for distributed fictitious invoices totalling $20 million and provided black market loans.

THE RUSSIAN MAFIA

The tradition of organized crime in Russia dates back to the imperial era and the tradition of *Vory v zakone* ("thieves in law") – criminals who regarded it as a matter of honour (punishable in the breach by death) never to cooperate with the authorities. Under Communism, organized crime was able to flourish because bribery and corruption were widespread. In economic hard times, corrupt officials and the Mafia profited from black-marketeering.

After the collapse of the Soviet Union, with the whole vast region in crisis and economic meltdown, the Russian Mafia reached a new level of power. One of the features of the modern Mafia is the diversity of its operations and its connections to apparently legitimate business. For example, members of the powerful Moscow gang the Solntsevskaya brotherhood were exposed by journalists in the late 1990s as being key players in a publicly traded company, YBM Magnex International Inc (a revelation which caused the value of the company's shares to collapse). One supposedly key figure is Semion Mogilevich. Wanted by the BFI and Interpol, he was was detained in Moscow in connection with a tax evasion in January 2008. The Izmaylovskaya gang is another major group, reported to have offshoots in Tel Aviv, Paris, Toronto, Miami and New York City.

The Obschina ("community") gang is slightly different from other Mafia groups within Russian borders. A Chechen group, it is reputed to have been formed in 1974 by a student at Moscow University who went on to become a leader of the resistance to Russian rule. Unlike other organized crime in the region, the Obschina has links to a nationalist ideology that is widely supported in the Islamic world – and so racketeering intersects with politics in this case.

Russian organized crime has spread internationally and is of great concern to law enforcement officials. Speaking during a BBC *Panorama* investigation into the Russian Mafia, 22-year-veteran FBI Special Agent Bob Levinson said: "Criminals are coming in who are wealthier and more vicious than any other criminals that you or anybody on the continent have ever seen. As far as I'm concerned, they're the most dangerous people on earth. People are more afraid of the Russian Mafia than they are of even the Colombians, the American Mafia or the Sicilians and Italian Mafia."

In the US, the Russian Mafia has made its home in the Brighton Beach neighbourhood of Brooklyn, New York, but is expanding. Cities with a Russian Mafia presence have pushed for more police officers to fight the problem. As Bob Yousefian, the mayor of Glendale, California, put it: "We're getting to the point that we have this huge elephant standing in the middle of the room, and we all have closed our eyes. We have an issue. We need to deal with it."

Godfather of Cocaine, simply said of him: "Escobar was to cocaine what Ford was to automobiles."

He was born in 1949 on the outskirts of Medellín, central Colombia. His background was comfortable, although not wealthy. As a teenager he developed a lifelong taste for marijuana and rebelliousness. He

HUMAN TRAFFICKING

Trafficking in people is a modern-day form of slavery – a new type of global slave trade in which perpetrators prey on the most weak, primarily women and children, for profit and gain. Victims are coerced by fraud into the sex trade or hard labour. Often the labels the victims of human trafficking are saddled with – "illegal immigrants", "juvenile delinquents", or "drug mules" – are conesquences of being forced to commit crimes.

In 2008, the US Department of State published a major report on the phenomenon of human trafficking. "The reality [is] that human beings continue to be bought and sold in the twenty-first century", wrote Condoleeza Rice in an accompanying letter that spoke also of a "growing abolitionist movement". The numbers are staggering. According to the report, 800,000 people are trafficked across national borders each year. Mostly this means women and girls (up to fifty percent of them minors) who are being forced into commercial sexual exploitation.

And that number does not include those who are trafficked within national borders. "Women, eager for a better future, are susceptible to promises of jobs abroad as babysitters, housekeepers, waitresses, or models", the report states, "jobs that traffickers turn into the nightmare of forced prostitution without exit." Countries are categorized in the report according to the severity of the problem there. Those countries regarded as the worst offenders (a classification known as Tier 3) are: Algeria, Burma, Cuba, Fiji, Iran, Kuwait, Moldova, North Korea, Oman, Papua New Guinea, Qatar, Saudi Arabia, Sudan and Syria.

A March 2008 study released by Shared Hope International was startling for many reasons, but foremost among them were its findings about Las Vegas. The report revealed that more than four hundred children had been found working as prostitutes in Vegas during a single month in 2007, and described the city as "a hub for child sex trafficking". Police in 2007 arrested 157 juveniles for prostitution-related charges there, with 153 arrests the year before.

In an eighteen-month US study released in December 2007, California was identified as a top destination for human traffickers. According to the report by the California Alliance to Combat

dropped out of education at sixteen and gravitated towards the petty street crime that was endemic in the area. The Escobar legend has it that he made a start by stealing headstones which he then cleaned up for sale, but his activities were probably more mundane: street cons, selling smuggled cigarettes and fake lottery tickets. He then moved into car theft, then kidnapping, proving himself capable of staying calm under pressure and meting out violence without hesitation. He was always ambitious, and his career received a boost when he became known for the kidnapping and killing of an unpopular, exploitative factory-owner in 1971.

Escobar was always able to portray himself as a kind of Robin Hood and he nursed that reputation later with calculated acts of charity for Medellín slum-dwellers. In the 1980s, he founded his own newspaper, the *Medellín Cívico*, which from time to time ran

Trafficking, the problem in the Mexican-border state reaches beyond the sex trade, because of migrant farm and construction workers, domestic-help employees, and service industry workers in hotels, restaurants, and clothing factories. The US government's Office to Monitor and Combat Trafficking in Persons (or TIP) has estimated that each year between 14,500 and 17,500 people are trafficked into the US.

In the UK, a woman from Prague, who eventually escaped her captors, was sold for 50 euros. After she was sold, she worked at a restaurant in Samlesbury, Lancashire, and then was taken to an isolated Vicarage Road restaurant where she was forced to work during the day in a kitchen; at night she was used for sex by staff members. Police in February 2006 raided the restaurant as well as a private home in Manchester and arrested five people. Each was charged with human trafficking for sexual exploitation. The 22-year-old victim, who suffered from epilepsy, testified against her captors.

In Anchorage, Alaska, in 2001, six Russian women were recruited to perform Russian folk dances for a cultural tour of Alaska. But when they arrived, their passports, visas and plane tickets were confiscated and they were forced to perform so-called exotic dances in topless strip clubs. The women were able to notify the authorities, and eventually one Russian and three US citizens were charged in a 23-count indictment for luring women to Alaska with the purpose of enslaving them. The US Department of Justice in 2006 charged nine people connected to an international sex trafficking ring. The ring smuggled women into the United States either against their will or with promises of a new life. The women were forced to work as prostitutes in illegal brothels, usually in Asian-themed massage parlours and spas. The network ran throughout the US with the profits funnelled back to the Northwest to fund Asian organized crime operations.

These examples demonstrate the immensity of the problem. But progress is being made. One huge step – and one which further illustrates the scale of human trafficking – is that the governments of Vietnam and Cambodia have recently finally made human trafficking illegal.

admiring profiles that stressed Escobar's social conscience. In one such article, quoted by author Mark Bowden, an interviewee spoke of the emotional pain that injustice caused Escobar: "I know him, his eyes weeping because there is not enough bread for all the nation's dinner tables. I have watched his tortured feelings when he sees street children – angels without toys, without a present, without a future." Escobar was the founder of Medellín Without Slums, a housing charity with a mission to improve slum conditions.

By the mid-1970s, he had moved into the cocaine business that would bring him almost unimaginable wealth. A decade later he would own fleets of boats, property around the world and eighteen residences in Medellín alone. He had so much money that sometimes it was impossible for him to know what to do with it and it was simply buried. His lifestyle was self-indulgent and unlimited. He would play amateur soccer games on professional pitches with top announcers paid to commentate, as if it was a professional tournament. He hosted huge parties at his country estate east of Medellín, where he indulged his taste for the bizarre, encouraging friends to climb naked up trees or eat insects. Built in 1979, the complex on the Magdalena River reflected his lavish and exotic tastes: hundreds of zoo animals, artificial lakes and, in pride of place, a bullet-ridden 1930s sedan car that the drug kingpin claimed had belonged to Bonnie and Clyde.

Medellín became a boom town on the back of the surge in the cocaine trade prompted by the soaring popularity of the drug in the US. Employment was up, and construction thrived. In 1978, he was elected as a substitute city council member in Medellín, and in 1982, he was elected to Congress. As a congressman, Escobar had automatic judicial immunity and could no longer be prosecuted under Colombian law for crimes. He was also entitled to a diplomatic visa, which he used to take trips with his family to the United States. Escobar was a key player in Colombia and his business hugely benefited the national economy. The government recognized this surreptitiously by, for example, making it possible for banks to convert unlimited amounts of US dollars into Colombian pesos.

During his reign, Escobar bribed countless government officials, judges and other local politicians. He was known to personally execute subordinates who didn't cooperate, and he assassinated anyone he viewed as a threat. Corruption and intimidation characterized the Colombian system during Escobar's heyday. He had an effective strategy that was known as "plata o plomo", which translated into English means "silver or lead". In other words, if you didn't accept a bribe you'd be facing a bullet. Escobar was believed

Pablo Escobar: the gangster with civic pride.

to be personally responsible for the killing of three Colombian presidential candidates, all competing in the same election. He was also believed to be the mastermind of the 1989 bombing of Avianca airlines Flight 203 that killed 100 and the truck bombing that killed fifty-two and injured 1,000 outside a security building in Bogotá, Colombia. Some analysts have said

Escobar was behind the 1985 attack on the Colombian Supreme Court by left-wing guerillas, which resulted in the murder of half the judges in the court.

Near the end of his second term in office, the US president **Ronald Reagan** signed National Security Decision Directive 221, which declared the drug trade a threat to national security – and therefore a military problem, not just a matter for law enforcement. In 1988, with the election of George Bush as US president, the tide started to turn against Escobar. The Bush administration made the drug war a priority. Crack had started to appear in American inner cities and cocaine was taken increasingly seriously, rather than seen as simply a yuppie party drug.

At the end of the decade, after more than one anti-trafficking candidate had been assassinated, Colombia had a reforming government at odds with Escobar. Led by Colonel **Hugo Martinez**, the police Search Bloc was formed to break his power. Many of its members were killed by Escobar loyalists, but Menendez was dedicated and unbending – and he refused the $6 million pay-off Escobar offered him if he would only back away.

Gradually the net tightened. In 1992, Escobar went into hiding. Then, on 2 December 1993, the day after his birthday, he was located by a joint US-Colombian task force, hiding out in a middle-class Medellín neighbourhood. Escobar attempted to escape by climbing up on the roof of the house. He was spotted by Colombian National Police, and then shot after an exchange of gunshots. Escobar died aged 44, having suffered gunshot wounds to his legs, back and a fatal one to his head, behind his ear. For the officers' safety, their identities were never made public.

After Escobar's death, the Medellín Cartel fragmented and the cocaine market was taken over by the rival Cali Cartel until the mid-1990s, when its leaders, too, were either killed or captured.

For further investigation

📖 **Mark Bowden,** *Killing Pablo: The Hunt for the World's Greatest Outlaw* **(2001)** This book describes in detail, through meticulous research and interviews, Pablo Escobar's rise and fall.

📖 **William Cran & Stephanie Tepper** The Godfather of Cocaine **(1997)** A PBS film about Pablo Escobar and his Medellín cartel.

🌐 tech.mit.edu/V113/N62/escobar.62w.html An article by Peter Eisner with *Newsday* about Escobar's murder.

EAST END VILLAINS: THE KRAY TWINS

In the annals of London criminality, perhaps only Jack the Ripper exceeds the Kray brothers in notoriety. Yet unlike the Victorian serial killer, the pair are surrounded by a mist of sentimentality: despite being convicted murderers, the Krays came to personify an idea of the East End as a tightly knit cockney community where loyalty to family and tradition was dominant. Courteous and softly spoken in front of the television cameras, the brothers managed to create an image of themselves that bore no relation to the brutal reality of their day-to-day existence: extortion, fraud, punishment beatings, bribery and killing.

Identical twins, they were born on 24 October 1933 in Hoxton, a poor district of the large East London borough of Hackney. **Reginald** ("Reggie") was the stockier, quieter of the pair. **Ronald** ("Ronnie", also sometimes called "The Colonel") was more flamboyant and ambitious, and he was also prone to mood swings and compulsive violence. The incidents were numerous. For example, one night in the mid-1960s, a man named Joe wanted to borrow £5 from Ronnie in a club on the Fulham Road in West London. He didn't do himself any favours, making his request with a bad joke: "With all that weight you've put on, Ron, you look as if you could afford it." Nobody said a word. Ronnie finished drinking and left with his companion, but after a short while returned. "I want a word with you in private", he told Joe. "What for?" Joe asked. Ronnie replied: "You'll see." The whole room watched as Joe went to the toilets with Ronnie. After Ronnie had left, Joe was found slumped in a corner. Someone later described the state of him. He "had half his face beside him on the floor", as one witness put it. He survived the attack, but was thereafter known by the grim nickname of "Tramlines". Another particularly nasty incident of Ronnie's involved a knife-sharpener that he had heated in a gas flame. He used the implement on a man's face in the manner of a branding-iron.

Indeed, early on in his criminal career, Ronnie Kray was confined to a psychiatric ward, suffering from "prison psychosis" – a catch-all term for what in Ronnie's case was paranoid schizophrenia. A telegram arrived at his mother Violet's house on Vallance Road in Bethnal Green: "Your son Ronald Kray certified insane." This took place in the late 1950s, during a three-year sentence for assault that he was serving following a rare slip-up. He had been sent to Wandsworth Gaol but later had been transferred to a laxer prison, Camp Hill on the Isle of Wight. Other prisoners, many of them due for release, wisely steered clear, which exacerbated Ronnie's paranoia.

The East End that the Kray twins grew up in was closer to the world of Charles Dickens' *Oliver Twist* than the area it is today: Hoxton and the adjoining district of Shoreditch are now beloved of artists, fashionistas and the media. Between the wars, men still made a living from petty crime, street cons and market trading. The young toughs boxed and both Krays had success in the fight game as teenagers (it was said that Reggie had the makings of a champion). It was the twins' ruthlessness and the fact that they worked as a team that set them apart from other cockney villains. While Ronnie had been losing his mind in prison, Reggie had made a success of a new club, The Double R, on the Bow Road. He brought in his older brother Charlie to help out, before opening a gambling den on the same street as the Bow police station. He had a natural talent as a ruthless businessman and manager. The trouble was that when Ronnie was finally released, he added a combustible extra element to the mix. Ronnie savoured the violence; he fancied himself as Al Capone. He liked to hold court, surrounded by foot soldiers and the dissolute aristos and showbiz celebs who had started to become fascinated by the brothers' vicious reputation. This was a life like no other cockney villain had had before. They were feared and respected in equal measure: whenever the Krays bloodied their hands, there were always alibis and a wall of silence surrounding the crime scene.

In their triumphal years during the 1960s, the Kray twins outgrew their East End roots, making inroads into gambling and protection rackets in other parts of the city. They moved in social circles that were far removed from Bethnal Green. In 1964 the *Sunday Mirror* newspaper ran a story insinuating that **Lord Boothby** (a former aide to Winston Churchill) and Ronnie were involved in an improper relationship.

Backed by the prime minister, Harold Wilson, who feared a scandal near election time, Boothby protested and threatened to sue. Even though the story was true, the paper backed down and paid the peer the huge sum of £40,000.

It seemed that not even a society scandal could stick to the Krays, let alone any criminal charges. However, one Scotland Yard detective, **Leonard "Nipper" Read** had got the Krays' scent and was determined to take them down. The Boothby cover-up was a setback, as some of the evidence he had acquired could no longer be used as a result. But when he was promoted to the Murder Squad, Nipper painstakingly built up his case.

Finally, on 8 May 1968, he was able to arrest not only the twins but also their closest henchmen. Having taken both the gangsters into custody, it was now (relatively) safe for witnesses to come forward. And eventually both twins were convicted of murder on 4 March 1969 for the killing of **Jack "The Hat" McVitie**. Ronnie received an additional

They were always kind to their dear old mum: Reggie, Charlie and Ronnie (from left to right).

murder sentence for shooting dead **George Cornell**, who had called him a "fat poof". The twins were each sentenced to serve thirty years. At the time, these were the longest such sentences ever handed down.

Following his imprisonment, Ronnie was again certified insane. He died on 17 March 1995 in Broadmoor Hospital (a high-security prison). At his funeral three weeks later, huge crowds gathered on the Bethnal Green Road to witness the old-style procession, complete with a glass hearse drawn by six plumed horses. Given permission to attend, Reggie was, according to the *London Tonight* news show, "greeted like a returning hero". Suffering from inoperable cancer and having in fact spent more than thirty years in prison, Reggie was released on 26 August 2000 to spend the last weeks of his life in freedom. He died on 1 October, leaving behind the legacy of a remarkable, unsavoury legend.

For further investigation

John Pearson The Profession of Violence: The Rise and Fall of the Kray Twins **(1985)** An award-winning account by a former *Sunday Times* reporter who interviewed the brothers and those around them.

ⓦ youtube.com/watch?v=D1Qc_8DoUCs 1960s TV interview footage of the twins.

ⓦ youtube.com/watch?v=iG_62SSJitY *London Tonight* coverage of Ronnie Kray's funeral.

Street gangs

LOS ANGELES STREET GANGS: BLOODS & CRIPS

Successive waves of migration to the West Coast of the US have resulted in California being home to a bewildering array of street gangs, biker gangs, Triads and other criminal outfits. The lesser-known groups include the **Mongols MC**, an "outlaw" motorcycle band founded in 1969 and based in the southern part of the state (though it has chapters elsewhere, including in Scandinavia). The Mongols have an unfortunate record of being successfully infiltrated by federal agents, leading to arrests and convictions for violent crimes and racketeering. In October 2008, a judge granted a controversial injunction to ban the club logo, which depicts a Mongolian warrior wearing shades. Also active are the Satanas, a Filipino American street gang in Los Angeles; the United Bamboo Gang, a large Taiwanese Triad; the Mara 18, one of several gangs whose membership is largely drawn from LA's El Salvadoran, Guatemalan and Honduran communities (the gang is known simply as El Criminal in El Salvador); and the Black Guerilla Family, an African-American prison gang with a hard-left agenda of overthrowing the government.

Los Angeles is the metropolis of street gangs, gangland central. Perhaps its most notorious gangs are two African-American outfits, the Bloods and the Crips. The Crips started in the neighbourhoods of West Los Angeles around 1970. The smaller neighbourhood gangs consolidated and joined forces under the leadership of Stanley "Tookie" Williams and Raymond Washington. Soon, other gangs started renaming themselves, incorporating the word Crips into their new names: gangs such as the Main Street Crips, Kitchen Crips, 5 Deuce Crips, and Rollin 20 Crips appeared on the streets. There are estimated to be at least thirty thousand Crips – but unlike the hierar-chically organized Mafia and Asian gangs, this mainly black gang is more of a loose federation. Williams wrote a memoir, *Blue Rage, Black Redemption*, in which he termed the Crips a "fighting alliance".

In 1971, a Crips group was formed in Compton. It called itself the Piru Street Boys and became powerful and well-organized. It has been in the nature of the

CRIMINAL TATTOOS

Throughout the world, gang members and prisoners have used tattoos as a visible way of declaring their allegiance and signalling facts about their criminal background. The tattoos in some cases are crude and simple; in others they are intricate and ornate, painstaking works of extraordinary craftsmanship.

Prisoners in Britain and also members of the football-hooligan "Ultras" groups, mark their hands with the acronym "A.C.A.B." (All Cops are Bastards, sometimes jokingly watered down as Always Carry a Bible). The letters are marked on the upper part of each of the four fingers, with a variant being just to have a dot in the place of each letter.

In the US a teardrop tattoo by the eye can indicate that its wearer is a murderer. Three dots in a triangle between thumb and forefinger, or by the eye, often indicates gang membership. The white supremacist Aryan Brotherhood favour a shamrock (also widely used outside gangs) or, to signal their malevolence, "666" disguised by some other design. The Nuestra Familia use the number "14" or four dots in a square. Californian street gang members commonly have their three-digit area code tattooed.

Yakuza tattooing ("Irezumi", meaning the insertion of ink) usually involves the complex clan crest depicted on the body. Some gang members have a black ring on the arm for each crime committed. The remarkable all-body tattoos that some members favour have taken sometimes hundreds of hours to make. They represent the man's fortitude in enduring prolonged pain as well as his defiance of social norms (in Japan tattooing is almost exclusively identified with criminality).

Perhaps the most remarkable tattoos belong to Russian criminals. They are highly symbolic and a strict code governs their use – wearing unearned tattoos will lead to violent reprisals and loss of gang rank can be punished by the burning off of tattoos with caustic magnesium. A rose tattoo, which is a mark of the Russian Mafia, is often the centrepiece of complex designs – though they are often roughly drawn (because no instruments are available in Russian prisons) using ink made with soot and urine. These designs incorporate deck-of-cards motifs (hearts, for example, indicate that the wearer is a prison sex object) and Egyptian symbols such as the ankh sign. In the Russian culture tattooing is also used as a form of branding, forcibly inflicted on someone in order to stigmatize him.

loosely organized black gangs that bloody feuds develop in the absence of a regimented structure, and so it was with the Pirus, who broke off violently from the rest of the Crips, calling themselves Bloods instead. The rivalry and factionalism continues today.

One of the Crips' founding members was a man called Buddha, who wore a blue bandanna together with blue jeans, shirt and braces. When he was killed in 1973, gang mourners wore similar bandannas as a mark of respect and, with that gesture, the Crips adopted the gang colour that identifies them. Crips gang members wear some blue article of clothing: shoelaces, hat, hair rollers, canvas belt. In some cities, members wear light blue. They generally write their graffiti in blue, tagging their gang name on walls to mark their territorial boundaries and to publicly taunt their enemies or rivals. They use terms like "BK" (Blood Killer) and "PK" (Piru Killer). Crips refer to one another as "Cuzz" and use the letter "C" to replace the letter "B" in their conversations and writings ("Meet me at the cusstop" or "that guy has crass calls"). Conversely, Bloods wear the colour red and refer to one another as "Blood", "Piru" or "CK" (Crips Killer). In the past, black gang members eschewed tattoos, but that's changed; today, members are tattooing themselves in the same manner as the traditional Hispanic gangs.

GANGS OF NEW YORK: WESTIES, BLACK SPADES, LATIN KINGS

Alongside Chicago and Los Angeles, New York is the other major US gang metropolis. Organized crime took root there in the nineteenth century. Its history is recounted in the classic 1928 book by Herbert Asbury, *The Gangs of New York: An Informal History of the Underworld*. The city's many now-defunct gangs include the **Five Points Gang** (Italian), the **Whyos** and **Dead Rabbits** (Irish) and the **Eastman Gang** (Jewish). In recent years, gang membership has declined, due to more effective policing, gentrification of traditional neighbourhoods and other cultural shifts. The **Westies**, an Irish American outfit, were powerful in the 1960s, under the leadership of Mickey Spillane (who was no relation to the writer). Later, in the 1990s, the Westies came under the leadership of a Yugoslavian – **Bosco "The Yugo" Radonjich** – and the gang hooked up with John Gotti's Gambino mob. But with the Hell's Kitchen neighbourhood cleaned up and renamed Clinton, and with Gotti dead, Radonjich returned to Europe. After a series of successful police busts, the outfit no longer seems to be a force. The African-American **Black Spades** gang, a fierce and vicious group in the 1970s, dispersed as black gang culture was increasingly transformed by hip-hop music, and the financial success it brought many former gang members.

The **Latin Kings** gang started in Chicago, Illinois. It has a complex structure and an elaborate mythology. When its leader, Luiz Felipe, a.k.a. **King Blood**, was convicted of organizing multiple murders in 1996 and went to prison, Antonio Fernandez, known as King Tone, assumed leadership of the Latin Kings. He embraced Puerto Rican nationalism, declaring a shift in the gang's activities towards focusing on improving the lives of the community's poor. Aspirations aside, the disturbing reality of the gang, as revealed on surveillance tapes, still took in assault, drug dealing, kidnapping and homicide.

Around the time of these revelations, which were connected to the FBI initiative Operation Crown, King Tone publicly declared he had reformed and was helping troubled youth. It was reported by the *Miami New Times* that he was working as a mail clerk in a New York advertising agency. However, in 1999 Tone began serving a sentence for an unrelated charge for drug-dealing, though his case is likely to be subject to parole consideration, for he has already served a considerable part of his sentence.

Most of the Latin Kings are proud of their gang affiliation and will display it by wearing a Latin Kings

PIRATES, BIKERS & THE UNKNOWN MAFIOSI

In 2008, the problem of Somali pirate gangs hit the headlines, adding a new dimension to the mythology of organized crime. Well armed and equipped with hi-tech surveillance equipment, the Somali pirates have become increasingly audacious since their emergence in the early 1990s during the civil war in Somalia.

The successful 2008 film *Gomorrah* prompted interest in the world of the "other Mafia", the Camorra of the Campania region of Italy (which includes Naples). The Neapolitan mob became especially infamous for running rubbish disposal scams which resulted in household and industrial, often highly toxic waste being carelessly dumped, causing severe pollution. The other regional crime gang in Italy is the 'Ndrangheta (which translates as the "Honoured Society"), which operates in the Calabria region at the southwest tip of Italy.

Biker gangs were also in the news in 2008, when seven members of the UK branch of the Outlaws gang were convicted in Birmingham of a drive-by shooting of a Hells Angels member. With chapters throughout the US and Western Europe, the Harley-Davidson-riding Hells Angels Motorcycle Club has routinely been investigated by police for gang violence, drug running, fencing of stolen goods and extortion.

Also in the US, there are several prison gangs which have expanded beyond the walls to become significant criminal organizations. Membership of these gangs is usually dictated by ethnicity. The major white gangs are the Aryan Brotherhood and the Nazi Lowriders; the major Hispanic gangs are La Eme (the "Mexican Mafia"), who have ties to the Aryan Brotherhood, and the Neustra Familia. African-American prison gangs derive from street gangs such as the Bloods and the Crips.

Another group with a fearsome reputation for violence are the Yardies – Jamaican gangsters involved in particular with drugs and gun crime in their home country and in the UK. However, police do not always classify Yardies as being part of the organized crime phenomenon because, unlike Mafia groups or Asian gangs, they do not have a hierarchical command structure.

tattoo or other gang identifier. The main identifying paraphernalia of the Latin Kings is the colour of their clothing – black and gold – which may be supplemented by black and gold beads worn around the neck. In 1994, the Latin Kings merged with the Latin Queens and became known as the Almighty Latin King and Queen Nation (ALKQN). Some members claim to have abandoned their criminal past, claiming kinship with the Black Panthers and the Puerto Rican nationalist Young Lords.

Criminal gang culture can evolve into something less violent and more community-focused. But there remains the seemingly eternal tendency for violent men to join together for violence and money and belonging. "For the most part the old time gangster was apparently very courageous", Herbert Asbury wrote in his preface to *The Gangs of New York*, "but his bravery was in truth a stolid, ignorant, unimaginative acceptance of whatever fate was in store for him; it is worthy of note that the gangster invariably became a first rate soldier, for his imagination was seldom equal to the task of envisioning either himself or his victim experiencing any considerable suffering from the shock of a bullet or the slash of a knife." Perhaps that description is still apt in the age of sub-machine-guns and criminal profits numbered in the billions of dollars; beyond degrees of scale, the modern mobs are nothing new.

For further investigation

A&E, Gangland: One Blood (2008) Gang detectives, former Bloods members and the mother of a victim of a fatal gang drive-by hit discuss the status of street violence and where it is today.

knowgangs.com An education-based information base for gangs.

DIRTY COPS &
BAD APPLES

POLICE DO NOT ENTER CRIME SCENE

Dirty cops & bad apples

Police corruption comes in a variety of shapes and sizes - from a simple looking-the-other-way on everyday minor infractions to major scandals of involvement in drug trafficking and money laundering. The worst of these stories go well beyond a mere stretching of the law. Tales of abuse, corruption, and even murder committed by those the world has charged with maintaining social order regularly hit the headlines. In some countries, it's a bona fide social problem, as new police officers earn salaries so low that they would qualify to go on the dole. Increasing their own incomes through corrupt means is a temptation some officers can't resist.

The LAPD

THE BEATING OF RODNEY KING

The most infamous instance of police brutality in recent history is the beating of **Rodney King**, an African-American cab driver. The footage captured on a witness's videotape was shocking. It showed an African-American man being tasered, stamped on, and kicked by police in 1991. More than fifty baton blows and several kicks were inflicted on King. The beating caused a worldwide scandal, and raised urgent concerns about racism and corruption within the Los Angeles Police Department.

The video footage showed a police supervisor standing by, watching LAPD officer **Theodore Briseno** stamping on Rodney King's shoulder, causing his head to hit hard against the asphalt. Three officers were charged with excessive force and held over for trial. The images of three baton-armed white officers savagely beating a defenceless black man were sent across the world via the airwaves: it seemed to be an open-and-shut case of police abuse and brutality. Polls taken after the beating revealed that more than ninety percent of Los Angeles residents who viewed the tape believed officers had used excessive force in their attempts to arrest King.

The case ended up, however, with the polar opposite results of what everyone had expected, and what the media predicted. Despite the videotape, an all-white jury in Simi Valley concluded a year later that the evidence was insufficient to convict the officers.

The same day the verdict was read, riots broke out in the inner city of Los Angeles. The civil unrest lasted four long days: a riot of major proportions, it was only the second of its kind in the history of California. The first had been the Watts riot, in the summer of 1965, which had had a similar spark. On the third day of the LA riots, Rodney King went on TV and made a plea for the violence to stop: "People, I just want to say, you know, can we all get along?" were his famous words. Rioting ended a day later, but the last line of King's plea became something of a joke among radicals, and was quickly the butt of late-night talk-show jokes.

It took seventeen thousand US National Guard officers, called into active duty and ordering the area under martial law, to control the violence. All told, 34 people – 28 of whom were African-American – were killed. The 1072 people injured included 773 civilians, 90 Los Angeles police officers, 136 firefighters, 10 national guardsmen, and 23 people from an assortment of government agencies, including the FBI and DEA. More than a hundred of those injured were shot. More than four thousand people were arrested. Much discussion and debate has since taken place, but the riots appeared to be caused by the long-standing resentment by Los Angeles' working-class black community, which is within South Central Los Angeles, over treatment by police.

After the riots, the United States Justice Department indicted four LAPD officers for federal civil rights violations against the four officers involved in the beating. The federal trial, unlike the state case, focused on the officers' training and relied less on the videotape evidence. A jury found Sergeant **Stacey Koon** and Officer **Laurence Powell** guilty. They each were sentenced to thirty months in a California state prison. The jury found officers Timothy Wind and Theodore Briseno not guilty and acquitted them of all charges.

As for King, his lawsuit against the Los Angeles Police Department and the city of Los Angeles eventually settled for $3.8 million, with a chunk of that going towards paying his lawyers' fees.

THE RAMPART DIVISION SCANDAL

In early 2003, Los Angeles County district attorney **Steve Cooley** announced that his office was wrapping up its investigation into what was termed the Rampart police corruption scandal – named after the police station at the centre of the investigation. The Rampart debacle was the biggest dirty-cop scandal to hit the Los Angeles Police Department in more than half a century. In the end, former police officer **Rafael Perez** implicated seventy officers in wrongdoing. As a result of his questioning of police procedures, more than a hundred prior convictions were thrown out and thousands more were re-investigated.

The Rampart is an area that covers eight crime-ridden square miles west of downtown Los Angeles. With 375,000 residents and 350 police officers, the barrios of Rampart are home to the highest concentration of gang members in all of Los Angeles: 60 gangs, comprising as many as 8000 members. The Rampart Division also routinely has led the city in arrests for homicide, drug activity, and violent crime.

DA Cooley pointed out that a key figure in the case – former LAPD officer **Nino Durden** – had impli-

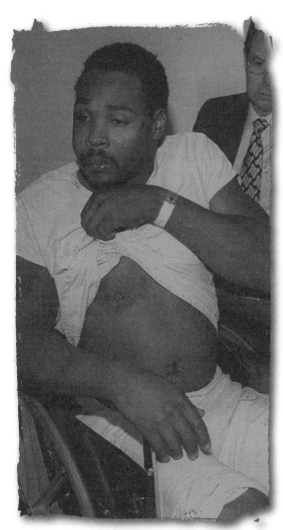

Rodney King shows the bruises he sustained at the hands of four Los Angeles police officers.

cated only himself and his partner, **Rafael Perez**, in any police wrongdoing. That could not have been further from the truth. Durden, in fact, told investigators that he and many of his colleagues routinely planted evidence, framed suspects, lied in court to obtain convictions, covered up misconduct, and even shot innocent people. An independent panel picked up the investigation where DA Cooley left off.

It was the worst corruption scandal in the chequered history of the LAPD. The corruption, which appeared to be systemic throughout the department, particularly within the special investigation units, first came to public attention with the admission of Officer Rafael Perez that he had helped frame an innocent man.

The Rampart investigation began in August 1998 after the 32-year-old Perez was arrested for stealing a million dollars' worth of cocaine from a police evidence vault. On 8 September 1999, Perez signed a plea bargain to serve just five years in prison, on condition that he assist in uncovering corruption within the Los Angeles Police Department. Perez eventually brought to light wrongdoings that he claimed were not unique to the Rampart, but endemic in such special police units. Perez declared that bogus arrests, perjured testimony, and the planting of "drop guns", or "throw downs", on unarmed civilians were commonplace. In exchange for less time inside, Perez spilled the beans. His story unfolded over several months, but what he told investigators rocked the LAPD to its very core. The *Los Angeles Times* described the Rampart saga as "the worst corruption scandal in LAPD history".

While Perez ended up implicating some seventy officers in wrongdoing, only Perez and his partner Durden were sent to prison and only twenty cops were suspended or fired because of the scandal. However, the fallout was enormous, with the scandal putting the city's criminal-justice system into a state of tumult. The district attorney released a list of 3300 people who had been convicted on the testimony of the 20 cops who were suspended or fired because of the scandal. The investigation forced the review of those cases by the DA's office to determine if the convictions had actually been justified. When the dust had settled, more than a hundred convictions by the officers in question were tossed out – and many more sought fresh appeals. Civil lawsuits were filed by people claiming they were assaulted or framed by police officers. None of the cases went to trial; they were simply settled. The city attorney's office estimated the potential cost of settling the suits at $125 million.

The *Los Angeles Times*, quoting the LAPD, reported that: "Rampart officers stole drugs from dealers and then used street prostitutes to sell the narcotics for their own profit." The LAPD also told the *Times* that officers who belonged to a so-called CRASH unit, operated like the gangs they were supposed to police. Los Angeles councilman Joel Wachs was reported afterwards as saying the scandal "may well be the worst man-made disaster this city has ever faced".

For further investigation

📖 **Richard Melville Holbrook** Political Sabotage: The LAPD Experience, Attitudes Toward Understanding Police Use of Force **(2004)** A studied look into the culture of police corruption and use of force, including the Rampart investigation.

Ⓦ pbs.org/wgbh/pages/frontline/shows/lapd/scandal A list of stories, including a timeline, posted on PBS's site that covers the LAPD's Rampart scandal.

The NYCPD

More than half a dozen major scandals involving the New York City Police Department have occurred within the last century. The **Knapp Commission** first brought attention to the NYPD in 1972, when it released results of more than two years of investigations into alleged corruption. The findings were startling: bribery, especially among narcotics officers, was extremely common. As a result, many officers were prosecuted and even more lost their jobs.

MAFIA COPS: LOUIE EPPOLITO & STEPHEN CARACAPPA

The most famous dirty cops in recent US history are **Louie Eppolito** and **Stephen Caracappa**, who were charged and convicted of being paid assassins for the mob. They were accused of being on the Gambino family payroll at the same time that they were collecting their New York City Police Department paycheques, while the boss of the Lucchese crime family referred to Eppolito as his own "crystal ball".

After their arrests, the pair of detectives were often referred to as "Mafia cops". However, the criminal case against them ended as dramatically as it started when the most egregious charges – racketeering and murder – were tossed out.

Eppolito and Caracappa were actually well into their respective retirements when they were arrested, having both moved to Las Vegas in the mid-1990s. About ten years later, on 9 March 2005, they each were charged by federal prosecutors for taking part in eight gangland murders, including working as contract hit men in the 1990 slaying of Gambino capo **Edward Lino**. The wide-ranging conspiracy described in the indictment was alleged to have started in New York City in the early 1980s, continuing in Las Vegas (despite their retirement from police work) right up until Eppolito's and Caracappa's arrests.

While an active-duty police officer, Eppolito was one of the most highly decorated cops in the history of the New York City Police Department. His father, Ralph Eppolito, was a hit man for the Gambino family; his uncle James was a Gambino captain known by the moniker of "Jimmy the Clam". Instead of following his family's footsteps into organized crime, Louie instead surprised his family in 1969 by becoming a police officer – the same year his future partner Stephen Caracappa joined the force.

Joseph Miedzianowski was a former agent with the US Bureau of Alcohol, Tobacco, Firearms and Explosives who has been described as Chicago's "most corrupt police officer". He was convicted in 2001 of masterminding a cocaine ring and supplying weapons to the very street gangs he was tasked with policing. Diane Klipfel and Michael Casali, a married couple, claimed they had received repeated threats after they accused him of corruption, and were awarded $9.5 million in damages in 2007.

The partners' careers began innocently enough on the East Coast. Both eventually made the rank of police detective and worked the streets of Brooklyn, the neighbourhood they had grown up in. Eppolito claimed to have avoided the Mafia lifestyle to become a crime-buster. The move led everyone – including his family – to believe that Louie had taken the straight and narrow. On the morning of 24 November 1984, Eppolito's path took a very different turn. Details of a lengthy police probe into corruption were leaked to the *New York Daily News*. Eppolito was suspended from the department and denied the charges made against him – of having provided inside information to the mob. In a departmental trial, the circumstantial evidence was deemed insufficient and he was

exonerated. Still, he felt betrayed.

"I knew my life as I had known it was over", Eppolito wrote in his book *Mafia Cop* about how he felt when the article was released. "No matter what I did for the rest of my life, I'd be classified as a member of organized crime." He began doing exactly what he had been exonerated of: working for the mob.

By this time Steve Caracappa was Eppolito's trusted police partner, and he joined Eppolito in his new career as a mob insider. Caracappa was then a member of NYPD's elite Organized Crime Homicide Unit. While on the job, the pair provided inside information to gangsters; Eppolito supplied details to the Mafia about police informants that often had fatal implications.

Louie worked for the NYCPD until 1990; Caracappa

THE SHOOTING OF AMADOU DIALLO

Not all controversy concerning the police's actions can be put down to corruption: heavy-handedness can sometimes cause problems. As the world learned that an unarmed West African immigrant had been shot and killed by four plain-clothes New York City police officers, a firestorm of controversy and outrage erupted. The undercover officers had been assigned to the Bronx. Wearing blue jeans, sneakers, and hooded sweatshirts, they jumped out of their car and headed straight for Diallo. When the officers mistook Diallo's wallet for a gun, they fired off forty-one rounds, hitting Amadou Diallo nineteen times. The 23-year-old died instantly.

Diallo was a college student from Guinea who worked as a street vendor. He had studied at the International School in Thailand and at the Computer Institute in Singapore, an affiliate of

Cambridge University; he'd moved to the US in 1996 for post-grad computer science studies. In the early morning hours of 4 February 1999, he was standing in the vestibule of his apartment building, on Wheeler Avenue in the Soundview section of the Bronx, when four officers cruised by in their unmarked car.

They stopped, because – as they later explained – Diallo fitted the description of a serial rapist. All four – Kenneth Boss, Sean Carroll, Edward McMellon, and Richard Murphy – were members of the NYPD's elite Street Crimes Unit, which has been credited with reducing crime and seizing hundreds of illegal weapons. The officers said they had thought Diallo had pulled a gun. It was his wallet.

The shooting prompted demonstrations in New York City, where a coalition of religious leaders,

retired two years later, to a disability pension. If anything, the pair's stories became even more extraordinary after they moved to Las Vegas, that hub of organized crime where first the Jewish mob and then the Italian mafiosi had skimmed money from casinos for years.

Life in Vegas was good to them. Caracappa worked as a private investigator, and Eppolito landed bit parts in movies, playing either cops or bad guys. Louie bought a four-thousand-square foot, half-million dollar home on Silver Bear Way in a western section of town with his wife Frances and his elderly mother. The southwest-style architecture featured a custom-designed swimming pool with statues of naked figures on the desert landscape. A year later, Steve, with his wife Monica, moved across the street from the Eppolitos to a similar house. The former partners appeared to lead quiet, albeit fancy, lifestyles in a gated community in the Mojave Desert.

However, in the desert, the life of Louie Eppolito was anything but innocent. Eppolito and Caracappa were regulars at Casa di Amore, an Italian restaurant in an older section of town known as a favourite for ageing mafiosi. The pair dabbled in racketeering, while Eppolito also found time to run a few cons. He found easy marks in at least two elderly women who were conned out of their life's savings in exchange for their life stories. Eppolito, a bit-part actor and part-time screenwriter, convinced at least two women that he could turn their stories into Hollywood blockbusters.

He promised, for a $45,000 fee, to write and sell

activists, and politicians accused police of engaging in racial profiling – the inclusion of racial or ethnic characteristics in determining whether a person is likely to commit a particular type of crime.

The officers were indicted on charges of second-degree murder and reckless endangerment. The trial took place in February 2000 and ended with the officers' acquittal after two days of deliberations. Diallo's family filed a further legal complaint, but the US Justice Department declined to prosecute the officers.

In April, a panel of police commanders decided not to discipline the four officers who killed Amadou Diallo, because they concluded that the men had not violated police guidelines. The panel did, however, order the officers to undergo retraining in police tactics. Diallo's parents then filed a negligence lawsuit against the city of New York alleging gross negligence, wrongful death, racial profiling and other violations of Diallo's civil rights.

In January 2004, five years after Diallo's death, the city agreed to pay $3 million to his family. In announcing the settlement, Michael Cardozo, counsel for the city, said: "The mayor, the police department, and the city deeply regret what occurred and extend their sympathies to the Diallo family."

The shooting prompted an investigation into racial profiling and ended in the commissioner implementing an anti-profiling policy in 2002. Diallo's mother, Kadiatou, set up a foundation, with a prominent board of New York business and political figures, to promote racial tolerance and improve police–community relations.

77-year-old Thelma Inglehart's story in a screenplay. Instead of writing a script, he left the Las Vegas woman deeply in debt. Eppolito is also accused of conning sixty-year-old former Sands Hotel call girl Jane McCormick – whose claim to fame is that she once had an affair with Frank Sinatra – out of $20,000.

Additionally, Eppolito somehow found the time to deal methamphetamine and launder money. At one point he hooked up with a Bonanno associate in Florida. What Louie did not know, however, was that the associate was wired and taping their talks for the FBI.

For back home, some of the pair's former fellow cops still harboured suspicions that their two retired colleagues had committed murder. They worked with investigators, sharing their suspicions with them. Investigations into one 1990 case proved to be fateful for the infamous pair of Mafia cops. It looked like a classic gangland hit: a bullet-riddled body was discovered that November in an abandoned Mercedes-Benz on a Brooklyn highway. The dead man was Edward Lino, a Gambino family captain who had helped kill Paul Castellano, the boss of all bosses. The mob hit catapulted John Gotti into power. To top it off, a dead gangster showed up on the Belt Parkway, and police began to try and solve the murder. They had little to go on. It was one murder among many in the late 1990s between warring Mafia families.

Law enforcement officers and federal agents made the rounds, questioning gangland sources and informants. A Brooklyn hit man turned snitch gave them a tip in 1994 that two corrupt detectives were responsible for Lino's death. Then, in 2003, detective Thomas Dades, working in the NYPD's Investigative Squad of the Intelligence Division, stumbled onto an informant who provided solid enough material for Dades to begin investigating it as a state murder case. As the investigation uncovered even more crimes, the

THE REAL SERPICO

Frank Serpico, a cop who worked for the New York City Police Department in the 1960s, refused to go along with his fellow officers and accept bribes. Instead, during the last few years of his twelve-year career, he reported the officers in question. But his reports fell on deaf ears. As a result, his fellow officers chastised him, and his life was in danger as an undercover officer working dangerous assignments with officers who no longer trusted him.

It wasn't until Serpico went public with the story, informing *The New York Times*, that his allegations were taken seriously. The *Times'* story prompted then-New York City mayor John Lindsay to appoint a commission to investigate the department-wide corruption within the NYCPD. "Through my appearance here today", Serpico testified, "I hope that police officers in the future will not experience the same frustration and anxiety that I was subjected to for the past five years at the hands of my superiors because of my attempt to report corruption ... We create an atmosphere in which the honest officer fears the dishonest officer, and not the other way around.

"The problem is", he continued, "that the atmosphere does not yet exist in which honest police officers can act without fear of ridicule or reprisal from fellow officers." His dramatic story was made into a movie, his part played by Al Pacino.

case snowballed, turning into a massive federal racketeering indictment. A federal indictment of Eppolito and Caracappa was issued in March 2005.

Louie Eppolito and Steve Caracappa were dining with associates at Piero's, a trendy, upscale Italian restaurant just off the Las Vegas Strip across from the Las Vegas Convention Center. As they ordered their meals, they were completely unaware of what was about to go down. Agents with the FBI, Drug and Enforcement Agency, and Alcohol, Tobacco, and Firearms were surrounding the restaurant as they prepared to take Eppolito and Caracappa into custody.

Instead, about a dozen heavily armed DEA, ATF and FBI agents – one with a sub-machine-gun – stormed the restaurant, throwing the lean Caracappa and the barrel-chested Eppolito against a wall and handcuffing them. Eppolito was armed with a .45-calibre semiautomatic handgun tucked in his waistband. On top of their federal charges, the pair was accused by Las Vegas and New York City authorities of a variety of crimes, from running drugs to laundering money. Glusman, the owner of the restaurant, was all over the TV news the next morning complaining that his restaurant had been made the scene of a raid. He told reporters he did not understand why agents didn't simply arrest the

Louie Eppolito exits Brooklyn federal court on Wednesday 22 March 2006, having been accused of being on the payroll of a mob underboss for $4000 a month.

pair at their homes.

The reason for such public arrests became clear afterward, when the indictment listed the pieces of evidence taken during a raid of Louie Eppolito's home. Inside the house located in a middle-class suburb, agents found more than a hundred guns, including two AK-47 assault rifles and a gold Luger pistol. Federal agents had not wanted to go to the men's homes, because of the intelligence they'd gathered telling them about the cache of guns and Eppolito's two-hundred-pound Mastiff dog.

Eppolito and Caracappa were arrested and booked into a downtown Las Vegas jail. Each was charged with eight murders, two attempted murders, murder conspiracy, obstruction of justice, money laundering and drug distribution. It was one of the worst corruption cases in the New York Police Department.

"These corrupt former detectives betrayed their shields, their colleagues and the citizens they were sworn to protect", said the Brooklyn lawyer **Roslynn Mauskopf** on the day following their arrests. "For years they were on retainer with the mob. They were paid handsomely for participating directly and indirectly in the murders and attempted murders of eleven individuals and for disclosing highly confidential law enforcement information to their mob benefactors."

On the morning of 11 March 2005, with his partner by his side, Louie Eppolito stood before acting US Magistrate Jennifer Togliatti and grinned at the Media. The cockiness he was known for on the streets was still very much apparent. Caracappa, on the other hand, appeared shaken. His face was ashen and expressionless. The gravity of the charges appeared to have hit him. The extent of the crimes each faced were nothing

to scoff at: eight murders, two attempted murders, conspiracy to commit murder, drug distribution, and money laundering.

Jennifer Togliatti was no stranger to the police world. Her father, George, was a career cop – a 25-year veteran and special agent to the FBI's Las Vegas office. At the time of the partners' arrests, the senior Togliatti was the top cop at the Nevada Highway Patrol. Eppolito and Caracappa's lawyers claimed prosecutors had based their case against the two decorated police officers on allegations made by mob informants who were trying to avoid life sentences in exchange for damaging information about the pair.

On 6 April 2006, Eppolito and Caracappa, after a three-week trial, were convicted on all charges. Two months later, Eppolito, inmate number 04596-748, and Caracappa, prisoner number 04597-748, were each sentenced to life in prison.

But almost two years later, in January 2008, there was a shock decision. US District Court Judge Jack Weinstein threw out the racketeering and conspiracy convictions against the two former detectives on a technicality. The murder convictions, however, remained. The judge, according to the written ruling, cited a conflict with the federal five-year statute of limitations as to his reason for tossing out the convictions. As a matter of law, the judge wrote, after Eppolito's and Caracappa's retirement from the New York Police Department, by early 1990 "the conspiracy that began in New York in the 1980s had come to a definitive close".

Under US federal criminal law, crimes alleged in a racketeering conspiracy have to have occurred within five years of the suspects being indicted. The judge emphasized in his ruling that even though there

charges had run out. In his 77-page ruling, the judge noted that the trial "overwhelmingly established" the guilt of Eppolito and Caracappa in the mob-related killings and other crimes, but he said the legal issue compelled him to overturn the convictions and instead acquit them. They were entitled to a retrial, he said, and he ordered that a new one be scheduled.

Even though the judge had reversed the duo's convictions, he nevertheless denied bail and ruled that they remain behind bars, calling them "flight risks". Eppolito and Caracappa remained, for the time being, in prison, awaiting a retrial. The convictions were eventually reinstated in September 2008 and in March 2009 both received life sentences. Both protested their innocence as sentencing loomed. "I'm a big boy, I'm not a child," Eppolito said. "The federal government can take my life. But they can't take my soul, they can't take my dignity. I never hurt anybody ... I never did any of this."

Today, the former cops are on 23-hour-a-day lockdown in the Metropolitan Detention Center, a federal penitentiary on Twenty-ninth Street in Brooklyn, New York, near where Louie Eppolito and Steve Caracappa grew up and became lifelong friends. They live in solitary confinement.

For further investigation

Lou Eppolito & Bob Drury Mafia Cop (1993) Louis Eppolito, before his arrest, wrote a memoir with author Bob Drury and claimed he avoided the mob ties of his father and grandfather.

Greg B. Smith Mob Cops (2006) This book gives graphic details of the circumstances that led to the fall of two decorated cops.

reportbadcops.com A site dedicated to stamping out bad cops.

Stephen Caracappa: one of the worst apples in the barrel.

was little doubt that Eppolito and Caracappa had "kidnapped, murdered, and assisted kidnappers and murderers", the judge had no choice but to let them go: the five-year statute of limitations in the conspiracy

Across the US

ANTOINETTE FRANK: A COP-KILLING COP

In the early 1990s, the case of a killer cop rocked the New Orleans Police Department and outraged a nation. The department was, at the time, severely short-handed. By 1992, crime in the Big Easy was rampant and murders were on the increase. The department needed more officers, but the policy of only hiring from within Orleans Parish limited recruiters' access to qualified candidates.

Antoinette Frank had wanted to be a police officer from the age of sixteen. When she belonged to New Orleans Police Explorer, a cadet scheme, she wrote in a letter: "I perceive myself to be a strong young woman with guts and who is willing to endure any obstacles to become the best law enforcement officer I can be."

In the spring of 1992, Antoinette's dream became a reality, even though a department psychologist had ranked her as a poor candidate. Antoinette's standardized personality assessment score was "poor" and the lowest score possible in the areas of tolerance, open-mindedness, and impulse control. She was ranked "below average" in stability, maturity, and in the likelihood of her adjusting well to organizations. The psychologist cited Frank's lack of tolerance and flexibility and suggested a psychiatric evaluation. At the conclusion of the evaluation, the psychiatrist who interviewed Frank rated her as unacceptable in integrity, forthrightness, and willingness to accept responsibility. "I do not feel ... the applicant is suitable for the job of police officer." After she failed the civil service psychiatric evaluation,

Antoinette Frank hired her own physician to evaluate her, and that doctor found her fit.

The department reconsidered. After all, Antoinette fitted the profile the department was looking for – she was a young female from an ethnic minority – and

THE NEW ORLEANS POLICE DEPARTMENT

The New Orleans Police Department has seen its fair share of police corruption scandals. In 1994, a dozen officers were convicted in a cocaine distribution and murder-for-hire scandal. It came out in a September 2000 report reporting that "a 1994 crackdown on police corruption [had] led to 200 dismissals and upwards of sixty criminal charges, including two murder convictions of police officers." Investigators, the report said, "discovered that for six months in 1994, as many as twenty-nine New Orleans police officers protected the cocaine supply warehouse containing 286 pounds of cocaine. The FBI indicted ten officers who had been paid nearly $100,000 by undercover agents."

The investigation, however, ended abruptly when officer Len Davis "successfully orchestrated the execution of a witness." It happened after New Orleans resident Kim Groves, under the protection of law, was killed. It was revealed in court that Davis – known as Robocop in the low-income housing project where the victim lived – ordered Groves' death after she filed a brutality complaint against him. Paul Hardy, the hitman for Davis, was convicted in connection with Groves' murder.

she was hired as a patrol officer with the New Orleans Police Department. She graduated from the police academy in July 1993 and was issued New Orleans Police Badge Number 628. However, after she began her active career, serious concerns from fellow officers about her behaviour were expressed. These concerns were ignored.

On Saturday 4 March at 1.50am, the 23-year-old Antoinette Frank let herself into Kim Anh, a family-owned Vietnamese restaurant in eastern New Orleans where she had moonlighted as a security guard. It was the third time she had visited the restaurant that night and she had stolen the front-door key. She was not alone: accompanying her was a drug dealer named **Rogers LaCaze**, who Frank is thought to have been having a relationship with. Chau Vu, the daughter of one of the restaurant's owners, was worried and bolted for the kitchen. Ronald Williams – Frank's partner in the police force – was inside the restaurant at the time, waiting to be paid for his night's work. Like Frank, he also moonlighted at the restaurant. As he went to see what was wrong, he was hit at the top of his spine by a bullet fired by La Caze. Frank then walked into the kitchen and executed Chau Vu and her brother before fleeing with her accomplice in a battered Toyota. But she returned later in a patrol car in response to an emergency call on her police radio, acting as if she knew nothing of the crime.

What she did not know, however, was that a third sibling, hiding in a walk-in refrigerator, had watched the events unfold. The witness identified Frank as the killer. Frank was taken to police headquarters for questioning, where she confessed to the crimes.

Antoinette Frank was for eleven years Louisiana's only woman on death row. The last woman executed in the state was Toni Jo Henry in 1942. Frank has appealed both the convictions and her death sentence. After a judge signed her death warrant, she was scheduled to be executed by lethal injection on 15 July 2008. She has had repeated stays of execution, the latest being a Louisiana Supreme Court decision in November 2008. She remains, however, a death row inmate.

For further investigation

📖 **Chuck Hustmyre** Killer with a Badge (2004) This book covers the story of Antoinette Frank's time on the New Orleans police force, her corrupt activities, and her ultimate arrest and trial.

🌐 trutv.com/library/crime/gangsters_outlaws/cops_others /antoinette_frank Within this site, listed under "Gangsters and Outlaws", is an in-depth account by author Chuck Hustmyre of the Antoinette Frank case.

🌐 democracyinaction.org Information about Antoinette Frank and women before her who have been executed in Louisiana. The site also includes statistics.

In 2008, former police officer Wayne Strawhorn, dubbed "Mr Big" by prosecutors, lost an appeal against his 2006 conviction for trafficking the chemical pseudoephedrine, an ingredient commonly used to illegally manufacture methamphetamine. While working as a drug squad detective for Victoria police in Australia, Strawhorn was discovered selling the chemical to one of the area's highest-profile drug dealers.

THE POLICE CODE OF SILENCE

When police officers perjure themselves on the witness stand during trials to protect one of their own, they call it "testilying". The practice runs rampant throughout some of the biggest police departments in the United States. To understand this unwritten but closely adhered to rule, the US National Institute of Ethics did the most extensive research ever conducted on the rule. Between February 1999 and June 2000, 3714 officers and academy recruits from 42 different states participated in the institute's study. The findings mark the first time law enforcement has ever been able to learn the truth about the code and the problems it causes. The study recognized that the "Blue Wall of Silence", as it's been called, is difficult for outsiders to break through.

The study concluded that the American criminal justice system and, in particular, law enforcement, has been negligent in not resolving the negative social impact of the code. It also concluded that, because of the code, serious misconduct in law enforcement has been covered up. It went even further, concluding that some police departments have shown they are incapable of policing themselves. One solution to the problem offered by the study was that written policies be provided to protect whistleblowers from being ostracized or threatened.

According to a 1998 report by the international Human Rights Watch entitled "Shielded from Justice", fourteen big cities were examined. Over a more than two-year period, they looked at Atlanta, Boston, Chicago, Detroit, Indianapolis, Los Angeles, Minneapolis, New Orleans, New York, Philadelphia, Portland, Providence, San Francisco, and Washington, DC. The study found that police brutality was endemic in all of those cities.

One example of a code of silence that has persisted for years is the recent corruption discovered within the Chicago Police Department. It's nothing new to Chicago. The city became a symbol of police brutality in 1968 as overzealous police officers attacked protesters outside the Democratic National Convention, all recorded by broadcast reporters. In the years after, Chicago police have been known to commit acts of brutality. "Abusive Chicago police officers have been allowed to perpetuate abuse in Chicago with virtual absolute impunity", Craig Futterman, a police critic and law professor at the University of Chicago, told CBS's Chicago local affiliate Channel 2 after three officers were charged with a home invasion in December 2006.

CRAIG ALAN PEYER, CHP TROOPER

Two days after Christmas 1986, twenty-year-old **Cara Knott** looked in her rear-view mirror and saw the lights of a California Highway Patrol trooper's vehicle. She was driving south on Interstate 15 in San Diego, from her boyfriend's house in Escondido to her parents' home in El Cajon, east of San Diego.

Cara, a student at San Diego State University, was nearing the Mercy Road exit in Rancho Penasquitos, a high-end but somewhat rural area, when a red light flashed from the roof of a car following closely behind her white 1967 Volkswagen Beetle. Cara started to turn her car onto the shoulder of the freeway, but the trooper directed her to continue on to Mercy Road. She did as she was told.

This was the stretch of road regularly used by **Craig Peyer**, a highway patrol veteran of thirteen years. He would pull over dozens of young women for minor traffic violations. He would use the bullhorn on his patrol car to order them to drive down the deserted, isolated dirt road. Once there, off the freeway, he would attempt to flirt with them, ask about their personal lives, and sometimes lecture them about vehicle safety.

By 10.30 that night, Cara's parents and boyfriend, expecting her to have finished the 45-minute drive home many hours earlier, contacted police to find out if there had been any accidents on the route travelled by Cara. When her parents learned no traffic accidents had been reported, they headed out on their own to try to find their daughter. Her sister and brother-in-law joined in the search. At around 5.30am they found Cara's VW abandoned with the key in the ignition at the end of Mercy Road. They called police. About three hours later, and less than a mile from her car, officers discovered Cara Knott's body under the Old Highway 395 bridge, which Mercy Road dead-ended into. Cara's skull had been smashed. She had been strangled with plastic rope and her body tossed over the former highway bridge to the canyon floor below.

Twenty-one days later, trooper Craig Peyer was arrested. The frightened community learned that Cara's death was at the hands of a veteran officer. It was later revealed in court that Craig Peyer used to ominously brag: "There are two people you don't piss off in this world: God and a Highway Patrolman – and not necessarily in that order." On the remote road, no one but Peyer could have heard Cara's screams. Peyer had returned to his station after his shift, bloodied and with scratches on his face. He told a fellow trooper that he had slipped and fallen into a chain-link fence.

After news of Peyer's arrest became public, more than twenty women came forward, telling of their experience with the same trooper who also pulled them over on the isolated road. Peyer was fired. He was first tried in 1988. The jury was deadlocked, and a mistrial was declared. The same year, Peyer was tried a second time, and the jury convicted him of murder.

Craig Peyer is currently serving a sentence of 25-years-to-life behind the walls of the California Men's Colony, a medium-security federal prison in between Los Angeles and San Francisco. The prison has been called a "country club" and the "garden spot" among California prisons, because of the vocational, educational, and psychological treatment programmes they have there, designed to rehabilitate inmates. According to published reports, Peyer spends his days working as a prison electrician.

In January 2004, after fifteen years in prison, Peyer went before the California Board of Parole. Present at the emotional hearing was Joyce Knott, Cara's mother. Afterward, the board denied his parole. Then, four years later, in January 2008, he went before the board a second time and, once again, was denied parole. Commissioners in both hearings named the seriousness of the murder and the former trooper's potential risk to the community as reasons for the denials. During both hearings, Peyer protested his innocence.

For further investigation

Ⓦ people.com/people/archive/article/0,,20099196,00.html A 1988 feature article in *People* magazine, by Kristin McMurran, detailing the Cara Knott case.

Ⓦ signonsandiego.com/news/metro/20040106-9999_1n6peyer .html This link includes the *San Diego Union-Tribune's* coverage of Craig Peyer's 2004 parole hearing.

Further afield

THE PERTH MINT SWINDLE

Dirty cops are common enough in Hollywood crime movies, but few real life-events come as close to echoing the plot lines of those scenarios as the celebrated **Perth Mint Swindle**. In June 1982, 49 gold bars worth $653,000 were taken by three separate couriers in exchange for three false cheques. They were to be delivered to an office a few kilometres away. But the gold and the couriers then vanished into thin air – the gold via Jandakot Airport. No one was hurt but the audacity of the raid and the ease with which security had been bypassed shocked Australia.

However, it didn't take too long before the Western Australian police had suspects in their sights. **Peter**, **Brian** and **Ray Mickelberg** were three brothers who could hardly be said to have been hardened criminals, with only a $50 fine for a licensed gun on the trio's collective records.

Detective Sergeant **Don Hancock**, a known tough cop amongst the local force, led the investigation. He was backed up by a junior policeman, Tony Lewandowski. Hancock had a deserved reputation for securing convictions, whereas Lewandowski was made of softer stuff. When the pair interviewed Peter – the youngest and potentially most pliable of the brothers – at Belmont police station, nobody else was around to observe proceedings. The officer in charge left soon after the suspects arrived. What happened next was vigorously contested for over twenty years over seven appeal trials. According to the police's version, Peter confessed and implicated his brothers in the crime. Instead, Mickelberg always contended, that account was fabricated. Peter was stripped naked, seated and punched innumerable times by Hancock in the interview. He said Hancock told him, while he grabbed his throat: "This is where you die, you little fucker." A confession later emerged, but Mickelberg always claimed it was forged. It was enough to convict Peter and Ray Mickelberg for sixteen and twenty years respectively. Brian, the third brother, served nine months in prison before being released on appeal, later dying after an aircraft crash. The other two brothers served time in Fremantle prison, which retains a reputation for being one of Australia's hardest incarceration facilities.

Peter and Ray fought against the conviction near single-handedly, but they had one ally, journalist Avon Lovell. A crusading local newshound, he had already made a nuisance of himself with reports into local corruption, and his interests in researching organized crime. Lovell was never convinced of the evidence but his life was irrevocably transformed on the publication of *The Mickelberg Stitch* in 1985, contesting the police's version of the story. It was subsequently banned by the authorities, leading to his bankruptcy

COERCED CONFESSIONS

Confessions are considered to be the strongest pieces of evidence that law enforcement can bring into the courts. The circumstances under which confessions are given, however, are often points of disagreement for defence lawyers fighting to keep their clients out of prison.

According to the Innocence Project, 156 inmates have been exonerated, of which 37 (some 24 percent) had earlier "confessed", since 1982. It's a startling revelation. Researchers Steven Drizin and Richard Leo analysed 125 cases of proven false confessions taken during police interrogations. "These 125 proven false confessions", the authors of the report say, "should put to rest any doubts that modern psychological interrogation techniques can cause innocent suspects to confess."

In August 2002, after more than seventeen years in prison because of his confession, Eddie Joe Lloyd walked out of prison a free man after being pardoned and released. His pardon marked the 110th US case based primarily on DNA evidence. Lloyd had confessed to murdering a sixteen-year-old Michigan girl, despite being innocent. According to his lawyer, the police tricked him by telling him that if he confessed, it would encourage the real killer to come forward. As soon as he signed the confession, he was arrested, tried, convicted, and sent to prison for life. That was in 1985.

After unsuccessfully appealing his case, Lloyd contacted the Innocence Project and asked that his DNA be tested against the remaining evidence from the crime scene. An analysis of DNA proved that Lloyd was not the one responsible for the teen's death.

According to Saul Kassin, professor of psychology at Williams College in Massachusetts, tactics used during interrogations of suspects often include minimization, where the seriousness of the crime is downplayed to make suspects believe he or she won't get in trouble if they confess. Another technique is to make suspects sit through hours of interrogations, prompting them to falsely confess just to get out of the interview room. Giving suspects evidence from the scene of the crime is also a technique.

The Innocence Project believe that the first step in preventing such false confessions is to teach interrogators how to properly conduct interviews. The next step is to implement the recording of all interrogations, from beginning to end, so that there's no doubt what was said to prompt a suspect's confession. Since some American police departments have made recordings mandatory, the number of false confessions has decreased, according to the Innocence Project's findings.

and several hundred court appearances defending his journalistic integrity.

Whilst the Mickelbergs languished in jail between their frequent appeals and Lovell fought legal actions brought by the police against him, his publisher and his distributors, Hancock rose to become head of Perth CIB before retiring to run a pub. It was only then, in 2002, that the tide turned. After getting into a dispute with local toughs, Hancock was murdered in Rivervale by a car bomb.

Lovell sought further interviews with Lewandowski, who eventually confessed to the journalist who had been on his tail for so many years. The guilt had clearly played on Lewandowski's tormented mind when he protested in a recorded interview that he had wanted to set the record straight – and that the ordeal of staying silent had ruined his life. "I was up at, like, 11 o'clock at night and I just sort of ... sat in the lounge room or somewhere and just drank piss, because I was so mentally fucked for being involved in this", was how he put it. The detective declared there was "no way" he could have defied his superior, indicating his own family would have suffered if he had come clean, at least whilst Hancock was still alive. The Mickelbergs were released but – just before Lewandowski was to stand trial for perjury in May 2004 – the distraught police officer committed suicide.

This might appear to have closed the case on two "bad" cops, but there were further twists to the tale. The Western Australian police were still not convinced and the assistant police commissioner indicated he was dissatisfied with the decision to release the Mickelbergs. The brothers moved to sue the Western Australian government for libel, setting the tone

for a protracted legal wrangle concerning terms for compensation for the pair, which related not only to the false imprisonment but to claims against five other officers connected to the case.

The tussle went to the very top. Western Australian attorney general **Jim McGinty** offered $500,000 to the acquitted pair, but he initially required them to drop the case against the other five officers. Detractors pointed to a possible conflict of interest – which McGinty has always denied – as one of the five was a personal friend of McGinty's. He was none other than political colleague Bob Kucera, the officer in charge of Belmont police station on the night of the interview. Kucera after a long police career had subsequently moved into politics.

During the long years of appeals, the Western Australian Police Union had collected $1 a week from members to support their legal action against Lovell and his publishers and distributors to uphold the ban against his book – which was subsequently lifted. So naturally when McGinty dropped the requirement for the brothers not to pursue the case, the Western Australian Police Union were said by the local press to be "seething". Many officers have found it hard to reconcile themselves to the brothers' acquittal. Even the disgraced Lewandowski – despite his own guilt about his involvement in the coerced

John Swift, onetime Gold Coast Casino Squad chief, and Carl Gibson, a former Coast detective, had each been previously jailed for corruption and perjury. But that didn't stop them getting hired as investigators for the State Government Department on the Australian Gold Coast. Their 2004 convictions were only discovered three years later; they had slipped through the cracks because only those applying for law enforcement jobs (as opposed to investigation positions) had criminal background checks carried out prior to employment.

confession – went to his grave with no doubts about the brothers' guilt whatsoever. "I'm convinced that they did it and that's the end of the story", he stated. No new evidence has, however, arisen to back up Lewandowski's accusation.

The case has never been closed and remains unsolved. There have been vague rumours of unnamed local businessmen being behind the crime, and the suggestion that Hancock himself may have had a hand in it. In the long run, the questionable methods used to secure the original conviction have served to complicate matters significantly. Only a fraction of the gold has ever been recovered – part of it being a tantalizing 55 kilograms dumped in 1989 outside a Perth TV station, with a note addressed to one of the station's reporters, protesting the Mickelbergs' innocence. It would appear that someone somewhere knows the truth.

For further investigation

Avon Lovell **The Mickelberg Stitch** (1985) The brave book that ignited the controversy.

news.com.au/perthnow/story/0,21598,23079642-948,00 .html. Local news report detailing the latest on the Mickelberg lawsuits

sixtyminutes.ninemsn.com.au/article.aspx?id=259181 Transcript of a remarkable TV report shortly after Lewandowski's suicide with compelling interview material.

RIO CRACKDOWN

Rio de Janeiro is a popular tourist destination, but it is one of Latin America's most violent cities, riven by drugs, poverty, and waves of gang violence. It is also infamous for the strong-arm tactics used by its police against drug gangs that control the city's hillside favelas (shantytowns). In 2006, more than 2400 homicides were registered in Rio.

A massive crackdown was launched in January 2007 when the government assigned significant numbers of federal and local police to the city's six hundred slums in an effort to oust the violent gangs and bandits who well-nigh govern most of them. Brazilian state governor **Sergio Cabral** requested the crackdown after a wave of violence in December 2006 that killed nineteen people, including seven civilians who died in a burning bus.

The 2007 initial crackdown involved 250 law enforcement officers – military and local police – who raided the **Vila Cruzeiro** slum in northern Rio that overlooks seaside apartment buildings. A shootout ensued, leaving two police officers injured, one gang member dead, and five other gang members injured during the twelve-hour siege. As part of the Rio crackdown on gang-related crime, a paramilitary group of five hundred had converged on the slum area the week before. The group was tasked with patrolling highways and guarding state borders to prevent drug and arms smuggling. Brazil's National Security Force – seven thousand specially trained officers – was created in 2004 after police patrol officers had difficulty quelling extreme violence.

The problem of violence in Rio, however, is not only the work of gangs. According to a November

Rio de Janeiro's governor Sergio Cabral, left, and General Ferreira, of the National Security Force, during a ceremony in Rio on 16 January 2007 launching an operation to battle a wave of gang violence.

executions were carried out by "police death squads". According to Brazil's state Public Security Institute, police killed 870 civilians during the first eight months of 2007. A coalition of 35 nongovernmental organizations, in response to the rash of killings, issued a public statement, saying: "For ten months, the Rio population has repeatedly watched arbitrary executions of supposed traffickers." The police department has countered such criticisms, claiming that most people killed by police were criminals.

2005 investigative report by the BBC, hundreds, if not thousands, of people are shot each year by the Brazilian police. And killings by members of the Rio police force are nothing new. Deaths at the hands of the police, however, had gone mostly unpunished because of public approval ratings for the new gang crackdown.

In 2004 alone, 983 people were killed by police officers. During the first half of 2007, police killings increased 25 percent from the same time the year before. A former police official told the BBC that

But, to cite one recent example of alleged police brutality, Brazilian authorities reported in June 2008 that active police officers suspected of being part of a Rio paramilitary group were involved in the torture of four people. The four – consisting of two journalists, their driver, and a local resident – told authorities they were captured and tortured by the militia police while doing an undercover story in a slum west of the city. They were abducted, beaten, and abused via electric shocks.

Militias, such as the one with which those corrupt cops were involved, are known as both "Men in

Black" and the "Galacticos", and are widely believed to control a portion of the city's shantytowns. The situation is similar to Tijuana, Mexico, where underpaid officers end up having to moonlight as security guards to make ends meet, and then find themselves in compromising situations – protecting drug dealers at night while fighting the same criminals during the day.

Rio has a lengthy history of officers making deals with drug gangs that give the traffickers free reign in slums, as long as they stay away from the city's affluent beach communities. The crackdown, however, is a sign that the long-standing, unofficial agreements between police and drug lords are ending.

For further investigation

ⓦ news.bbc.co.uk/2/hi/americas/4463010.stm An investigative article by BBC News about the execution of "thousands" by police.

ⓦ thepeninsulaqatar.com/Display_news.asp?section=World _News&subsection=Americas&month=October2007&file= World_News200710208306.xml An article by Reuters news services about criticism of Brazilian authorities for alleged heavy-handed police activities in Rio.

ⓦ english.people.com.cn/90001/90777/90852/6287253.html This short article includes statistics of police killings in Rio.

WILLIAM DUNCAN MCKELVIE

A celebrated investigator for the UK National Criminal Intelligence Service, Detective Sergeant **William "Duncan" McKelvie** proved to be a bad apple. He tipped off a gang of fraudsters based in Marbella, Spain, about a confidential police investigation. McKelvie, from Esher, Surrey, was scheduled to retire from the force in 2005.

The fraudster's ploy, planned between 2002 and 2004, was to exchange a forged bond for half a billion dollars. When the National Crime Squad opened an investigation into the cheque fraud, McKelvie alerted Robert Miles, a former colleague of his who had left the force in 1989 and who was also involved with the fraudsters. McKelvie, a respected investigator who had risen through the ranks of his department, was also accused of contacting international banks to see whether officials were suspicious or not.

But it was when Miles presented the forged bond at banks that the attention of the officials was caught, prompting an investigation. McKelvie tracked the probe, and, at one point, generated a false intelligence report in an effort to throw investigators off track – and away from the trail of Robert Miles.

McKelvie was arrested in 2004 for using official information for personal gain. The official charges included perverting the course of justice and improper conduct. Lawyers for both suspects argued that Miles had been the victim of a fraudster – a businessman based in Johannesburg – and that he had simply called on his former colleague and co-defendant, McKelvie, for assistance. Brian O'Neill, representing Miles, told the court: "If you believe you are a victim of a fraud perpetrated by a South African fraudster, who better to turn to for help than your close friend who is an expert in detecting African fraud?"

The argument didn't work. McKelvie, who was tried in Southwark Crown Court, was found guilty of three counts of misconduct in a public office and sentenced to two years in prison. For his part, Miles, originally from Towcester, Northamptonshire, was also tried and found guilty of aiding and abetting McKelvie, although the panel acquitted him of conspiracy. He was sentenced to one year in prison.

For further investigation

Ⓦ bucksfreepress.co.uk/misc/print.php?artid=757785 An article, published in the *Bucks Free Press*, about the McKelvie and Miles court cases.

Ⓦ news.bbc.co.uk/2/hi/uk_news/england/southern _counties/5079086.stm The BBC's coverage of the convictions of a detective and former officer for their involvement in a plot to forge a half-million-dollar bond.

LESSER
VIOLATIONS

Lesser Violations

Some crimes, such as violent homicide, are so horrendous that reactions to them are fairly uniform - horror, astonishment, or perhaps anger or fear. Others, such as white-collar crime, parking offences or blasphemy can arouse anger, rage or even pity for the perpetrators. How we feel about such lesser violations when they reach court - or the newspapers - will vary.

Of course, a crime is still a crime, even when it hangs upon a technicality. Yet that precept can be taken to ludicrous extremes: a strict, unreflective upholding of every law on every statute book across the world would be both absurd and impractical. Whether it's blasphemy or parking offences, the letter of the law often comes up against norms of average human behaviour: the debates may not be just about under-lying values of society but also about the severity of a law's application. Are criminals always in the wrong? Or are the laws sometimes the real problem? There are various categories of criminal behaviour that elicit mixed reactions.

Do the perpetrators deserve the strictest punishment – or our pity? With these "lesser violations" it seems the jury will remain out.

Celebrity misdemeanours

WINONA RYDER GOES SHOPPING

One case of theft that garnered worldwide media attention was the arrest of a well-known American movie star. On December 12, 2001, **Winona Ryder**, a twice Oscar-nominated actress – who at the time was earning around $6 million a film – was arrested in Beverly Hills, California. The charge sent shockwaves through Hollywood. Ryder was accused of shoplifting designer clothes and accessories, including hats, handbags, tops and hair accessories from the posh **Saks Fifth Avenue** department store on the trendy Rodeo Drive in Beverly Hills.

Shoplifting – the act of taking items or cash from a retail outlet – is one of the most common crimes clogging the court system. The ultimate costs, if stores do not recoup them, are often absorbed by the paying customers through higher price tags. Organized shoplifters run in gangs and are called **boosters**.

Ryder was caught red-handed; she was forced to take on an unwanted real-life role as a defendant in court. Ninety minutes of surveillance videotape from cameras showed her taking some twenty items as she moved through the store, but only paying for a handful of pieces. The video also showed Ryder examining a white-fringed Gucci slip dress with a retail value of $1,595. Ryder was seen removing the dress from its hanger and throwing the item over her arm. Among other items, she was also observed hanging onto an $80 pair of cashmere socks, a $525 Dolce & Gabbana purse, and a $200 headband. As she walked through the different departments, Ryder wore a black hat with a price tag hanging with a string from the rim. After she had entered two dressing rooms, the hat disappeared into a shopping bag, along with a sundry of other items. At the end of her shopping spree, Ryder was observed chatting with a sales clerk and then paying more than $3,000 for a leather bomber jacket and two tops.

Security guards in the basement of the store watched their screens before swooping down on their suspect. The store's videotape surveillance captured Ryder leaving the store and then immediately being confronted by security officers, who had followed her to the exit doors. They took the shopping bags from her and led her back into the store. All told, the booty Ryder was accused of stealing was worth $5,550 (around £3,900). According to court transcripts, she initially told security officers that a director had suggested she shoplift as preparation for a movie role.

A hefty team of eight prosecutors, put together by Los Angeles district attorney **Stephen Cooley**, handled the case. Cooley filed four felony charges against Ryder in what was described by one British newspaper as a "show-trial", especially since the prosecution had demanded that the trial be televised. Ryder, for her part, hired noted defense attorney **Mark Geragos** – famous for representing pop singer Michael Jackson.

Negotiations for a plea bargain, for Ryder to plead guilty for a lesser crime, failed at the end of summer 2002. The district attorney went after Ryder with everything he had. As pointed out by Joel Mowbray from the *National Review*, the prosecution was not ready to offer the actress a misdemeanour, no-contest plea – deals that are routinely handed out to thousands of other defendants in similar cases. And while Ryder's attorney told the judge his client offered to pay for the clothes, the prosecution would not allow it. (Ryder later sent a cheque to the store, which executives have refused to cash.)

On 1 February 2002 Winona Ryder was formally charged with four counts of felony grand theft and possession of a controlled substance. She pleaded

Ryder arrives on the second day of the preliminary hearings. Her arm (in sling) was injured negotiating hoards of photographers.

not guilty and was released on a $20,000 bail bond. The international attention on the case was comparable to that of a high-profile murder trial, despite it being a non-violent crime against a business, not a person. The channel *Court TV* provided gavel-to-gavel coverage of the trial, which got underway on 24 October 2002. *Court TV* also posted a page on its site entitled "Shopping With Winona", where readers could click onto photos of clothing and see exactly what merchandise was in Ryder's shopping bags and under her overcoat that day. A circus atmosphere surrounded the case, as often happens with celebrity trials. Outside the courthouse, droves of fans wore "**Free Winona**" T-shirts.

During the trial, Ryder – whose films include *Girl, Interrupted*, *Beetlejuice*, *Little Women*, *The Age of Innocence*, and *Mr. Deeds* – was also accused of having used drugs without prescriptions. According to a probation report, over a three-year span, Ryder had filled up to 37 prescriptions written by twenty doctors, using six different aliases. The defense produced the written prescriptions for the drugs that the police found in her purse, and the prosecution consequently dropped the charge, because she had been taking painkillers after breaking her arm. Deputy district attorney **Ann Rundle** said that the heavy prosecution had been undertaken so that Ryder would "take responsibility for her conduct" and not out of vindictiveness, as the defense had claimed.

Ultimately, on 6 November 2002, a Los Angeles jury convicted Ryder of grand theft and vandalism (for damaging the items by cutting off the security tags – an act described in court as "slice and dice") but she was acquitted on the third felony charge of burglary. She faced up to three years in prison. But in December 2002, the judge sentenced her to three years' probation and 480 hours of community service, and imposed $3,700 in fines, plus $6,355 restitution to Saks Fifth Avenue. She was also ordered to attend psychological and drug counselling. By 2004, she had paid her fines and completed 480 hours of community service at the City of Hope Medical Center in Duarte, California. In the end, the felony convictions were reviewed and on 18 June 2004 the felonies were reduced to misdemeanours. "I want to compliment you on your behaviour on probation" judge **Elden Fox** told the then-32-year-old actress during a court hearing wherein her lawyer asked that the convictions be reduced. As for Ryder's acting career following the trial, she went into a self-imposed exile and relocated from Los Angeles to San Francisco, to be near her parents, Mike and Cindy Horowitz.

After a six-year hiatus, in 2007 Ryder returned to work with three new movies: *The Ten*, *Sex and Death 101* and *The Last Word*. That same year, she spoke out for the first time since about the shoplifting offence. "I didn't have this tremendous sense of guilt, because I hadn't hurt anyone," she told *Vogue* magazine for its August 2007 cover story. "Had I physically harmed someone or caused harm to a human being, I think it would have been an entirely different experience."

Nevertheless, Ryder had been publicly humiliated. "I never said a word," Ryder told *Vogue*. "I didn't release a statement. I didn't do anything. I just waited for it to be over. The attention was what was embarrassing." Ryder also told the magazine that one day the news of her arrest was the lead story in broadcast media, over and above a piece about the suspected capture of **Osama bin Laden**.

For further investigation

Ⓦ cjonline.com/stories/110702/usw_ryder.shtml An Associated Press story about Winona Ryder's shoplifting conviction.

📖 **Us Magazine (ed.)** Winona Ryder **(1997)** A compilation of articles about Ryder published over the years in *Us Magazine*.

MORE SHOPLIFTING IN THE HEADLINES

California also witnessed one shoplifting case in which the punishment for one citizen's theft went to an extreme. While Winona Ryder did not serve any time in prison for lifting more than $5,000 worth of clothing and accessories, **Leonardo Andrade** was sentenced in 1995 to half a century in prison for stealing $153 worth of videotapes from Kmart. He had two previous convictions for theft, so his case fell under the **three-strikes law** – he received fifty years. His lawyers took the case to the US Supreme Court, where they argued that his sentence was "cruel and unusual punishment". **Gary Ewing**, a repeat felon whose prior convictions included burglary and robbery, also went to prison under the three-strikes mandate, serving a 25-to-life sentence for shoplifting three golf clubs from an El Segundo, California, pro shop in 2000. The US Supreme Court upheld both Andrade and Ewing's sentences, leaving them incarcerated.

In yet another high-profile shoplifting-related case, former brigadier general **Janis Karpinski** was demoted in the aftermath of the Abu Ghraib torture and prisoner abuse scandal for dereliction of duty, making a material misrepresentation to investigators, failure to obey a lawful order and shoplifting.

WORST ALIBI IN THE WORLD

In 2002 man in Ohio offered up one of the oddest reasons for a break-in – one involving busting into a car. The accused was discovered naked from the waist down and told police a leprechaun had let him into the car the night before. The 36-year-old suspect was caught early one morning inside a car, naked from the waist down. According to the *Cincinnati Enquirer*, the man had broken into the parked car the night before and fallen asleep. The car owner discovered the individual the next morning and called police. He reportedly told officers afterwards that he had taken drugs and imagined that it was a leprechaun who had let him into the car. For his nakedness, the man was charged with public indecency and, because the car's speakers had been removed, criminally damaging property.

Karpinski, who served as military police commander at Abu Ghraib, apparently failed to inform the army, as required when filling out an official document, about an alleged 2002 arrest at MacDill Air Force Base on a misdemeanour charge of stealing a bottle of perfume from a US military store. She has always denied any guilt. A 2005 Fox News posting suggested that the army said that only the shoplifting and dereliction of duty charges were "substantiated". The Pentagon has always refused to release the evidence for the alleged offence and Karpinski has claimed instead that the charges may have been part of a scapegoating campaign to draw the attention of the public away from high level establishment involvement in the Abu

Ghraib prisoner abuse scandal.

Claude Allen, US president George Bush's longtime domestic policy advisor, also had a shoplifting-related skeleton in the closet. It became known after he suddenly resigned from his post on 9 February 2006. It was not immediately clear why, but then the public learned Claude Allen was under investigation for a form of shoplifting known as "refund fraud" at the Target chain of stores. Refund fraud is when someone buys an item at a shop, then goes back to the shop later with the receipt, picks up an identical item off the store shelves, and then "returns" the unpaid-for item at the customer service desk in exchange for a refund. (Quite often, a refund fraudster may pull the same scam using discarded receipts found outside the shop.) A month later, on March 10, 2006, Allen was charged.

According to the Montgomery County police department, Allen was arrested and charged with felony theft and felony theft scheme. A departmental press release, stated that Allen carried out about 25 fraudulent "refunds" in Target and Hecht's stores in Maryland. On 2 January, a Target employee apprehended Allen after observing him receiving a refund for merchandise he had not purchased. Target then contacted the Montgomery County Police. According to published reports, both the Target chain and the police had been observing Allen since October 2005. He was only ever once caught red-handed, however.

Items Allen stole by refund fraud included a computer printer, a Bose home stereo system, a Snoopy alarm clock, a copy of **Michael Moore**'s documentary *Dude, Where's My Country?* and the hip-hop album

STEERING CLEAR OF THE LAW

One notable traffic case involved a "scofflaw" from Harlingen, Texas. Valerie Ortiz Sanchez amassed 76 traffic violation arrest warrants and fees totalling nearly $20,000, which spanned more than a decade. The fines and offences went undetected until she was pulled over in a routine traffic stop in 2007 by a Harlingen officer. When the traffic cop discovered the warrants, he arrested the 31-year-old.

The majority of the warrants stemmed from sundry infractions such as speeding, driving without insurance, having no inspection sticker, having an expired vehicle registration and expired driver's license, and failing to appear in court. In 2002 alone, warrants were issued to her for failing to use a seatbelt for a child passenger, disregarding a no-pass zone,

speeding, and failing to appear in court. Why she was not arrested sooner was anyone's guess.

In January 2008, Ortiz Sanchez was to appear in municipal court in Harlingen to answer to an outstanding $15,000 in fines, but she didn't show. At that point, she still had warrants pending in the Texas cities of Harlingen, San Benito, La Feria, and Brownsville.

A day after missing her scheduled court appearance, Ortiz Sanchez went to the courthouse after seeing her story on TV news. Once there, a Harlingen municipal judge struck a deal with her and dismissed at least twenty of the order citations. Then he allowed her to pay $250 a month until the fines were satisfied. If she missed even one payment, a judge would reinstate the warrants and fines.

Efil4Zaggin by NWA (Niggaz With Attitude).

For further investigation

Ⓦ **slate.com** Slate An in-depth article about former Bush aide Claude Allen and the phenomenon of refund fraud.

PARIS HILTON'S TRAFFIC TRANSGRESSIONS

The traffic violations of **Paris Hilton** made headlines across the globe. In May 2007, she was convicted of driving under the influence of alcohol in California. She was first placed on three-years' probation and her driver's license was suspended. Then, in a foolish moment, she took her car out for a drive. She did so at night, without her headlights on and, predictably, was pulled over, whereupon it was discovered that her license had been suspended. The case ultimately ballooned from not driving with a valid license into a sentence of 45 days in the county jail.

The heiress to the Hilton Hotel fortune had knowingly violated her probation for a previous traffic offense by driving without a valid license, as a Los Angeles county superior court judge pointed out, during a two-hour hearing. The prosecutor, for his part, told the court that Hilton thought she was above the law. He described her as a "**scofflaw**" – someone who habitually breaks the law and fails to answers summons to appear in court.

The next mistake made by Hilton was to blame someone else. She told the judge that her publicist

DRIVECAMS

In vehicles, DriveCams are the newest technology being utilized by not just police agencies but individuals too. While many police vehicles are equipped with DashCams (which attach to the dashboard), the latest in-car digital cameras are attached to rear-view mirrors. An insurance company in 2007 launched a pilot program in three US states by offering free spy camera technology to parents whose teenage children are new drivers. Since its launch, other insurance companies have come on board, offering similar programs, including onboard GPS (Global Positioning System) and email notification systems, for teen drivers. With DriveCams, one camera lens faces the driver and a second lens points at the road. The camera records audio and video images of both the road and the driver when motion sensors detect sudden changes in the car's behaviour, such as swerving, heavy braking, sudden acceleration, or collisions. The cameras, triggered by bad driving, send signals to remote computers, which send emails to parents, who in turn can log on to a DriveCam Website and observe their children's driving habits in real time (with a ten-second delay). The DriveCam company also offers coaching from experts for errant drivers.

said she could drive for work-related purposes. She apologized and said she would never knowingly have driven without a license. The judge, however, was unimpressed and rejected her claim; he ordered her to turn herself in by 5 June that year. "Probation is revoked – 45 days in jail," he decreed. Hilton stood before the judge stunned and tearful. But the ruling had been made and the decision was final. As the packed courtroom cleared, Paris's mother, **Kathy Hilton**, was heard yelling to the prosecutor: "You're pathetic."

Hilton initially only stayed in prison for three days. Her early release proved controversial: she was remanded to house arrest and had to wear an ankle bracelet. She was quickly ordered back to jail by the judge, and LA county sheriff's deputies picked up the tearful socialite at her Beverly Hills home in a black-and-white police vehicle.

Paris was released 23 days later. She walked out of the jail just after the stroke of midnight to a waiting swarm of 200 reporters and photographers. She has managed to stay out of trouble since.

For further investigation

Ⓦ msnbc.msn.com/id/19102663 MSNBC's coverage of Paris Hilton's two-hour sentencing hearing.

Obscenity, blasphemy & free speech

In England and Wales, obscenity laws have been governed by various rulings on obscene publications. The UK's obscenity laws date back to the eighteenth century – to English common law. The first conviction, which occurred in 1727, was of **Edmund Curll** for the publication of *Venus in the Cloister, or The Nun in her Smock* under the common law offence of disturbing the King's peace, setting a legal precedent for other convictions. Since 1857, the Obscene Publications Act, a series of obscenity laws, was used to enforce the censorship of obscene material in England and Wales, until 1929, when Irish law separated from English law on that issue. These common-law ideas of obscenity formed the original basis of obscenity law. But differentiating between indecent and obscene material is difficult at best.

It's also a freedom-of-speech issue that has not fully been settled in the UK and US. Although one lawsuit brought by an evangelical minister against one high-profile smut peddler attempted to do so...

THE LARRY FLYNT STORY

It started after *Hustler* magazine publisher **Larry Flynt** – one of the most outspoken opponents of US obscenity laws – thumbed his nose at US prosecutors when he opened a store in Cincinnati, Ohio, in 1997

– the only sex shop in the area – and began selling sexually explicit videos, as well as the pornographic magazines that he had been publishing since 1974. During the ensuing suit, the controversial pornography publisher ended up becoming an out-and-out defender of free speech.

After Flynt's company began selling the videos, authorities watched and waited. And then, in 1998, they accused Flynt and his younger brother Jimmy with having sold a pornographic video to a fourteen-year-old boy at the Hustler Books, Magazines, and Gifts store. Ohio's strict laws define obscenity as material "with a dominant tendency to activate lust by displaying sexual activity ... that tends to represent human beings are mere objects of sexual appetite." Flynt's latest court outing drew national attention

Larry Flynt takes the oath in court, on 6 March 1978. During a recess on the same day, he was shot.

and reminded the public of a previous case. In 1988, standing before the US Supreme Court, Flynt successfully argued his case using the First Amendment, which was designed to protect freedom of speech. He was fighting off a lawsuit by the Reverend **Jerry Falwell**, about whom *Hustler* had published a raunchy satire. In their decision, the supreme court justices ruled that pornographic parodies are protected speech – in essence expanding the legal protections for parody and satire. At the same time, the supreme court overturned the $200,000 award that the Falwell had won against Flynt, who has been dubbed the "patron saint of smut." The ruling solidified Flynt's image as an underdog champion for the US First Amendment.

Back to Larry Flynt's 1999 case. On the third day of jury selection, he managed to avoid a trial – and a possible prison term if convicted – on obscenity charges by signing a plea deal with prosecutors. In exchange for a light sentence, Flynt agreed to remove all sexually explicit videos from Hustler News & Gifts, the Cincinnati store that was managed by his brother Jimmy. In exchange, prosecutors allowed the Flynt brothers to substitute their corporation, charging the company and not the Flynts with two counts of pandering obscenity. The prosecution also dropped thirteen other charges which involved the illegal sale in 1997 of an explicit video to a fourteen-year-old boy. The video, *Jet Striker Underground*, was among those removed from the store, as per the plea bargain stipulations. They faced 24 years in prison and fines of $65,000. With the plea arrangement, a judge in Hamilton County instead levied a total fine of $10,000 against Hustler Corporation on two counts of pandering obscenity.

However, Flynt wasn't done with his campaigning.

THE SHOOTING OF LARRY FLYNT

On 6 March 1978, Joseph Paul Franklin, using a high-powered rifle, shot Flynt and his lawyer in an ambush outside a county courthouse in Lawrenceville, Georgia.

Gene Reeves, a lawyer who was walking next to Flynt when the gunman opened fire, ended up in a coma for twenty days. Flynt was left paralyzed because of damage from a bullet to his spinal chord. He lost all motor control below his waist. The would-be assassin reportedly was angry over Flynt's pronographic magazine illustrations showing interracial couples. Yet Franklin, an avowed white supremacist and former Klansman, was not arrested until two years later, in 1980. He was indicted in connection with Flynt's shooting but was already facing murder charges elsewhere, so wasn't prosecuted. In 1993, in an unrelated case, Franklin was convicted of murder for shooting Jewish worshippers. He was sentenced to life in a Missouri prison, where he sits on death row.

After a lengthy recuperation period, Flynt, who has described his magazine as a vulgar flagship "for the 'Archie Bunkers' of America," resumed his professional life. He spends most of his days in an $80,000 gold-plated wheelchair. He was surgically outfitted with a penile implant – a hydraulic, inflatable prosthesis – to restore his ability to get an erection.

In 2003, Flynt ran for governor of California. His slogan was "Vote for a Smut-Peddler Who Cares". Flynt also made political news as President **Bill Clinton**'s unexpected ally amid allegations of infidelity, when Flynt ran an October 1998 ad offering up to $1 million for information about sexual affairs to anyone who could show him proof that members of Congress involved in Clinton's impeachment were themselves involved in sexual escapades. No one took Flynt up on his offer.

For further investigation

📖**Larry Flynt** Sex, Lies and Politics: The Naked Truth **(2004)** Partly an autobiographical account of his own life, and partly a critical view of the George Bush administration, which, he argued stripped Americans of their civil liberties.

🎬**Milos Forman** The People vs. Larry Flynt **(1996)** A movie starring Woody Harrelson as the controversial pornography publisher and Courtney Love as his wife.

BLASPHEMY

Blasphemy, like obscenity, is another legal hot potato. Though some US states still have blasphemy laws on the books from their founding days, they are rarely, if ever, enforced. Even as blasphemy laws remain on the books, the US Supreme Court's expansive interpretation of the First Amendment to the US Constitution makes it likely that any blasphemy prosecution today would be regarded as an impermissible establishment of religion. Along with the US, most other Western societies have retreated from strict enforcement of blasphemy laws but the existence within those societies of various hard-line devout factions, sensi-tive to insults to their faith has frequently challenged this unspoken consensus.

British blasphemy

Britain provides a notable example of both the longer history of blasphemy and current tensions. Whilst blasphemy – the willful cursing, denouncing, reviling, or reproaching of God – is a crime in some countries, in Great Britain, prosecutions have been rare. In fact, the last person in Great Britain to be sent to prison for blasphemy, which was illegal in Britain and in most US states during the nineteenth century, was **John William Gott** on December 9, 1921. Gott had three previous convictions for blasphemy when he was prosecuted for publishing two pamphlets titled *Rib Ticklers or Questions for Parsons* and *God and Gott*. In these pamphlets Gott satirized the biblical story of Jesus entering Jerusalem (Matthew 21:2-7) comparing Jesus to a circus clown. Gott was sentenced to nine months' hard labour despite suffering from an incur-able illness, and died shortly after he was released. The case became the subject of public outrage.

There was even more outrage eighty-six years later when Britain protested against the November 2007 arrest in Sudan of a British schoolteacher accused of insulting Islam by allowing her students to name a class teddy bear Muhammad. Britain's Prime Minister **Gordon Brown** issued a protest. The protest prompted much debate, because Britain also had its own law making blasphemy a crime. As the *Boston Globe* pointed out, "Downing Street was standing on diplo-matic quicksand". With its own blasphemy law still in effect, some considered it hypocritical or at least inconsistent for Britain to complain about the arrest. Talks ensued about doing away with the old law.

That same law had, in fact, has also been invoked a year earlier. That time a Christian group unsuccessfully tried to prosecute the British Broadcasting Corporation for transmitting a recording of the musical *Jerry Springer: The Opera i*n which a fantasy Jesus character is depicted as a sexual deviant in a large nappy, singing that he feels "a little bit gay". Then, in a 148 versus 87 vote in March 2008 in Britain's House of Lords, the law against blasphemy was abolished. The controversial vote came after a heated two-hour debate. It came into force in July 2008. Most remaining blasphemy laws in Western democracies are either little used or about to be tossed out. "It is crystal clear that the offenses of blasphemy and blasphemous libel are unworkable in today's society," said Baroness **Kay Andrews** as she introduced the historic amendment in the House of Lords.

Shades of blasphemy

Some cultures, like Sudan's, disapprove of speeches and writings which defame the deity of their respective established religions. Those restrictions often have the force of law. In countries governed under Islamic law, the concept of blasphemy is broad and embraces many kinds of disrespect toward religion. In Iran, blasphemy laws extend to the disrespect of clerical members of the government – the areas of religion, state and the judiciary are seen as intertwined. However when it came to the so-called "death sentence" of author **Salman Rushdie**, advocated through the means of Ayatollah Khomeini's *fatwa* – technically speaking, a clerical opinion on a point of Islamic law – the picture is murky. It is frequently asserted that a *fatwa* is not binding on anyone but its author and is not comparable to a Western style legal sentence that could simply be enforced. This was not however, how many interpreted the *fatwa* at the time and Rushdie still lives under threat of reprisals for what Khomeini clearly saw as blasphemous insults to Allah and Islam.

More recently in 2002, for example, a Pakistani Christian sentenced to death for blasphemy against Islam was acquitted by his country's Supreme Court in Islamabad. He had been in prison since his 1996 arrest in Punjab province. **Ayub Masih** was sentenced to death in 1998 for allegedly blaspheming the Prophet Muhammad, though lawyers defending Masih contended that the real motive behind the allegations were connected to a dispute over land. He was released in August 2002, following six years in the Multan Central Jail, and immediately had to flee to another country to escape threats from extremists, according to Amnesty International. In another case, this one in Afghanistan on September 29, 2005, **Ali Mohaqiq Nasab**, editor-in-chief of the women's rights magazine *Haqoq-e-Zan*, was arrested on charges of blasphemy and "insulting Islam." The charges arose because Nasab reprinted articles by an Iranian scholar criticizing the stoning of Muslims who convert to another religion.

Blasphemy is still punishable by death in Afghanistan. Officials used the articles as evidence to arrest the editor. Reporters Without Borders, which has said Nasab's arrest was in violation of international treaties signed by Afghanistan, has worked for his release since his arrest. In the meantime, a Kabul court sentenced Nasab to two years in prison at the end of a summary trial on blasphemy charges. He was subsequently released, but in 2008 it was reported (the pretext unknown) that he had been detained by the Iranian Ministry of Information.

The latest known conviction for blasphemy, which occurred in Afghanistan, ended in a death sentence. **Sayed Perwiz Kambakhsh** was arrested on October 27, 2007, in Mazar-i-Sharif, the capital of the northern province of Balkh, on blasphemy and "disseminating defamatory comments about Islam," according to reports about the case. Since the 2001 fall of the Taliban regime in Afghanistan, strict enforcement of Islamic codes has continued, and violations have been severely punished, including for blasphemy by the media.

After the Council of Mullahs and local officials pressured the court, Kambakhsh, a 23-year-old student journalist who wrote for a small newspaper called *Jahan-e Naw* (or *The New World*), was sentenced to death in January 2008. At the closed hearing, which lasted three minutes, Kambakhsh was not represented by council.

The head of the Afghanistan Independent Journalists Association has called the verdict unjust. The case was has been heard on appeal. In the meantime, the young journalist, who pleaded not guilty during the hearing, told the court that security forces tortured him, forcing a confession from him. He told the court he was innocent, stating: "I'm a Muslim and will never allow myself to insult my religion. These are totally lies." Kambakhsh's death sentence was later commuted but he was still ordered to spend 20 years in jail.

Free speech versus blasphemy?

In Europe, freedom of speech issues have also come in to play within a highly charged political context. The Parliamentary Assembly of the Council of Europe in Strasbourg on Jun 29, 2007, adopted a recommendation about blasphemy, religious insults and hate speech against persons on grounds of their religion. The recommendation set guidelines for member states of the Council of Europe for freedom of expression and freedom of thought, conscience and religion in respect of the European Convention on Human Rights.

This framework is supplemented by considerable relevant case-law overseen by the European Court of Human Rights in Strasbourg. However the latest challenge to the blasphemy status quo was ignited by the *Jyllands-Posten* Muhammad cartoons controversy, in which twelve editorial cartoons pictorially representing the prophet Mohammed were published in a Danish newspaper in 2005. Angry protests ensued across the world and it was claimed that the newspaper had committed offences against two sections of Danish law. The public prosecutor, however, did not find in favour of the complaint, citing criteria of public interest and freedom of speech. Republication of the cartoons in other European media spawned further criticism and outrage. So, in 2008, when a resolution "combating defamation of religions" was adopted by a majority at the United Nations, many saw it as a response to the *Jyllands-Posten* incident.

Blasphemy cases across the world may well be in long-term decline but that is not to say they might not stage a comeback or reappear in the guise of a select number of high-profile cases.

For further investigation

📖 **Joss Marsh** Word Crimes: Blasphemy, Culture, and Literature in Nineteenth-Century England **(1998)** Marsh's book explains how, in Victorian times, blasphemy gradually became more a crime more to do with taste than one of religious principles.

📖 **Dan Brown** The Da Vinci Code **(2007)** Subsequently made into a film, Brown's novel became an international hit in part because of its sensationalistic fictional claims – the discovery of a religious mystery protected by a secret society for two thousand years. Brown's book has routinely been decried for its blasphemy, but no attempt at prosecution has been forthcoming.

Ⓦ **rsf.org** Information from Reporters Without Borders, a group that fights for international freedom of the press.

THE "NATURAL FAMILY" CONTROVERSY

A heated dispute surrounding a resolution – one step short of an ordinance – in the city of **Kanab,** in the red-rock bluffs of southern Utah, made headlines across the US in 2006. The controversial resolution forbade an "unnatural family" and said "marriage between a man and a woman is ordained by God".

Kanab has a population of about 4,000, and is in Kane County, 300 miles south of Salt Lake City, where it is a gateway to some of Utah's prettiest red rock landscapes, including Zion and Bryce Canyon national parks. **Resolution 1-1-06R**, titled "The Natural Family: A Vision for the City of Kanab", was passed by the mayor and city council on 10 January 2006. It was no surprise that the lone dissenting vote was from a female member of the council. The resolution calls for marriages to be between a man and a woman "ordained by God". It also encourages young women to become "wives, homemakers and mothers" and young men to grow into "husbands, home builders, and fathers". "We look to a landscape of family homes, lawns and gardens busy with useful tasks and ringing with the laughter of many children", the resolution continues. Natural families were defined as consisting of a working husband, a stay-at-home wife, and a "full quiver of children". Some in town felt the resolution excluded a variety of other types of families, including those headed by widows, grandparents, and single parents. Residents also complained that the resolution overstepped its legal bounds, mixing church with state.

At the following city council meeting, residents in opposition – who only learned about the language in the resolution after it was passed – packed the Kanab public library. This was big news in a small town where they're lucky if ten people show up to watch small-time city hall in action. Many residents wore buttons that said "Quiverless". The opinion page of the weekly paper, *Southern Utah News*, included scathing letters from residents. One read: "The embarrassment this has brought to many of the locals here is unforgivable." Another said: "The next step here is the city government going around and painting a red 'X' on the non-natural family door." At a public meeting afterwards, following an hour-long discussion, Councilwoman **Carol Sullivan** made a motion to rescind the resolution. But because no fellow council members seconded her motion, it was too little, too late. The motion died, and the resolution remained.

The text of Kanab's Natural Family Resolution is identical to a draft resolution created by the **Sutherland Institute**, a conservative political think tank based in Utah that works toward public policy reform to reflect its notion of traditional values. The resolution also echoes language from the Church of Jesus Christ of Latter-day Saints, which has openly opposed gay rights. The Sutherland Institute wrote the draft resolution and sent it to every city in Utah. So far, officials in Kanab, a predominantly Mormon community, have been the only elected body to adopt the resolution for its municipality.

Syndicated travel columnist **Arthur Frommer** – founder of the Frommer's series of travel guides and books – wasn't happy and urged readers to boycott **Zion National Park** because the nearby city government was discriminating against gay men and lesbians. *Slate* magazine titled the debacle "We Are 'Natural Fam-il-y'" and a *New York Times* story about the resolution was titled "Welcome to Our Town. Or, Maybe Not." *The Times* wrote that "although the resolution is essentially symbolic, with no force of law, it hit Kanab like a thunderclap, creating divisions within the community and raising concerns in a tourism-dependent economy that people around the country might see themselves as 'unnatural' in Kanab's eyes and stay away."

Another blow to the city's main economy of tourism happened when a classic car club, because of the resolution, canceled a convention, costing a local inn $14,000 in revenue. Some businesses, in response, tried to counter the negative publicity with an "Everyone Welcome Here" campaign, posting stickers in windows of shops, restaurants, and hotels. Even so, Mayor **Kim Lawson** vowed not to back down from his stance on declaring that the first responsibility of state and local government is to protect a family structure – one that discourages families with foster children, single parents, adoptive parents, grandparents raising children, same-sex couples, and single people whose friends are their families. One of the ironies of the fracas is that the resolution is "non-binding", so is not in effect an actual law. But what it illustrates is that when the law shades close to dictating clear preferences on family morals, controversy and disagreement follow more or less inevitably.

For further investigation

Ⓦ www.salon.com/mwt/broadsheet/2006/01/25/kanab/index .html A column in salon.com opining about the "tolerance of intolerance" with resolutions like the one passed in Kanab, Utah.

Ⓦ kanab.utah.gov/artman/publish/council/article_187.shtml Meeting minutes from the Kanab, Utah, city council's discussion of the Natural Family Resolution.

ABSURD LAWS

THE US

Laws that outlaw outlandish activities or which strike out against relatively normal behaviour – and which exist mostly because they've *always* existed – don't appear to be going away anytime soon. Why some of these laws stay on the books is anyone's guess. Guido Calabresi, in his 1982 book *A Common Law for the Age of Statutes*, where he studies the history of lawmaking, complained that the US was "choking on statutes". He suggests throwing them out and resorting to common law, as suggested by **Oliver Wendell Holmes** a century earlier. During the nineteenth century, US Supreme Court Justice Holmes challenged the practice of retaining old laws. He believed that statutes should

SMITH AND BATEMAN'S CRIME SPREE

In the summer of 2005, college student Richard Smith and his "accomplice", Luke Bateman, both from Cornwall, England, embarked on a most unusual road trip: a cross-country crime spree. But it's not the kind you might think. The partners in crime travelled to US cities and towns that have what Smith called "absurd laws" still on their books. The partners' goal was to break laws in as many states as they could during the course of the summer. One of those laws they vowed to break, for example, was Utah's statute making it illegal to whale watch, even though the Southwestern state is landlocked.

They set off on their journey equipped with binoculars, vowing to hunt whales. And in Miami, where it's illegal for a man to wear a spaghetti-strapped dress, they planned to challenge that law too. The 25-state, cross-country stop began at the former Alcatraz island prison in San Francisco Bay in Northern California and ended in Hartford, Connecticut, where it's still illegal to cross the road while walking on one's hands. So that's what they did. Law enforcement officers in each of the cities ignored their antics. The most difficult law to break

was flying a kite in Washington, explained Smith afterwards in an interview with online magazine Anti. Because it's the US capital they are very strict about objects entering their airspace, Smith said. More importantly, because of the lack of stores in Washington, he had to make his own kite. The most attention from police the pair received was in Chicago, Illinois, when they were held at gunpoint by officers. They had just finished fishing while wearing pyjamas – behaviour that's illegal in the windy city. "However, this had nothing to do with the silly law I broke," Smith told Duggins. "It was due to the fact I had a Cornish flag on the parcel shelf of my car. They thought it was a gangland symbol and we were members". The officers released them and sent the "scofflaws" on their way. Even when they were caught by police in the act of breaking a law, they weren't arrested. In the end, Smith and Bateman successfully pulled off their crime spree, committing 25 in total. A year later, they landed a book deal for their efforts. The work was entitled *You Can Get Arrested For That: 2 Guys, 25 Dumb Laws, 1 Absurd American Crime Spree*.

adapt to society, instead of society having to adapt to outdated laws. "A very common phenomenon, and one very common to the student of history, is this," Holmes said at the time. "The custom, beliefs, or needs of a primitive time establish a rule or a formula. In the course of centuries, the custom, belief, or necessity disappears, but the rule remains." He proposed that laws be revisited.

Forbidden!

US state laws offer some of the richest pickings when considering the area of strange laws. The best tend to be both very specific and improbable at the same time even allowing for the passage of time. In Ohio, if you ignore an orator on Decoration Day – since renamed Memorial Day – by publicly playing croquet or pitching horseshoes within one mile of the speaker's stand, you can be fined $25. In Bexley, a tree-lined suburb of Columbus, Ohio, municipal ordinance number 223, enacted into law in 1919, prohibits the installation and usage of slot machines in outhouses – that is, outside toilets. In Baltimore, Maryland, it's illegal to take a lion to the cinema. It begs the question as to whether there once was a run on lions – or did lions break out of the Maryland Zoo in Baltimore? Nothing seems to explain the reason for having a law on the books that bans lions from walking into a cinema.

Governing clothing and apparel seems to have been a trend in past years, at least in two US states. In Carmel, New York, a man cannot go outside while wearing a jacket and trousers that do not match. And in Miami, Florida, it is illegal for men to be seen publicly in any kind of strapless gown. Women in Ohio are in theory prohibited from wearing patent leather shoes in public. Even laws governing health

can go too far. Take the one in Washington state that bans those suffering from the common cold from walking in public. That's one law, however, that residents in Washington wish *would* be enforced, especially during heavy cold and flu season.

Fun is out of the question, it seems, in Tinley Park, Illinois. The mayor has described his village as a "dynamic, progressive community" and a "great place to live, work, and play," yet in September 2000, his village enforced an ordinance making it unlawful to "play any games upon any street, alley, or sidewalk, or other public place except when a block party permit has been issued." In other words, the law prohibits even children from playing tag without a party permit. This ordinance was later repealed. Another place to take care is Jonesborough, Georgia, where it is illegal to say "Oh, boy." And in North Carolina, a 1913 law makes cussing on public streets forbidden in ninety-eight counties. In 1973, in a stunning move, the state legislator tried to amend the law, statute number 14-197, to include all 100 counties in the state. It didn't pass, and today two counties – Pitt and Swain – are the only outdoor places where North Carolinians can legally use obscenities within earshot of two or more people. Other examples of North Carolina laws that may have outlived their usefulness include a law that says it is illegal to commit "crimes against nature", which outlaws adultery and fornication between unmarried people. Another law bans unmarried couples from occupying the same bedroom in a hotel room and registering as husband and wife.

Here are some other absurd regulations that have yet to be revisited:

It is illegal to play cards against a Native American in Globe, Arizona.

It is illegal to drive around the town square in

Oxford, Mississippi, more than 100 times on a single occasion.

It is illegal to give lit cigars to dogs, cats, and other pets in Zion, Illinois.

In Little Rock, Arkansas, dogs are not allowed to bark after 6pm. It's not known which party gets arrested – the dog or its guardian.

In Arkansas, a man may also legally beat his wife – but not more than once a month.

In Texas and Ohio, the French wine Fat Bastard is banned (though it is distributed in 22 other states).

In Texas, it's illegal to shoot a buffalo from the second story of a hotel.

Antiquated law reform and its difficulties

Outdated laws often stay on the books because lawmakers and politicians don't want to appear as if they're condoning certain behaviour. It's considered the main reason why so many laws many people call silly are difficult to repeal. While laws like these are no longer enforced, they're often controversial and don't appear in danger of being repealed anytime soon.

Such was the case with US state lawmakers over the years who were hesitant to repeal consensual sex and sodomy laws. It took the highest court in the land to repeal them. With the sweep of a pen, Supreme Court justices invalidated long-established state anti-sodomy laws. Mutually consenting sex for citizens with a person of choice in the privacy of their own home is now a basic right in America, according to a 2003 ruling by the highest court in America. The ruling was based on the case of Lawrence versus Texas. The government

cannot forbid it, nor can discriminate against a person for choosing to exercise a basic right of citizenship. The ruling, in effect, took government out of people's bedrooms and, at the same time, opened the door for same-sex marriage.

North Carolina lawmakers did repeal a handful of non-political outdated laws. In 1994, they passed a bill that repealed a large number of the state's antiquated statutes. The bill included laws that banned dance marathons, forbade speaking indecent language on trains, bothering squirrels on the capital grounds in Raleigh, North Carolina, coasting downhill in a car, passing a horse without taking reasonable care, and prevented Communists from speaking at public institutions. In 2003, Nevada legislators voted unanimously to take an old law off its books that made it illegal to shear sheep within city limits. The statute, dating back to at least 1911, made it a misdemeanour for "any sheep to be penned, housed, or fed for the purpose of being sheared" within city limits. Legislators said, during a public session, that they did not know why the law existed. Why they chose that particular law was not made clear. Other outdated laws – seemingly nonsensical in today's world – remained in effect.

OutFront Minnesota, a gay rights group, campaigned successfully in late 2003 for repeal of a St. Paul ordinance that prohibited people from appearing in public in dress "not belonging to their sex". The group criticized the language of the ordinance "which dates from the late nineteenth century, has outlived any usefulness it may ever have had". Likewise, in North Dakota, the legislature voted in 2007 to repeal a centuries-old law that banned men and women from living together without a marriage certificate. The

DISORDERLY CONDUCT

Laws on drunkenness vary from country to country. In the UK and most states in the US, police have the authority to arrest offenders for drunken and disorderly conduct when they appear impaired. In San Francisco, public drunkenness, tolerated for years in this liberal city, was addressed in 2001 with a new ordinance: "Three chugs, you're in". It used to be that when police in San Francisco picked up inebriated citizens, they'd cite "public intoxication", put them in holding cells for twelve hours, and then let them go – even if they were repeat offenders. The long-standing policy was that the district attorney's office would not hold any drunks over for court, so the errant drinkers were released. Not any more. After the third offense, no more free passes. Instead, they get go-straight-to-jail orders, charges are filed against them, and offenders have to appear in court to answer for their behaviour. At the opposite end of the spectrum, in New Jersey a civil rights case was filed in a US federal court claiming that out of New Jersey's 566 municipalities, 74 were illegally enforcing ordinances that make public intoxication a crime. The arrests violate the rights to intoxication, according to the June 2008 suit. The lawsuit suit also claimed that such local laws were repealed in 1975 by New Jersey lawmakers,

making such arrests invalid. The outcome of the suit, on behalf of a Moorestown man arrested in 2007, was pending. Missouri, on the other hand, has no state public intoxication laws, protecting drinkers from criminal penalties. As a result, city and county municipalities are prohibited from enacting ordinances of their own. Nevada also has no public intoxication laws. In Montana, a state law addresses the issue, saying public intoxication is not a crime and may not be mentioned in an arrest record. While breathalizer tests and urine analyses can determine how intoxicated a person is, when it comes to disorderly conduct, it is mostly left to the discretion of police officers. Once the cases move through the legal system, the courts interpret the law. In California, soliciting a lewd act falls under the charge of disorderly conduct. So does public drunkenness. Peeping into windows and doors also constitutes disorderly conduct in the Golden State. In New York City, disorderly conduct statutes are most stringent on or near the public transit system. Dumping liquids and littering fall under the statute, as does spitting. Sleeping when it interferes with a transit worker, standing on or riding a skateboard or bicycle, and sitting on more than one seat are, in part, also considered disorderly conduct violations.

repeal said that living together "openly and notoriously" while being unwed would no longer be considered a sex crime. The old law went into effect in 1889 when North Dakota became a US state of the union. The repeal effected 23,000 unmarried state residents who lived with their partners, according to the US Census Bureau. **Tracy Potter**, one of the state senators who voted for the repeal, commented that "I don't think it's any of my business whether my neighbours have a marriage certificate or not. I certainly don't think the government has any role in regulating that type of morality." Similar laws in Florida, Michigan,

Mississippi, North Carolina, Virginia, and West Virginia remain on the books.

No legislating for vice

As for the practice of prostitution – the so-called "oldest profession in the world"– Nevada is one of just two US states that allows it, but only in counties with populations less than 400,000, and only in brothels, not on the streets. The other state is **Rhode Island**, where the act of sex for money is not illegal, but street solicitation and operation of a brothel are. Clark County, which includes the city of Las Vegas, is one of the counties in Nevada that does not allow legal prostitution (contrary to widespread public belief). Hookers, however, are regularly seen on streets soliciting would-be johns (clients).

Large mobile billboards advertise "Hot Babes Direct to Your Room". The phone book's yellow pages include about 150 pages of escort ads for "college teens", "mature women", "mothers and daughters", "petite Japanese women" and "Chinese teens in short skirts". The city's mayor, **Oscar Goodman** (a self-described former "mouthpiece for the mob," which he represented for years as a longtime criminal defense lawyer), has publicly said he wants prostitution legalized in controlled brothels and has proudly and publicly called his city an "adult playground".

On 15 May 1905, two blocks in the Las Vegas Townsite were set aside as the only places where alcohol could be sold without licensing restrictions. Block 16 soon evolved into the town's red-light district, offered locals and weary railroad travelers a variety of recreational opportunities, such as billiards and bowling. But Block 16 soon became infamous in the western United States for its string of saloons that offered drinking, gambling, and wide-open prostitution. The buildings were initially made of wood and tent canvas, but some saloon owners rebuilt them using bricks, mortar, and wood. From about 1906 to 1912, brothels were located in rooms in the rear, known as "cribs", in such Block 16 saloons as The Arcade, Double O, and Star Saloon, all on the east side of the downtown area. Despite local officials and residents' disapproval of Block 16 and its brothels, the city tolerated the block until early 1940s.

On December 2, 1941, city officials directed police to raid the block. Sixteen officers, including the police commissioner and police chief, arrested twenty-two women on prostitution charges. But after posting bail, the women returned and the brothels reopened. It wasn't until a month later that city commissioners voted to cancel all alcohol and slot machine licenses for Block 16 saloons. Without that, business slowed down to a halt and the saloons and brothels soon closed. In 1946, the wooden buildings were declared hazardous and they were demolished. Parking lots were put in their place behind what is now West Fremont Street.

Legal discriminations

The case of Brown versus Board of Education declared racial segregation unconstitutional in 1954. Afterwards, most – but not all – US states repealed their respective racial laws, referred to as "alien land laws". California's land laws, passed before World War II, were in effect until after the war. The laws denied "aliens ineligible to citizenship" – specifically non-native-born Asian Americans – the right to own property in the United States. The law remains in place in Wyoming and Florida. In New Mexico, a full constitutional amendment with voter approval was required – which is also the case with Florida – to repeal the alien land law. On November 8, 2006, a repeal of New Mexico's Alien Land Act placed on the ballot was approved. The law, adopted in 1921, amended the New Mexico constitution prohibiting land ownership by all immigrants ineligible for citizenship. The statute was typical of anti-Japanese immigration sentiments that were prevalent in the US in the early 20th century.

Discrimination also applies to US Army regulations barring homosexual men and women from military service. While the regulation remains on the books, it violates the US Constitution and cannot be enforced, according to an appeal disallowing a sergeant from re-enlisting in the Air Force. In 1982, the sergeant was refused re-enlistment after fourteen years of service and a good record. The refusal was based solely on the grounds that the sergeant was gay, a fact known by the Army since the officer's original enlistment fourteen years earlier.

Lawsuits fighting the army's regulation have been challenged in court. In the case of the sergeant, the United States Court of Appeals for the Ninth Circuit ruled that the Army was allowed, by use of "estoppel" – a legal way of preventing the reexamination or restatement of assumptions or facts concerning a case – to bar the officer from reenlisting in the military. The military's regulation provides for the discharge of any soldier who "evidences homosexual tendencies, desire, or interest, but is without overt homosexual acts". US courts of appeal have consistently upheld military regulations barring service by homosexuals.

For further investigation

📖 **Oliver Wendell Holmes** The Common Law **(1888)** A compendium of lectures and legal opinions offered by Justice Holmes.

Ⓦ **www.highwayrobbery.net** A site that talks about outdated laws for motorists.

Ⓦ **dumblaws.com** This site has been around since 1998, and not a lot has changed since then, because old laws continue to sit on the books, with most unenforced.

Ⓦ **usdoj.gov/osg/briefs/1989/sg890273.txt** The US Department of Justice's decision concerning open homosexuality in the military.

After Richard Gere swept Shilpa Shetty off her feet, tango-style, at an awards ceremony, burning effigies of Gere were beaten with sticks by protestors on the streets of India.

STRANGE LAWS FROM AROUND THE WORLD

The USA is not unique in retaining unusual statutes. Antiquated laws are not much different in Europe, Asia and elsewhere. Open challenges (often in the media) to religious and ethical codes are often the catalyst for controversial rulings, whereas antiquated customs, that no one has ever found time to repeal, are widespread.

Improper behaviour

A worldwide storm ensued in India recently over public displays of affection, such as holding hands and kissing, which are taboo and deemed in bad taste. The acts of affection are classified criminal offenses and can be prosecuted. So, when American actor **Richard Gere** embraced and kissed Bollywood actress Shilpa Shetty during a televised public appearance in 2007, it was not only considered to be in bad taste, but it was considered by some to contravene India's strict obscenity laws. A court in the western state of Rajasthan, in turn, ordered that Gere be arrested. The actor, who had already left India, faced a warrant against him that was issued for what officials in that country considered obscene behaviour. The offense occurred during an AIDS awareness event in Delhi when Gere swept Shetty into his arms, bent her backwards in a tango-style dance move, and kissed her. The forbidden kiss was televised.

For Shetty's part, because she did not resist Gere's advances, obscene charges were ordered against her too. Gere, a practicing Buddhist who frequently visits India, later apologized for the offence and any problems he may have caused for the actress. Shetty told a reporter that Gere's actions were a take-off from his recent film, *Shall We Dance?* (2004), calling it "a natural cute and loving impromptu gesture by Gere which was blown out of proportion due to improper projection by the gossip-hungry television media." Gere's lawyer, in the meantime, filed a document in an Indian court calling the charges "frivolous" and asking that the arrest warrant be dropped. In March 2008, a judge suspended the warrant and issued a statement. "Richard Gere is free to enter the country," said the Chief Justice of India, K.G. Balakrishnan, who headed the bench. "This is the end of the matter."

The closest the US has had to a parallel to this incident was of course the infamous "Nipplegate" controversy – the result of an alleged "wardrobe malfunction" when Justin Timberlake pulled back a part of singer **Janet Jackson**'s costume to momentarily reveal a breast and nipple. The latter was covered by a shield. Over half a million US viewers complained, leading to a record fine of $550,000 fine being imposed on CBS by the Federal Communications Commission as a national debate raged. However, in July 2008, the third US Circuit Court of Appeals threw out the fine on appeal , on the grounds that it was inconsistent with previous FCC policy, which had only acted on breaches of broadcasting considered "pervasive" enough to shock an audience. (Most reports calculated the incident as having lasted nine-sixteenths of a second). Related class actions and lawsuits from individual viewers were not successful either.

Overseeing the media in most Western countries now falls into the lap of an industry regulator rather than being handled directly, but as the Jackson incident reveals, pushing boundaries can see individuals or corporations being dragged into court.

Pressure to change

Pressure to modernize laws may often be due to the results of long term shifts in public opinion but the impetus can also come from commerce. In Germany, a coalition of major business executives joined forces calling for the revocation of laws that restricted discounts and free gifts to consumers. The businesses – McDonalds, Procter & Gamble, Marriott Hotels, VISA and AOL Deutschland – described the confining laws as "antiquated", forcing international companies to tailor advertising and messaging to the German market. But the group of companies didn't fight the laws alone. They enlisted the help of the consulting firm APCO Worldwide. Within eighteen months of APCO lobbying for a repeal, the laws were revoked. Eliminating the statutes saved German-based companies several hundred million euros a year.

The forces of modernization themselves have on occasion led to unusual restrictions. When the reforming Turkish leader Mustafa Kemal banned the fez hat in 1925, it was because he perceived it as a symbol of backwardness and colonial subjection. Turks were encouraged to adopt Western headgear and clothing instead. That said it is more usual for peculiar laws to date back much further – to the nineteenth century or earlier. Here are some choice examples.

Forbidden across the world

England, as you might expect, has much to contribute when it comes to antiquated laws. Several relate to aristocratic or official privileges, such as the law that stipulates that the head of any deceased whale found on the British coast is *de facto* the property of the king, whereas the tail (which might provide useful bones for her corset), would belong to the queen. The current monarch, one assumes, would be able to claim both ends. Another dated law requires royal naval ships coming into the Port of London to give the constable of the Tower of London a barrel of rum. Parliament, which is in part responsible for many UK laws still has a few odd ones of its own. Members of that venerable body need to be careful not to wear a suit of armour in the House and, likewise, should at all costs avoid dying there, which is also illegal.

A certain residual hostility to England's neighbours is enshrined in many local laws. Chester is a town where being Welsh, legally speaking, might have disadvantages. Welshmen are banned from entering the city before sunrise and not allowed to stay after sunset. Those that stay after midnight within the city walls may be legally shot at with a bow and arrow whereas in York (also only within city walls) Scotsmen carrying bows and arrows may be also be killed. Visitors to England attracted by the tradition and pageantry should be warned that when sending postcards back to friends and families that they could theoretically be convicted of treason if the stamp on the envelope has the head of the British monarch placed upside down. Nor should anyone stand within 100 yards of the Queen (or the monarch of the day) not wearing socks. Women in Liverpool are not usually allowed to go topless – the exception being if they are working in a tropical fish store. This strange exception makes about as much sense as the law dating back to Puritan times, which forbids the eating of mince pies on Christmas day. The reason why most English citizens have not been hauled before a magistrate or worse for eating mince pies is apparently due to the "doctrine of implied repeal" but that defense could in theory be challenged by the foolhardy or determined under the common law traditions of the country.

Europe also boasts some fine absurdities. The ruling that no citizen in France is permitted to call their pig "Napoleon" probably needs little explaining. More perplexing is the prohibition on UFO owners flying over or parking their craft in vineyards of the Rhone region. And why are people not allowed to kiss on public railways in (of all places) France?

The Swiss mania for order forbids the flushing of toilets in an apartment after 10pm and, on Sundays, clothes should not be hung out to dry nor cars washed. Strange then that drinking the famously potent liquor absinthe is not illegal but the producing, storing and selling it is. One region of Italy forbids local women christened Mary to work as prostitutes whereas in Denmark, before starting a car, drivers must first make a visual check to make sure no children are underneath the vehicle.

Throughout the Asia-Pacific region there are laws which reflect the traditions and reputations of specific countries. In Australia there are laws which offer a local parallel to the myriad and peculiar laws of US states as well as others resembling old favourites from their former colonial overlords, the British. Urban legend has it that sex with a kangaroo is banned outright, unless the perpetrator is drunk though mere legend it, in all probability, has remained. Morality also figures prominently in the lawmaker's psyche. Why else would women need to wear only neck-to-knee clothing in order to swim on Brighton Beach in Victoria? In a similar vein, pink hot pants (or other trousers) are forbidden to be worn there after midday on Sundays. Throughout Australia, taxi cabs are apparently compelled to carry a bale of hay in the boot – reminiscent of a similar ruling for London cab drivers – whereas an old rule (also supposed to be extant in England) allows urination in a public place, provided the act is undertaken by a man, aiming at the back sidewalk side wheel of a motor vehicle. More seriously, prior to the notorious 1996 gun massacre in Port Arthur, Tasmania it was legal to own an AK-47 firearm but not to be gay. The most frequently cited of Australia's questionable laws is however the Victoria state's insistence than only a licensed electrician may change a lightbulb. Singapore's laws, to some extent, bear out its reputation as being the "Switzerland" of Asia. Littering is especially frowned upon and, if convicted three times, an offender may find themselves cleaning the streets on Sundays. You should always flush public toilets and never urinate in a public lift. There are heavy fines as penalties and leaving chewing gum on subways is strictly forbidden and could even lead to jail. Selling chewing gum isn't allowed either. Taking into consideration the nuisance value of these activities, many would feel that this Singaporean "zero tolerance" policy has much to recommend it. However, crossing the street within 50 metres of a pedestrian crossing is also illegal in Singapore which might be one step too far in the direction of law or order for some pedestrians. Civil liberties advocates also have issues with some Singaporean legislation. Oral sex was forbidden (except as foreplay before procreative intercourse) until 2007, and gay sex remains illegal. The latter ban remained intact amidst concerns that this conservative society was unready and that change would be better left to develop unhurriedly.

Wherever you go in the world, fringe laws speak to wider moral concerns. In discussions of strange sex laws it is frequently reported that in Cali, a city in Columbia, a woman is only allowed to have sex with her husband. The first time this happens, her mother is required to be in the room to witness the act for it to be legal. Catholic restraint of a different kind may be glimpsed in the Bolivian law (in reference to the town of Santa Cruz) reported in the same lists which deems it forbidden for a man to have sex with a woman and her daughter at the same time. As with other such laws, it is extremely worrying to think that someone felt that a law was required for this kind of situation. Similarly worrying is the prohibition on having sex with alpacas in Peru. Such is the gravity of the problem that lawmakers also felt it necessary to outlaw young men from having a female alpaca live in their houses or apartments. No prosecutions relating to these offences have been recently reported so it can probably be safely assumed these "laws" (unlike those of Singapore) are forgotten, except as amusing urban legends.

Even so, these and numerous other questionable laws of their kind suggest that in this world it is clearly impossible to legislate for all kinds of behaviour *and* all kinds of lawmakers.

For further investigation

ⓦ **dumblaws.com** You can find listings of dumb laws on this website and links to dumb lawsuits and dumb criminals listings. Plenty of advertising links too.

ⓦ **business.timesonline.co.uk/tol/business/law/article2251280. ece** Strange laws listings from two UK websites.

▭ **Christine Green** The Little Book of Loony Laws **(2002)** As well as this self-explanatory compendium, Green has also produced sister volumes on loony driving laws, and loony sex laws.

CYBERCRIME

Cybercrime

On 30 July 2008, 42-year-old Briton Gary McKinnon received the news he was dreading. The House of Lords ruled that he could be extradited to the US to stand trial for hacking into Pentagon computers. McKinnon's lawyers had argued that his motive had been harmless: he simply believed he could find secret evidence of alien life forms.

What's more, the lawyers claimed, this overzealous but unemployed computer programmer could conceivably spend the rest of his life in prison if extradited – or even be classified as an "enemy combatant" and find himself in Guantánamo Bay.

McKinnon's case offers a glimpse into the world of hackers and cybercriminals, although the two classes of people are not always the same. Some hackers are intellectuals, idealists or anarchists. They claim to use computers as a form of self-expression and free inquiry, abiding by a code of ethics. But it's a fine line. One of the defining statements of the hacker subculture was written in 1986 by **Loyd Blankenship**, known

as the Mentor. Titled "The Conscience of a Hacker", it contains the statement: "We explore … and you call us criminals. We seek after knowledge … and you call us criminals." And it ends: "Yes, I am a criminal … My crime is that of outsmarting you, something that you will never forgive me for." But are hackers dissidents, renegades, free spirits, just geeks? Or are they thieves and vandals?

In their slang, there are three types of hacker. Their names derive from Western films: "**black hat**", "**white hat**" and "**grey hat**". The "black hat" is the bad guy. He (hackers are almost always male) breaks into computer systems without permission. The motives for such unauthorized intrusions vary: fun, profit, malice, political protest. McKinnon, for example, left messages on the government systems he hacked ("I said US foreign policy was akin to government-sponsored terrorism and I believed 9/11 was an inside job", *The Guardian* reported him as saying.) "White hats" – also known as "ethical hackers" – are often employed by companies to test system security or, in the case of a celebrated few, are industry stars. Among the "10 Most Famous Hackers of All Time" listed on ITSecurity.com, the white hats include **Stephen Wozniak** (co-founder of Apple), **Tim Berners-Lee** (widely credited as the inventor of the Internet) and **Linus Torvalds** (creator of the Linux operating system). They are tasked with searching for weak spots and system flaws, which can then be fixed. The "grey hats" are somewhere in between. They may trespass, exploring a network without permission, but won't cause any damage or steal any information. Most grey hats prefer anonymity, but one of the most famous, Adrian Lamo, delighted in informing the companies he penetrated of the holes in their security.

Black hats can cause massive damage and alarm. In particular, they can release computer viruses and "worms" that destroy data and disable computer networks. Law enforcement agencies across the world regard the threat from such "malware" – short for "malicious software" – as a major global criminal threat. There is a difference between a virus and a worm. A virus attaches itself to another program, and needs that program to be executed in order for it to be activated. A worm is more autonomous: once released, it can transmit itself across networks. But

first a worm has to get in, undetected. The best means of surreptitious entry is by means of a "Trojan horse" (or just "trojan"), a program that seems to have some useful function but in fact installs the malware as soon as it is run.

Malicious hacking often involves a con trick – what is known in computer security as "social engineering". Some of the most famous hackers, including Kevin Mitnick, relied on such cons – for example talking a company employee into divulging a password by pretending to be a colleague in need of it. Such activity is commonly done not online but over the phone. Its most widespread Internet manifestation is "**phishing**", when an email lures an unsuspecting recipient to a website which looks official but is in fact just a means of securing someone's confidential personal information (especially credit card details). Phishing is a highly lucrative criminal endeavour and its exponents are constantly refining their tactics in the hope of enticing new victims.

The digital revolution has changed crime just as it has changed much else. Though it often resembles age-old con tricks, malicious hacking is a crime for the twenty-first century. But it is not the only threat in the digital age. In everyday life, cybercrime emerges too: new forms of bullying and intimidation have arisen in the era of instant messaging, online networking and 3G mobile phones.

Gary McKinnon is taking his appeal against extradition to the European court. His fate is uncertain, but he may one day join the select ranks of celebrity hackers who, having served sentences for their crimes, reinvent themselves as commentators or security experts – who have ditched their black hats.

KEVIN MITNICK, AMERICA'S "MOST-WANTED CYBERTHIEF"

Go to kevinmitnick.com and you will find the website of **Mitnick Security Consulting**. On the front page, endorsements from satisfied clients include one from the US Federal Probation Office. But back on 16 February 1995, Mitnick was being written about in different terms, in a story by John Markoff on the front page of the *The New York Times*: "A Most Wanted Cyberthief Is Caught in His Own Web". The article explained how, over a period of years, Mitnick had become expert at infiltrating, vandalizing and embezzling from telephone networks as well as government, corporate and university computer systems. *Forbes* magazine has called Mitnick "the most famous hacker in history".

Born on 6 August 1963, Mitnick got involved in illegal activities in a low-tech way at age twelve when, using a hole punch, he forged bus transfer passes so he could go anywhere in the Los Angeles basin without having to pay. He grew up in a struggling family; friends and relatives were often in trouble with police. He seems to have coped through pranks involving electronics. With some friends, he once rigged the outdoor loudspeakers at a burger joint so that they emitted curses. On another occasion, they managed to rig the home phones of some people they disliked to announce "Please deposit 20 cents!" when picked up. His computer interest began when he became active on computer bulletin boards, using the handle "The Condor" (a name he took from the 1975 conspiracy movie starring Robert Redford) and then, mostly out of curiosity, began accessing the bulletin boards' systems. Armed with a personal computer and modem, he was able to commandeer a phone company's digital central office switch remotely simply by dialling in. The result was unlimited free long-distance phone calls. His skills improved and he became adept at hacking into computer systems.

In 1982, at the height of the Cold War, Mitnick is reputed to have broken into the top-secret military supercomputer of the North American Defense Command (NORAD) systems, an act which inspired the film *War Games*, starring Matthew Broderick, the following year. Mitnick continues to deny this: interviewed while in prison by Adam L. Penenberg of *Forbes* magazine, he insisted: "No way, no how did I break into NORAD. That's a complete myth." Then, in 1983, he was caught sitting at a computer in a University of Southern California terminal room in the midst of breaking into a Pentagon computer using the **ARPAnet** (Advanced Research Projects Agency Network) system. He was charged as a juvenile, convicted, and sentenced to six months at a California Youth Authority juvenile prison in Stockton, California.

Upon his release, plainly undeterred, he ordered a personalized licence plate that read "X HACKER", and set his sights on hacking the computer systems of large corporations. Once in, he caused computers to illegally transmit copies of source-code versions of unpublished software programs. The transmissions took place over interstate telephone lines, making the crimes federal offences. As well as having technical skills, Mitnick was a charming, credible con artist, and from the beginning, his successes came about through his "social engineering" skills. When he was finally apprehended, he was found with multiple fake

IDs and cloned mobile phones, which he used to gain sensitive information such as passwords. He would often obtain passwords by phoning up a company and pretending to be an employee.

In 1987 Mitnick was arrested again, for infiltrating the computer system at the **Santa Cruz Organization**, a California software company. He was convicted of a misdemeanour and given three years' probation. The following year, he was caught hacking into the Digital Equipment Corporation and stealing source codes for programs. He was charged with breaking into the company's system. His lawyer claimed Mitnick was "addicted" to computers. He was convicted but given a reduced sentence of one year in jail and ordered to participate in a counselling programme for his addiction. Eight months of his sentence in jail were spent in solitary confinement – because his jailers feared he'd use the telephone for hacking. Once freed in 1989, Mitnick went to work as a researcher for a private investigator and once again began hacking into computers. When he sensed the FBI was onto him, he went on the run for two years, travelling across the US, creating new identities along the way. The FBI labelled him a "cyber terrorist" and "computer outlaw".

He was arrested in 1995 when a dozen FBI agents converged on his apartment in Raleigh, North Carolina. According to *New York Times* reporter **John Markoff**, who would go on to co-author a controversial book on the Mitnick case, the hacker's downfall came when he crossed Tsutomu Shimomura, a thirty-year-old senior research fellow of the San Diego Supercomputer Center. On Christmas Day 1994, Shimomura noticed a sophisticated but unauthorized attempt to access his home computers from a terminal at Loyola University of Chicago. Shimomura alerted the FBI,

but also began his own extensive monitoring, tracking activity to telecom switching centres which in turn led to indications of suspicious access to the computer networks of such major companies as Motorola and Apple. Following the trail, Shimomura helped investigators, using cellular-frequency scanners, to track Mitnick to a Raleigh apartment block. "The story of the investigation", according to Markoff, "particularly Mr Shimomura's role, is a tale of digital detective work in the ethereal world known as cyberspace." But *Forbes* magazine offered another take on Mitnick: far from being a criminal mastermind, he was "a recreational hacker with a compulsive-obsessive relationship to information … just your average geek who has done some bad things in his life, and has paid the price".

After pleading guilty to wire and computer fraud charges through his lawyer, Mitnick asked that his guilty plea be withdrawn. A judge granted it and he was tried. He was convicted and sentenced to five years in a federal penitentiary. He was paroled on 21 January 2000 on the condition that for the next three years he use neither a computer nor a mobile phone. Just a few weeks after his release, Mitnick took up an invitation to give evidence to a Senate panel. He urged lawmakers at all costs not to ignore the danger posed by social engineering: "I rarely had to resort to a technical attack", he said. "Companies can spend millions of dollars toward technological protections and that's wasted if somebody can basically call someone on the telephone and either convince them to do something on the computer that lowers the computer's defences or reveals the information they were seeking." The former most wanted computer outlaw was well on his way to the other side of the security fence.

For further investigation

📖 **Tsutomu Shimomura & John Markoff** Takedown: The Pursuit and Capture of Kevin Mitnick, America's Most Wanted Computer Outlaw – By the Man Who Did It **(1996)** A first-person account, chronicled by journalist Markoff, of Shimomura's assistance to the FBI in the arrest of Mitnick.

📖 **Jonathan Littman** The Fugitive Game: Online with Kevin Mitnick **(1997)** Littman tells Mitnick's side of the story in the US government's case against him.

🌐 forbes.com/1999/04/05/feat.html A 1999 interview with Mitnick conducted while he was still in prison.

🌐 guardian.co.uk/technology/2002/dec/13/ g2.usnews An interview feature by *Guardian* reporter Oliver Burkeman.

KEVIN LEE POULSEN, A.K.A. "DARK DANTE"

This man was once considered to be a threat to US national security.

The staff biography that appears on the home page of Wired.com does not mention that **Kevin Poulsen**, its senior editor, had a previous career as a "black hat" hacker, which landed him in prison, having been charged with espionage (the first time such an accusation had been levelled at a hacker). Though he is a convicted criminal, Poulsen is legendary among hackers for his ingenuity and risk-taking. Using the alias "Dark Dante", Poulsen seemed able to find his way into even the most well-protected computer networks, and he became one of the US best-known cyberpunk outlaws.

Born in 1965, Poulsen was given his first computer when he was sixteen, and within a year had become efficient enough on the TRS-80 – an early portable affectionately called Trash-80 – to hack into the US Department of Defense's ARPAnet system through a backdoor on the University of California at Berkeley's military research. Guessing at a password, he tried the university's initials, UCB, and was allowed inside ARPAnet. The feat, for which he was never charged, earned him the label "the Hannibal Lecter of computer crime". His expertise was cracking government and military systems thought until then to be impenetrable. But he stumbled when he accidentally used his real name instead of his alias. In September 1983, agents from the Los Angeles district attorney's office went to his home and confiscated his computer. Because he was seventeen and therefore a minor, they didn't prosecute and instead warned him that his hacking was illegal. A few months later, Kevin graduated from high school, moved out of his parents' home and settled in Northern California. By day, he worked for SRI International, a nonprofit research institute headquartered in Menlo Park, California. But by night, he hacked into telephone systems, once reactivating old **Yellow Pages** escort service phone numbers for the benefit of an acquaintance in the business.

He was involved in more serious crimes too. In January 1990, he and two other men (one of whom also worked at SRI International) were charged with computer trespassing. Poulsen was specifically accused of obtaining classified flight information for a US military exercise. He was also charged with committing a physical burglary in order to steal data and equipment from **Pacific Bell Telephone Company**. Some of the information thus obtained was highly sensitive, including files that formed part of an FBI investiga-

Kevin "Dark Dante" Poulsen

tion into Ferdinand E. Marcos, the recently deceased president of the Philippines. Such were Poulsen's wiretapping skills, investigators said, that he listened in on Pacific Bell security staff discussing how to catch the thief.

When the indictment was issued Poulsen went on the run, and he evaded capture for seventeen months. But he did not stop hacking and it was while he was a fugitive that he pulled off a stunt that is still revered by hackers. The target was a radio station, KIIS-FM in Los Angeles, which every week ran a "Win a Porsche by Friday" contest. Listeners were invited to call in as soon as a particular sequence of songs had been played, with the 102nd caller winning a $50,000 Porsche 944. On 1 June 1990, Poulsen took control of the station's phone lines, guaranteeing he would win the car – which he duly collected.

When he was featured on NBC's *Unsolved Mysteries*, a crime-solving reality television show, the show's 1-800 telephone lines mysteriously crashed. But Poulsen was finally arrested in April 1991 soon after *Unsolved Mysteries* aired, when night-shift employees recognized him, tackled him in an aisle, and called the FBI.

There was a further twist in December 1992. A Federal Grand Jury in San Jose issued a further indictment, superseding the previous one, against Poulsen. This time – for the first time ever – espionage laws were used against a hacker. The new indictment related to the military flight orders, which were expressly marked as secret. Under the legislation, it is a crime to obtain such information even if it is not actually passed onto a foreign government. *The New York Times* reported Poulsen's outraged lawyer protesting against the charge: "The government is trying to turn Kevin Poulsen, a curious computer nerd, into Julius Rosenberg, and it just doesn't fit." Poulsen faced a $250,000 fine and five years in prison for each of the computer and telecommunications offences, and $250,000 and ten years for the spying charge.

In June 1994, Poulsen pleaded guilty to seven counts of mail, wire and computer fraud, money laundering, and obstruction of justice. He was sentenced to 51 months in federal prison and ordered to pay $56,000 in restitution. In addition, a judge forbade Poulsen, upon his release from prison, from using a computer for three years. At the time, it was the longest sentence ever handed down for hacking. Poulsen enjoyed brief celebrity in the tech world upon his release from prison and was the subject of a book, *Watchman: The Twisted Life and Crimes of Serial Hacker Kevin Poulsen*.

Now a reformed hacker, Poulsen has reinvented himself as a journalist, beginning in 2000 as editorial director for SecurityFocus, a California-based security research firm, before being hired by Wired.com. He established his credentials on the other side of the law in October 2006 when he helped police arrest a repeat sex offender by cross-referring MySpace pages to offender databases using an innovative automated script. His technique worked because the sex offender (who was subsequently jailed on a misdemeanour charge) had used his real name when he created his MySpace profile.

For further investigation

📖 Jonathan Littman The Watchman: The Twisted Life and Crimes of Serial Hacker Kevin Poulsen (1997) A controversial book about Poulsen, which includes details Poulsen has publicly disputed.

Ⓦ **phreakvids.com** Includes streamed video of *Unsolved Mysteries*' TV segment about Kevin Poulsen's crimes and arrest.

Ⓦ **wired.com/science/discoveries/news/2006/10/71948** Kevin Poulsen's account of identifying a sex offender on MySpace.

ADRIAN LAMO, "GREY HAT"

Hacking is often thought to involve complex computer programming, but this is not always the case. Access to computer networks can be achieved in other ways, such as social engineering. It is also possible to exploit vulnerabilities in networks: if a network is not securely configured, then the software that allows a company's employees to access the Internet from within a corporate system may also offer a way in for the vigilant trespasser. This was **Adrian Lamo**'s technique. In his words, if you randomly try enough doorknobs, you will sooner or later find one that rattles. Because Lamo isn't a technical whizzkid, some other hackers scorn him. **Oxblood Ruffin**, a member of the Cult of the Dead Cow hacker group, retorted: "It's like dancing. Anyone can dance. But not many people can dance like Michael Jackson." *Wired* writer Jennifer Kahn added: "Lamo's hacks are uncommonly witty and at times almost inspiring." For example, he once made his way into the customer service database of the now-defunct Excite@Home. Having gained access, he found the contact details of someone who had made a complaint which had not been answered for a year. Lamo phoned the customer and offered to forward to him all the company's internal mails about the complaint.

VLADIMIR LEVIN, THE CITIBANK HACKER

In 1994, in the first recorded case of bank robbery through a computer network, Vladimir Levin, a Russian computer programmer, began stealing from the giant finance group Citibank. By the time he was caught, he had managed to spirit away $10 million.

Having hacked into the Citibank computer network, Levin obtained a list of customer codes and passwords. Logging onto the Citibank system eighteen times over the course of several weeks, he wire transferred $11.6 million to accounts set up by accomplices in the US, Germany, the Netherlands, Finland and Israel. Levin conducted his illicit transactions during New York business hours so that the transfers would not look suspicious. Despite his cautiousness, bank officials became aware of his actions in the summer of 1994 when two Citibank customers complained that large sums had mysteriously disappeared from their accounts.

One transfer was for $26,800 and the other for $304,000. Bank officials notified the FBI. Accounts were flagged. FBI agents secretly monitored the illegal transfers from that moment on.

In March 1995 Levin was apprehended by officers from Scotland Yard at London's Stansted Airport, where he was preparing to catch a connecting flight to Moscow. Levin fought extradition to the US, but the House of Lords rejected an appeal in June 1997, and, thirty months after his arrest, he was extradited. He was initially charged with four counts of theft, totalling more than $10 million, and several counts of forgery, false accounting and computer misuse. But he agreed to a plea bargain and was convicted of stealing only $3.7 million. He was sentenced to three years in prison and ordered to repay Citibank $240,015. The company was eventually able to retrieve all but about $500,000 of the monies he had transferred.

Lamo was born in 1981 in Boston, Massachusetts. He completed all the required high-school tests a year early, enabling him to leave school, and then embarked on the life of what Kevin Poulsen called "a lone vagabond hacker who lives out of a weathered L.L. Bean backpack". Lamo's hacking was of the grey-hat variety. He gained unauthorized access to major corporate networks, but not for personal profit. Having rooted around, he would contact the IT security staff at the company concerned and inform them of what he had done. The companies he is known or alleged to have infiltrated include Yahoo!, MCI WorldCom, AOL Time Warner, Bank of America, McDonald's and Citigroup. Sometimes companies were even grateful for the security and risk-assessment information Lamo provided them with, but if ever offered payment he declined. Critics accused him of vanity and publicity-seeking, but the fact that he didn't gain financially from his actions and always used his own name, never seeking to disguise his identity, added to his reputation as a hacker whose activities were often illegal, but who operated according to a personal code of ethics.

This grey-hat hacker came undone in an encounter with the "Gray Lady" – the nickname given to *The New York Times*. In February 2002, Lamo caused more than

$25,000 in damages to the New York Times Company, in what would be his most notorious hacking transgression. After logging on – as usual giving his full name and cellphone number – he was able to gain access to the personal details of employees and other confidential information, including social security numbers for writers such as former UN weapons inspector **Richard Butler** and actor **Robert Redford**.

Lamo disclosed his handiwork to SecurityFocus (where Poulsen was then working), who contacted the New York Times Company, telling them about the breach and asking for a comment. Managers were not amused with the intrusion and contacted the police, who issued a warrant in August 2003. After five days on the run, Lamo turned himself in at a Starbucks coffeehouse in a suburb of Sacramento, California. He was ultimately convicted of hacking after he accepted a felony plea bargain. He was sentenced to serve six months on house arrest at his family's home near Sacramento. Lamo's supporters launched a website named FreeLamo.com to support him and his "fight for freedom".

He was ordered to pay $65,000 in restitution, and was given twelve months to pay it off. His three-year probation ended in June 2007. Today, Lamo works as a journalist, writing for online and print magazines.

JONATHAN JAMES

Jonathan James died suddenly and unexpectedly on 18 May 2008 at his home in Pinecrest, Florida, at the age of 24. Details of the cause of death were never released. "A computer genius by all definitions of the term, he routinely astounded friends, family, and governments with his accomplishments", stated the brief but pointed obituary in the *Miami Herald*. Also known as "c0mrade", James was in fact one of the most notorious of the "black hat" hackers. At the age of sixteen, he was convicted of breaking into the computers of the Defense Threat Reduction Agency (part of the US Department of Defense) and NASA. After his arrest in 1999, he admitted having intercepted thousands of emails and acquired software and highly sensitive data, including passwords. Being a juvenile, he served only six months in prison.

Shortly after completing his sentence, James gave a frank interview to US TV channel PBS's current affairs show *Frontline*, in which he explained the appeal of hacking. "You can control all these computers from the government, from the military, from large corporations. And if you know what you're doing, you can travel through the Internet at your will, with no restrictions. That's power; it's a power trip." He admitted to being shocked by the official response to his actions and dismayed by his six-month sentence. "While it's not as long as some other sentences, it's still a long time. And that's six months of me being surrounded by people that did these actual crimes, did bad things to other people, to humanity. And I'm surrounding myself with these people that are lower than myself", he protested. He insisted that what he had done was not harmful. "This is just harmless exploration. It's not a violent act or a destructive act. It's nothing."

For further investigation

Ⓦ securityfocus.com/news/296 Hacker-turned-journalist Kevin Poulsen's 2001 profile of the "helpful hacker".

Ⓦ wired.com/culture/lifestyle/news/2002/03/50811 A March 2002 Wired profile of Lamo before he was arrested.

THE "ILOVEYOU" VIRUS

The most destructive and costly computer bug ever released, the **"ILOVEYOU" virus** wreaked havoc worldwide by burrowing into email software. It is estimated that ten percent of all computers were infected; resulting business losses may have amounted to more than $5 billion. All because of an email that seemed to be a harmless valentine from an unknown admirer. The virus involved a form of social engineering: its apparently open-hearted message of affection engaged the curiosity and emotions of the person sitting down to work. Intrigued, perhaps a little excited, many people clicked on the attachment to find out more – only to realize too late that in doing so they had opened the door to a parasite on a mission to destroy.

The VBS/Loveletter worm came to light on 4 May 2000. Within hours the UK House of Commons email system was disabled, along with those of major businesses, universities and other organizations. The virus had first appeared in the Philippines, but it soon moved westward, to Hong Kong and then Europe and the US. It looked innocuous enough – an email with the subject line "ILOVEYOU" – but it was potentially lethal to computers operating the Outlook email client as part of the Microsoft Windows operating system.

The text of the message was brief: "kindly check the attached LOVELETTER coming from me", and there was an attachment labelled "LOVE-LETTER-FOR-YOU.TXT.vbs". IT departments were quick to realize the danger. The Yale University Library, for example, issued a warning at 10.25am on 4 May: "Do NOT open the attachment … do not send this message on, just delete it." But in many cases the warning came too late. Once opened, the attachment released the virus, which was programmed to delete computer files on the hard drive (MP3s, images, documents) and also, even more disastrously, to replicate itself. A copy of the mail would automatically be sent to other email addresses in the computer's Outlook address book. In this way the virus spread exponentially, crippling system after system.

This was not the whole problem. A further feature of the virus was its ability to lie dormant, in disguise, taking the appearance of a pre-existing file. If users later opened this file, thinking it unrelated to the virus, the Love Bug was back in business. Because virus-damaged files were overwritten instead of deleted, recovering lost files was difficult, if not impossible. Much of the damage, however, was in actuality the labour of getting rid of the virus and explaining to its recipients that the senders didn't mean to say "I love you". Along with large corporations, the Pentagon, the CIA and the British Parliament all shut down their email systems to stop the worm in its progress and to thwart further assaults. However, hackers quickly introduced copycats with new subject lines but the same dangerous code in the attached file.

On 25 May, **Michael A. Vatis** of the FBI's National Infrastructure Protection Center gave an official statement to the Senate Committee on Judiciary, warning of "a continuing upward trend in the damage caused by cyber crime", using the Love Bug as a key example. He expressed particular concern about the "polymorphic" capacity of the virus, its ability to mutate: "each new dissemination of it comes in a new guise and with slightly different code, which makes it harder for human recipients and anti-virus software to detect", he said. Each of the variants tried a slightly different social engineering tactic to dupe the recipient, from mysterious hint ("hehe…check this out") and titillation ("I Cant Believe I Have Just Received This Hate Email … Take a Look!") to duplicitous warning ("There is a dangerous virus circulating. Please click attached picture to view it and learn to avoid it"). A particularly sneaky variant derived the subject line from the name of a file the previous victim had recently been working on.

Within a day of the release of the virus, an antidote had been concocted. Narinnat Suksawat, a 25-year-old Thai computer engineer, released a therapeutic program, which he named Rational Killer. It removed the virus files and then retrieved system files, restoring them to working order. The threat posed by the "malware" (or malicious software) was now minimized.

In the complex language of computer programming, which combines sci-fi/fantasy and mythology with technical terminology, the Love Bug entered computers via a "backdoor trojan" (also known as a "Remote Access Trojan" or RAT), an application program that appears to be useful (for example, for viewing online videos) but in fact steals passwords and other data. The ILOVEYOU virus relied on a trojan which was found to be called Barok. When this was discovered, investigators were able to identify its author as someone using the name "Spyder",

who was traced to a technical college in Manila, the Philippines capital. That country's National Bureau of Investigation raided an apartment and three people were questioned, including **Onel de Guzman**, a student at the AMA Computer College. He admitted releasing the virus but not writing it. College authorities revealed that he had submitted a thesis proposal as part of his course; it was rejected because it concerned a password-stealing virus and so dealt unacceptably with illegal activity. But the evidence was circumstantial and anyway there was no Philippine law which obviously applied in this case. All charges against de Guzman were dropped.

For further investigation

- ⓦ archives.cnn.com/2000/TECH/computing/05/04/iloveyou A CNN news article describing the onslaught of the ILOVEYOU virus.

- ⓦ guardian.co.uk/technology/2003/aug/24/observerfocus .theobserver An *Observer* article by Paul Harris on virus writers and how they are caught.

- ⓦ pcworld.about.com/news/Nov132000id33392.htm A chronology of the investigation into the virus.

SVEN JASCHAN & THE SASSER WORM

Because of its market dominance, Microsoft has a significant stake in deterring the virus-writing that periodically results in huge damage to computers running its software and operating systems. Consequently in November 2003, the company teamed up with the FBI, Secret Service and Interpol to launch an Anti-Virus Reward Program aimed at

THE "LOGIC BOMB" THAT FAILED TO DETONATE

A "logic bomb" is a piece of computer code written to perform a particular destructive or malicious function when certain conditions are met. Unlike other viruses, its purpose is to carry out a targeted attack rather than to infect in a random and indiscriminate way.

Logic bombs have been used by disaffected employees to take revenge against their employer after dismissal, the bomb being set to go off some time after they have left the company. Since they tend to originate within a company's system, they are harder to detect because they do not need to break through firewalls or other defensive systems.

In early January 2008, a New Jersey man, Yung-Hsun "Andy" Lin, was sentenced to thirty months in prison and ordered to pay $81,200 as restitution to his former employer Medco Health Solutions, a large pharmacy benefits manager. Three years earlier, a colleague had discovered a logic bomb Lin had planted in the company's computer system, designed to erase prescription information for sixty million people in the US when activated on his birthday that April.

Lin had planted the bomb as revenge for the redundancy notice he expected to receive any day. He had been fearing lay-off since 2003, when the company began a process of restructuring. But ironically he never did get fired – until his planned revenge was discovered.

obtaining information on the creators and propagators of malicious code. Brad Smith, a Microsoft senior executive, declared: "These are not just Internet crimes, cybercrimes or virtual crimes. These are real crimes that hurt a lot of people. Those who release viruses on the Internet are the saboteurs of cyberspace, and Microsoft wants to help the authorities catch them."

Less than two years later, in July 2005, the first bounties were claimed. Microsoft paid out $250,000 to two unnamed informants whose tip-offs had led to the conviction of **Sven Jaschan**, a nineteen-year-old German computer science student, for writing and releasing the highly destructive Sasser and NetSky worms the previous year. The Sasser worm was first detected at the beginning of May 2004. It was a particularly effective virus because it did not require an attachment file to be downloaded in order to attack. Instead it took advantage of a problem which existed at that time in some versions of the Windows operating system. All it took was for affected users to make an Internet connection. The problem had to do with a component known as LSASS (Local Authority Security Authority Subsystem Service) – and the "Sasser" nickname was derived from that acronym. What this meant in practice was that a networked computer could be infected just by virtue of having an Internet connection. If the virus got into your computer, you would see a "System Shutdown" message which named the culprit ("lsass.exe"). Quick-witted users could type in a sequence of commands to prevent the shutdown, but that would not fix the problem because the system would too unstable to be useful and so would need to be rebooted anyway.

Though infected machines could be quickly fixed

with a software "patch", the immediate impact of the worm was massive. Whole computer networks were disabled. Rail passengers in Australia were stranded. A bank in Finland had to close all its offices. The British coastguard, Delta Airlines, Deutsche Post, the European Commission and the French stock exchange all suffered. It was estimated that a million computers were infected.

It took only days for police in Germany to trace Jaschan in the village of Waffensen near Rotenburg. The teenager initially protested his innocence, claiming that his intention had been to help users combat two other viruses, the **MyDoom** and **Bagle** worms, but he later admitted releasing Sasser on 29 April 2004, his eighteenth birthday. There were reports that he might be sued for damages. Interviewed shortly after his arrest by the weekly news magazine *Stern*, he was downcast: "I'm afraid that my life is in the trash can. What am I supposed to do if a lot of claims come? All I can do is apologize to everyone." One of the informants turned out to have been a classmate of Jaschan's. But the virus-writer did not seem to bear him any ill will, judging by his comments to *Stern*. "What am I supposed to do? I'm certainly not going to beat him up."

Because he was under eighteen when he created the virus, Jaschan was tried as a minor. On 8 July 2005, he was given a suspended sentence of one year and nine months after he was convicted of four counts of altering data and three counts of computer sabotage. He was also placed on three years' probation and ordered to serve thirty hours of community service in a retirement home. But the damage caused by Jaschan's creations didn't stop the teen from landing a position with a top German computer firm. In

German computer nerd Sven Jaschan walks into the court in Verden, northern Germany, on Friday 8 July 2005. He admitted he created 2004's Sasser computer worm virus.

September 2004, he was hired by firewall manufacturer Securepoint. The hire was controversial: in November 2004, H+BEDV Datentechnik, an anti-virus company, broke links with Securepoint. Its chief executive Tjark Auerbach was quoted as saying: "What would the customer think? If this engine misses a virus and a former virus writer is working for that company, that smells a little bit stinky."

For further investigation

ⓦ msnbc.msn.com/id/4890780/ MSNBC report on the impact of the virus.

ⓦ securityfocus.com/news/11242 Report on the conviction of Jaschan and the bounty paid to informants.

PHISHING

In January 2009, when many British people were in the process of filing their tax returns, a new "phishing" scam was widely reported in the UK press. Phishing is the attempt to "fish" for confidential personal information (passwords, bank or credit card details) by sending out mass emails that pretend to come from a trusted source.

In the case of the tax scam, emails were arriving with what looked like the logo of HM Revenue and Customs (HMRC). "Please update your account to the new EV SSL certification by Clicking Here", the mails read – and if you followed the link you were taken to a clone of HMRC's site. A similar scam promised recipients a tax refund. Clicking the link took victims to an official-seeming site which requested credit card details. Unlike older phishing scams, which promised the addressee some huge lottery win, this one mentioned moderate sums – £99.23 is the amount in one sample mail – which are more credible.

In October 2005 **David Levi** of Lytham, Lancashire, became the first person in the UK to be convicted of a phishing fraud. He was the leader of an identity fraud gang that stole nearly £200,000 by tricking more than 160 people into giving away their account details. The gang sent out emails to eBay vendors asking for personal details. Some people believed the links in the emails sent them to a secure eBay site. Instead, they were connected to the criminals' own computers. Using those stolen eBay credentials, the gang then accessed vendors' accounts and assumed their eBay identities. They then offered expensive items for sale, including laptop computers and designer watches. They collected the cash and never delivered the goods. Levi's five accomplices received sentences ranging from six months to two years in prison.

Phishing is big business. Estimates of the sums involved vary enormously, with some claiming that in the US the amount may have been as much as $3 billion in 2007. In the UK, the sum was estimated to have been over £20 million in 2005. Because the financial gain is potentially so large, fraudsters are continually developing new techniques.

One major trend (called "spear phishing" because it is focused rather than scattershot) is to target particular groups of people, carefully customizing the contents of the con-trick email so as to increase the chance of a catch. On 13 January 2009, the Dark Reading business security website reported another ingenious and disturbing variation, termed "in-session phishing", which looks like it may become the phishing of the future.

A user conducting online banking will be presented with a pop-up message saying that the online session has expired and that the username and password must be re-entered; if the customer complies, the information is sent directly to the fraudsters. It remains to be seen how common such tactics will become as criminals seek ever more effective means of defrauding Internet users.

For further investigation

Rachael Lining Phishing: Cutting the Identity Theft Line (2005) Written by a phishing security expert, *Phishing* offers step-by-step instructions on how to foil identity thieves.

online.wsj.com/public/article/SB112424042313615131-z_8jLB2WkfcVtgdAWf6LRh733sg_20060817.html?mod=blogs *Wall Street Journal* article about an experiment in anti-phishing education.

CRACKDOWNS: OPERATION BOT ROAST & OPERATION BLOSSOM

Launched by the FBI and the US Secret Service, **Operation Bot Roast** is a major initiative directed at "bot-herders". This is the name given to hackers who infect computers with malware and so gain remote control over a number of machines, known collectively as a "botnet". Some botnets, according to the FBI, are massive: tens of thousands of computers. With this control, bot-herders are able to steal user identities, launch spam mailings, engage in "click-fraud" (schemes which artificially inflate the number of visitors to a website), disrupt servers and crash sites. "The majority of the victims are not even aware that their computers have been compromised or their personal information exploited", said FBI Assistant Director **James Finch**, head of the bureau's Cyber Division.

In May 2007, a major arrest was made. Twenty-seven-year-old **Robert Alan Soloway**, owner of Newport Internet Marketing (NIM), was indicted on multiple charges, including mail fraud, wire fraud, aggravated identity theft and money laundering. Dubbed the "spam king" by prosecutors, Soloway had used botnets to send out millions of spam emails on behalf of clients. In order to stay ahead of law enforcers, he constantly changed domain names, moving from host to host. But in 2007 police finally caught up with him, and on 14 March the following year he pleaded guilty to two charges of fraud as well as to a charge of failing to file a tax return. He was sentenced to 47 months in prison and ordered to repay over $700,000.

Another major success for the FBI came in October 2008, the result of a collaboration with British, German and Turkish police. A two-year investigation culminated in the arrest of 56 cybercriminals who maintained the **Dark Market** site, a web forum for the buying and selling of stolen financial data (such as usernames and passwords, account details). The 2500 members had been carefully vetted to weed out those with suspect motives. Or so they all thought. In fact one of the site's administrators, username Master Splyntr, was an FBI agent. Cyber Division Assistant Director Shawn Henry commented: "What's worked for us in taking down spy rings and entire mob families over the years – embedding an undercover agent deep within a criminal organization – worked beautifully in taking down Dark Market."

On the other side of the Atlantic in April 2001, British home secretary **Jack Straw** unveiled a new elite police squad, the National Hi-Tech Crime Unit (NHTCU). Explaining the move, the deputy director general of the National Crime Squad, Bob Packham, said: "Looking to the future the equation is simple, money is going electronic and where money goes so will organized crime." The squad divided its work into two categories. "New crimes, new tools" was the first – hacking being the main example, where there is probably no other way to cause the same damage. "Old crimes, new tools" was the second, where the

crimes are traditional ones (fraud, identity theft, stalking and harassment) but carried out with new technology. The NHTCU's most high-profile undertaking was **Operation Blossom** (also referred to as Operation Buccaneer), an investigation into a plot to defraud the Japanese bank Sumitomo Mitsui. Although convictions of members of the so-called Drink or Die gang of hackers did ensue, the cost of the

PHILIP CUMMINGS, IDENTITY THIEF

In 1999, British-born Philip Cummings took a job as a customer support worker for Teledata Communications in Bay Shore, New York, a company that specialized in software that enabled banks to obtain personal credit histories from credit reference agencies. It was a relatively low-grade job, but Cummings was soon offered the chance to supplement his income when he was approached by a gang of Nigerian criminals eager to get their hands on the personal data to which his job gave him access. Another man, Linus Baptiste, acted as the go-between for Cummings and the gang, bringing Cummings the names of people whose details were wanted. Cummings left the company after less than a year, but managed to retain remote access to the computer system. By the time he, Baptiste and another man, Hakeem Mohammed, were put on trial in November 2002, it was thought that up to thirty thousand people had been compromised and defrauded, the total sum in the region of $50 million. At the time Kevin P. Donavan of the FBI said: "The defendants took advantage of an insider's access to sensitive information in much the same way a gang of thieves might get the

combination to the bank vault from an insider. The potential windfall was probably far greater than the contents of a bank vault, and they didn't even need a getaway car."

Once the gang had the credit histories and other data, they used that information to empty bank accounts, arrange fake loans and run up credit-card bills – all without the knowledge of the person concerned. The gang would also change the address on bank accounts in order to have cheque-books sent out to new addresses where the gang could collect them. Cummings and his accomplices received up to $60 for each credit history they passed on, a tiny sum in comparison with what was being stolen. As US Attorney James Comey put it, "with a few keystrokes, these men picked the pockets of tens of thousands of Americans, and in the process, took their identity, stole their money, and swiped their security".

At the time, it was the biggest identity-theft fraud ever uncovered. In January 2005, Cummings was sentenced to fourteen years' imprisonment. Handing down the sentence, the judge told him the damage he had caused was "almost unimaginable".

operation was in the region of £220 million (of which £18.4 million went on legal aid to the defendants). In May 2006, the squad was transferred to the newly formed **Serious Organized Crime Agency** (SOCA) and renamed SOCA e-Crime. In an embarrassing development, in September 2008, it transpired that the police had lost control of the NHTCU's domain name, which had been bought up opportunistically by a German firm. The site now provides "Computer Information Resources".

For further investigation

Ⓦ fbi.gov/cyberinvest/cyberhome.htm Website of the FBI's Cyber Investigations operation.

Ⓦ forbes.com/technology/2008/03/31/cybercriminals-hacking -jail-cx_ag_0331cybercrime.html *Forbes* magazine's reporting on Robert Soloway and the Operation Bot Roast investigation.

CYBERBULLYING & MEGAN MEIER'S SUICIDE

Most teenagers in the developed world now conduct a large part of their social life online. They cannot remember a time before email, instant messaging, texting and Internet social networking. These communication tools mean that most young people's lives involve a level of daily peer-to-peer interaction unheard of in earlier decades. The downside is that with the advent of this new technology have come novel and often extremely unpleasant forms of bullying and intimidation, known as "cyberbullying". According to the US National Crime Prevention Council (NCPC),

examples include pretending to be someone else while online, spreading lies and rumours, tricking others into revealing personal information, sending or forwarding insulting text messages, and posting pictures of someone without their consent.

The consequences of such bullying can be devastating. In 2006, a phoney MySpace account was created in the name of a nonexistent sixteen-year-old boy named **Josh Evans**, who appeared good-looking and had a troubled background ("when I was seven, my dad left me and my mom and my older brother and my newborn brother … poor mom yeah she had such a hard time … finding work to pay for us after he left", the profile stated). "Josh" flirted with thirteen-year-old Megan Meier, who lived in O'Fallon, Missouri. But then things turned nasty. Megan received a message saying the world would be a better place without her. Megan's reply, according to *The New York Times*, was chilling: "You're the kind of boy a girl would kill herself over." After an argument with her mother about her MySpace use, Megan went to her bedroom and hanged herself. Within hours, the Josh Evans profile had been deleted from MySpace.

A month after the death, a neighbour informed the Meiers that the Josh Evans profile had in fact been set up by Lori Drew, a local woman, whose daughter had argued with Megan in the past. The information was passed on to the authorities, but at first it seemed no charges would be brought. Then, in an ABC interview, Ashley Grills, a friend and employee of Drew's, admitted she had been involved and named Drew as ringleader. The details were out. The story became major news and sparked furious online debate.

A case finally came to court in November 2008 in Los Angeles, where MySpace is based. Drew was charged with conspiracy and three violations of an anti-hacking law, the Computer Fraud and Abuse Act. It was argued that Drew had broken the MySpace terms of use. Ashley Grills was granted immunity in return for testifying against Drew. The jury reached a verdict on 26 November, finding Drew guilty of three charges of computer fraud (there was deadlock on the charge of conspiracy). Los Angeles US Attorney Thomas P. O'Brien, who had made it his mission to bring the prosecution, said after the verdict: "If you are going to attempt to annoy or go after a little girl and you're going to use the Internet to do so, this office and others across the country will hold you responsible."

For further investigation

Ⓦ **meganmeierfoundation.org** Anti-bullying foundation set up in Megan Meier's name by her family.

Ⓦ **newyorker.com/reporting/2008/01/21/080121fa_fact_collins** A January 2008 *New Yorker* article by Lauren Collins on the Megan Meier case.

Ⓦ **us/27myspace.html** *New York Times* report on the "guilty" verdict in the Megan Meier suicide case.

CAUGHT IN THE ACT

The Internet may have prompted the rise of new crimes and new criminals; but it's also opening up new avenues for law enforcement agencies and others trying to combat more "traditional" crimes. You no longer need expensive video surveillance equipment installed in your home to catch burglars: webcams will do the trick. Crooks are unknowingly being watched via webcams as the technology becomes more affordable and savvy consumers get tiny cameras for their personal computers. That was the case in 2005 when a webcam in Cambridge, England, caught a burglar in the act. Homeowner Duncan Grisby, a software engineer, had set up the camera after his home was burgled on an earlier occasion. As soon as Grisby's computer detected motion from a sensor he'd installed, the camera started taping. The images were simultaneously sent to an email address. The teenage burglar, Benjamin Park, a repeat offender, actually stole the computer, but the evidence had already been sent across cyberspace. "It was better than a burglar alarm", according to Detective Sergeant Alan Page, head of Cambridgeshire Police Burglary Squad, "and when Park initially denied breaking in to the property we were able to simply show him the footage." On 15 February 2005, Park pleaded guilty and a magistrate in Cambridge handed down an eleven-month jail term.

In 2007, an Orange County, Florida, man experienced something similar. Only in this case, he watched in horror, from his desk at work, as a burglar rifled through his home – and through his wife's lingerie drawer. Thomas Arline was alerted after motion sensor cameras installed in his home triggered the sending of an email. He logged onto his system and watched the crime in real time on his PC, soon attracting a crowd of bemused colleagues. He called the police, but by the time they arrived the burglar was gone. Still, the video footage is there, ready to act as evidence when the burglar (whose face is clearly visible in the images) is caught.

Index

R

S

Listen Up!

"You may be used to the Rough Guide series being comprehensive, but nothing will prepare you for the exhaustive Rough Guide to World Music . . . one of our books of the year."
Sunday Times, London

Covers iPod touch, iPod nano, iPod classic and iPod shuffle

THE ROUGH GUIDE to
iPods & iTunes

6TH EDITION · THE GLOBAL BESTSELLER

"Mind-expanding and irresistible"
Mark Ellen, The Word

THE ROUGH GUIDE book of
Playlists

5000 SONGS YOU **MUST** DOWNLOAD

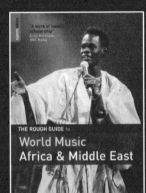

"A work of lunatic scholarship"
Andy Kershaw, BBC Radio

THE ROUGH GUIDE to
World Music
Africa & Middle East

The songs · the singers · the stories · the soul

THE ROUGH GUIDE to
Soul and R&B

Peter Shapiro

Rough Guide Music Titles

The Beatles • The Best Music You've Never Heard • Blues • Bob Dylan • Classical Music
Heavy Metal • Jimi Hendrix • iPods & iTunes Led Zeppelin • Nirvana • Opera • Pink Floyd
Book of Playlists • The Rolling Stones • Soul and R&B • Velvet Underground • World Music

Lost classics · Hidden gems · Amazing stories

THE BEST MUSIC YOU'VE NEVER HEARD

Musical splendours off the beaten track

THE ROUGH GUIDE to
Jimi Hendrix

Richie Unterberger

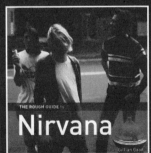

THE ROUGH GUIDE to
Nirvana

Gillian Gaar

www.roughguides.com
MAKE THE MOST OF YOUR TIME ON EARTH

ROUGH
GUIDES